DUNDEE DISTRICT LIBRARIES

REFERENCE SERVICES

FOR REFERENCE ONLY

TRADE MARK
LICENSING

TRADE MARK LICENSING

By

NEIL J. WILKOF
B.A. (Yale University), J.D. (University of Chicago),
Ph.D. (University of Illinois)
Law Offices of Neil J. Wilkof
Adjunct Lecturer of Law, Bar-Ilan University

Tax section contributed by
NIGEL EASTAWAY
Moores Rowland

LONDON ● SWEET & MAXWELL ● 1995

Published in 1995 by
Sweet & Maxwell Limited
of South Quay Plaza
183 Marsh Wall, London E14 9FT
Typeset by Selwood Systems,
Midsomer Norton.
Printed and bound in Great Britain
by Hartnolls Ltd., Bodmin

No natural forests were destroyed
to make this product only farmed
timber was used and re-planted.

A CIP catalogue record for this book
is available from The British Library

ISBN 0 421 44510 6

To my wife Leah, and to my children, Abigail, Shira, Renana and Jonathan:
It's finally over. It's time to be a husband and father again.

Acknowledgments

Over the four-year span during which this book was written, I was fortunate to receive the assistance and encouragement of numerous colleagues. Without their help, this book would not have been completed.

I wish to especially thank Dr. Jeremy Phillips (London), who provided the initial impetus and encouragement, Nigel Eastaway (London), whose insight and eloquence grace his contribution to the section on taxation, Nadine Parker (New York City), Ellen Shankman (Rehovot), and Daniel Taub (Jerusalem), who each read a portion of the text and provided the sorely needed virtue of perspective, and David Metzger (Chicago), who was particularly gracious in sharing his wisdom on several aspects of U.S. law.

The I.T.T. Chicago-Kent College of Law allowed me to make use of its excellent research facilities during the summer of 1991 as a visiting lecturer of law. My several visits to the law library of Queen Mary and Westfield College enabled me to identify and ponder numerous authorities under U.K. law.

I wish to acknowledge the contribution of the following persons: Sally Abel (Palo Alto), Robert Anderson (London), Doris Bandin (Madrid), Abraham Bell (Jerusalem), Michael Blakeney (London), William Bullinger (Washington), Sheldon Burshtein (Toronto), Simon Cohen (London), Trevor Cooke (London), Douglas Deeth (Toronto), Susan Upton Douglas (New York City), Professor Gerald Dworkin (London), Caroline Easter (Brussels), Allen Gabriel (Los Angeles), Stephen Goldberg (Pretoria), Beth Goldman (Palo Alto), Margaret F. Goldstein (New York City), Linda Harland (London), Alison Harrington (Reading), Laurence Jacobs (London), Lionel Kestenbaum (Jerusalem), Sheldon Klein (Washington), Charles Laff (Chicago), Dr. Shelly Lane (London), Howard Levy (New York City), Morag MacDonald (London), Christopher Morcom (London), Sally Nicolson (London), John Olsen (London), Elise Orenstein (Toronto), Mark Partridge (Chicago), David Petterson (London), Mark Radcliffe (Palo Alto), Mary Hutchins Reed (Chicago), Joanna Reeseby (London), Catherine Rothwell (London), Andrea Rush (Toronto), Anna Sharpe (Melbourne), Peter Silverman (New York City), E. Susan Singleton (London), Martin Stern (Chicago), Richard Sutton (Leeds), Donald Turner (London), Thomas Vinje (Brussels), Professor Joshua Weisman (Jerusalem), Andrew White (London), and Lindsey Wrenn (Leeds). If I have forgotten anyone, please accept my apologies.

Sweet & Maxwell and its entire staff variously succored, supported and encouraged me throughout the project.

The errors, of course, are all mine.

Neil J. Wilkof
Ra'anana, Israel
October 27, 1994

Contents

CONTENTS

Table of Cases

National Legislation

Table of Statutory Instruments

E.C. Treaties

E.C. Legislation

1. Trade Mark Licensing: A Subject Worthy of Separate Treatment

INTRODUCTION

The purpose of this book is to describe the law and practice of trade mark   **1–01**
licensing. By trade mark licensing is meant any arrangement by which one
party consents to the use of its trade mark in accordance with specified terms
and conditions. Trade mark licensing spans a wide spectrum, ranging from a
subsidiary's use of the trade mark of its parent, in which the licence may be
oral or even implied, to a lengthy written agreement between unrelated parties
located on different continents.

The rationale for a separate work on the subject is that trade mark licensing
differs sufficiently, both in conception and in practice, from other forms of
intellectual property licensing, such as patents, copyright and know-how, to
warrant separate treatment and discussion. To understand trade mark licensing, it is not enough to be familiar with the principles of intellectual property
generally, or merely to apply the licensing principles applicable to patents,
know-how and the like. Rather, the successful practice of trade mark licensing,
be it negotiating, drafting, or enforcement, requires an appreciation of the
distinctive character of this form of intellectual property licensing.

Trade Mark Licensing – A Multi-Billion Dollar Business

In its broadest form, trade mark licensing is a multi-billion dollar activity   **1–02**
that pervades the ways in which goods and services are distributed, marketed
and sold, both domestically and internationally. Because of the diversity and
scope of trade mark licensing, it is difficult to quantify precisely the extent of
its activity. One study concluded that over $50 billion worth of licensed
consumer goods were sold at the retail level in the United States in one year
alone.[1]

Nor is trade mark licensing limited to any single country or region.
Wherever consumer markets exist, manufacturers and other purveyors of
goods and services have found licensing a preferred means for the marketing,
distribution and advertising of their products. It is expected that the use of
trade mark licensing will expand with the collapse of the barriers between
East and West in Europe, and regions such as the Far East become increasingly
more consumer oriented. One need only take notice of the great interest in

---

[1] Bryer, 'Sublicensing Intellectual Property Rights in the United States,' *The Licensing Journal*,
March 1989, p. 4.

franchising that has been demonstrated in Eastern Europe to appreciate the attraction that trade mark licensing holds as a way of doing business.[2]

Diversity of Trade Mark Licensing

1–03   The commercial scope of trade mark licensing is matched by the diversity of circumstances in which the licensing takes place, and the variety of issues to which it gives rise. This can be better appreciated by considering the following examples:

(a) Company X manufactures and sells its swim-wear products under its own trade mark. All of its manufacture is currently done locally under contract. Company X now wishes to expand its business into foreign markets. It considered a distribution agreement, the establishment of a wholly owned foreign subsidiary, and the creation of a joint venture in the foreign country, before deciding to enter into a formal licence agreement with a foreign licensee.

(b) Company A owns a well known trade mark used in connection with certain products in the beverage industry. Company X now wishes to license the use of the mark on various unrelated goods, including shirts, luggage, and perfume. Company A has no previous experience with any of these products, but it believes that the cachet of its mark will encourage sales of these additional products.

(c) Company M is negotiating a distribution agreement whereby a new Company D will be established to distribute its products. Company D insists that its name must include Company M's trade mark. Company M rejects this demand, but does allow a portion of the mark to be included in Company D's name. Subsequently, Company D adopts its name as a trade mark and begins to distribute other goods under the trade mark.

(d) Company P manufactures and sells certain consumer goods worldwide under its trade mark. It distributes its products in foreign countries either through a wholly owned subsidiary or an exclusive local distributor. Ownership of the local trade mark varies, sometimes belonging to the local entity and sometimes remaining with Company X. Competing parallel or grey market goods bearing the genuine trade mark of Company X are now being imported into these foreign countries.

1–04   Each of these examples addresses a different aspect of trade mark licensing:

In (a), the issue is how to take advantage of one's established trade mark in order to market and sell the product in new markets.

In (b), the trade mark proprietor seeks to benefit from the reputation of his trade mark in new product areas.

In (c), the question of trade mark use by the distributor is raised.

In (d), the problem of grey market and parallel import goods is posed.

The common thread that runs through all of these examples is that each

---

[2] Zeidman and Avner, 'Franchising in Eastern Europe and the Soviet Union,' *DePaul Business Law Journal*, Vol. 3, 1991, no. 2, pp. 307–338.

of them describes a situation in which one party allows another to use the goodwill or reputation that the first party has acquired in its mark.

The scope of these examples may seem broader than the common understanding of trade mark licensing. However, upon reflection, it should be readily appreciated that the forms of trade mark licensing are as diverse as the ways in which goods and services themselves are distributed, marketed and sold in connection with commercial marks and symbols. It is the diversity of these practices that makes trade mark licensing worthy of separate attention.

Problems with the Industrial Property Orientation

Despite the central role that trade mark licensing plays in modern commerce   1–05
and trade, the tendency has been to refrain from addressing it as a distinct form of intellectual property licensing. While the licensing of intellectual property rights is hardly a neglected subject, this literature has tended to focus on the industrial aspect of intellectual property protection, namely, patents and know how. The result is that patent and know how licensing becomes the focus for the licence even when, as with trade marks, the underlying rights and the commercial considerations clearly require separate and discrete attention. The practitioner who is primarily interested in trade mark licensing, in relying on this industrial property orientation, faces several obstacles in applying this approach to trade mark licensing.

Industrial Property Does Not Address Certain Fundamental Elements of a Trade Mark Licence

The industrial property orientation will be of limited application for certain   1–06
fundamental elements of trade mark licensing. A primary example is quality control. The requirement of quality control creates obligations between the trade mark licensor and licensee, and may provide for certain consequences that are not present with other intellectual property rights, if these obligations are not satisfied.[3] Another example is the question of the duration of the licence. The maximum term of a patent licence is limited by the term of the patent.[4] After the expiration of the patent, the licensee is entitled to use the invention without the permission of the owner of the patent. The patent licence has come to an end.

However, the termination of the patent licence need not bring to an end the commercial relationship between the parties, especially if the patented product has enjoyed commercial success, or where know-how or technical assistance continues to be provided. A trade mark, by contrast, is potentially of unlimited duration, provided that it is renewed on a timely basis. Should an agreement provide for both a patent and trade mark licence, under modern law, the trade mark licence does not come to an end with the termination of the patent. Indeed, both the patentee and licensee may continue to reap the benefits of the patented product, even after its expiry, if the trade mark

---

[3] See Chap. 6, paras. 6–23 to 6–28, paras. 6–41 to 6–47.
[4] In the U.K. the term is 20 years from the date of the patent application, while in the U.S. it is 17 years from the issuance of the patent.

associated with the product continues to enjoy and attract custom.[5] Thus, the fate of the trade mark licence will not necessarily depend upon the term of the patent.

Protection of The Trade Mark May Be at Odds with the Exploitation of Other Intellectual Property Rights

1–07   The industrial property orientation may also be at odds with specific aspects of a trade mark license. This can be seen in the issue of genericness.

One of the distinctive features of trade mark law is that if a trade mark has come to be identified as synonymous with the goods, such as escalator and aspirin, it may be deemed to be generic. As such, it can no longer be the property of any single proprietor. This is because the trade mark no longer serves to distinguish the goods of the proprietor from those of its competitors, but has come to identify the goods generally.

Genericness may be most at odds with other intellectual property rights when the product is too successful, and the trade mark becomes synonymous with the name of the product itself.[6] The trade mark proprietor must take all corrective steps to ensure that the mark does not become generic. Such measures are usually directed towards third parties, such as the trade media and other traders in the goods, but it may be also directed to personnel of the proprietor and to other parties related to the proprietor, including licensees. In the absence of such measures (assuming that they are effective), a proprietor could lose his rights in the mark because of the failure of his licensees to use and monitor the mark properly.

Nothing similar to genericness, whereby rights are lost because the product is too successful, can be found in connection with any other intellectual property right. Indeed, the opposite is true: an industrial property licence may be formulated with the hope that the product succeeds so well that its trade mark will come to identify the product. Thus, not only is the issue of genericness singular to trade marks, but it may also conflict with the goal of a successful patent or know-how licence.

Common Legal Features of Intellectual Property Licences

1–08   It would be misleading, however, to imply that a trade mark licence is wholly unrelated to the licensing of other intellectual property rights. While this book will focus on what is distinct about trade mark licensing, it is important to recognise that at a certain level of generality, all intellectual property licences share common legal features. These features can be summarised as follows:

---

[5] Consider, *e.g.* whether the artificial sweetener known as 'NutraSweet' will continue to enjoy commercial success after the patent expires, and competing brands are available on the market, due to the wide-spread recognition of the mark.

[6] *e.g.* 'Yo-Yo.'

A Licence Is the Grant of an Intellectual Property Right

A licence is first and foremost the grant of an intellectual property right from   **1–09**
the licensor to the licensee. It is the essence of each of these separate rights,
whether a patent, trade mark, copyright or other, that will shape the substance
of a particular licence agreement.

It is not a simple matter to describe concisely what is the common
ground between the various intellectual property rights. Perhaps the best
characterisation is that each of them provides for a certain type of conduct,
be it the exploitation of a patent or the use of a trade mark on goods, that
can be carried out only by the consent of the proprietor of the right. The
substance of the various rights will differ, but they all share the feature that
they prevent others from exercising these rights without the permission of the
rights holder. Even the statement that each of these rights may be used with
the consent of the rights holder is in a sense misleading. The right to license
a trade mark was not always recognised, and indeed the right was once in
grave legal doubt.[7] Even today, the law may impose certain conditions on a
trade mark licence, such as quality control, that are not required for the
validity of licensing of other forms of intellectual property.[8] Not all licensing
of intellectual property is created equal.

Perhaps the most that can be said about the common ground between these
rights is that both commercial and legal conventions have attached substantive
significance to the fact that patents, trade marks, copyright and the like have
all been brought under the rubric of intellectual property.[9]

Intellectual Property Licences are Usually in the Form of a Contract

Licences are typically in the form of an agreement that is subject to the law   **1–10**
of contract. A licence is merely the grant of the right to use certain intellectual
property. For the licence to have commercial significance, the actual terms
and conditions of the grant must usually be specified in an agreement between
the parties. Thus, while it is the grant of the intellectual property right that
enables its licensed use by the licensee, it is the contract that spells out how
the parties will carry out the agreement to their mutual benefit.

While there is no set of standard contract provisions that necessarily applies
to all intellectual property licences, several categories of provisions, in addition
to the grant of the licence itself, are often found. Royalties or other consideration should be provided for and the terms of their payment described,
standards of performance regarding the licensed right should be spelt out,
and the duration and conditions of termination should be specified. Whatever
the precise content of these and other provisions of the licence agreement,
their construction will be in accordance with the general principles of contract
law.[10] Since both intellectual property rights and contract rights are involved,
complete adjudication of the licence arrangement may be subject to two or

---

[7] See, below, Chap. 2, paras. 2–03 to 2–17.
[8] See, below, generally Chap. 6.
[9] Cornish, *Intellectual Property, Patents, Copyright Trade Marks and Allied Rights* (2nd ed.,
1989), para. 1–001.
[10] See generally, Chaps. 10, 11, 12 and 15 for discussion of the contract elements.

more jurisdictions, the law of each country in which an intellectual property right has been granted under the licence, and the law of the country governing the construction of the contract itself. The result is that the adjudication of a contract involving an intellectual property licence may be more cumbersome than a conventional commercial agreement.[11]

Intellectual Property Licences Involve a Consideration of Other Subject-Matters

1–11   While intellectual property licences are usually viewed in terms of the interrelationship between intellectual property and contract rights, other types of concerns are involved. Three of the most important are taxation, product liability and competition law. Each of these topics is discussed separately later in this book.[12]

OTHER INTELLECTUAL PROPERTY RIGHTS

1–12   While the focus of a trade mark licence is, obviously, trade mark rights, it is important, nevertheless, to have an appreciation of the other intellectual property rights as well. There are three reasons for this:

(a) It is not unusual for a trade mark licence to be part of an arrangement where one or more other intellectual property rights are also involved. The interrelationship between these various intellectual property rights must be understood.

(b) An awareness of the differences between trade marks and the other intellectual property rights will enable one to understand better the particular requirements of trade mark licensing.

(c) As indicated previously, the industrial property rights especially patent and know-how, commonly serve as the model for intellectual licensing generally, even when the underlying premises of the industrial property model depart from the special requirements of trade marks.

Given the particular importance of patent, know-how and copyright licensing, a brief consideration of each of these rights, particularly as they apply to licensing, is considered below.

Patents

1–13   While the patent laws may differ somewhat from country to country, it is possible to describe the characteristics of patents generally.

---

[11] See, *e.g. Apple Corps Ltd v. Apple Computer Inc.* [1992] F.S.R. 431 (Ch.D.).

[12] See, *e.g.* Chap. 14, paras. 14–33 to 14–65 concerning taxation; Chap. 14, paras. 14–14 to 14–32 concerning product liability in the E.C.; and Chap. 12, paras. 12–54 to 12–57, and Chap. 13 concerning competition law.

Basic Elements of the Patent

A patent is an invention that is novel (*i.e.* was not known at the time of the application nor was anticipated by the prior art), non-obvious in comparison with the prior art and which constitutes a genuine creative advance, and is capable of industrial application. The invention may be either a product or a process.

An invention that satisfies these requirements may be granted a patent. The grant enables the proprietor of the patent to exploit the patented invention on an exclusive basis for a fixed period of time. Upon the expiration of the patent, the invention enters the public domain and it is free for anyone to use.

The scope of protection accorded under the patent is defined in the patent claims, which set out precisely what is new and non-obvious about the invention. It is not a requirement of the patent grant that the invention be reduced to an actual product or process. It is, however, a condition of the grant that the proprietor make a full and public disclosure of the invention. Thus, the patent system seeks to add to the stock of useful knowledge, by conferring upon the proprietor a monopoly for a limited period of time, during which he may exploit the invention on an exclusive basis.

A Patent is a Negative Right

A patent is a negative right, because the patent grants to its proprietor the   **1–14** right to prevent others from carrying out certain activities (popularly described under U.S. law as 'to make, use or sell') in relation to the invention that is the subject of the patent. A party that carries out any of these activities without the permission of the proprietor is liable for patent infringement.

Licence is a Covenant Not to Exercise the Negative Right

It is the consent of the proprietor, under specified terms and conditions, not   **1–15** to exercise its negative right under the patent with respect to a third party, that forms the basis of a patent licence. Under a patent licence, the licensee is promised that if he makes, uses or sells a product or process in accordance with the patent claims, he will not be sued by the proprietor. In exchange for this promise, the licensee usually undertakes to pay consideration to the proprietor, typically in the form of royalties based on some measure of the use of the patent by the licensee.

Thus, the foundation of a patent licence is permission by the inventor to a third party to exploit the invention for commercial or technological purposes. The motivation for entering into the licence can vary. The inventor may not have the financial or technical resources to commercialise his invention, or he may wish to take advantage of the expertise and resources of the licensee to further develop his invention.

A patent licence may be either exclusive or non-exclusive. Under an exclusive licence, the licensee is guaranteed that no other licensee nor the proprietor itself will exploit the invention within a defined territory. The guarantee of exclusivity serves as the inducement for the licensee to make certain investments and expend substantial effort in exploiting the invention. A non-exclusive licence furnishes no such guarantee of exclusivity, and it is essentially a covenant not to sue on the part of the proprietor. Whatever the motivation for its grant, the licence (especially if it is an exclusive licence) protects the licensee from competition from third parties for a limited period of time. At the same time, it shields the licensee from attack on grounds of infringement.

Know-How

Basic Elements of Know-How

1–16 Know-how (or confidential information) is less easily described than a patent, with which it is often compared and contrasted, and definitions of know-how, both formal and informal, abound, depending upon the jurisdiction.[13]

One way to understand know-how is that it constitutes the sum total of one's stock of confidential knowledge which enjoys some type of value. It can range from technological and scientific secrets to commercial information such as customer lists and marketing data. It may even extend to professional techniques and methods. If knowledge or information has value and has been disclosed in confidence, then the knowledge or information may well be protected as know-how. The key elements of know-how are that it is *confidential* (*i.e.* it has not been publicly disclosed) and that it has *commercial or technological significance*. There is no registration of know-how. Whereas the hallmark of the patent system is disclosure of the patent in exchange for the grant of a monopoly for a limited period of time, the foundation of know-how is that its subject-matter remains secret. As long as such secrecy is maintained, the protection of rights in the know-how continue without limitation of time.

Uses of Know-How

1–17 A patent licence may be of practical use only if the patentee also makes available certain know-how necessary to implement the invention. In other situations, the know-how may have significant commercial or technological value, but it may not be eligible for patent protection. Alternatively, the know-how may be patentable, but its proprietor may not seek patent protection because of its limited practical duration, preferring instead to exploit the technology or knowledge in confidence.

Know-How and Trade Mark Licensing

1–18 A trade mark licence may be ancillary to a know-how (or patent) licence. The reverse is also true; know-how may be a part of a trade mark licence. This

---

[13] See the U.S. Supreme Court decisions, *Kewanee Oil Co. v. Bicron Corp.*, 416 U.S. 470 (1974) and *Aronson v. Quick Point Pencil Co.*, 440 U.S. 257 (1979), for attempts to understand the nature of know-how under U.S. law. The English law approach to the subject has been well expressed in *Saltman Engineering v. Campbell Engineering*, 65 R.P.C. 203 (1949) and *Coco v. A.N. Clark (Engineers) Ltd* [1969] R.P.C. 421.

is especially true in connection with quality control, where the manufacture or production of the goods is dependent on the provision of know-how from the licensor to the licensee. Thus, a trade mark licence will frequently concern itself with know-how as well.

Advantages and Disadvantages of Know-How as a Protectable Right

The open-ended nature of know-how with respect to both its subject matter 1–19
and the duration of its protection carries with it both advantages and disadvantages. On the one hand, the broad definition of know-how means that its protection may be enjoyed over a wide array of technological and commercial secrets without any obligation to ever disclose its contents. On the other hand, since the essence of the protection is confidentiality, the owner of the know-how must be on constant guard. A secret that is disclosed, even improperly, may well never be recaptured, and the relief available may not compensate for the loss or damage caused by the disclosure.

Befitting its protean nature, a know-how licence is less easily described than a patent licence. True, the know-how licence is essentially an agreement to pay royalties or other consideration in exchange for the right to use certain disclosed knowledge or information on an exclusive or non exclusive basis. However, know-how is not a negative right in the same sense as a patent. This is because know-how is essentially a confidence rather than a prohibition against use of the know-how *per se*. One does not infringe rights in the know-how; instead, one breaches the terms of confidence under which the know-how has been disclosed. Any person who has developed or arrived at the know-how independently, without breaching the confidence of the proprietor, is free to do so. This is not so with regard to a patent, where any unauthorised use by a third party, no matter how innocent, is an infringement.

Nature of the Know-How Licence

Because of the nature of know-how, the contents of a know-how licence tend 1–20
to be less given to precise definition than those of a patent licence. This is compounded by the fact that, in comparison with a patent, the licensing of know-how is more likely to be on-going in nature. Moreover, to the extent that the know-how is part of continuing research and development, it becomes more and more difficult to disentangle the know-how from the sum total of the final product.

All this uncertainty has particular implications for termination of the know-how licence, when the task of trying to specify what technology and knowledge is to be returned to the proprietor of the know-how often proves to be a daunting task. Thus, a know-how licence requires from the parties not only contractual good faith, but a large degree of mutual trust and good will as well. However, patent licensing and know-how licensing both fall within the field of industrial property in the accepted sense. They share a common purpose, namely, to enable the commercial production or manufacture of a product through the use of the patent or know-how. In each case, the licensor makes available to the licensee certain knowledge or information that the licensee would otherwise not be permitted to use. In the absence of the licensed knowledge or information, the licensee would be less likely or would be unable to manufacture or produce the product.

Copyright

Copyright Protects Certain Types of Works

1–21 Copyright is concerned with protecting the results of man's creative expression against unauthorised copying or reproduction by others. Copyright is a territorial right, but the widespread membership of countries in several international arrangements, most notably the Berne Union, has provided a common floor for rights and protection at the international level.[14] Historically, four categories of works were protected by copyright: literary, artistic, musical and dramatic works. Subsequently, in response to advances in technology, other types of works, such as sound recordings, films, broadcasts, and computer software, have been accorded copyright protection.

Originality and Expression

1–22 It will readily be noted that there is great variety in the types of works that are protected by copyright. Still, there are two basic characteristics that are common to all protected works.

(a) The work must be original. This means at a minimum that the work must have originated with the author and must not have been taken or adapted from some other source.[15]

(b) The work must constitute the expression (or fixation) of an idea rather than the idea itself. Thus, while one could not claim copyright in the idea for a story in which the children of two feuding families fall in love with tragic consequences, a particular version of this story is protected with tragic consequences, a particular version of this story is protected against copying. It is not always easy to distinguish between idea and expression, particularly in such areas as computer software and useful works. Still, this distinction between unprotected idea and protected expression is fundamental to copyright.

With the principal exception of the U.S., there is no registration of copyright. It subsists the moment that the work is created in a fixed form.

---

[14] It is noted that the U.S. only joined the Berne Union in 1989.

[15] Under U.S. law, the originality requirement may also include an element of creativity. See *Feist Publications, Inc. v. Rural Telephone Service Co., Inc.*, 113 L.Ed. 2d 358 (1991). Note, however, that the distinction between idea and expression may not be so clear-cut under English law. In the recent judgment rendered on February 24, 1994 in the case of *Ibcos Computers Ltd. v. Barclays Mercantile Highland Finance Ltd* (H.C. unreported) Jacob J. stated that '[t]he true position is that where an "idea" is sufficiently general, then even if an original work embodies it, the mere taking of that ideal will not infringe. But if the "idea" is detailed, then there may be infringement. It is a question of degree.'

Categorisation is Central to Copyright

The definition and categorisation of a work is central to the operation of the   1–23
copyright system, because the categorisation determines: (a) whether or not
the subject matter is protected under copyright; (b) if so, what type of
protected work is involved; and (c) what rights are conferred upon the owner
of the copyright in the work.

For instance, (a) Is the stylised drawing of a girl dressed in blue a work?
(Answer: 'yes'); (b) Is the drawing a protected work? (Answer: 'yes', it is an
artistic work); and (c) What rights are conferred upon the proprietor of the
drawing? (Answer: 'the right to prohibit unauthorised copying or reproduction,
adaptation, issuing or distributing copies to the public.')

Most simply put, copyright protects against the unauthorised copying of a
work, or its adaptation into another medium, such as making a movie based
on a protected short story. The emphasis on protecting works against copying
makes copyright easy to understand, but it serves as a limit on the protection
that it accords its owner, since it does not extend to the underlying idea.

Copyright Licences

A copyright licence is an undertaking by the owner of the copyright that the   1–24
licensee may copy the protected work. However, a copyrighted work may be
used in numerous ways, each of which may be the subject of a separate
licence. For example, a book may be translated, it may be serialised, and it
may be turned into a television screen play. Each of these copyrighted uses
of the book may be licensed to a different licensee. Indeed, it is quite unlikely
in such circumstances that a single licence would be given whereby one person
would be granted the right to exercise all these rights. Or, to take the example
of the stylised drawing of the girl, a licence could be given to allow
reproduction of the drawing for use only on various articles of clothing.
Under such circumstances, the licence would not allow the licensee to use the
figure on the cover of a notebook (for instance), and any such use by the
licensee would be copyright infringement.

Unlike a patent or know-how licence, a copyright licence is less likely to
have as its aim the manufacture or production of a product or a process.
(Computer software is the one major exception.) On the other hand, copyright
licensing has become a favoured method of character merchandising. Given
the variety of subject matters that can be protected by copyright, it is difficult
to furnish a single characterisation that would apply to all licensing situations.

TRADE MARKS ARE DIFFERENT

It is the distinctive elements of trade mark licensing that are the focus of this   1–25
book. At the heart of the matter, trade mark licensing is different from other
intellectual property rights because trade marks are different from patents,
know-how, copyright and so on. To understand trade mark licensing, one
must have an appreciation for the law of trade marks.

Protection under U.K. Law[16]

1–26   Until most recently, registered trade marks were governed in the U.K. by the Trade Marks Act 1938, as amended, and service marks were governed by the Trade Marks (Amendment) Act 1984, as amended (collectively: 'the Trade Marks Act 1938').[17] Trade marks refer to marks used in connection with the manufacture and sale of goods, e.g. soft drinks or motor vehicles, while service marks relate to marks used in connection with the provision of services, e.g. banking or insurance. Since service marks were not accorded protection under the Act until the 1984 enactment, the experience with service mark protection, and by extension, service mark licensing, is still in its formative period under U.K. law. Unless otherwise required under the circumstances, any reference in this book to a trade mark is intended to include a service mark as well.

The emphasis above on the words 'until most recently' reflects the fact that a new trade mark code, entitled the Trade Marks Act 1994, which replaces the Trade Marks Act 1938, has recently been enacted in the U.K.[18] The Trade Marks Act 1994 implements the E.C. Council Directive of December 21, 1989, to approximate the laws of the member states relating to trade marks (the 'Trade Marks Directive'), as well as to bring about a general modernisation of the law of trade marks in the U.K.[19] It also gives effect to various proposals for change in the trade mark laws in the U.K. contained in the White Paper of the Department of Trade and Industry entitled 'Reform of Trade Mark Law' (the 'White Paper').[20]

In line with the Trade Marks Directive and the White Paper, the Trade Marks Act 1994 provides for broader protection of trade marks and service marks than is currently available under the Trade Marks Act 1938. Regarding licensing, the Trade Marks Act 1994 eliminates the substantive examination

---

[16] The leading treatise on trade marks under U.K. law is Kerly, *Law of Trade Marks and Trade Names* (12th ed., 1986).

[17] 1 & 2 Geo. 6, c. 22; 1984 Trade Marks (Amendment) Act (c. 19); and Patents, Designs and Marks Act 1986 (c. 39); and Copyright, Designs and Patents Act 1988 (c. 48). Despite the fact that the 1938 and 1984 enactments, governing trade marks and service marks, respectively, are virtually identical, they were in fact enacted as separate legislative codes. A separate code was provided for service marks because it was argued that prior to when the 1984 enactment came into effect, there had been no legal recognition of service marks as a form of intellectual property.

[18] Trade Marks Act 1994 (c. 26). It is noted that the U.K. had delayed its implementation of the Trade Marks Directive beyond the mandated date of December 31, 1992. The implications of this delay on the status of the Trade Marks Act 1938, particularly to the extent that it is inconsistent with the mandatory portions of the Trade Marks Directive, have been debated. See, e.g. Nissen and Karet, 'The Trade Marks Directive: Can I Prevail if the State Has Failed?' [1993] 3 E.I.P.R. 91. With the enactment of the Trade Marks Act 1994, the practical effect of these debates can be assumed to be moot.

[19] First Council Directive of December 21, 1988 to approximate the laws of the Member States relating to trade marks (89/104/EEC).

[20] Reform of Trade Marks Law, Department of Trade and Industry, Cm 1203 (1990). As well, the Trade Marks Act 1994 *inter alia*: (i) makes provision for the Trade Mark Regulation of the E.U. (not yet enacted); (ii) allows effect to be given in the U.K. to the Protocol relating to the Madrid Agreement regarding the International Registration of Trade Marks, thereby enabling the U.K. to ratify the Protocol; and (iii) satisfies various other international obligations concerning trade marks arising under the Paris Convention for the Protection of Industrial Property.

of a licence arrangement as a prerequisite to recordal of the licensee as a registered user, while still providing for a recordation system to make the existence of a licence more patent to third parties. The Trade Marks Act 1994 also specifies the rights of exclusive and non-exclusive licensees so recorded, in the event of an infringement of the registered trade mark.[21]

With the enactment of the Trade Marks Act 1994, it appears that for a time there will be something of a dual system with respect to trade mark licences, depending upon when the licence was granted. The Trade Marks Act 1938 will apply to a licence that a licence granted before the commencement of the Trade Marks Act 1994, *i.e.* October 31, 1994, while the Trade Marks Act 1994 will apply to a licence granted after that date.[22]

This book will make reference to both the Trade Marks Act 1938 and the Trade Marks Act 1994, as appropriate, in discussing the relevant portions of each in connection with the licensing of a registered trade mark.

Trade Marks and Service Marks Defined

Section 68 of the Trade Marks Act 1938 defined a trade mark and a service   **1–27** mark thus:

Trade Mark:

> 'a mark used or proposed to be used in relation to goods for the purpose of indicating, or so as to indicate, a connection in the course of trade between the goods and some person having the right either as proprietor or as registered user to use the mark, whether with or without any indication of the identity of that person...'

Service Mark:

> 'a mark (including a device, name, signature, word, letter, numeral or any combination thereof) used or proposed to be used in relation to services for the purpose of indicating, or so as to indicate, that a particular person is connected, in the course of business, with the provision of those services, whether with or without any indication of the identity of that person...'

Section 1(1) of the Trade Marks Act 1994, in accordance with the Trade Marks Directive, contains a single definition for both trade marks and service marks, thus:

> 'In this Act, a "trade mark" means any sign, capable of being represented graphically which is capable of distinguishing goods or services of one undertaking from those of other undertakings.
>
> A trade mark may, in particular, consist of words (including personal names), designs, letters, numerals or the shape of goods or their packaging.'

---

[21] Trade Marks Act 1994, ss. 25, 28–31.
[22] Trade Marks Act 1994, Sched. 3, para. 9. See, *infra*, Chap. 4, para. 4–32, n. 89.

A Trade Mark Protects a Connection in the Course of Trade

1–28   Under both sets of definitions, it is not the words or symbols of the trade mark per se, nor the product to which the mark refers, that is protected. Indeed, the product itself need not be the subject of any distinct intellectual property protection. Rather, it is the connection between the goods and the proprietor as symbolised by the trade mark that is protected. A trade mark enables the proprietors to distinguish his goods from those of others, and to protect the commercial association that is created between the mark and the product. As long as this association between the mark and the product is maintained, the trade mark remains effective.

Registration of a Trade Mark

1–29   To register a trade mark, an application is filed, and the mark is examined for registrability. Two major criteria determine registrability:

(a) Is the mark of the type that may be registered? The principal concern here is whether the mark is distinctive, *i.e.* whether it distinguishes the source of the goods or services to which it refers. A mark is not distinctive if it relates primarily to the goods or services to which the mark applies, or to a character or quality thereof, rather than to the source of the goods.[23] Taking its cue from the Trade Marks Directive, the Trade Marks Act 1994 refers to a mark that is refused registration on this basis as an 'absolute ground' for refusal.[24]

(b) Is the mark identical or does it resemble a mark that has already been registered in respect of the same or similar goods, *i.e.* is the mark deceptive or is it likely to cause confusion with the other mark or symbol? Here, as well, taking its cue from the Trade Marks Directive, the Trade Marks Act 1994 refers to a mark that is refused registration on this basis as a 'relative ground' for refusal.[25]

1–30   Unlike U.S. law, use of the trade mark is not a prerequisite to registration.[26] The registration of the mark on the Register is prima facie evidence of the validity of the rights therein.[27]

Registration of the Trade Mark Licence

1–31   The licensing of a registered trade mark was permitted under the Trade Marks Act 1938, subject to examination of the licence and its being recorded on the Register. The recordation of the licence in this manner, which is popularly referred to as a 'registered user' registration, was permissive rather than mandatory, but significant advantages flowed from the recordal.[28]

    As noted above, the Trade Marks 1994 continues to provide for the

---

[23] Trade Marks Act 1994, s. 3(1), (2).
[24] Trade Marks Act 1994, s. 3.
[25] Trade Marks Act 1994, ss. 5–8. The scope of protection accorded the prior mark with respect to the registration of a later mark has been broadened under the Trade Marks Act 1994.
[26] See below, para. 1–35.
[27] Trade Marks Act 1994, s. 2(1).
[28] See generally, Chaps. 3, 4, for discussion of the registered user provisions.

registration of a trade mark licence, but with a radically different focus. The new Trade Mark Act eliminates any substantive examination of the licence arrangement. The primary purpose of the registration is to put third parties on notice of the existence of the licence.

Regardless of whether or not the licence is registered, the use of a trade   1–32
mark under a licence does not directly relate to the manufacture of a product; indeed, a trade mark has no direct connection with protecting inventive advance and industrial application. Instead, the trade mark licence principally allows the licensee to take advantage of the goodwill that the mark enjoys, or has the potential for acquiring, in the marketplace. By virtue of its goodwill, a trade mark has the power to attract, convince and sell products in the marketplace. The trade mark licence thereby offers the licensee the opportunity to benefit from the goodwill in the mark in its marketing, distribution and advertising.

The key is to ensure that the licensed use of the trade mark maintains the commercial connection between the goods or services and the trade mark proprietor. If this connection is not maintained, the validity of the trade mark itself may be opened to challenge. The maintenance of the commercial connection touches on perhaps the most unique aspect of trade mark licensing, namely the requirement of quality control. The licensor must take steps to guarantee that the licensee's use of the trade mark does nothing to harm the commercial connection created by the mark.[29]

Unregistered Trade Marks

Unregistered trade marks are protected under the law of passing off.[30] In the   1–33
case of an unregistered trade mark, there is no presumption that the mark or symbol has come to be associated with the plaintiff. Rather, the plaintiff's goodwill must be proved in court. The status of the purported license of an unregistered trade mark under law in the United Kingdom is uncertain.[31]

Protection under U.S. Law

While there certainly are material differents between the Trade Marks Act   1–34
1938 and the Trade Marks Act 1994 on the one hand, and the U.S. trade mark law on the other, the broad brush strokes of the two systems are not dissimilar.

Registered trade mark rights are principally regulated under the Trademark Act of 1946, as amended, popularly known as the Lanham Act.[32] Both trade marks and service marks have been protected by the Lanham Act since its

---

[29] See Chap. 6, for discussion on quality control.
[30] See generally Wadlow, *Passing Off* (1990). See also Trade Marks Act 1994, s. 2(2).
[31] See Chap. 3, paras. 3–14 to 3–19.
[32] The Trademark (Lanham) Act of 1946, ss. 1–50, 15 U.S.C. 1051 *et seq.*, as amended. As a precise matter, the Lanham Act regulates trade marks at the federal level only, *i.e.* interstate commerce or commerce with a foreign country. The Lanham Act also addresses unregistered marks and symbols. There are also statutory schemes for registration of trade marks by the various individual states, but the reach of protection under state registrations is limited, save for a claim based on dilution. This book will focus on federal rights under the Lanham Act.

enactment. The Lanham Act defines a trade mark and a service mark in a manner similar to that of the Trade Mark Act.[33]

As in the U.K., registration is granted following application and examination. The principal grounds for registrability are that the mark is distinctive, *i.e.* that it is neither descriptive of the goods, nor identical or similar to another mark either registered or in prior use. As a practical matter, federal registration of a mark is often more readily obtained in the U.S., than in the U.K. under the Trade Marks Act 1938. As well, the scope of protection granted to a registered mark in the U.S. was broader than that accorded under the Trade Marks 1938. This may well change under the Trade Marks Act 1994.

Use Requirement for Trade Mark Registration

1–35　U.S. law departs from U.K. law in its requirement that there be actual use of the trade mark prior to registration. This requirement follows from the common law foundation of trade mark protection, namely, that trade mark rights are derived from use and not from the mere adoption of a mark. Thus, federal registration does not create trade mark rights, but merely extends such rights.[34] The use requirement has been modified in part under the 1988 amendments to the Lanham Act, which gave recognition to the right to file an application to file on an 'intent-to-use' basis. However, registration will not issue until the applicant has provided evidence of actual use of the mark.[35]

Licensing Permitted Under The Lanham Act

1–36　Licensing is permitted under the Lanham Act under the concept of a 'related company.' A 'related company' is in effect a licensee that uses the trade mark subject to the quality control of the licensor.[36] There is no registration of a related company, and the test for the validity of the licence is whether the standard for quality control has been met.

A Licence as Opposed to an Assignment

1–37　A clear distinction should be made between the assignment and the licensing of a mark. Proprietorship of a trade mark, being a form of intellectual

---

[33] Thus (Lanham Act, s.45):
  A trade mark is 'any word, name, symbol, or device, or any combination thereof–(1) used by a person ... to identify and distinguish his or her goods, including a unique product, from those manufactured or sold by others and to indicate the source of the goods, even if that source is unknown.'
  A service mark is 'any word, name, symbol, or device, or any combination thereof–(1) used by a person ... to identify and distinguish the services of one person, including a unique service, from the services of others and to indicate the source of the services even if that source is unknown.'

[34] A similar view regarding use of a mark as a prerequisite was once held under U.K. law as well, but it was changed in the Trade Marks Act 1905.

[35] Lanham Act, s.1(b). The date of the application will be deemed the constructive date of first use. However, no registration will issue unless the applicant establishes actual use of the mark within a prescribed statutory period.

[36] Lanham Act, ss.5 and 45. See, *infra*, Chap. 5, for discussion of the 'related company' doctrine.

property, may be transferred or assigned to a third party. Once the assignor parts with ownership, it no longer has any further right to use the trade mark, unless the assignee licenses back a right of use to the assignor.[37]

A licence, on the other hand, merely purports to grant a right of use of the trade mark to the licensee. Such use by the licensee may, under appropriate circumstances, actually provide the basis for the licensor's claim of validity in the trade mark. The licensee does not, however, obtain any right of proprietorship in the mark itself.

Conclusion

This book will be divided into three principal parts. The first part will discuss the foundations of trade mark licensing. The second part will compare and contrast licensing from related forms of trade mark use by third parties, and will consider the contract aspects of trade mark licensing. The third part will focus upon related aspects of a trade mark licence. The book will conclude with an annotated trade mark licence, together with cross references to the main body of the text to highlight issues raised in the annotation.

1–38

---

[37] See, *infra*, Chap. 6, paras. 6–48 to 6–63, for discussion on assignment and licence back.

2. Trade Mark Licensing and the Functions of a Trade Mark

INTRODUCTION

Trade mark licensing is distinguished from other forms of licensing, in general, **2–01** and intellectual property licensing, in particular, by the fact that it deals with trade marks. This observation is not intended simply to state the obvious, but rather to emphasise that one cannot understand trademark licensing without an appreciation of the legal foundation of trade marks.

It has been said that there is no area of trade mark law that is 'murkier' than licensing.[1] This uncertainty is due in no small measure to the historical foundations of trademark law generally. While trade mark licensing continues to change and expand, it derives from legal roots that continue to be essential. Thus, the historical development of trade marks must be the starting point for understanding trademark licensing.

The Functions of a Trade Mark

The historical development of the concept of a trade mark can perhaps best **2–02** be understood in terms of the functions that the mark serves in trade.

Over time, six functions have been noted in connection with the use of trade marks: identification, physical source, anonymous source, quality, advertising and merchandising. It should be emphasised that these functions have not always been consciously recognised in such terms. Indeed, the early history of trade mark law and doctrine has been described as a combination of 'what actually happened with myth drawn from decisions over the years ...'[2] Nevertheless, a certain consensus has developed about these functions, and they have been recognised by commentators and judges as a useful way of understanding trade mark law. The nature and scope of trade mark licensing is a direct consequence of the functions that a trade mark has been understood to serve. Hence, trade mark licensing can only be appreciated against this historical backdrop.

---

[1] Bereskin, 'The Source Theory of Trade Mark Law and its Effect on Trade Mark Licensing,' *Patent and Trademark Institute of Canada Review* (1986), p. 322.
[2] Kerly, *Law of Trade Marks and Trade Names* (12th ed., 1986), p. 1, n.2.

Trade Mark Licensing has Moved in Step with the Function of a Trade Mark

2–03   At one time, it was commonly held that trade mark licensing was not permitted at law, because licensing was viewed as incompatible with the sole function of a trade mark, namely, the identification of the source of the goods. Use of the mark by a licensee, being a person other than the proprietor of the mark, was deemed deceptive, since the licensed use no longer designated the source of the goods.[3] Later, a trade mark was understood as serving a related function, the assurance of a consistent expectation of quality in respect of the goods. With the recognition of the quality function of a trade mark, trade mark licensing was permitted, subject to some provision of quality control over the licensee.[4]

In the United Kingdom and other countries influenced by English law, statute has provided for the recordal of the licensee as a registered user, which sets restrictions on the licensee's use of the trade mark.[5] Even if the recordal of a licence is no longer deemed to be mandatory,[6] or where no recordal of a registered user has ever been required (such as in the U.S.), the validity of the licence rests upon the notion of control with respect to the licensee's use of the trade mark.[7] What is common to each of these situations is that the right to license a trade mark is predicated on quality control.

More recently, there has been a growing sense that a trade mark enjoys independent value beyond that of identifying and distinguishing the goods or services of the trade mark proprietor.[8] Under certain circumstances, the mark not only signifies that the proprietor stands behind the goods or services identified by the mark, but that the mark itself enjoys a certain drawing power or cachet, whereby the consumer wishes to be identified with the mark itself. The proprietor of the trade mark will likely wish to engage in licensing to take advantage of the commercial attraction of the mark itself. Here, the extent to which a mark may be licensed in such a fashion, and if so, under what conditions, has not been fully resolved.

This chapter will discuss the interrelationship between the changing understanding of a trade mark, and the nature of trade mark licensing.

---

[3] See, *infra*, paras. 2–04 to 2–17.
[4] See, *infra*, paras. 2–18 to 2–26; see generally Chap. 6 and McCarthy, *Trade Marks and Unfair Competition* (1st ed.) Chap. 3.
[5] See, *infra*, generally Chap. 3. The Trade Marks Act 1994 provides for the registration of licensees, but has done away with any substantive examination of the licence arrangement. See generally Chap. 4.
[6] See Chap. 3, paras. 3–04 to 3–19.
[7] See generally Chap. 6. In Canada, the registered user system has recently been abolished by virtue of the Amendments to the Trade Marks Act of June 9, 1993 (R.S. c. T–10, s. 1). As a result, the Canadian approach to licensing now more closely resembles that taken in the U.S.
[8] See paras. 2–27 to 2–33.

THE IDENTIFICATION FUNCTION

A Trade Mark and the Identification of Ownership

The antedecents to the modern concept of trade marks can be found in certain   2–04
uses of a mark to identify the ownership of goods or the person responsible
for its manufacture. Two such types of marks have been noted.

The Merchant's Mark

The first was a 'merchant's' mark that was voluntarily affixed to the goods
by the owner of the goods. The purpose of this mark was to establish
ownership of the goods, either for the benefit of illiterate clerks, or to assist
the Admirality Court in connection with goods brought before it after recovery
from piracy or a shipwreck. In this situation, the mark served as evidence of
the identity of the owner of the goods.[9]

The Craftsman's Mark

The second was a 'craftsman's' mark that was applied to the goods and
served to identify the craftsman that produced the goods. The mark was
personal in nature inasmuch as it identified the work of a single craftsman.
This type of mark has also been described as a 'regulatory production' mark,
since its affixation was often compulsory, either by statute, administrative
order or regulation of a guild or municipality. In this sense, its purpose was
punitive and restrictive in nature, since it enabled a person either to trace the
source of defective craftsmanship, or to identify goods that were being
smuggled into an area in which another guild enjoyed a monopoly.[10]

It is with the craftsman's mark, as used in connection with the cutlery and
clothier trades, that we find the beginning of the use of a trade mark to
identify the source of the goods. In the cloth industry, as rivalry developed
between various groups of cloth makers, a mark was employed to identify
the collective origin of the goods. Identity of individual cloth makers was less
important.[11] In the cutlery industry, the identification of individual craftsmen
was apparently more important, although there, as well, marking was done
within the context of the Cutlers' Company.[12]

No Licensing in Pre-Modern Use of Marks

More typically, however, a mark did not serve even this limited form of   2–05
identifying the source of the goods. Given the local nature of trade prior to
the Industrial Revolution, sellers and buyers personally knew each other.
Thus, the mark was not relied upon to convey information about the source

---

[9] Schechter, 'The Rational Basis for Trademark Protection,' 40 Har. L.Rev. 813, 814 (1927). See
generally, Schechter, *The Historical Foundations of the Law Relating to Trade Marks* (1925),
p. 20.
[10] Bereskin, 'The Sources and Theory of Trade Mark Law and its Effect on Trades Mark
Licensing, *Patent and Trademark Institute of Canada Review* (1986).
[11] *ibid.*
[12] Bereskin, 'The Rational Basis for Trademark Protection,' at p. 324.

21

of the goods, since they could readily be inspected by the customer before making the purchase. In these circumstances, the issue of licensing did not arise.

THE SOURCE FUNCTION

The Trade Mark as an Identifier of Source

2–06   With the advent of the Industrial Revolution, the proximity between producers and purchasers waned, as more and more goods began to be transported over greater distances. With these changes in the nature and scope of manufacture and distribution, the power of the guild to inspect and regulate goods declined. The function of the mark changed apace. It no longer merely served a punitive or regulatory role. Rather, it became the badge of the proprietor, whereby the purchaser could rely on the mark as identifying the source of the goods bearing the mark, even if the source was removed from direct contact with the ultimate purchaser. The courts struggled to keep abreast with this fundamental change in the commercial function of the mark.

Protection of Marks Based on Deceit

2–07   At the outset, protection for marks was based on a claim for deceit, whereby use by the defendant of the plaintiff's mark or symbol served to deceive the purchaser.[13] As early as the 17th century, a case is reported in which the court apparently recognised an action in tort where the defendant used the plaintiff's mark on its own, inferior goods.[14]

By the mid-19th century, the action for deceit was firmly established at both law and equity, irrespective of whether or not inferior goods were involved, and even if there was a certain fiction. The foundation of the action was based upon proof of fraudulent intent of the defendant with respect to diversion of the plaintiff's goods, while the deceit actually occurred in connection with the confusion on the part of the purchaser.

The focus on deceit made it difficult at first to conceive of trade marks as a form of property. However, in the great case of *Millington v. Fox*,[15] Cottenham L.C. was prepared to enjoin misuse of a trade mark on the basis of infringement, without the necessity to show that there had been an intention to deceive on the part of the defendant. What was important was that the plaintiff had established 'title' to the marks. Under such circumstances, equity could be called upon to assist the 'proprietor' in enforcing its rights to that 'title.'

This view of a trade mark as a form of incorporeal property did not totally displace the concern with deceit. Even as Parliament wrestled with enacting legislation for the protection of trade marks, the focus remained, in the words

---

[13] *Sykes v. Sykes* (1824) 3 B. & C.
[14] *Southern v. How* (1618) Popham 144.
[15] (1838) 3 My. & Cr. 338.

of one contemporary commentator, to deal with 'the repression of common law frauds and cheats, and not merely to prevent the using or pirating of trade marks.'[16] Moreover, there developed a suspicion by liberals of the time that recognition of a property right in trade marks would have an adverse affect on the competitive position of later entrants in the market.

The Trade Mark as a Property Right

Nevertheless, the view of trade marks as a unique form of property became more and more accepted, and its legal contours began to take a recognisable form. This was given particular impetus in a series of judgments by Lord Westbury, who expressed the view that there was a property right in trade marks, whereby the proprietor could dispose of the right and enforce it even as against innocent infringers.[17]   2–08

From the vantage of historical hindsight, Lord Diplock characterised the nature of the property right in trade marks on the eve of the enactment of the Trade Marks Registration Act (1875) thus:

'... [It] shared with patents and with copyright ... that it was a monopoly, that is to say, it was a right to restrain other persons from using the mark. But it was an adjunct of the goodwill of a business and incapable of separate existence disassociated from that goodwill.'[18]

As noted in the words of Lord Diplock, unlike a patent or copyright, where the property right inheres in the invention or the work itself, there is no trade mark right in the word or symbol *per se*. Thus, from its outset, the trade mark was not viewed as a property right in the symbol *per se*, but rather a right that derived from the association of the mark with certain goods, and the goodwill that was created as a result of the association.

Similar Development in the U.S.

Across the Atlantic, a similar recognition had been made by the United States Supreme Court in 1879 in the Trade Mark Cases: 2–09

'The right to adopt and use a symbol or device to distinguish the goods or property made or sold by the person whose mark it is, to the exclusion of the use of that symbol by all other persons, has long been recognized by the common law and the chancery courts of England and of this country, and by the statutes of some of the States. It is a property right, for which damages may be recovered in an action at law and the violation of which will be enjoined by a court of equity, with compensation for past infringement.'[19]

---

[16] Words of William Hindmarch, Report from the Select Committee on Trade Marks Bill in Reports of Committees, 1862, 12 Session Papers, Q. Nos. 2611, 2727, 2749, 2752, 2757, as quoted in Schechter, *supra*, 'The Rational Basis for Trademark Protection,' at p. 820, n. 33.
[17] Wadlow, *Passing Off* (1990), para. 10–07 and the citations contained in accompanying n. 61.
[18] G.E. Trademark, [1973] R.P. c. 297 at p. 325 C.H.L.
[19] *Trade Mark Cases*, 100 U.S. 82 (1879).

Source as Integral to the Property Right

2–10   The recognition of a trade mark as a special form of property right, based on the goodwill embodied in the mark, was integrally linked with the notion that the mark served to indicate the source of the goods. The mark served to inform the purchaser about the actual origin of the goods. Relying upon the trade mark, the purchaser understood that the goods bearing a certain trade mark emanated from a single source.

This was the basis for the proprietor's goodwill. If a third party later began to use the mark for its own goods and, as a result, a purchaser might be confused about the source of the goods bearing the mark, the proprietor was entitled to enjoin the confusing use.

Incompatibility with Licensing

2–11   Trade mark licensing was viewed as inconsistent with the function of a mark as an indicator of the actual source of the goods because a licensee, being a person other than the proprietor, could never be the actual source of the goods. As a result, use by the licensee might invalidate the trade mark, because a purchaser would be deceived about the source of the goods identified by the mark.

Stated another way, a licensee was compared unfavourably with the assignee of a trade mark to whom all of the good will and business of the assignor had been transferred. The law early on recognised the right to assign a trade mark under proper conditions, since the essential unity between the mark and the source of the goods as indicating a trade connection between them was not altered. A licensee, on the other hand, would be using the mark in respect of the goods in the absence of any actual transfer of the goodwill and business. Here, even if the licensee had obtained the authority of the licensor to use the mark, the connection in trade between the mark and the physical source of the goods has been destroyed. Either the proprietor of the mark was no longer the source of the goods, or the licensee, rather than the licensor, would be erroneously held to be the proprietor of the mark. In both situations, licensing would be inconsistent with the function of the trade mark as identifying the actual source of the goods, working a deception on the public.

Incompatibility Also Recognised Under Early U.S. Law

2–12   The incompatability between trade mark licensing and the view that a trade mark served to identify the actual source of the goods, was expressed in the landmark American judgment *Macmahan Pharmacal Co. v. Denver Chemical Mfg. Co.*, where the court stated as follows:

> 'An assignment or license without such a transfer is totally inconsistent with the theory upon which the value of a trademark depends ... Disassociated from merchandise to which it properly appertains [the mark] lacks the essential characteristic which alone gives it value, and becomes false and deceitful designation.'[20]

---

[20] 113 F. 468 (8th Cir. 1908).

The *Bowden Wire* Case

In the United Kingdom, the jurisprudence of trade mark licensing had been   2–13
framed by the judgment of the House of Lords in the case of *Bowden Wire
v. Bowden Brake*.[21] The facts of this landmark judgment warrant particular
attention.

The plaintiff was the patent holder of a product known as Bowden Wire
for use *inter alia* in brakes for bicycles and motorcycles. The plaintiff also
engaged in the actual manufacture of brakes for bicycles. The defendant
acquired that portion of the plaintiff's business which was concerned with
the manufacture of brakes for bicycles, together with a license for the use of
the patent as well as any trade marks. In fact, no trade marks had been used
in association with bicycle brakes at the time of the transfer. Subsequently,
the plaintiff registered one trade mark for brakes for velocipedes and other
road vehicles, and a second trade mark for related component parts and
accessories. It then granted a licence to the defendant to use the first trade
mark with respect to bicycle brakes. The term of the trade mark licence was
co-extensive with the duration of the patent licence.

The market for bicycle brakes diminished, while the trade in brakes for
motorcycles increased dramatically. After the expiry of the plaintiff's patents,
the defendant sought to use the trade mark in respect to motorcycle brakes.
The plaintiff sued, and the defendant responded with a motion to remove the
trade marks from the Register on the grounds that the registration was
invalid.

The trial court ruled in favour of the plaintiff, subject to an amendment to
the first trade mark registration. The Court of Appeal reversed this decision,[22]
holding that the trade mark licence had been granted in respect of goods,
brakes for bicycles, which had been the subject of a prior assignment to the
defendant. As a consequence, the trade marks could not identify the plaintiff
as the course of the goods, and were thus calculated to deceive. The
registrations were accordingly ordered to be expunged.

The House of Lords agreed with the Court of Appeal, holding unanimously
that the registrations were invalid.[23] In so ruling, their lordships emphasised
that the licences were inconsistent with the function of the trade mark as an
indicator of source. This ruling was expressed most pointedly by Lord Shaw,
who stated that

> '[t]he Appellants permitted another firm (not their own firm) to imprint
> upon goods not manufactured by them, the Appellants, but by the other
> firm, a Trade Mark belonging to the Appellants and by law incapable
> of such assignment.'[24]

Lord Dunedin expressed the principle slightly differently:

> 'By registration they affected to tell the public that goods in the class
> and of the description specified, marked with the registered mark, were

---

[21] (1914) 31 R.P.C. 385.
[22] (1913) 30 R.P.C. 45 and 580.
[23] See n. 21 above.
[24] (1914) 31 R.P.C. 385 at 395.

their goods; that is to say, manufactured, or at least put on the market by them. But in reality, with their assent, the mark was, in practice, adhibited to goods which were not put on the market by them, but manufactured by or which were of composite manufacture and put on the market by the Brake Company.'[25]

While the precise reach of the *Bowden Wire* judgment continues to be debated, their lordships were clear on the point that the source function was deemed to be incompatible with the licensing of a trade mark. A proper assignment, that is, where the trade mark was assigned together with the underlying goodwill and business, did not offend this principle, because the mark continued to identify a single source for the goods. Any other transfer of a trade mark, including by way of licence, would be deceptive regarding the source of the goods.

ANONYMOUS SOURCE

Actual Source Deemed Too Narrow

2–14   As the scope of commerce expanded, it became increasingly unlikely that a purchaser would actually know the precise identity of the source of the goods. This could mean that the purchaser was unaware of the identity of the individual craftsman or workman who made the goods. More typically, it meant that the purchaser might not know the identity of the manufacturer.

If the function of a trade mark had been limited to the identity of the actual source of manufacture of the goods, the trade mark right would have become largely irrelevant. For example, under this narrow view, it could have been argued (and was) that the Standard Oil Company could not assert rights in its *Nujol* mark because the goods had been sold in the United Kingdom through and by the name of its local sales agent, The Anglo-American Company. Thus, the public could not identify the actual source of the goods.[26] If the function of a trade mark was to be limited in this manner (and the argument was rejected only on appeal),[27] the commercial value of trade mark protection would have become nil.

The response of the courts was to reconceive the notion of source, whereby a trade mark served its function so long as it indicated a single, albeit anonymous source, for the goods. So long as the trade mark served to indicate this single source for the goods, it did not matter that the purchaser could not identify the actual entity that stood behind the mark.

Recognition of the Anonymous Source Function in the U.K.

2–15   In the well-known *Yorkshire Relish* case, Herschell L.J. expressed the kernel of the anonymous source function of a trade mark as follows:

---

[25] (1914) 31 R.P.C. 385, pp. 392–93.
[26] *Re McDowell's Application*, 43 R.P.C. 313 (1926).
[27] *ibid* pp. 337, 339.

'I do not mean that in the minds of the public the name of the manufacturer was identified, but that it meant a particular manufacture, and that when a person sold "Yorkshire Relish", as the defendants did, by selling it as "Yorkshire Relish", and calling it "Yorkshire Relish", they represented to the public that it was that manufacture which was known as and by the name of "Yorkshire Relish." '[28]

It did not matter whether a purchaser could give the actual name of the producer of the goods, so long as the mark had come to indicate goods that emanated from a single source. Deception occurred if a purchaser was misled about this source, even if he could not identify it with precision. In the words of Warrington L.J., in rejecting the application of the *Nuvol* trade mark in light of the opponent's prior rights in the *Nujol* mark:

'... The deception which I think the registration would be calculated to produce is that the two products emanate from the same source, and for the purposes of the present question it does not, in my opinion, matter whether the public do, or do not, know what that source is.'[29]

Recognition of the Anonymous Source Function Elsewhere

American courts adopted the same approach. One court expressed the   2–16
anonymous source function of trade marks as follows:

'When the courts speak of the public's identifying the source or origin, they do not mean thereby that the purchasing public can identify the maker by his specific name or the place of manufacture by precise location. What they mean by such expression is that the purchaser of goods bearing a given label believes that what he buys emanated from the source, whatever its name or place, from which goods bearing that label have always been derived.'[30]

Further, it had been recognised early on that the identification by a mark of source was not limited solely to the actual manufacturer. Kay J., in the 19th century Australian case of *Wine Importers Ltd*, observed that a trade mark 'means the mark under which a particular individual trades, and indicates the goods to be his goods, either goods manufactured by him or goods selected by him, or goods which, in some way or other pass through his hands in the course of trade.'[31] During the same period, the U.S. Supreme Court had expressed a similar position. In the famous case of *Menendez v. Holt*, the Court held that a dealer in flour had obtained the exclusive rights to the trade mark. The Court stated that '[t]he brand did not indicate by whom the flour was manufactured, but it did indicate the origin of its selection and classification.'[32] This view was also reflected in the definition of a trade mark under the Trade Marks Act 1905, where a mark was defined as

---

[28] *Birmingham Vinegar Brewery Co. Ltd v. Powell* [1897] A.C. 710, 715.
[29] *McDowell's Application, supra*, p. 337.
[30] *Manhattan Shirt Co. v. Sarnoff-Irving Hat Stores*, 164 A. 246, aff'd 180 A. 928.
[31] *Wine Importers Ltd* (1889) 41 Ch.D. 278.
[32] 128 U.S. 514, 520 (1888).

indicating a connection in the course of trade with the proprietor 'by virtue of manufacture, selection, certification, dealing with, or offering for sale.'[33]

The Source Function Explained

2–17   The relationship between the notions (1) that the source function of a trade mark has not been limited to the actual manufacturer of the goods, and (2) that a trade mark can relate to a single, albeit anonymous source, can be explained thus. The former merely reflects the fact that in modern commerce, various associations between the mark and the goods may be made by the consumer. The concept of anonymous source complements this understanding by further recognising that the precise identity of the source of the mark, however source is understood with respect to the use of a trade mark, need not be precisely known.

Still, the relaxation of the source function to connote a single, anonymous source could not, by itself, work any fundamental change with respect to the legal status of licensing. So long as a trade mark was viewed solely in terms of indicating the source of the goods, whether or not the source could be identified with specificity, the use of the mark by a licensee would continue to be viewed as conceptually inconsistent with that function.

THE QUALITY FUNCTION

Quality Control

2–18   Nevertheless, the anonymous source function paved the way for a reconceptualisation of the role that trade marks played in the marketplace, because it drew attention to the importance of the mark as an indicator of quality. Lying at the heart of the anonymous source function was the notion that some person or entity stood behind the goods identified by the trade mark. It could be asked, however, why the indication of anonymous source, standing alone, was so important for the purchaser.

The answer that emerged was that, perhaps more than where the goods came from, what interested the purchaser was whether the trade mark could be relied upon to indicate that the goods were of a certain quality. The trade mark thus created an expectation regarding quality, and allowed the purchaser to safely rely on the expectation. Quality did not mean a warranty. Nor did quality necessarily mean a luxury product. Not every automobile needed to be a Lambourghini, every hotel The Ritz, or every watch a Rolex, in order for the trade mark to serve its quality function. Rather, the trade mark was the consumer's assurance of constancy, consistency and predictability concerning quality with respect to repeated purchases of goods bearing the trade mark.

---

[33] s. 3. See also, *infra*, Chap. 8, paras, 8–01 to 8–16, for discussion of contract manufacturers.

Control is the Touchstone

The key test of this quality function was control.[34] If the proprietor of the   2–19
trade mark exercised some form of control over the goods sold under the
trade mark, then the expectation of the purchaser regarding quality would be
satisfied. A soft drink could be produced by licensed bottlers, or baked goods
could be sold by various subsidiaries of the proprietor. If the proprietor
exercised such control over the use of the mark, whether by himself directly
or by others under this direction, the proprietor could continue to be deemed
the source of the goods. Thus, the source function of a trade mark became
interwoven with the notion of control.

Licensing and Quality Control

Once it was recognised that a trade mark could indicate the source of control   2–20
over the use of the marks with respect to the goods, the legal position of
licensing changed. Provided that the licensor exercised satisfactory control
over the use of the trade mark by the licensee, it did not matter in principle
whether the goods actually emanated from the proprietor of the trade mark,
or from someone under his control.

In either situation, the notion that the mark identified a single source with
respect to the quality of the goods was preserved. As a result, a licence no
longer needed to be viewed as inconsistent with the function of a trade mark.
The issue was not whether or not licensing was permitted, but rather under
what conditions it could take place.

The *Radiation* and *J.H. Coles* Cases

Even before the enactment of the Trade Marks Act 1938, in which licensing   2–21
was explicitly recognised within the framework of the registered user provisions,[35] one can find instances in which licensing was apparently upheld on
the basis of a recognition of the quality control function. The two leading
judgments in this regard are *Re Radiation*[36] and *J.H. Coles Proprietary Ltd v.
Need*.[37] These judgments can be seen as presaging the practice of the use of
house mark and distribution franchising, respectively.

The Radiation Case

In the *Radiation* Case, the applicant for registration of a trade mark was the   2–22
parent of a group of associated companies. All manufacture and sale of the
goods under the mark were carried out by the associated companies rather
than by the applicant, which nevertheless maintained overall policy supervision
over the articles that were to be sold under the mark, and also exercised
control over the design and quality of the manufacture. The Comptroller-

---

[34] See Chap. 6, for discussion of quality control.
[35] ss. 28 and 29; see *infra*, Chap. 3.
[36] (1930) 47 R.P.C. 37.
[37] (1934) 50 R.P.C. 379.

General rejected the argument that the relationship between the applicant and the associated companies rendered the mark deceptive. Applying a 'practical' approach to the question, it was held, by virtue of the corporate relationship between the entities and the actual control that was exercised by the applicant, that:

> 'I ought not to say that the form or constitution of the "Radiation" group of Companies is such as to prevent the Applicants from holding a Trade Mark which indicates the connection of the whole group of Companies under the conditions I have described. The Mark "Radiation" in this case becomes in effect the House Mark of the whole group, in addition to which each associated Company (or Branch) may properly use its own individual Mark.'[38]

However, the force of this judgment as a recognition of the validity of licensing, at least under circumstances of intra-corporate control, was tempered by the alternative holding of the case. Thus, the Comptroller-General stated that even if it was wrong to treat the whole group as users of the House Mark in this fashion, one could still view the Applicant as either 'selecting' or 'dealing with' the goods.[39]

The J.H. Coles Case

2–23 In the *J.H. Coles* case, the Privy Council ruled on a request by the owner of a small chain of retail stores in Australia that a licensee using the trade name and business name of the licensor be enjoined from continuing their use after the termination of the licence. The Privy Council reinstated the injunction, it having been granted in the first instance but subsequently quashed by the Court of Appeal. It emphasised that the licence arrangement had not been carried out with deceptive intent, and that it was therefore valid and enforceable.[40] Presumably, there had been sufficient control over the licensee to indicate a course of trade between them, even if the licensee did not really use the names in connection with goods but rather the retail services of the plaintiff.[41]

Judgments such as in the *Radiation* and *J.H. Coles* cases were hardly determinative of the question as to the conditions under which trade mark licensing would be a permissible exercise of the quality function. The answer to that question would have to await the enactment of the Trade Marks Act

---

[38] (1930) 47 R.P.C. 37 at 43.
[39] (1930) 47 R.P.C. 37 at 44.
[40] (1934) 50 R.P.C. 379 at 387–388.
[41] More recently, quality control was well expressed by Whitford J. as follows:
'If one buys a dressing gown bearing the trade mark 'McGregor', one may never know and may not be concerned to enquire who in fact made the dressing gown in question; but if one buys a dressing gown and finds it satisfactory one would feel, if one were buying another dressing gown bearing the same brand name at a later stage, that one could reasonably expect it to be of similar quality to the first dressing gown. In the same way, it is customary for people to make recommendations to their friends by reference to brand names for goods; and, upon a recommendation being made, the purchase is carried out in the confidence that the article purchased will be of similar quality to that sold to the friend making the original recommendation.' *McGregor T.M.* [1979] R.P.C. 36, 51.

1938, with its explicit provisions for permitted use of a trade mark by a registered user.[42] Nevertheless, these judgments reflect the fact that the quality function, with its emphasis on control, could enable a court to give effect to the use of a mark by a licensee.

Quality Control Also Recognised in the U.S.

In the U.S. as well, prior to the enactment of the Lanham Act in 1946, which gave express recognition to licensing a 'related company',[43] courts on occasion had showed a readiness to recognise certain licensing arrangements. These results may be understood in terms of control by the licensor over the licensee. Two recurring types of situations can be identified from that period in which such control was determinative.

Control Over the Main Ingredient of a Product

In one line of cases the trade mark proprietor controlled the main ingredient of the product, and sometimes exercised control over its manufacture by the licensee as well. The leading examples of this were the cases involving the franchise bottling and distribution arrangements of the Coca Cola company, where the validity of the licensing arrangements was sometimes put in issue.[44]

In another variation, a licensor would authorise a licensee to use its patents and know-how in addition to the grant of the trade mark license.[45] Here as well, some courts would give effect to the license if they found that the licensor had exercised active quality control in the manufacture of the goods under the licence. While it was not always articulated, these judgments can be understood in terms of the quality control that was provided by the licensee.

Financial Control

The other type of case was where the trade mark proprietor enjoyed financial control over the entities that used the trade mark. Here the courts were divided as to whether mere financial control was enough.[46]

The Continuing Relevance of the Source Function

With the enactment of the Trade Marks Act 1938 and the Lanham Act 1946, licensing was given statutory recognition, albeit subject to certain restrictions which are discussed elsewhere.[47] However, the quality function did not replace the notion of source as the foundation of trade mark law. On the contrary, the respective definitions of a 'trade mark' under the Trade Marks Act 1938,

2–24

2–25

---

[42] See, *infra*, Chap. 3.

[43] See Chap. 5 for discussion on 'related company'.

[44] See, *e.g. Coca Cola Bottling Co. v. Coca-Cola Co.*, 269 F. 796 (D. Del. 1920).

[45] See, *e.g. Smith v. Dental Products Co.* 140 F.2d 140 (7th Cir), cert. denied, 322 U.S. 743 (1944).

[46] *cf. Keebler Weyl Baking co. v. J.S. Ivins' Son*, 7 F. Supp. 211 (E.D. Pa. 1934) with *Re United States Steel Corp.*, 23 U.S.P.Q. 145 (Comm'r 1934).

[47] See *infra*, Chaps. 3, 4 and 5.

and the Lanham Act, as amended, both explicitly adopted the notion of a trade mark as indicating the source, albeit anonymous, of the goods.[48]

Recognition of the Quality Function in Connection with Licensing

2–26   Reference to the quality function of trade marks is found in connection with the statutory provisions dealing with licensing. The quality function is explicitly referred to in the definition of a 'related company' under the Lanham Act,[49] and is clearly implied in the Trade Marks Act 1938 by the references to control over the use of the mark by a registered user.[50]

In both statutes, the recognition of the quality function was wedded with control so as to confer statutory authority to trade mark licensing. Thus, trade mark licensing was the principal beneficiary of this recognition of the quality function.

THE ADVERTISING FUNCTION

2–27   With the growth of advertising and promotion in modern commerce, trade marks increasingly come to be used apart from the goods to which they were actually applied. It was observed that the use of a trade mark in this way served a somewhat different function, namely, that the mark might become the very instrument for creating demand for the goods. This view was well expressed by Schechter as follows:

> '... [T]oday the trademark is not merely the symbol of goodwill but often the most effective agent for the creation of goodwill, imprinting upon the public mind an anonymous and impersonal guaranty of satisfaction, creating a desire for further satisfactions. The mark actually sells the goods. And, self-evidently, the more distinctive the mark, the more effective is its selling power.'[51]

---

[48] s. 68(1) of the Trade Marks Act 1938 defined a trade mark as a 'mark used or proposed to be used in relation to goods for the purpose of indicating, or so as to indicate, a connection in the course of trade between the goods and some person having the right either as proprietor or as registered user to use the mark, whether with or without any indication of the identity of that person.' There is a parallel statutory definition for a service mark.
s. 45 of the Lanham Act defines a trade mark to 'include any word, name, symbol, or device, or any combination thereof ... to identify and distinguish his or her goods, including a unique product, from those manufactured or sold by others and to indicate the source of the goods, even if the source is unknown.' The definition in pertinent part concerning service marks is similar. It is noted that the Trade Marks Act 1994 does not explicitly refer to a trade mark as indicating origin, despite a proposed amendment to that effect. Norman, "Trade Mark Licences in the United Kingdom: Time for Bostitch to be Re-evaluated": [1994] 4 E.I.P.R. 154. 157.
cf. with the recent judgment of the European Court of Justice. *IHT International GmbH v. Ideal-Standard GmbH.* C-9/93 (June 22, 1994), in which the court emphasised the mark as an indicator of origin, and the exercise of quality control as the basis for applying the doctrine of exhaustion. Chap. 13. *infra*, paras. 13–08 to 13–11.
[49] s. 45.
[50] s. 28. It should be noted that no explicit reference to quality control is made in ss. 28–31 of the Trade Marks Act 1994, which governs the explicit registration of licensees.
[51] Schechter, *supra*, n. 9, 'The Rational Basis for Trade Mark Protection', at p. 819.

In other words, through a trade mark, its proprietor 'may "reach over the shoulder of the retailer" and across the latter's counter straight to the consumer.'[52]

The psychological attraction of trade marks in this sense was graphically described by Justice Frankfurter of the United States Supreme Court in the following words:

'If it is true that we live by symbols, it is no less true that we purchase goods by them. A trade mark is a merchandising short cut which induces a purchaser to select what he wants, or what he has been led to believe that he wants. The owner of a mark exploits this human propensity by making every effort to impregnate the atmosphere of the market with the drawing power of the congenial symbol.'[53]

In Criticism of Advertising

The advertising function of trade marks has long engendered opinion both for and against. On the negative side, some have viewed the psychological pull of trade marks as irrational, allowing the trade mark proprietor to manipulate the consumer's psyche by artificially differentiating its product from those of its competitors. For example, there may be no substantial difference between a certain brand of soap and that its competitors. Through advertising, however, consumers can be made to prefer one brand of soap over the others.   **2–28**

The result can be that the proprietor enjoys a monopoly power over the price of the product and may even be able to prevent the entry of competitors into the market. In the words of one commentator writing over forty years ago, '[i]mmoderate regard for entrenched brand-name interests can freeze the pattern of industries . . .'[54]

In Favour of Advertising

Those arguing in favour of the advertising function emphasise that the use of the trade mark in advertising complements the source and quality functions of a trade mark by enabling the consumer easily to identify the product. Under this view, advertising of the trade mark actually reduces the cost to the consumer, because it provides the consumer with a short-hand way of being certain that he is obtaining the product that he wants.[55] Use of the trade mark in advertising may thus be both rational and efficient. Moreover, proponents of the advertising function favour less paternalism in the attitude of authorities towards consumer choice, and less hostility to the notion of consumer attraction to symbols. They argue that the vicissitudes of the   **2–29**

---

[52] Schechter, *supra*, p. 818.
[53] *Mishawaka Rubber & Woolen Mfg. C. v. SS. Kresge Co.*, 316 U.S. 203, 53 U.S.P.Q. 323, 325 (1942).
[54] Brown, 'Advertising and the Public Interest: Legal Protection of Trade Symbols,' 57 Yale L.J. 1165 (1948).
[55] See, *e.g.* Nelson, 'Information and Consumer Behavior,' 78 J. Pol. Econ. 311, 312 (1970).

market, rather than any legal or administrative action, should determine the ultimate commercial fate of products and the trade marks that they bear.

Licensing and Advertising

2–30   However, even if one views the advertising function favourably, the question remains as to what it implies for trade mark protection and use. The source and quality functions protect the proprietor against deception with respect to the use by another of an identical or similar trade mark on competing goods. Licensing has been woven into this framework, albeit with some difficulty, on the ground that quality control serves the source and quality functions.

The advertising function is different. Its role is principally psychological, serving to strengthen the 'identity and hold upon the public mind of the mark or name.'[56] Thus, the licensing of a trade mark is not directly connected with the advertising function, although a trade mark licence will typically address the use of the licensed mark in advertising and promotion.[57]

Perhaps the most that can be said is that the advertising function of a trade mark may be part of a licence arrangement, but this function does not replace the source and quality functions as the basis for a trade mark licence.

THE MERCHANDISING FUNCTION

The Trade Mark as a Good in Itself

2–31   But it is not merely that the trade mark itself draws custom to the goods. At some point, the trade mark itself may be seen as the object of the custom, either because of a desire by a purchaser to be identified with the sponsor or source of the mark, or because of the status or cachet that the mark itself is perceived to project. The trade mark no longer serves to sell the goods, but it serves to sell itself. Thus, one purchases a jacket bearing the emblem of a well known university because one wishes to be identified with that institution. Or one purchases a book containing the image of a fanciful character that has acquired success on television or in the movies. Or one purchases a wide array of diverse products, all carrying a certain name or symbol, because a certain status has become associated with this name or symbol.

To the extent that the proprietor can enforce trade mark rights in these marks or symbols, he can also seek to make commercial use of them. Since it is unlikely that the proprietor is in a position himself to commercialise the trade mark on goods far removed from those which he manufactures, the only feasible way to do so under such circumstances is by licensing the use of the trade mark to others. Indeed, in each of these situations, licensing may be the *raison d'etre* for the commercial use of these marks.

---

[56] Schechter, *supra*, n. 9, 'The Rational Basis for Trademark Protection', p. 825.
[57] See Chap. 15, para. 7, the provisions regarding advertising in the Annotated License Agreement.

Enforcement of Merchandising Rights

The law in the U.S. has been more willing to embrace these licensing 2–32
arrangements within the framework of conventional trade mark law, despite
the fact that it is the trade mark itself that is being merchandised.[58] In the
U.K., the jurisprudence under the Trade Marks Act 1938 has been less likely
to sanction such practice under the trade mark law, on the ground that such
use is mere trafficking in the mark per se, even if the licensor purports to
exercise quality control.[59]

However, the Trade Marks Act 1994 has eliminated any reference to
trafficking. One may, therefore, expect a relaxation of the legal position in
the U.K. regarding the merchandising function of a trade mark. As a result,
there will likely be a convergence, if not a complete identity, between the
respective approaches under U.K. and U.S. law with respect to the merchandising of trade mark rights.

Merchandising Challenges the Classical Foundations of Trade Mark Licensing

With the rise of merchandising, trade mark licensing can be viewed as having 2–33
come full circle. The source function of trade marks was understood as
conceptually inconsistent with licensing. Later, with the recognition of the
trade mark as an indicator of a single, albeit anonymous, source of the goods,
and the perception that trade marks had come to be relied upon as a indication
of quality, trade mark licensing became permitted, subject to the exercise of
quality control.

The development of the merchandising function of trade marks has forced
the question of how far trade mark licensing may extend. The issue is whether
the exploitation of the word or symbol in this way, where the sole or primary
identification is with the word or symbol rather than the goods, and where
the word or symbol is applied by a licensee to diverse goods, can be deemed

---

[58] The registration of a trade mark for promotional purposes was recognised by the Trademark
Trial and Appeal Board of the U.S. Patent and Trademark Office in the case of *Re Olin Corp.*,
181 U.S.P.Q. 182 (1973). In that case, the applicant was granted registration of a mark in the
form of a stylised 'O' for T-shirts. It was reasoned that the mark informed the purchasing
public of the source of the manufacture of Olin products, although not necessarily of the
source of manufacture of the T-shirts. This is called 'secondary source' identification.
The notion of secondary source identification was extended in the case of *Re Paramount
Pictures Corp.*, 213 U.S.P.Q. 1111 (1982). The Board allowed registration both of the title of
the U.S. television series 'Mork and Mindy', as well as of a large picture of the stars of the
series.
Note as well the following statement of the well-known U.S. judge of the U.S. 7th circuit
court of appeals, Judge Richard Posner. He observed that "[i]n an age when fashion-conscious
consumers wear T-shirts emblazoned with the trademarks of consumers products and owners
of Volkswagens buy conversion kits to enable them to put a Rolls-Royce grille on their car, it
is apparent that trade names, symbols and design features often serve a dual purpose, one part
of which is functional in the sense of making the product more attractive, and is distinct from
identifying the manufacturer or his brand to the consumer." *W. T. Rogers Co. Inc. v. Keene*
228 U.S.P.Q. 145, 145 (8th Cir. 1985). See generally, Kozinski, "Trademarks Unplugged." *The
Trademark Reporter*, vol. 84, no. 4, 1994, pp. 441–459.
[59] See, *infra*, Chap. 3, paras. 3–35 to 3–41, for discussion of this issue.

to function as a trade mark. Again, as in the earliest days of the modern trade mark right, the commercial practice of trade mark licensing may be at odds with the legal framework that governs trade mark use.[60]

---

[60] For a view that there is no incompatability, see Parks, ' "Naked" is Not a Four-Letter Word: Debunking the Myth of the "Quality Control Requirement" in Trademark Licensing,' *Trademark Reporter*, Vol. 82, 531.

3. The Registered User System in Transition: the Historical and Conceptual Background

The registration of trade mark licences and the whole registered user system **3–01** have never seen such diversity as now. With the inception of the registered user provisions as part of the U.K. Trade Marks Act 1938, various jurisdictions with an English law tradition incorporated these provisions in one form or another as part of their local trade mark laws. (The U.S. was the most notable exception.) While there are some differences in the precise form in which the registered user system was legislated and implemented in these various countries, there was a basic uniformity in the approach taken.

This uniformity is no longer the case. The most notable change has taken place in the United Kingdom itself. With the enactment of the Trade Marks Act 1994, the registration of trade mark licences at the Registry will continue, but the underlying purpose of the registration has been changed. Registration is now primarily intended to encourage the legal transparency of the transaction, rather than to protect the public against deception.[1] Thus, law in the United Kingdom, as the progenitor of the registered user system, has undergone a radical departure in conception. This can be compared with jurisdictions such as Israel, which continues to maintain the registered user system intact, or Canada, which has recently eliminated the system in its entirety.[2] To understand better the contours of this rapidly changing legal landscape, it is helpful to consider the historical and conceptual underpinnings of the registered user system. These are considered in the next sections of this chapter, which then also goes on to discuss the licensing of unregistered marks, character merchandising and trafficking in the context of the registered user system.

---

[1] Trade Marks Act 1994 (s.28). See also the '*Reform of Trade Marks Law*', Department of State and Industry, Cm. 1203 (1990) (hereinafter: the White Paper), especially paras. 4.34–4.39. See Chap. 4, for discussion of the operation of the registered user system under the Trade Marks Act 1938 and the changes brought about under the Trade Marks Act 1994, and Chap. 5, for discussion of the approach taken under U.S. practice.

[2] The registered provisions under Israel law are contained in the Trade Marks Ordinance, (New Version), 5732–1972, ss.50–52. The changes in the Canadian law are contained in Amendments to the Trade Marks Act, June 9, 1993, R.S. c. T-10, s.1. It is anticipated that material changes in the registered user requirements under the trade mark laws of South Africa and Australia will soon take place.

The Eve of the Registered User System

3–02   The increasing use of trade mark licensing in trade was not lost upon the U.K. Parliament as it set out in the 1930s to revise the Trade Marks Act 1905. Moreover, a handful of judgments, such as the *Radiation*[3] and the *J.H. Coles*[4] cases, had shown that the courts were on occasion prepared to recognise some form of trade mark licensing, when accompanied by adequate quality control or other assurances that no deception would occur by virtue of the licensed use.[5] It was not surprising, therefore, that the Goschen Committee Report on the Law and Practice relating to Trade Marks pointed to the fact that statutory recognition of some form of licensing would be appropriate as part of the recommended revisions to the Trade Marks Act. The Report noted that '[a]nother important question we have to consider is whether and if so to what extent, the existing trade mark law ... should be altered in order to authorise other persons to use his trade mark upon their goods.'[6]

The arrangement that was ultimately adopted as part of the Trade Marks Act 1938, whereby licensing, under certain terms and conditions, was recognised as valid within the registered trade mark scheme, has popularly come to be known as the 'registered user' system.[7] Under this scheme, the Trade Marks Act 1938 would provide for registration of the licensee as a registered user of the trade mark upon examination of the licence arrangement by the Registry.

Approval and Registration

3–03   The registered user provisions brought together two considerations: the recognition that quality control, if properly maintained, would reduce the likelihood that licensing would work a deception on the public, and the belief that the public interest would be served by providing for approval and recording of a licence on the Trade Marks register. This combination of approval and registration, whereby the administrative authority was empowered to review the contractual or other relationship between the parties as a condition for the registration of the licence, made trade mark licensing unique amongst the licensing of different intellectual property rights.[8]

---

[3] *Re Radiation* (1930) 47 R.P.C. 37.
[4] *J.H. Coles Propriety Ltd v Need* (1934) 50 R.P.C. 379.
[5] See, *supra*, Chap. 2, at paras. 2–21 to 2–23.
[6] Cmd. 4568 (1934); see also *Hollie Hobbie T.M.* [1983] F.S.R. 138, 141, 142.
[7] See Chap. 4, *infra*, paras. 4–32 to 4–39, for a discussion of some of the provisions of the registered user system under the Trade Marks Act 1938.
[8] *cf.* the application of the 'related company' doctrine under U.S. practice in the absence of a registered user scheme, Chap. 5. Consider as well the relationship between a recordal of a licence under the Trade Marks Act 1994 and the Restrictive Trade Practices Act 1976, especially Sched. 3, para. 4(2), which exempts the licence agreement from the scope of the RTPA if the only restrictions relate to: (i) the description of the goods; and (ii) the method or process of manufacture of the goods.

Registered User Registration: Mandatory or Permissive?

The enactment of the registered user provisions in the Trade Marks Act 1938   **3-04**
left open the question of the precise relationship between the status of the
licensing of a registered trade mark and the legal effect of a registered user
registration.[9] In particular, the question remained as to whether or not the
registerd user provisions were mandatory, *i.e.* whether a trade mark licence
was valid only if the arrangement was registered in accordance with the
registered user provisions. Two stages can be identified in the understanding
of this relationship.

In the first, valid trade mark licensing was understood as being limited to
a registered user agreement approved by and recorded on the Register. Under
this view, not only was the licence itself of no effect if not registered, but the
validity of the registered trade mark might be in jeopardy by virtue of the
putative licence.[10]

In the second, a registered user registration was deemed to be merely
permissive: registration conveyed certain advantages to the parties, but did
not establish the validity of the licence nor did its absence necessarily impair
the validity of the registered trade mark.[11] As long as it could be shown that
a trade mark licence arrangement was not deceptive, it would not be
invalidated simply because the licensee had not been registered as a registered
user.

The second view was the one that became generally accepted, but it was
never explicitly endorsed by the House of Lords, and remnants of the earlier
view could still be found.[12] Each of the two stages is described further below.

---

[9] The discussion that follows addresses the licensing of a registered trade mark. See generally,
Norman 'Trade Mark Licences in the United Kingdom', (1994) 4 E.I.P.R. 154. See, *infra*,
paras. 3-14 to 3-19, regarding the licensing of an unregistered trade mark.

[10] See discussion, *infra*, at para. 3-06.

[11] The following advantages of a registered user registration under the Trade Marks Act 1938,
even if the registration was merely permissive, have been cited:
(i) The permitted use of the trade mark by the registered user was deemed use by the
proprietor, and it could be relied upon by the proprietor to defeat a challenge to invalidity of
the trade mark based on a claim of non-use.
(ii) The registration was deemed prima facie evidence that the Registrar had examined and
approved the quality control arrangements between the parties.
(iii) The registered user could take action for infringement under specified circumstances.
(iv) The registration was valid against an assignee of the proprietor.
(v) A sole registered user was protected against the appointment of additional registered
users, while a non-sole registered user was protected against a subsequent appointment of a
sole registered user.
(vi) An applicant for registration of a trade mark could base the application on the intended
use of the registered user.
Davy, *Licence Design, But Don't Endanger Your Trade Mark*, E.C.T.A, no. 4 (1987). See also
the discussion of the advantages of a registered user registration, *per* the *Bostitch* court, *infra*,
para. 3-09.
See Chap. 4, paras. 4-05 to 4-25, for discussion of the benefits of registering a trade mark
licence under the Trade Marks Act 1994.

[12] See, for instance, the comments of Falconer J. in the *Levi-Strauss* decision, *infra*, at 3-05.

The View that Valid Licensing was Limited to a Registered User Registration

3–05   Under this view, a valid trade mark licence was limited to a registered user registration. This position was well expressed by a commentator, writing shortly after the enactment of the Trade Marks Act 1938, as follows:

> 'By section 28 of the Act of 1938, a system of registered users is introduced. In view of this, it is difficult to maintain the view hitherto held, that a licence is necessarily a fraud on the public. It may still be argued that a licence is normally calculated to lead to deception, so that it is contrary to public policy to recognise as lawful any licence which has not been passed by the Registrar.'[13]

More recently, the registered user system was described by Falconer J., who noted that it made

> '... a very considerable departure from what had been the position in trade mark law, both at common law and under registered previous trade mark statutes, that is that a trade mark cannot be licensed ... Accordingly, the rights being granted by the registered user provisions as a limited form of licenseship were very carefully circumscribed because of that position – it was such a departure from what had gone before.'[14]

It must be noted that the observation of Falconer J. was expressed after the *Bostitch* decision, which held that the registered user provisions were merely permissive.[15] Consider as well the ruling by Lord Diplock in *Star Industrial Company Limited v. Yap Kwee Kor*[16], regarding whether the licensing of an unregistered trade mark should be permitted when there is sufficient quality control. Lord Diplock rejected the suggestion, stating that it was the 'intention of Parliament in the United Kingdom, to confine these novel statutory rights to registered trade marks...'[17]

An Unregistered Licence could Invalidate the Trade Mark Registration

3–06   Under the view that a registered user registration was mandatory, not only was valid trade licensing limited to a registered user registration, but the trade mark registration itself could be put at risk. Thus, in the *Turmix T.M.* case, the House of Lords noted, in *obiter*,[18] that a trade mark licence that was not registered in accordance with the provisions of the registered user provisions invalidated the registration of the trade mark.[19]

However, since the issue of the registered user registration and its effect on the validity of the trade mark was not argued before the House of Lords, the

---

[13] Kerly, *Law of Trade Marks and Trade Names* (7th ed.), p. 450, quoted in Ennis, 'Is a Registered User Necessary?', *In Honor of Heinz Dawid*, at p. 209.

[14] *Levi Strauss v. The French Connection Ltd* [1982] F.S.R. 443, 445, Falconer J.

[15] For discussion see, para. 3–08.

[16] [1976] F.S.R. 256 (P.C.).

[17] *ibid.* at 272.

[18] *T. Oertli A.G. v. E.J. Bowman (London) Ltd* [1959] R.P.C. 1.

[19] The requirements of s.28 of the Trade Marks Act 1938 were not complied with in regard to this licence; accordingly the registration of the mark was invalidated.

questions of whether or not a registered user registration was mandatory, and whether the failure to register the registered user invalidated the underlying trade mark registration, could not be held to have been conclusively resolved by that judgment.

The View that the Registered User Provisions Were Merely Permissive

The notion that a registered user registration was mandatory came under serious challenge in a series of judgments, for the most part in the 1960s.   3–07

The Authority of the Radiation Case

One difficulty with the view that a registered user registration was mandatory, was that the position could not be squarely reconciled with the result in the *Radiation* case.[20] That judgment was understood to stand for the proposition that a trade mark licensing arrangement between a parent and a subsidiary, particularly when there was also evidence of adequate quality control, was not ipso facto invalid, despite the absence of a registered user registration. The *Radiation* decision was given in 1929, well before the registered user system went into effect.[21]

Several cases, in considering the continuing authority of the *Radiation* case to particular licensing arrangements of a registered trade mark outside of the registered user system, did not challenge the validity of the *Radiation* judgment itself, that is, that a trade mark licence could be valid outside of the registered user system. If this was the situation, however, it would have meant that the registered user provisions could not be viewed as mandatory. Most notably, in the *Firemaster* T.M. case, the *Radiation* decision was understood to hold that the trade mark licensing arrangement was valid since the parent-applicant had exercised close quality control of the use of the trade mark by its subsidiaries prior to the filing of the application. In applying this principle, the *Firemaster* court ruled that no such control was found in the facts before it, and the result reached in the *Radiation* case was thereby distinguished. The holding of the *Radiation* case itself, however, was not challenged.[22]

The *Radiation* decision was briefly discussed as well, in obiter, by Cross L.J. in the *GE T.M.* Case. There, while the result reached in the *Radiation* case was questioned, it was not rejected as authority.[23]

The Bostitch Decision

The more direct attack on the position that the registered user provisions   3–08

---

[20] See, *supra*, n. 3.
[21] See, Chap. 2, para. 2–22, for a discussion of the *Radiation* case.
[22] *Firemaster T.M.* [1965] R.P.C. 40. Query whether the result in the *Firemaster* case, even on its facts, is correct, in light of later jurisprudence which suggests that the very fact of a parent-subsidiary relationship itself is deemed sufficient control. Kerly, *Law of Trade Marks and Trade Names* (12th ed.), paras. 2–16 and 10–41; *Trade Marks Registry Work Manual*, Chap. 27, Registration of Users, at para. 27–30(b); *cf.* with the *BP T.M.* Case, *infra*, at 3–16.
[23] [1970] R.P.C. 393, 394.

were mandatory came from the judgment of Lloyd-Jacob J. in the *Bostitch* decision.[24]

In that case, the foreign proprietor of several registered trade marks had permitted its U.K. distributor to manufacture and sell certain goods under the trade marks, when war-time conditions had made import impractical. The distributor-licensee was not registered as a registered user of the trade marks. The distributor-licensee continued to manufacture and sell under the trade marks for a period of nearly 15 years, after which the parties had a falling out. In the ensuing dispute, the distributor-licensee sought to expunge the registrations of the trade marks, on the ground that the absence of any registered user registration had rendered the trade mark registrations invalid.

The Court rejected the licensee's argument. It held that '[t]here is nothing anywhere in this section to justify the view that an arrangement between a registered proprietor of a trade mark and a party concerned to use such mark requires to be registered, still less that in its absence of registration, its effect upon the validity of the mark, if called in question, will be any way different.'[25]

Thus, the test for the validity of a trade mark licence was not whether or not there was a registered user registration, but whether the licence arrangement was deceptive. The key to the validity of a trade mark licence was whether or not the licence arrangement had destroyed the trade connection between the proprietor of the trade mark and the goods.[26] In the words of the Court, the section of the Trade Marks Act 1938 (section 28) containing the registered user provisions

> '... is not a mandatory but a permissive section, and cannot fairly be construed to provide a protective cover for any trade mark use which would otherwise be deceptive or confusing.'[27]

The result in the *Bostitch* case was recently relied upon to conclusively establish the same principle in South Africa, namely, that registration of a registered user is merely permissive. The test, as stated by the court there, is whether the licensed use 'is such as to deprive it of its very reason of existence, namely, as a mark which should distinguish the proprietor's goods from the goods of other makers.'[28]

Bostitch: Change in the Trade Connection Between the Proprietor and the Goods?

3–09   It has been suggested that the result in the *Bostitch* case can also be understood on the basis of section 62 of the Trade Marks Act 1938. That section provided that a change in the trade connection between the proprietor and the goods,

---

[24] *Bostitch T.M.* [1963] R.P.C. 183.

[25] *ibid.*, at 195.

[26] *ibid.*, at 197.

[27] *ibid.*, at 195.

[28] *Sportshoe (Pty) Ltd v. Pep Stores (SA) (Pty) Ltd,* 1990 (1) SA 722, 730. Note the virtually identical language expressed by the *Bostitch* court on p. 197. It has also been cited with approval by the High Court of Australia. *Pioneer Electronic Corporation v. Reg.* [1978] R.P.C. 717, 727, 728.

that is, from direct manufacture to a licence arrangement based on quality control, was not ipso facto deemed to be deceptive.[29] This understanding does not appear to have been judicially adopted by later courts.

Why Register a Registered User? – The View of the *Bostitch* Court

The fact that registration was permissive did not, in the eyes of the *Bostitch* **3–10** court, mean that a registered user registration was of no legal significance. The court indicated several advantages to registering a registered user:

(a) The registration of a registered user constituted prima facie evidence that the use of the trade mark in accordance with the licence arrangement was not deceptive or likely to cause confusion.

(b) Use of the trade mark by the registered user was deemed to be use by the proprietor, and it could be relied upon by the proprietor should the trade mark be attacked on the grounds of non-use.

(c) The registration of the registered user protected the registered user against a claim of infringement by the proprietor, provided that the registered user satisfied the conditions and restrictions of the permitted use under the registration.

(d) The registration provided the registered user with a limited right to sue a third-party infringer.[30]

Despite these advantages, however, the absence of a registration did not render a trade mark licence, or the underlying trade mark registration, invalid.

The British Petroleum Case: Use by an Affiliate

The *Bostitch* decision was subsequently relied upon where an affiliate of the **3–11** proprietor had not been registered user of the trade mark. Here, as well, it was held that the failure to record use by a registered user did not serve as the basis to invalidate the trade mark.

The *British Petroleum* court noted as crucial that the licensee apparently used the trade mark subject to the same conditions or restrictions that governed the use of the proprietor's other trade marks, for which there were registered user registrations.[31] This result was not inconsistent with the *Radiation* decision, that case not being referred to in the judgment. Nevertheless, like the *Radiation* decision, the result reached by the *British Petroleum* court suggested that mere use of a trade mark by a subsidiary was not enough, without quality control, to establish the necessary trade connection.[32]

---

[29] *Kerly* (12th ed.), para. 13–24.

[30] *Bostitch, supra*, at 195.

[31] *British Petroleum Company Limited v. European Petroleum Distributors Limited* [1968] R.P.C. 54, 63.

[32] This result should be compared, however, with the declared practice of the Trade Marks Registry, which tended to treat a parent-subsidiary relationship under the Trade Marks Act 1938 as sufficient, without further proof of quality control, to establish a valid licensing arrangement, because there is presumed to be a convergence of aims between the parties. *Work Manual, supra*, n. 22, paras. 27–30(b), 59–60. See also Ennis, *supra*, n. 13, stating that use of a trade mark by a subsidiary or licensee is sufficient, even in the absence of quality control.

The GE Case: Bostitch Approved

3–12   The principle of the *Bostitch* decision was also reaffirmed in connection with the tortuous trade mark dispute between the British company, General Electric Co. Ltd (GEC), and the U.S. concern, General Electric Company (GE).[33] This case involved a motion by GEC to expunge the registration of the trade mark 'GE' by the U.S. company, in the context of the use of the trade marks *Mono-GE-Gram* and *Simplex* GE in the U.K. by certain affiliates of the U.S. company.

There, it was accepted without challenge that the *Bostitch* decision established that the registered user provisions are merely permissive, and that if adequate quality control can be shown, the failure to register the licence does not destroy the validity of the trade mark.[34] The matter at issue before the trial court was whether the *Bostitch* rationale could be extended to the licensing of an unregistered trade mark as well. It was held that it could.[35]

The Position of the Registry

3–13   It has been held in proceedings before the Trade Marks Registry, citing the *Bostitch* decision and the dictum of Lord Cross in the *GE* case, that the registered user provisions are not mandatory.[36] The Registry, relying on the *Bostitch* case, has also indicated in its practice manual that the registered user provisions are merely permissive.[37]

Licensing of an Unregistered Trade Mark

3–14   The *Bostitch* case dealt only with the status of licensing registered trade marks outside the scope of the registered user requirements. Accordingly, it did not settle the status of licences involving unregistered trade marks. This is so despite the commercial reality, whereby unregistered marks are thought to be the frequent subject of licensing arrangements. There is case law both for and against the validity of such licences, but the question has not yet been conclusively resolved.[38] The Trade Marks Act 1994 does not address the subject.

What was at stake in the question of whether an unregistered trade mark can be licensed? Several points are worthy of mention:

---

[33] [1973] R.P.C. 297, H.L., rev'g [1970] R.P.C. 339, C.A.; rev'g GE T.M. [1969] R.P.C. 418.

[34] *GE*, *supra*, at 457 (Graham J.); at 372 (dictum) (L. Salmon), and at 395 (dictum) (L. Cross).

[35] Neither the Court of Appeal nor the House of Lords ruled directly on this point, however.

[36] *Molyslip T.M.* [1978] R.P.C. 211, 218.

[37] *Work Manual*, *supra*, n. 22, para. 27–3.

[38] The legal status of the licensing of an unregistered trade mark has been well-described in Lane, below, n. 41. It should be noted that the protection of unregistered marks (a mark is defined by the Trade Marks Act 1938 as including 'a device, brand, heading, label, ticket, name, signature, word, letter, numeral, or any combination thereof'), is a species of the broader category of passing-off, which protects goodwill against a misrepresentation that is likely to deceive. Passing-off is not limited to marks as defined above. See generally, Wadlow, *Passing-Off* (2nd ed., 1994.)

(a) In the absence of an unequivocal right to license an unregistered trade mark, the legal basis on which the licensor may exploit the mark through the receipt of royalties and fees from third-party use of the mark is less certain.

(b) Use of a registered trade mark by a registered user (and perhaps even by an unregistered user, if the *Bostitch* requirements are satisfied) was deemed to inure to the benefit of the proprietor. This enables the proprietor to claim constructive use of the mark. It also prevents the licensee from asserting any right of proprietorship of its own by virtue of the licensed use. If no licensing of unregistered trade marks is recognised, the licensor may be on less certain legal footing in claiming goodwill by virtue of the licensed use, and may be more vulnerable to a claim by the licensee that the rights in the mark belong to him (the licensee).

(c) The right of the licensee to take action against unauthorised use of the mark by other parties is uncertain.

A Licence of an Unregistered Trade Mark: A Thing Writ in Water

One view maintains that a licence of an unregistered trade mark is of no legal effect, or, as expressed by one judge, it is merely a 'thing writ in water.'[39] This position finds support in the words of Lord Diplock in the judgment of the Privy Council in *Star Industrial Company Ltd v. Yap Kwee Kor*.[40] Here, the plaintiff, a Hong Kong company trading in tooth brushes in Singapore ceased doing business there due to import restrictions. The tooth brushes had been traded under a certain mark, but the mark had never been registered in Singapore. Subsequently, the plaintiff entered into an agreement for the establishment of a company in Singapore to manufacture and sell tooth brushes under the trade mark. One half of the share capital of the new company was owned by the plaintiff; the other half was owned by two other companies in which the plaintiff had no financial interest.

The new company obtained the exclusive right to use the plaintiff's know-how and the trade mark in respect of the tooth brushes. It is not clear from the decision whether the grant of the trade mark was by way of an assignment, albeit limited in time, or an exclusive licence.[41] The issue was whether the plaintiff had a passing-off action against a rival trader that sold tooth brushes under similar get-up and marking. No claim was made on behalf of the new company.

In affirming judgment in favour of the defendant, Lord Diplock held that there was no basis for finding that the licensing of an unregistered law trade mark is countenanced either at common law or by extension from the registered under provisions.

As to the common law, Lord Diplock dismissed the result in the case of *Warwick Tyre Company*, in which some form of licensing of an unregistered

3–15

---

[39] *Tavener Rutledge Ltd v. Trexalpalm Ltd* [1975] F.S.R. 479, 486 (Walton J.)
[40] [1976] F.S.R. 256.
[41] [1976] F.S.R. at 270; Lane, *The Status of Licensing of Common Law Marks* (1991), at pp. 38, 39.

trade mark appeared to have taken place. He found that the *Warwick Tyre* decision rested on the premise, rejected by the House of Lords, that there is a passing-off right in the mark as a form of property, distinct from the goodwill or reputation that attaches to the use of the mark.[42]

Lord Diplock Criticised

3–16 It has been pointed out that Lord Diplock's reasoning, in dismissing the *Warwick Tyre* case, is flawed. Rather than citing the case squarely for the proposition that licensing is possible at common law, and then expressly rejecting this proposition, he merely rejected the legal premise on which the case rested, namely, that an unregistered mark is a species of property.[43] Accordingly, the judgment cannot be held on a fair reading to have unequivocally rejected the proposition that licensing of an unregistered trade mark, where there is sufficient quality control, is *per se* impermissible at common law.

The GE Case—Licensing of an Unregistered Trade Mark

3–17 In contrast to Lord Diplock's ruling in the *Star Industrial* decision is the judgment of Graham J. in the *G.E.* case. There, the judge stated that he found no reason to distinguish between the licensing of a registered, as opposed to an unregistered, trade mark. It was true, the court noted, that the *Bostitch* case concerned a registered trade mark. However, there was the nothing to limit the reasoning of the case to registered trade marks only.

In all situations involving the licensing of a trade mark, the key is whether there is sufficient quality control to prevent deception in the use of the mark by the licensee. Thus, Graham J. stated that

> '[i]n so far as unregistered common law marks are concerned, the principles to be derived from the cases are quite consistent with and can be applied in present day conditions, and, in my judgment, result in the position at common law being parallel with the position under the statute.'[44]

This position was approved on appeal, albeit *obiter*, by Cross L.J., who noted that

> 'the licensing of a mark, whether registered or unregistered, does not deprived it of the character of a trade mark providing that the owner of the mark retains sufficient connection in the course of trade with the relevant goods, which connection can be maintained.'[45]

---

[42] *Warwick Tyre Company Ltd v. New Motor and General Rubber Co. Ltd* [1910] 1 Ch. 248.
[43] See Lane, *supra*, n. 41, at pp. 39–40.
[44] [1969] R.P.C., *supra*, at 455.
[45] [1970] R.P.C., 339, at 395.

Should the GE Case Be Limited to its Facts?

In considering these judicial statements in favour of licensing unregistered   3–18
trade marks, the facts of the *G.E.* case must be taken into account. The marks
at issue were deemed to be unregistered (*i.e.* common law marks) because
they were applied to goods that fell outside of the specification of goods that
were covered by the registration. As such, there was no material difference
between the control exercised over those goods that were within the scope of
the specification of the registration, and those goods that were deemed to fall
outside the scope of the registration. The mark was the same and the control
was presumably the same.

In such circumstances, it is understandable why the court declined to
distinguish between the registered and unregistered 'portions' of the mark, so
as not to accord different treatment to each. The application and extension
of the result in the *Bostitch* case to the licensing of unregistered trade marks
should be seen in this context. Whether the same result would obtain in a
situation where the only marks at issue are unregistered marks, even when
quality control can be shown, is less certain.[46]

The Ninja Turtle Case: Are Unregistered Trade Marks Next?

The recent judgment in the *Ninja Turtles* case contains a tantalising suggestion   3–19
that some future English court may be more likely to recognise generally the
licensing of an unregistered trade mark.[47] The court in that case held that a
claim for passing-off was established when the defendant used humanoid
turtle characters on goods that created a misrepresentation that they were
licensed by the proprietor of the Ninja Turtle characters. The plaintiff had
granted use of the Ninja Turtle characters in over 150 licence agreements in
the United Kingdom, and had maintained close quality control over its
licensees.

The court distinguished three earlier cases in which a claim of character
merchandising had been rejected. In each of them, the court noted, the
plaintiff 'was concerned with licensing rights in a name as opposed to licensing
rights in what is undoubtedly copyright material. It may be that different
factors appear in such a case, though those cases may, given the change in
trading habits, require reconsideration on a future occasion if the evidence
before the court is different.'[48] This is a suggestion that the use of an
unregistered name or word may be recognised as licensible, at least under
certain circumstances.

---

[46] One commentator has noted, in connection with Graham J.'s pronouncement regarding equal
treatment for the licensing of registered and unregistered trade marks, that '[t]here has been,
however, little enthusiasm in the UK for such a wide principle in relation to common law
marks.' Lane, *supra*, n. 41 at p. 21, n. 68.
[47] *Mirage Studios v. Counter-Feat Clothing Company Ltd* [1991] F.S.R. 145.
[48] *Mirage Studios*, *supra*, at 158. The tendency to recognise a merchandising right in unregistered
marks and symbols has been even more pronounced in Australia. See, *e.g.* the so-called
Crocodile Dundee cases: *Hogan & Anor. v. Koala Dundee Pty. Ltd* (1988), ATPR para. 40–
902; and *Hogan & ors. v. Pacific Dunlop Ltd* (1988) ATPR para. 40–914.

ALTERNATIVES TO A REGISTERED USER

3–20   Even if a registered user registration was merely permissive under the 1938 Act regime, the advantages that could be derived from the registration made it attractive in many instances.[49] However, there were circumstances in which the trade mark proprietor would prefer to avoid the entire issue of a registered user, for example because of the expense involved or the required commitment to quality control. Several lines of decisions address circumstances in which the court has dealt with the issue of whether or not a registered user is appropriate. These decisions can be divided into two categories: (a) Cases where no licence arrangement was found; and (b) cases where the applicant was not required under subsection 29(1)(b) of the Trade Marks Act 1938 to apply for trade mark registration on the basis of intended use by a registered user.

No Licence Arrangement Found

3–21   On occasion, it has been held that what might appear to be a trade mark licence arrangement is not a licence at all. Instead, direct use of the trade mark by the proprietor is found. Under such conditions, the problems of whether the licence is valid, and whether a registered user registration is appropriate, do not arise.

The Manus Case

3–22   A notable example is the *Manus* case.[50] There, the exclusive distributor had been granted a manufacturing licence by the foreign manufacturer during World War II in order to maintain a supply for the goods in the local market under the foreign manufacturer's trade mark. The court held that no trade mark licence arrangement had been created, and that the goodwill in the trade mark and the rights therein had remained at all times with the foreign manufacturer.[51]

    The rationale of the *Manus* case is not wholly clear, and its result may have been influenced by the view, no longer accepted, that a registered user registration was mandatory, whereby the manufacturer as licensor may have lost its rights in the trade mark for failure to register the licence. To avoid what in effect would have resulted in a forfeiture of proprietorship in the trade mark, the court may have preferred to rule that no licensing arrangement existed. In any event, under the later view, the foreign manufacturer would have been permitted to establish a valid licensing arrangement through a showing of proper quality control, even in the absence of a registered user registration.[52]

---

[49] See, *supra*, n. 11, for some of the advantages of a registered user registration under the Trade Marks Act 1938.

[50] *Manus v. Fullwood & Bland* [1949] Ch. 208, 66 R.P.C. 71; aff'g [1948] R.P.C. 329.

[51] *Manus, supra*, paras. 3–07 to 3–13.

[52] See, *supra*, paras. 3–07 to 3–13.

Direct verses Licensed Use

The distinction between (1) direct selection or sale by the proprietor of trade   3–23
marked goods manufactured by a third party, and (2) manufacture and sale
by a licensee, is not always clear. When this type of situation occurs, it may
be possible to characterise the relationship between the parties either as direct
use by the trade mark proprietor or as controlled use by the licensee.[53]

Under section 68 of the Trade Marks Act 1938, a trade mark was defined
as indicating 'a connection in the course of trade' between the goods and
either the proprietor or the registered user.[54] The required connection included,
but was not limited to, such direct acts of use of the trade mark by the
proprietor as the 'manufacture, selection, dealing with, or offering for sale'
of goods, all of which were all explicitly identified in the definition of a 'trade
mark' under the Trade Marks Act 1905.[55]

The connection in the course of trade also included a permitted use of the
trade mark by the licensee under the registered user provisions, where there
was no direct use of the trade mark by the proprietor, but controlled use by
the registered user. As stated above, the line between the two, that is, direct
use of the mark by the proprietor, and controlled use of the trade mark by
the licensee, has not always been clear.

The Australian Pioneer Case

A notable example is the *Pioneer Electronic* Case in Australia, decided under   3–24
similar law.[56] There, the High Court spoke of 'selection or quality control or
control of the user in the sense in which a parent company controls a
subsidiary', as if selection, quality control, and financial control all describe
an identical relationship between the proprietor of the trade mark and the
goods.[57] The Australian High Court went on to conclude that:

> 'It does not appear ... to make any difference whether he uses it [the
> trade mark] on goods manufactured overseas by the registered proprietor
> by affixing labels, advertising and the like, or by selecting those goods,
> and selling them with the marks on them in Australia, as well as by
> advertising them, displaying them with the marks either originally placed
> on them or those placed on or attached to the goods or the advertising
> material by the licensee.'[58]

The Radiation Case: Both Direct and Licensed Uses Possible

Given this uncertainty between direct use and licensed use of the trade mark,   3–25
it is not surprising, perhaps, that on occasion the registry refused to distinguish
between them in ruling on the registability of a trade mark. This is particularly

---

[53] See the discussion of trade mark licensing and contract manufacturers, Chap. 8, paras. 8–01
to 8–18.
[54] The leading judgment is *Aristoc v. Rystra*, 62 R.P.C. 65, H.L.
[55] s.3.
[56] *Pioneer Electronic Corporation v. Register* [1978] R.P.C. 716.
[57] *ibid.* at 727, Aickin J.
[58] *ibid.* at 729, Aickin J.

likely when financial control is involved. In the *Radiation* decision, the Comptroller-General indicated that its decision to register the trade mark could be based on two alternative grounds, namely, (a) that the applicant exercised quality control over the use of the house mark by its affiliate, or (b) that the applicant had used the trade mark to indicate its 'selection' or its 'dealing with' the goods in question.[59] The upshot was that the court could choose to characterise the use as direct use of the trade mark by the applicant or registrant, thereby avoiding the issue of whether a licence arrangement had been shown.

Use of the Trade Mark By Associated Companies

3–26 The *Radiation* decision recognised the applicant's exercise of quality control over the use of the trade mark by a subsidiary. It is unclear whether, in the absence of the quality control relationship, mere financial control of the applicant would have been sufficient in that case. There have been subsequent decisions, however, where valid trade mark use by the affiliate company was held to be justified, even in the absence of a finding that a licence relationship was present.

The Astronaut T.M. and Kidax (Shirts) Cases

3–27 In one case, it was found that where two companies were effectively under the control of the same persons, the fact that the watches were sold under the trade mark 'Astronaut' by one company did not support a claim of rectification of the trade mark on the ground that there had been no actual use of the trade mark by the other, who was the proprietor.[60]

The court made it clear that there was no '... question of some other party as a registered user or that there was any assignment which has not been registered. This is not a case where there is even a suggestion of a licence, if such were permissible under the trade mark law.'[61] Nevertheless, the court rejected the motion to expunge the trade mark. It held that the proprietor was deemed to have selected the goods sold by the associated company, either by having marked the goods or having instructed others to do so. This was so, even if, in the words of the court, '... there been some failure in legal formality', so long as the user of the trade mark 'was in the family.'[62]

A similar result was reached in *Kidax (Shirts) Ltd's Application*[63] in which an unregistered trade mark had been used 'side by side' for a short period of time without a licence by companies under the same effective ownership and control. The court held that the trade mark could still be registered, where the applicant undertook to register the 'side by side' user of the trade mark as a registered user.

No explicit reliance was laid by the *Kidax* court upon the applicant having

---

[59] *Radiation*, *supra*, n. 3, at 42–44.
[60] *Astronaut T.M.* [1972] R.P.C. 655.
[61] *ibid.* at 666.
[62] *ibid.* at 672.
[63] [1959] R.P.C. 295, [1960] R.P.C. 117.

exercised its selection function with respect to the goods, nor had a licence relationship been claimed (even though the applicant undertook to file prospectively a registered user application). Nevertheless, the court was prepared to overlook 'a reprehensible carelessness' in attending to the legal formalities, when the used was made by various entities belonging to a single overall organization.[64]

Registered User Registration Sought Even If It May Not Be Appropriate

The cases discussed above represent instances in which the claim of a licence   3–28
arrangement was avoided. On occasion, the opposite also occurred, namely, a registered user registration was sought even when the existence of a licence arrangement was questionable. This was most likely to happen in connection with an exclusive distributor.

Licence Arrangement Claimed by a Distributor

It is generally held that the sale of marked goods by a distributor is not   3–29
deemed use of the mark. Registration of the distributor as registered user was therefore unnecessary.[65] However, a registered user registration conferred upon the distributor a right of action for infringement, which could even enable the distributor to take action to prevent parallel imports, if permitted by law. Under such circumstances, registration of the distributor as a registered user was sometimes sought. The question then became one of whether the registry would register the distributor as a registered user. For example, registration of a subsidiary as a registered user was initially denied in the Australian case of *Pioneer Electronics*[66], in part, because the claim of a licence arrangement was 'contrived' in order to allow the subsidiary to prevent parallel imports by exercising its right of action. The registered user registration was ultimately approved on appeal, presumably because the parent-subsidiary relationship, together with contractual provisions for quality control, were found to give rise to a proper licence arrangement.[67]

Reliance on Use of the Trade Mark by a Licensee To Support a Trade Mark Application

A somewhat different issue is raised by a line of cases which addressed   3–30
whether a licensor applying for trade mark registration could (by virtue of the licence) claim to be using or intending to use the trade mark itself, or whether it had expressly to rely on use of the trade mark by a registered user to supports its claim of use. Section 17(1) of the Trade Marks Act 1938 provided that a proper applicant for trade mark registration was any person

---

[64] *Kidax, supra,* at 300, 301.
[65] *Trade Marks Registry, Work Manual,* Registration of Users, Chap. 27, para. 27–03. See also Chap. 4, paras. 4–41 to 4–42.
[66] *Pioneer Electronics, supra,* n. 56, at 725.
[67] See, Chap. 4, paras. 4–41, 4–42, for discussion regarding registration of the distributor as a licensee.

'claiming to be the proprietor of a trade mark used or proposed to be used by him ...', *i.e.* that the applicant was using, or intending to use the trade mark directly. Subsection 29(1) provided, however, that, an application for registration should not be refused, even if it appeared that the applicant itself did not use or propose to directly use the trade mark, if the applicant could show that a bona fide registered user was intended.[68]

The issue here was to what extent direct use of the trade mark by the applicant would be found, thereby obviating the need to claim use through a registered user.

Reliance on a Registered User Was Unnecessary Where Companies Are Associated

3–31   The registry recognised that when use of a trade mark by members of a group of companies family was involved, it could not require that the application be based on subsection 29(1)(b), even though direct use of the trade mark by the applicant had not been unequivocally made out.

A similar decision was reached where, the applicant was an individual who actually traded through a company that he owned equally with his wife, and for which he served as the Managing Director.[69] It was argued that the application was ineffective because the applicant neither satisfied the requirements of section 17, since he personally did not use the trade mark, nor subsection 29(1)(b), since no registered user application had been filed.

The Assistant Registrar rejected the argument. Relying on the *Astronaut* decision,[70] he held that the involvement of the applicant in the company constituted a sufficient trade connection between himself and the goods to meet the requirements of section 17. Accordingly, there was no necessity to apply under subsection 29(1)(b). In the words of the Assistant Registrar:

> 'It is true ... that the mark in suit could have been sought to be registered under the provisions of section 29(1)(b) of the Act, with [the Applicant] as Registered Proprietor and [the Company] as Registered User. That, however, would be at [the Applicant's] option. He elected to seek registration under section 17(1) with himself as proprietor of the mark.'[71]

The *Pussy Galore* Case: Where neither Section 17 nor Section 29 Applied

3–32   However, there were situations in which neither direct use nor use by a registered user might be found. This would occur when the mere intention to appoint a registered user was not sufficient to satisfy the requirements of

---

[68] Under section 32(3) of the Trade Marks Act 1994, an application for registration of a mark 'shall state that the trade mark is being used, by the applicant or with his consent, in relation to those goods or services, or that he has a bona fide intention that it should be used.'

[69] *Re Application No. 1117385 by Ajit Singh Maker Trading as Oriental Fashions and the Opposition No. 16953 by A & C Modes* (unreported).

[70] Above, para. 3–27.

[71] *Oriental Fashions, supra,* n. 69, at 4. Under the provisions of subs. 32(3) of the Trade Marks Act 1994, above, n. 68, this result can be understood as representing either direct use by the applicant, or use by the company with the applicant's consent.

licensed use by a registered user under subsection 29(1)(b), and yet there was no direct use by the applicant. In such circumstances, the application would have to fail.

This was the result in the *Pussy Galore* case.[72] There, the applicant intended to merchandise goods containing the words 'Pussy Galore' and several related words taken from Ian Fleming's novels, but it was held that the application failed under both section 17 and subsection 29(1)(b). This was so because the applicant neither intended to use the trade marks itself, nor had it had firmly identified any licensee, that is, it had not submitted an application for a registered user, as required under subsection 29(1)(b).

Quality Control and Financial Control: Two Different Bases?

In considering the above cases, it is apparent that intended use of the trade mark by a third party licensee was treated differently from intended use by an entity controlled by, or related in some material fashion to, the applicant. In the former situation, some evidence of the specific arrangements for quality control, preferably by means of a formal contract, was required. In the absence of a definite, bona fide licence arrangement, no direct use of the trade mark by the applicant would have been found. 3–33

In the latter situation, the mere fact of financial control in respect of the party using the trade mark was capable of being sufficient to establish direct use without any need to rely on a registered user registration, and the application could then proceed under section 17. Nevertheless, under such circumstances, the registry would not have rejected an application based on subsection 29(1)(b), citing the *Radiation* case as authority.[73] In other words, both direct use and use by a registered user could be claimed as the basis for an application under the identical set of facts.

A Dual Answer

The registry's position on this point can be viewed as coming full circle back to the ambiguity raised by the *Radiation* decision itself. Was the right of proprietorship based on direct use by the parent, or did it have to rely on evidence of a quality control relationship within the meaning of the registered user provisions? The answer seems to have been, at least in some situations, both. 3–34

Given this, it is arguable that the more correct answer may be that neither provision under the Trade Marks Act 1938, direct use under section 17 or use by a registered user under subsection 29(1)(b), exclusively applied when financial control was found. Accordingly, liberties were taken with both

---

[72] *'Pussy Galore'* T.M. [1967] R.P.C. 265. The view has been expressed that the result reached in this case will have been 'swept away' by the Trade Marks Act 1994. Richards, 'Looking Forward to the New UK Trade Mark Statute,' Autumn Conference of the Institute of Trade Mark Agents, October 1991, p. 7 (unpublished). Query, however, whether a mere statement of intention to use the mark through a licensee unascertained at the time of the application will necessarily satisfy the requirement of a bona fide intention to use the mark?

[73] *Work Manual*, *supra*, n. 65, para. 27–59.

sections so as to allow an application to proceed under either basis.[74]

Character Merchandising and the Problem of Trafficking

3–35   One particular question that arose under subsection 29(1)(b) of the Trade Marks Act 1938 was whether an application filed under that subsection was appropriate in the light of the specific prohibition under section 28(6) against registering a licence that amounted to 'trafficking' in a trade mark. Under section 28(6), if a licence arrangement would facilitate trafficking a trade mark, the Registrar was obliged to refuse registration of the licensee as a registered user.

3–36   In practice, the provisions of section 28(6) were relied upon sparingly by the Registry in refusing registration of a registered user, but were most notably at issue in the *Hollie Hobbie* case.[75]

The *Hollie Hobbie* Case

3–37   In the *Hollie Hobbie* cases, the House of Lords upheld the decision of the Registrar, who had refused the registration of 12 applications for a trade mark comprising the name and well-known likeness of an imaginary girl to be used in connection with a wide variety of goods. The applications had been filed under subsection 29(1)(b) by a U.S. greeting card manufacturer for use on various goods other than greeting cards. However, registration was refused under section 28(6), on the ground that the planned arrangement amounted to impermissible trafficking in the trade mark.

Definition of Trafficking

3–38   The term 'trafficking' was not defined in the Trade Marks Act 1938, and each of the courts in the *Hollie Hobbie* case wrestled with the question of its meaning. No single understanding emerged, but three definitions offered during the course of the case are noteworthy:

   (a) Trafficking was 'treating the mark itself as a source of income without any existing reputation attaching to the mark for the [particular class of] goods concerned.'[76]
   (b) Trafficking 'extends to any conduct carried out or intended to be carried out in respect of a mark or a proposed mark with a view to commercial gain which is not a bona fide exploitation of that mark in pursuance of the true function of a trade mark, namely its use "in

---

[74] Financial control may be more easily understood in terms of the notion of 'consent' under s.32(3) of the Trade Marks Act 1994.

[75] *Re Hollie Hobbie T.M.* [1984] F.S.R. 199, H.L.; [1983] F.S.R. 581, C.A.; [1983] F.S.R. 138. In addition, the notion of trafficking had occasionally been relied upon by a party seeking to challenge the validity of a trade mark registration. See, *e.g.*, *Tradam Trading Company (Bahamas) Limited's T.M.* [1990] F.S.R. 200.

[76] Assistant Registrar Myall, as reported in [1984] F.S.R. 199 at 206, H.L.

relation to goods for the purpose of indicating, or so as to indicate, a connection in the course of trade between the goods and some person having the right either as proprietor or as registered user to use the mark".[77]

(c) '[T]rafficking in a trade mark context conveys the notion of dealing in a trade mark primarily as a commodity in its own right and not primarily for the purpose of identifying or promoting merchandise in which the proprietor of the mark is interested. If there is no real trade connection between the proprietor of the mark and the licensee or his goods, there is room for the conclusion that the grant of the licence is a trafficking of the mark.'[78]

Quality Control Not Sufficient

Notably, impermissible trafficking was found in the *Hollie Hobbie* case despite the fact that the applications for registration had been accompanied by licence agreements providing for some form of quality control over the various marked goods. In the view of the House of Lords, the actual quality control exercised by the applicant was 'slight'.[79] More importantly, the Court could discern no general rule that 'the mere ability to control quality is always to be sufficient to establish the required connection.'[80]   3–39

Were There Clear Principles on Which a Finding of Trafficking was Based?

It can be said that none of the opinions explains, on principled grounds, why the proposed use of the *Hollie Hobbie* mark amounted to trafficking, while the use in a merchandising sense of other well-known marks, such as *Coca Cola*, on a variety of goods, did not. Perhaps the ultimate test was the one simply expressed by Lord Brightman in the form of the following question: '[I]f a commercial activity such as that falling to be considered by your Lordships in the instant case is not trafficking in a trade mark, what is?'[81]   3–40

On the other hand, Lord Bridge, while concurring with the refusal to register the *Hollie Hobbie* trade mark applications, expressed his dissatisfaction with the 'trafficking' provision under section 28(6), and urged its parliamentary repeal. In his Lordship's view, such character merchandising 'deceives nobody.'[82]

---

[77] Buckley L.J. [1983] F.S.R. 581 at 591, C.A.
[78] Lord Brightman [1984] F.S.R. 199 at 209, H.L. See also the judgment in the case of *J. Batt and Co.'s Trade Marks* (1898) 15 R.P.C. 262; (1899) 16 R.P.C. 11, H.L., the only previously reported case in which the term 'trafficking' was applied in a trade mark context.
[79] [1984] F.S.R. 199 at 208.
[80] *ibid.* at 208 (Lord Brightman); see also the observation of Dillon L.J. in the Court of Appeal, who rejected the proposition that 'the mere inclusion in an agreement of quality control provisions provides automatically a trade connection where otherwise there would be none.' [1983] F.S.R. 581 at 588.
[81] [1984] F.S.R. 199 at 207, H.L.
[82] *ibid.* at 202, H.L.

Trafficking Under the Trade Marks Act 1994

3-41 The provisions requiring the Registrar to refuse to record a licence on the ground that the use would facilitate trafficking in the mark have been eliminated by the Trade Marks Act 1994. Nevertheless, the new legislation does not contain any provisions that specify the precise boundaries of acceptable licensing practices in respect of characters and the like.

In particular, the suggestion that 'less desirable' forms of trafficking be prohibited under the new Act, such as speculative filings for registration without any intent by the applicant to use the mark, was not adopted. It was reasoned that no reasonable person would undertake to invest in a mark that had no substantial economic value. Further, a person who later might wish to adopt and use such a mark in the course of trade could seek to cancel any speculatively registered mark on the ground of non-use and that the filing of the mark had been made in bad faith.[83]

In light of the above, the scope of valid character merchandising under the Trade Marks Act 1994 must be viewed as not fully settled.

---

[83] White Paper, 'Reform of Trade Marks Law', Cm. (1990) para. 4.41. Note as well that three distinct types of character merchandising from the point of view of trade mark law can be identified:

(i) The use on a variety of goods of a cartoon or similar character, such as Hollie Hobbie, having no independent trade mark significance.

(ii) The use of a well-known mark, such as 'Coca Cola', on goods, such as clothes, distinct from its primary identification.

(iii) The use of a mark, such as the figure of an alligator on clothing, which arguably serves both to decorate the goods and to identify the source of the goods as well. White Paper, op. cit., at para. 4.43.

4. The Registration of Licensees in Transition

A Change in the Legal Landscape

Nowhere have recent events so changed the legal landscape of trade mark   **4–01**
licensing than in connection with the registration of licences.

The registered user provisions under the United Kingdom Trade Marks Act
1938 were enacted against the backdrop of a concern that the public should
be protected by the Registrar against deception. In accordance with this view,
the registered user provisions were formulated with the idea of relying on the
administrative scrutiny of the Registrar as the front line of protection.[1] With
the registered user requirements that were in place since 1938, this chapter
would, until recently, have focused primarily on the substantive and procedural
provisions of the Trade Marks Act 1938 dealing with this issue. Such is no
longer the case.

As has been noted,[2] the focus on the role of the Registrar as the principal
watchdog of the public interest has given way to a realisation that it is the
trade mark proprietor who has the most immediate interest in protecting the
value of its trade mark, by ensuring that the mark is not being used by the
licensee in a deceptive manner.[3] Accordingly, the registered user provisions
have been increasingly perceived as out of touch with the licensing needs of
traders and the protection of their trade marks in the marketplace. The result
of this perception has been a legislative trend towards either the abolition, as
in Canada,[4] or the modification, as in the U.K., of the provisions for
registration of a licensee.[5]

While the registration of licensees will not disappear under the Trade
Marks Act 1994, the focus of the registration will change by the elimination
of any substantive examination of the quality control provisions of the licence.

---

[1] White Paper, '*Reform of Trade Marks Law*', Cm. 1203 (1990), para. 35–36.
[2] See, generally, Chap. 3.
[3] White Paper, *supra*, para. 4.36. A similar view appears to characterise the trade mark regime
in the Benelux countries, where marks are registered without any substantive examination. All
challenges to a registered trade mark are then left to the initiative of interested parties.
[4] See n. 14, *infra*, regarding the new Canadian legislation.
[5] As an aid to the interpretation of the Trade Marks Act 1994, there is the White Paper, which
set out as long ago as 1990 the views of the Department of Trade and Industry on the shape
of a new trade marks act in general, and the registered user provisions and the treatment of
licences in particular. An excellent summary can be found in Richards, 'Looking Forward to
the New U.K. Trade Mark Statute,' a paper delivered to the Autumn Conference of the
Institute of Trade Mark Agents, October 1991. Note as well that the provisions regarding the
Community Trade Mark do not require the recordal of a trade mark licence. See, *infra*, Chap.
13, para. 13–45.

The mechanics of the registration will be modified accordingly. This chapter
will discuss this transition under the Trade Marks Act 1994 in the light of
the registered user practice under the Trade Marks Act 1938.[6]

The Registered User Provisions Under the Trade Marks Act 1938 Were Treated as Permissive

4–02 Even under the Trade Marks Act 1938, the registered user provisions were
treated as permissive rather than mandatory.[7] Provided that adequate quality
control was maintained, a trade mark licence was not invalidated simply
because it had not been recorded under the registered user provisions.
Moreover, while certain advantages were said to attach to a registered user
registration, notably that (a) the permitted use of the trade mark by the
registered user was deemed to be use of the mark by the licensor, in the event
that the mark was challenged on the ground of non-use, (b) the registration
was prima facie evidence that the Registrar had found that adequate quality
control exists, and (c) the registered user had a limited statutory right of
action against a third party infringer, it was certainly the case that not all
licences of registered trade marks were registered under the 1938 Act. Thus,
'it is thought that many licensing arrangements are not recorded in the
register.'[8]

Legal Transparency: The Changed Focus of the Registration of a Trade Mark Licensee

4–03 Under the Trade Marks Act 1994, the focus of the registration of a trade
mark licensee will be dramatically changed. Unlike other jurisdictions that have
recently amended their trade marks laws, most notably Canada, registration of
the licence has not been abolished under the 1994 Trade Marks Act.[9] On the
contrary, the registration of licences will be encouraged, albeit with a different
purpose in mind.

The grant of a licence of a registered trade mark under the Trade Marks
Act 1994, is a registrable transaction. However, the underlying rationale for
the registration of a trade mark licensee will no longer be to ensure that the
quality control and other requirements which guard against public deception
have been met. That is primarily the responsibility of the trade mark
proprietor. Rather, the registration of the licence agreement will serve the
'interests of legal transparency.'[10] The intention is essentially that the registration of a licensee will put third parties on notice regarding the existence
of the licence arrangement. In addition, to encourage registration, only a

---

[6] It should be noted, however, that some form of registered user requirement is still in effect in
certain other jurisdictions. In these jurisdictions, the principles of the U.K. system with respect
to registration under the Trade Marks Act will presumably continue to apply.

[7] See Chap. 3, paras. 3–07 to 3–10.

[8] White Paper, *op. cit.*, para. 4.38.

[9] *cf.* n. 14, the amendment to the Trade Marks Act in Canada, which abolished the registration
of registered users.

[10] White Paper, para. 4.38.

registered licensee under the Trade Marks Act 1994 will enjoy a statutory right to bring an action for infringement, although there are certain differences between an exclusive and non-exclusive licensee in this regard.[11]

The requirements for registration are significantly simplified. In particular, the new law provides that a trade mark may be licensed for some or all of the goods in respect of which it is registered, and for all or part of the U.K.[12] In order to register the licence, an application must be filed setting out certain prescribed information, such as the identity of the licensee and the date and duration of the licence, but without the need for any substantive examination of the licence by the Registrar.

Quality Control Still Remains Important

As we have seen, quality control is not a requirement for registration of a   4–04 trade mark licence. This is not to say that quality control has become irrelevant. The focus, however, will now be on the interest of the proprietor in protecting his interest in the trade mark as a valuable piece of property. The exercise of quality control will be the vital means by which to accomplish this, 'ensuring that the value of that property is not reduced by misuse, either because the use of the mark has become deceptive or misleading, or because the mark has become generic.'[13] As a practical matter, therefore, the exercise of quality control will remain a central feature of a trade mark licence.[14]

Two Important Provisions: Notice and the Licensee's Right of Action

There are two main areas in which the registration of a licence under the   4–05 Trade Marks Act 1994 are particularly important: (a) notice about the licence to third parties and (b) the licensee's right of action.

---

[11] See, *infra*, paras. 4–07 to 4–25, for discussion on right of action.
[12] Trade Marks Act 1994, s. 28(1). This provision follows Art. 8(1) of the Trade Marks Directive. See also, *infra*, para. 4–45.
[13] Richards, n. 5 *op. cit.*, p. 10. See also, White Paper, para. 4.36.
[14] See, generally, Chap. 6, for discussion on quality control. By comparison, in June 1993, the provisions requiring the registration of a registered user (s.50) were completely eliminated from the Canadian Trade Marks Act (Bill S-17, Intellectual Property Improvement Bill). In its place, the law will validate a licence arrangement which meets the substantive requirements of the section, *i.e.* that the licensee derives its use of the trade mark from the proprietor of the trade mark, and the proprietor exercises control of the licencee's use of the trade mark. In such a situation, use of the trade mark by the licensee is deemed always to have had the same effect as use by the owner.
The section also contains a new provision regarding the marking of the goods, whereby if the fact of the licensed use of the trade mark and the name of the proprietor of the mark properly appear, there is an assumption that the use is licensed and that quality control is being exercised.
A further provision extends the right to license a trade mark which forms part of a composite mark or a trade name.
Legislation materially altering or eliminating the registered user requirements is also likely under the trade mark laws of South Africa and Australia.

Notice of Licence to Third Parties

4-06   A written licence signed by the licensor is a 'registrable transaction' under the Trade Marks Act 1994. As such, upon proper application by the licensee to the Registry, the grant of the licence may be registered on the register.[15] Until an application for registration of a licence under a registered trade mark has been made, the licence transaction is ineffective against an innocent third party that acquires any conflicting interest. This provision is of particular practical significance to an exclusive licensee.[16] Moreover, a person will have no right of action as a licensee under the Trade Marks Act 1994 unless an application for the registration of the licence as a registrable transaction has been made.[17]

The rule relating to notice also applies to a party which has a security interest over the registered trade mark under which a licence has been granted. It would appear, therefore, that if the security interest is properly registered, the right of the secured party chargee to foreclose on the security interest is subject to the rights of the registered licensee.[18] More generally, it is intended that this scheme of registration will ease the burden of resolving conflicting claims of priority of rights in the trade mark. Such disputes may arise between the licensor and licensee, a licensee and a secured party, or between one licensee and other licensees, in a situation where the licence purports to grant conflicting exclusive rights to more than one licensee.[19]

The result of the registration system is that the licensee which is first to register prevails in most instances in which a claim of priority is raised, even if the date of execution of that licensee's agreement is later than the date of the licence agreement of the conflicting licensee.[20]

The Registered Licensee's Right to Bring an Action

4-07   Under the Trade Marks Act 1994, extensive provision is made for the right of action of a licensee. As noted above, the prerequisite for a claim of action by a licensee is that the licence of the registered trade mark has been properly registered. Assuming that the license has been registered, the following provisions apply with respect to the licensee's right of action.

Exclusive Licensee and Non-Exclusive Licensee Distinguished

The Trade Marks Act 1994 distinguishes between an exclusive and a non-exclusive licensee. An exclusive licence is defined as 'a licence (general or limited) authorising the licensee to the exclusion of all other persons, including the person granting the licence, to use a registered trade mark in a manner

---

[15] Trade Marks Act 1994, s. 25(1).

[16] Trade Marks Act 1994, s. 25(3)(a).

[17] Trade Marks Act 1994, s. 25(3)(b).

[18] Richards, n. 5, above, p. 13.; see, generally, on charges over a trade mark, Chap. 14, para. 14–13, *infra*, n. 5.

[19] *ibid*. pp. 14–15.

[20] *ibid*. p. 15. However, there may be an exception to this rule if the second licensee, although first to register, was aware of the existence of the first licence agreement. See, *e.g.* s. 25(3)(a).

authorised by the licence. The expressions 'exclusive' and 'non-exclusive' licensee shall be construed accordingly.'[21] The exclusive licensee has these same rights against any successor in title, and the licence will bind the successor in title in the same way that it bound the person granting the person granting the licence.[22]

General Provisions Regarding Licensee's Right of Action

The provisions authorising the right of action of a licensee underwent material   4–08
change during the legislative development of the Trade Marks Act 1994. In its initial form, a sharp distinction was drawn between the right of action of an exclusive, and non-exclusive licensee, respectively, whereby the right of action of an exclusive licensee was likened to that of an assignee as a matter of law.[23] Views were expressed that such a provision would have the effect of dissuading the granting of an exclusive licence. This is because the proprietor stood the risk that the exclusive licensee, in bringing on its own an action for infringement, would lead to a situation in which the defendant successfully countersues for expungement of the mark from the registry.

In the final form of the Bill, the provision that likened the exclusive licensee to an assignee as a matter of law was eliminated. In its place, section 30 of the Trade Marks Act 1994 contains general provisions governing the right of action of a licensee, either exclusive or non-exclusive. These general provisions are then made subject to an exception under section 31 in the situation where the licence agreement itself provides that the exclusive licensee shall have the same rights and remedies as if the grant of the licence had been an assignment, and the exclusive licensee may thereby bring an action in his own name.[24]

Under the general provisions regarding the right of action, a licensee, unless the licence provides otherwise, is entitled to call upon the proprietor to take infringement proceedings 'in any matter which affects his interests.'[25] If the proprietor refuses to take action or fails to do so within two months of having been called upon to do so, the licensee may bring an action in his own name as if he were the proprietor.[26] In a case where the licensee brings an action in his own name, the licensee may not, without leave of court, proceed with the action unless the proprietor is either added as a plaintiff or is joined as a defendant. This requirement does not apply, however, to the granting of interlocutory relief upon application of the licensee alone[27]. A proprietor that is joined as a defendant in this manner is not liable for any costs in the action unless he takes part in the proceedings.[28]

---

[21] Trade Marks Act 1994, s. 29(1).
[22] Trade Marks Act 1994, s. 29(2). Generally, a licence is binding on a successor in title to the licensor, unless the licence provides otherwise. s. 28(3).
[23] Trade Marks Bill (HL Bill 5), s. 16(1).
[24] See, paras. 4–09 to 4–12, for discussion of right of action of an exclusive licensee.
[25] Trade Marks Act 1994, s. 30(2).
[26] Trade Marks Act 1994, s. 30(3).
[27] Trade Marks Act 1994, s. 30(4).
[28] Trade Marks Act 1994, s. 30(5).

Right of Action of an Exclusive Licensee Having Rights and Remedies as if Assignee

4–09   As noted above, an exception to the general provisions regarding the right of action of a licensee is made for an exclusive licensee under limited circumstances. Thus, the licence may contain a provision that the exclusive licensee has the same rights and remedies in respect of matters that take place after the grant of the licence, as if there had been an assignment. In such a situation, the exclusive licensee may, in accordance with the terms of the licence and the provisions of section 31 of the Trade Marks Act 1994, bring action for infringement in its own name against any person other than the proprietor of the registered mark.[29] If there is no such provision in the licence agreement, however, an exclusive licensee will not be deemed a assignee for the purpose of the exclusive licensee's right of action. An exclusive licensee that has the rights and remedies of an assignee under section 31(1) is also deemed for the purposes of section 30 as if he were the proprietor of the registered mark.[30]

4–10   The rights and remedies of the exclusive licensee under section 31 of the Trade Marks Act 1994, and in particular, the provisions relating to the proprietor in connection with infringement, are deemed to be concurrent with those of the proprietor.[31] In addition, the exclusive licensee having the rights of an assignee may avail himself of any defence that would have been available were an action to have been brought against him by the proprietor.[32] Similarly to the general provisions regarding the licensee's right of action, the exclusive licensee having the rights of an assignee may not, without leave of court, proceed with an action unless the proprietor is either joined as a defendant or added as a plaintiff, to the extent that the exclusive licensee having the rights of an assignee and proprietor have concurrent rights of action.[33] A proprietor will be liable for costs only if it takes part in the action as a defendant. Notwithstanding these provisions, the exclusive licensee may be granted interlocutory relief alone.[34] The proprietor of the registered trade mark must notify any exclusive licensee who has a concurrent right of action before the proprietor seeks an order for delivery up of infringing goods, materials or articles. If the exclusive licensee makes the appropriate application, the court may take into account the provision of the licence when granting an order for delivery up.[35]

Right of Action is Subject to a Contrary Agreement

4–11   The licensee's right to call upon the proprietor of the registered mark to take infringement proceedings is subject to contrary provision of the licence agreement.[36] With respect to the right of action of an exclusive licensee

---

[29] Trade Marks Act 1994, s. 31(1).
[30] Trade Marks Act 1994, s. 30(7). Presumably, this applies to a sub-licence situation.
[31] Trade Marks Act 1994, s. 31(2).
[32] Trade Marks Act 1994, s. 31(3).
[33] Trade Marks Act 1994, s. 31(4).
[34] Trade Marks Act 1994, ss. 31(4), (5).
[35] Trade Marks Act 1994, s. 31(7).
[36] Trade Marks Act, s. 30(2).

deemed to be an assignee, the parties may by agreement to the contrary alter certain portions of section 31 (subsections (4)–(7)). These subsections cover the following issues: the joinder or addition of the proprietor, the right of the exclusive licensee to be granted interlocutory relief alone, the proprietor's liability for costs in the action as a defendant, the assessment of damages and apportionment of recovery, and a request for an order for delivery up.[37] Regarding subsection 31(8), it is ambiguous whether or not the agreement to the contrary be in writing ('subject to any agreement to the contrary'), although the absence of a written agreement may give rise to difficult issues of proof.

There may be several motives on the proprietor's part for excluding the licensee from having a right of action. The proprietor may not wish to relinquish its sole control over the enforcement of the trade mark, or be ordered by the court to share any monetary recovery with a licensee. Further, at least with respect to a licensee subject to section 30, the proprietor may not wish to be limited to the particular time schedule specified by the relevant statutory provisions.   **4–12**

The converse will be true as far as the licensee is concerned. Thus, depending upon its bargaining power, the licensee can be expected to resist a provision in the licence agreement excluding it from a right of action.

The Registered Licensee's Right to Monetary Relief in an Action for Infringement

Closely related to the right of action of a licensee under the Trade Marks Act 1994 are provisions governing the assessment of damages and the apportionment of monetary relief between the proprietor and a licensee.   **4–13**

General Provisions

In an infringement action brought by the proprietor of a trade mark, any loss that a non-exclusive licensee has either suffered or is likely to suffer in respect of the infringement shall be taken into account. The court may give such directions to the plaintiff as the court deems appropriate to hold the proceeds of such monetary recovery on behalf of licensees.[38]   **4–14**

Exclusive Licensee Deemed an Assignee

Where an action for infringement is brought by either the proprietor or the exclusive licensee that is deemed an assignee under section 31, and the proprietor and the exclusive licensee have or had concurrent rights of action, the following provisions govern the awarding and apportionment of monetary relief: **4–15**

---

[37] Trade Marks Act 1994, s. 31(8).
[38] Trade Marks Act 1994, s. 30(6).

Assessment of Damages

    (a) The court, in assessing damages, must take into account the terms of the licence and any monetary remedy that has been awarded or is available to either of them with respect to the infringement.

    (b) No account of profits shall be directed if an award of damages has been made, or if an account of profits has been directed in favour of either of them.

    (c) Where an account of profits is directed, the court shall apportion the profits between the proprietor and the exclusive licensee in such manner as it 'considers just', subject to any contrary agreement between the parties.[39]

Application of These Provisions Regarding an Exclusive Licensee

4-16   The provisions apply whether or not the proprietor and the exclusive licensee are both parties to the action for infringement. Where they are not both parties, the court may give such directions as it deems appropriate regarding the extent to which the party to the proceedings is to hold the proceeds of any monetary relief on behalf of the other.[40]

Prerequisite to Monetary Recovery: The Licensee Must Be Registered

4-17   A licensee is not entitled to an award of either damages or an account of profits in respect of an infringement of the registered trade mark that occurs after the date of the licence agreement but before the date on which the particulars of the licence are registered, subject to the following:

    (a) The application for registration of the particulars of the licence has been made within six months of the date of the written licence agreement; or

    (b) The court is convinced that it was not practicable for the application to have been made within the six-month period, and the application was made as soon thereafter as was practicable.[41]

The Parties May Provide in the Licence Agreement for the Award of Recovery

4-18   Given the novelty of the provisions regarding the awarding and apportionment of monetary recovery, it remains to be seen how they will be applied in practice.[42] Parties that wish to have greater certainty in connection with the apportionment of recovery may perhaps do so by including explicit provisions on this point in the licence agreement.

---

[39] Trade Marks Act 1994, s. 31(6), (a), (b), (c).
[40] Trade Marks Act 1994, s. 31(6).
[41] Trade Marks Act 1994, s. 25(4).
[42] *cf.* the result in the U.S. case of *Original Appalachian Artworks Inc. v. S. Diamond Associates Inc.*, 911 F.2d 1548 (11th Cir. 1990). See also discussion, Chap. 10, paras. 10–28 to 10–30.

A Comparison: The Right of Action of the Registered User under the Trade Marks Act 1938

Under section 28(3) of the Trade Marks Act 1938, the registered user had a   **4–19**
right of action for infringement only if he first called upon the proprietor to
sue, and the proprietor then either refused or failed to take action within the
period of two months after having been called upon to do so.

The scope of the registered user's right of action under the Trade Marks
Act 1938 was narrowly construed by the courts. Most notably, in the *Levi
Strauss* case, the court rejected an attempt by the foreign proprietor of the
U.K. registered trade mark to join its wholly-owned U.K. subsidiary, which
was registered as a registered user, as a party to the infringement action.[43]
Falconer J. stated the relevant principles as follows:

'Registered usership is entirely a creature of this statute and, so far as
the rights which the registered user may exercise are concerned, they are
to be found in subsection (3) of section 28 ... This seems to me to be a
complete code of the rights of the registered user, certainly in so far as
the bringing of actions for infringement is concerned, and it seems to me
quite clear that the only circumstances that the statute provides for in
which the registered user may be a plaintiff is where he has called upon
the proprietor to take proceedings in respect of the infringement in
question and the proprietor after the stipulated period of two months
has either refused to do so or had neglected to do so ... There are no
other provisions for a registered user to be the plaintiff in a registered
trade mark infringement action.'[44]

Can the Proprietor Refuse to Sign the Application for Registration?

Is it possible for the licensor to exclude the licensee's right of action by simply   **4–20**
refusing to sign the application for registration of the licensee? Under the
Trade Marks Act 1938, the answer with respect to the registration of a
registered user was generally yes. Under the Trade Marks Act 1994, however,
the licensee is apparently allowed to file for registration on his own behalf.
Indeed, it is in the particular interest of the licensee to register the licence,
since the registration will serve to provide notice to a third party about the
transaction, and will confer the right to take action for infringement under
either sections 30 or 31, as appropriate.[44a]

The Trade Marks Act 1994 provides that the application for registration

---

[43] *Levi Strauss & Co. and Levis Strauss (U.K.) Ltd v. The French Connection Ltd* [1982] F.S.R.
443.
[44] *ibid.* pp. 444–445. The result reached in the *Levi Strauss* case runs counter to the earlier
suggestion by a leading commentator that it is 'proper for a user who has been damaged by
infringement to be joined as a plaintiff in an action by the registered user of the mark.' Kerly
(12th ed.), para. 15–06. But note the case of *Portakabin Ltd v. Powerblast Ltd* [1990] R.P.C.
471, where both the proprietor and the registered user of the two trade marks at issue, which
had apparently been the subject of an assignment and licence back arrangement, were allowed
to maintain a joint action for infringement.
[44a] See, *supra*, paras. 4–05 to 4–19.

of a 'registrable transaction' may be made by a person claiming to be entitled to an interest in or under a registered trade mark. The grant of a licence is specified as a 'registrable transaction' within the meaning of this section.[45] Thus, a licensee is a party with a registrable interest in the licence. The right of the licensee to apply for registration of the licence fits with the aim of the Trade Marks Act 1994 of encouraging legal transparency in the licence relationship. A concern arises if the licensee is able to register itself as a licensee of the registered trade mark without any opportunity for the proprietor's views to be heard. This problem would, in principle, appear to be most acute if the licence is oral. Since, however, a licence is not deemed effective for purposes of registration under the Trade Marks Act 1994 unless it is in writing (at least signed by the grantor), there is no practical concern in regard to an oral licence.[46]

Other Provisions in Connection with the Bringing of an Action

4–21   As noted, the Trade Marks Act 1994 confers upon the proprietor a right to override by agreement the statutory provisions in respect of the right of the licensee to call upon the proprietor to bring an action for infringement.[47] The precise scope of this right will ultimately have to be determined the courts. Several types of provision regarding the rights and obligations of the parties in connection with the bringing of an action for infringement can be identified.

The Licensee's Right of Action as the Agent or Representative of the Proprietor

4–22   Can the parties authorise the licensee to sue as the agent or representative of the proprietor? The validity of such an arrangement was recognised, albeit *obiter*, by the Israel Supreme Court under the somewhat different registered user provisions of the Israel Trade Marks Ordinance, which confers on the registered user no independent right of action whatsoever.[48]

Duty to Notify the Proprietor of an Infringement

4–23   The licence agreement may provide that the licensee shall notify the proprietor of any third party infringement of the trade mark. It would appear that this contractual obligation to notify is separate from any statutory entitlement of the licensee to call upon the proprietor to take action against infringement.

The opposite contractual obligation may also be found, namely that the proprietor has a duty to notify the licensee in the event that the proprietor decides to take action against an infringer. Such an obligation does not seem to be inconsistent with the provisions of the Trade Marks Act 1994. In particular, the proprietor has a fixed period of time from the receipt of a request from the licensee in which to take action against the infringement, but there is no mention of any obligation on the part of the proprietor to notify the licensee of his decision.

---

[45] Trade Marks Act 1994, s. 25(2)(b).
[46] Trade Marks Act 1994, s. 28(2). See generally, Chap. 11.
[47] See paras. 30(2), (3).
[48] *Ampisal (Israel) Ltd v. Naimi*, P.D. 37(3) 198 (in Hebrew).

Right to Terminate for Proprietor's Failure to Take Action

May a licence include a provision permitting the licensee to terminate the   4–24
licence if the proprietor does not take action against the infringer?

It would appear that such a provision is not inconsistent with the Trade
Marks Act 1994, provided that the proprietor has the full statutory period of
time following the receipt of notice from the licensee in which to take action.
A licensee, when confronted with a third party infringement which the
proprietor does not wish to challenge, but having limited resources of his
own with which to maintain the action, may wish to invoke such a provision
if the infringement has adversely affected the continuing viability of the
commercial arrangement. Conversely, the proprietor is under no general
obligation to take action upon being called upon to do so by a licensee.
However, the proprietor may wish to clarify this point by including an express
provision in the agreement stating that it is under no such obligation.

Indemnification

A provision is sometimes included in the licence agreement to the effect that   4–25
if the licensee brings an action for infringement, it will indemnify and hold
the proprietor harmless from any damage or expense resulting from the
bringing of the action.

Of principal concern is the possibility that a defendant to an infringement
action will successfully countersue for the expungement of the registration.
This is particularly acute in connection with an exclusive licensee. The
provisions of the Trade Marks Act 1994, which provide that the parties to
the licence agreement may agree to treat the exclusive licensee as if it were
an assignee, would appear to authorise the exclusive licensee to sue on its
own behalf. The exclusive licensee could thereby put the registration of the
mark in jeopardy. An indemnification undertaking from the exclusive licensee
to the proprietor may provide the proprietor with some comfort, and encourage the exclusive licensee to consult with the proprietor before bringing an
action.

The Licensee's Right of Action: A Comparison with U.S. Law

The provisions regarding the licensee's right of action under the Trade Marks   4–26
Act 1994 can be contrasted with the situation in the U.S. under the Lanham
Act. There is no statutory provision under the Lanham Act regulating the
right of a trade mark licensee to sue for infringement. Accordingly, the scope
of the trade mark licensee's right of action has been formulated by case law.
In this context, the distinction that has been drawn is between the licensee's
right of action for infringement of a registered, as opposed to an unregistered,
trade mark.

Licensee's Right of Action for a Registered Trade Mark

Section 32(b) of the Lanham Act provides that the 'registrant' may seek relief   4–27 for infringement of a registered trade mark.[49] Section 45 of the Act defines a registrant to include 'legal representatives, predecessors, successors and assigns.'[50] The question is whether the term 'registrant' in this context extends to the licensee of the registered trade mark. The better view is that it does, at least with respect to an exclusive licensee.[51]

In a leading case, it was observed that an exclusive trade mark licensee is deemed to be an assignee within the meaning of the Lanham Act and, therefore, has standing to take action for infringement of the registered trade mark.[52] On the other hand, a non-exclusive trade mark licensee is not deemed to be an assignee.[53] The analogy was drawn with a patent licensee's right of action, where an exclusive licensee enjoys a right of action, but a non-exclusive licensee does not.[54] The touchstone of an exclusive licence has been described as a prohibition upon the proprietor from competing with the licensee in the licensed territory.[55] However, the precise definition of what constitutes an exclusive licence remains unsettled.

A right of action has been recognised when the exclusive licensee is the wholly-owned subsidiary of the proprietor of a registered service mark[56] and has even been recognised when the licence agreement was not put into evidence, but there was convincing oral testimony establishing the existence of the exclusive licence.[57]

Right of Action of a Distributor

4–28   U.S. courts have on occasion failed to make a clear distinction between an exclusive licensee and an exclusive distributor.[58] As a result, certain judgments can be construed as holding that an exclusive distributor has a right of action. The better view, however, is that an exclusive distributor lacks such standing.[59]

Licensee's Right of Action for an Unregistered Trade Mark

4–29   On the other hand, the right to bring an action under section 43(a) of the Lanham Act on account of the unauthorised use of an unregistered mark, or

---

[49]   15 U.S.C. 1114(b).

[50]   15 U.S.C. 1127.

[51]   But see, contra, The Panatech Corporation v. Carl Zeiss Inc., 96 U.S.P.Q. 261 (S.D.N.Y. 1953); Volkswagenwerk Aktiengesellschaft v. Dreer, 224 F. Supp. 744, 746, 140 U.S.P.Q. 54, 55 (E.D. Pa. 1963).

[52]   Quabaug Rubber Co. v. Fabiano Shoe Co. Inc., 195 U.S.P.Q. 689 (1st Cir. 1977).

[53]   ibid. 195 U.S.P.Q. at 692–93, n. 8; see also Alfred Dunhill of London Inc. v. Kasser Distillers Products Corp., 350 F. Supp. 1341, 175 U.S.P.Q. 586 3588 n. 1 (E.D. Pa. 1972), aff'd per curiam 480 F. 2d 917, 178 U.S.P.Q. 449 (3rd Cir. 1973).

[54]   Quabaug, supra, n. 52 at 962. The leading case is the U.S. Supreme Court decision of Waterman v. McKenzie, 138 U.S. 252 (1891), which was later applied in the trade mark context in the case of Bourjois Co. v. Katzel, 260 U.S. 689 (1923).

[55]   Quabaug, supra, n. 52 at 692.

[56]   Century 21 v. R.M. Post Inc., 8 U.S.P.Q. 2d 1614, 1615; Alfred Dunhill of London Inc. v. Kassser Distillers Products Corp., n. 53.

[57]   Wynn Oil Co. v. Thomas, 5 U.S.P.Q. 2d 1944, 1949 (6th Cir. 1988).

[58]   Most notable is G.H. Mumm Champagne v. Eastern Wine Corp., 142 F.2d 499, 61 U.S.P.Q. 337 (2d Cir.), cert. denied, 323 U.S. 715 (1944); Browne-Vinters Co., Inc. v. National Distillers and Chemical Corp., 151 F.Supp. 595, 114 U.S.P.Q. 483 (S.D.N.Y. 1957).

[59]   DEP Corp. v. Interstate Cigar Co., 622 F.2d 621, 206 U.S.P.Q. 673 (2d Cir. 1980).

for a false or misleading description and representation, extends more broadly to 'any person who believes that he or she is likely to be damaged by such act.'[60]

Applying this statutory standard, the court has granted a right of action to a non-exclusive licensee,[61] to a licensee that is not in direct competition with the defendant,[62] to the estate of Elvis Presley (which receives royalty payments from merchandising the name and likeness of the late entertainer),[63] and even to an exclusive distributor.[64]

However, the U.S. courts have not recognised a right of action for infringement in favour of an exclusive licensee against its own licensor, even if the parties had provided by contract that the licensee had a specified right of action against third parties, on the ground that only a contract claim between the licensor and licensee was at issue.[65]

Right of Action and Exclusion By Virtue of Contract

Registered Trade Mark

As indicated above,[66] U.S. courts have recognised the right of action of an exclusive licensee of a registered trade mark. However, there is nothing under U.S. law that would prevent the parties from contractually excluding a right of action by the licensee. It would appear that neither a non-exclusive licensee nor an exclusive distributor has a right of action with respect to a registered trade mark.[67] Here again, however, the exclusion can be made explicit in an agreement between the relevant parties.   **4–30**

Action Brought Under Section 43(a) of the Lanham Act

As we have seen, the scope of a licensee's right of action under section 43(a) may be broader than the right of action under a registered trade mark.[68] It is even more essential, therefore, that in this situation, a licensor wishing to exclude a non-exclusive licensee, or even a distributor, does so explicitly in the licence or distribution agreement.   **4–31**

The Application Procedure for Registration of a Registered User Under the 1938 Act

Despite the significant changes to the registration of licensees under the Trade   **4–32**

---

[60] 15 U.S.C. 1125(a).
[61] *Quabaug, supra*, n. 52 at 693.
[62] *London v. Carson Pirie Scott & Co.*, 4 U.S.P.Q2d 1148, 1150 (N.D. Ill. 1987).
[63] *Estate of Elvis Presley*, 211 U.S.P.Q. 415 (D.N.J. 1981).
[64] *Ferrero U.S.A. Inc. v. Ozak Trading Inc.*, 18 U.S.P.Q. 2d 1052, 1056 (D.N.J. 1991). Note, however, that the court appears to be incorrect in its ruling that the right to bring an action under Section 32(a) also extends to 'any person', rather than to the 'registrant.'
[65] *Silverstar Enterprises, Inc. v. Aday*, 218 U.S.P.Q. 142 (S.D.N.Y. 1982).
[66] See *supra*, paras. 4–26 to 4–27.
[67] See *supra*, para 4–27.
[68] See *supra*, para. 4–29.

Marks Act 1994, there are three reasons why we should consider briefly the registration procedure of registered users under the Trade Marks Act 1938. First, the procedure may serve to guide jurisdictions which still maintain a fully fledged registered user system. Secondly, aspects of the procedure remain instructive in understanding the approach taken under the new law with respect to the registration of licensees. Third, there are transitional provisions under the Trade Marks Act 1994 which provide that certain aspects of practice under the registered user provisions remain relevant.[69] Registration of registered users under the Trade Marks Act 1938 was governed principally by sections 28(4) and 28(5).

Form of Application

4–33   Pursuant to section 28(4), the application had to be made jointly by the proprietor and the proposed registered user. In addition, a statutory declaration had to be filed by the proprietor or on its behalf. The declaration set out the relationship between the parties, the degree of control over the permitted use, the goods in respect of which the registration was proposed, any conditions or restrictions, whether the registered user was to be the sole registered user, and the time limit, if any, for the permitted use. The Registrar could also require further documents, information or other evidence in connection with the application. An oral licence agreement was not sufficient to establish the existence of the licence for the purposes of registration of the registered user.

Examination of the Application

4–34   Under section 28(5), the Registrar had to examine the application and determine whether it was contrary to the public interest. The notion of the public interest was ill-defined and apparently little relied upon in practice. The Registrar could then register the user agreement in accordance with any conditions or restrictions that he deemed appropriate.

---

[69] Under Sched. 3, s. 9(2), existing entries of registered users under s. 28 of the Trade Marks Act 1938 shall be transferred to a register to be maintained under the Trade Marks Act 1994, and shall henceforth have effect as if they were made under s. 25 of the Trade Marks Act 1994. This means that that the right to take action under either s. 30 or s. 31 will now apply, unless the parties take measures to provide otherwise (Cook, 'The Trade Marks Bill 1994', Seminar Paper, June 16, 1994).
A pending application for registration of a registered user shall be treated as an application for registration of a licence under s. 25(1) of the Trade Marks Act 1994, subject to any amendments in the application to conform to the new registration requirements (Sched. 3, s. 9(3)). A pending proceeding for variation or cancellation of registration of a registered user shall be dealt with under the Trade Marks Act 1994, and any necessary alteration then made to the new register (Sched. 3, s. 9(5)). See also, *infra*, paras. 4–46 to 4–48.
However, under Sched. 3, 5.9(1), s. 28 (licensing of a registered trade mark) and s. 29(2) (rights of an exclusive licensee against the grantor's successor in title) apply only to licences granted after the commencement of the Act. The Trade Marks Act 1938 will continue to apply to licences granted before commencement.

Quality Control and Other Conditions and Restrictions on Registration

The principal issue in accepting the application for registration of the registered   4–35
user was the matter of control with respect to the specified goods or services.[70]
In addition to the requirement of quality control, other conditions for
registration of the licence particularly territory, duration, and termination,
were also noteworthy.

Territory

A territorial restriction was allowed to limit use of the trade mark to a defined   4–36
area within the U.K. In addition, there was apparently a practice of registering
a registered user lying outside the U.K. whose intended use of the mark was
also outside the United Kingdom.[71] This situation is to be distinguished from
that in which the export itself qualified as trade mark use.

The purpose of restricting the licensed use of the trade mark to use outside
the U.K., which would appear to lie outside of the territorial scope of the
registration, was to satisfy the requirements of certain jurisdictions for which
a registered user registration in the United Kingdom might be a prerequisite
for registration in those jurisdictions. This is thought to have been a rare
situation.[72]

Duration

The registration did not need to specify any limitation on the period of time   4–37
of the licensed use. If no time limit was specified, it would appear that the
period was co-extensive with the duration of the trade mark registration. If
a specific duration was intended, it was advisable to expressly state this in
the licence agreement.

Termination Due to a Failure to Adhere to Quality Control

The licence agreement could contain a termination clause which enabled the   4–38
proprietor to terminate the permitted use if the registered user failed to adhere
to the quality control provisions. Such a provision could be registered as part
of the conditions of control.[73]

Sole Licence

The statutory declaration had to indicate whether it was a condition of the   4–39
licence agreement that the registered user was to be the sole registered user.
The term 'sole registered user' was not defined in either section. Presumably,
however, it was distinct from an 'exclusive' licence, the difference being that
a sole licence did not preclude the licensor from using the trade mark in the

---

[70] *Trade Marks Registry, Work Manual*, Registration of Users, Chap. 27, para. 27–33. See
generally on quality control, Chap. 6.
[71] *ibid*. para. 27–43.
[72] *ibid*. para. 27–209.
[73] *ibid*. para. 27–35. Note also Art. 8(2) of the Trade Marks Directive, which provides that the
contravention of the quality control provisions of a licence agreement gives rise to a claim of
infringement.

territory, while an exclusive licence would have that restrictive effect on the licensor's activities.

The concern over whether or not the licence was 'sole' focused on the status of the registered user *vis-à-vis* other registered users, rather than on the relationship between the registered user and the proprietor. Thus, a term providing for a sole registered user protected the registered user against the appointment of additional registered users. Conversely, the absence of such a term appeared to protect the non-sole registered user against any later attempt to displace it with a sole registered user. In the event that there were multiple registered users, there was nothing in the registered user provisions which required that their respective terms and conditions should be identical.

Two Issues of Continuing Relevance

4–40   In addition to the provisions discussed above, the registered user provisions under the Trade Marks Act 1938 addressed two matters of general relevance to trade mark licensing which are still worthy of attention. They are: (a) What constitutes permitted use of the trade mark by the licensee? (b) To what extent does the licensee's use count as use of the mark by the proprietor?

Is Use of a Trade Mark by a Distributor a Licensed Use?

4–41   The major question raised in this context under the Trade Marks Act 1938 was whether use of the mark as indicating a connection in the course of trade between the goods and the registered user includes use of the trade mark by a distributor, retailer or contract manufacturer.[74] Under the Trade Marks Act 1938 the answer was that it did not. The Registry took the position that 'the sale of goods or provisions of services by agents, wholesalers, or retailers is not, in any sense, a 'use' of the mark by such persons.'[75] Since the registration of a licensee under the Trade Marks Act 1994 does not require substantive examination by the registry, can a distributor or other such person acquire a statutory right under section 30 to call upon the proprietor of a registered trade mark by simply registering itself as a licensee?

Use of the Trade Mark in Connection with Bulk Products

4–42   A related situation under the Trade Marks Act 1938 occurred where the proprietor provided a person with the product, such as chemicals or spirits,

---

[74] Under the Trade Marks Act 1938, the definition of 'trade mark use' by the registered user under s. 28(1) was 'use ... in relation to goods with which [the registered user] is connected in the course of trade'. This was consistent with the definition of a trade mark under s. 68 of the Trade Marks Act 1938. There, a trade mark was defined as a mark that is used in relation to goods for the purpose of 'indicating a connection in the course of trade' between the goods and the proprietor or the registered user of the mark. The motivation for registering a distributor as a registered user was to assuage an 'over-anxious' proprietor concerned with protecting his trade mark registration. Work Manual, para. 27–4.
[75] Work Manual, para. 27–4; see, generally, *infra*, Chaps. 6, 7 and 8.

in bulk for resale, and the goods were packaged under instructions from the proprietor. If the person handling the goods was to take some further action which might affect the quality of the goods, a registered user registration was appropriate to provide for the requisite quality control. The mere breaking down of the goods into smaller quantities, however, did not justify a registered user registration, since the trade connection indicated by the trade mark remained between the proprietor of the trade mark and the goods.[76]

Authorised Use of the Trade Mark Inures to the Benefit of the Proprietor

It was a central notion under the Trade Marks Act 1938 that authorised use   4–43 by a third party of a registered trade mark was deemed to be use of the mark by the proprietor. This principle lay at the heart of the rationale by which the validity of trade mark licensing, in giving expression to the quality function of trade marks, was recognised.[77] Controlled use of the trade mark by the licensee did not lead to deception with respect to the expectation of quality in the goods connoted by the trade mark and, thereby, established the required connection in the course of trade between the goods and the registered user.

This principle was expressed under section 28(2) of the Trade Marks Act 1938 as comprising two components: (a) a permitted use will be deemed to be use by the proprietor of the mark, and shall not be deemed to be use by any other person; and (b) should the trade mark be challenged on grounds of non-use (under section 26 of the Trade Marks Act 1938), or should use of the trade mark by the proprietor be relevant for any other reason, the permitted use will support the proprietor's claim of use. The converse is that if the use was not a permitted use, for whatever reason, it would not be deemed to inure to the benefit of the proprietor. In particular, if the proprietor itself did not use the trade mark, then the registration of the trade mark might be vulnerable to cancellation on the basis of non-use. In one case, it was the registered user itself that successfully sought to cancel the registration on this ground.[78]

Deemed Use Is Still Important Under the New Act

Under the Trade Marks Act 1994, it is a ground for revocation of a registration   4–44 that no 'genuine use' has been made of the mark in the U.K. for an uninterrupted period of five years following registration in respect of the goods or services for which the mark is registered by either 'the proprietor or with his consent'.[79] The term 'consent' appears however, to be broader

---

[76] Work Manual, para. 27–38. See also the U.S. Supreme Court decision in *Prestonettes Inc. v Coty*, 264 U.S. 359 (1924), in which the Court held that mere repackaging or rebottling is 'collateral' use which is not unauthorised trade mark use, provided that the public is not otherwise deceived. Stated in terms of the Trade Marks Act 1938, such 'collateral' use of the trade mark does not connote a connection in the course of trade between the repackager and the goods. See also, *infra*, Chap. 7, para. 7–19.

[77] See, Chap. 2, paras. 2–18 to 2–30, regarding the quality function of trade marks and its relationship with trade mark licensing.

[78] *McGregor T.M.* [1979] R.P.C. 36.

[79] Trade Marks Act 1994, s. 46(1).

than use by a registered licensee. In particular, there is no requirement that the licensee be registered, nor even that the consent be in writing, for the proprietor to defend the mark from revocation on the ground of non-use.

Authorised Use of the Trade Mark May Not be Deemed to be Use of a Related Service Mark

4–45 The nature of the mark that is the subject of the authorised use should be carefully noted. In particular, the authorised use of a trade mark will be deemed to inure to the benefit of the proprietor of the trade mark, but it may not be deemed to apply to a related service mark.[80] Thus, in the interests of legal certainty, it is recommended that the proprietor either establishes direct use of the service mark, or ensures that the service mark is also the subject of the licence.

VARIATION, CANCELLATION AND TRANSFER OF THE REGISTERED LICENCE

Variation and Cancellation

4–46 Sections 28(8)–(10) of the Trade Marks Act 1938 and the implementing rules set out procedures by which a registered user registration could be varied or cancelled. In the light of the goal of legal transparency, the Trade Marks Act 1994 provides that rules may be promulgated with respect to the following:

4–47   (a) The amendment of the registered particulars relating to the licence so as to reflect any alterations in the terms of the licence;
    (b) The removal of the registered particulars either where:

        i. The registered particulars relating to the licence were granted for a fixed period of time, and that time period has expired; or
        ii. Where no time period has been indicated, and having regard to such period as may be prescribed, the Registrar notifies the parties of his intention to remove the particulars from the Register.[81]

4–48 One possible thorny issue is the matter of cancellation on the ground that the licence agreement has been breached. If the cancellation is contested, it was conceivable, under the Trade Marks Act 1938, that the Registrar would have had to construe the contract between the parties, or rule on whether a breach of the underlying contractual relations between the parties had occurred.

---

[80] For example, it has been held that the performance of financial services under the VISA mark is a service separate and distinct from the trading of travellers cheques and credit cards bearing the same mark, in relation to which the mark is separately registrable as a trade mark. *VISA T.M.* [1985] R.P.C. 323.
[81] Trade Marks Act 1994, s. 25(5).

However, in *Actomin Products Ltd*,[82] Lloyd-Jacob J. held that the issue of whether non-observance of the provisions of an advertising clause amounted to a 'material change' in the terms of the registered user was not a suitable proceeding before the Registry for cancellation of the registration. The proper procedure was for the parties to seek a declaration of their rights under the contract, and then to apply to the Registrar for cancellation. The Court observed as follows:

'The **Registrar** is expected to have profound knowledge of the law relating to trade mark registration, and an acquired facility of resolving questions of deception or confusion in the use of trade marks in the course of trade ... It is unreasonable to expect him to decide contested issues as to the existence, construction, or observance of contractual stipulations which have no significant relation to trade mark law or practice.' (Emphasis in original.)[83]

This observation would appear to remain relevant under the provisions of the Trade Marks Act 1994, to the extent that the amendment and removal of a registered licence is an administrative act. All other issues connected with the enforcement of rights in the underlying trade mark licence agreement are within the exclusive authority of the courts.

The Licensee's Right of Assignment or Other Transfer

Prohibited Under the Trade Marks Act 1938

Under section 28(12) of the Trade Marks Act 1938, the assignment or other   4-49
transfer of the registered user's right under the registration was prohibited. This prohibition could occur in two situations. In the first, the registered user would purport to assign its rights under the licence to a third party, while, in the second, the registered user would grant a sub-licence. Under the registered user provisions, both the assignment of the registered user's right and the sub-licensing of the right were prohibited.

The right of the proprietor to assign or otherwise transfer its right in the mark was not prohibited. Unlike the registered user, the proprietor's right of assignment of the trade mark was in no way subject to the registered user registration, to the extent that the Registry neither informed the registered user of the assignment nor questioned the registered user's relationship with the new proprietor.[84]

---

[82] *Actomin Products Application* (1952) 69 R.P.C. 166; (1953) 70 R.P.C. 201.

[83] *supra* (1953) 10 R.P.C. at 203.

[84] This highlights the fact that a permitted use under a registered user registration was viewed solely in terms of the registration, irrespective of any rights arising under the contract between the parties. Another way to view this is that the registered user registration enjoyed a legal life of its own, even if it is inconsistent with the underlying commercial arrangement between the parties. Any change in the identity of the registered user, other than by way of the cancellation of the previous registered user registration and registration of the new user, in the case of an assignment, or a separate registered user registration, in the case of a sub-licence, was not permitted. This position was explained thus: 'The registration of the registered user creates rights which are good against the entire world, not just the proprietor, and it continues to bind the mark to the user until it is cancelled, irrespective of the identity of the proprietor.' Work Manual, para. 27–184.

Rights of Assignment and Sub-Licensing under the New Act

4–50   The Trade Marks Act 1994 does not expressly prohibit the assignment of the licensee's rights in a registered licence. Presumably, such an assignment would be reflected as an amendment to the registered particulars relating to the registered licence.[85] Such a provision clearly serves the interests of legal transparency.

Sub-licensing is also permitted under the Trade Marks Act 1994.[86] It appears that the sub-licensee may register his right in a manner similar to the licensee and will be treated like a licensee. For example, presumably, under subsection 30(2), the sub-licensee now enjoys the right to call upon the proprietor to take action against an infringer and, if the proprietor fails to do so, the sub-licensee may bring the action himself.[86a] The comments noted above regarding the right of the proprietor to exclude by contract the licensee's right to take action is equally applicable to the sub-licensee.[87]

Application for Registration Based on Proposed use by a Licensee

4–51   Under the Trade Marks Act 1938, an application filed under section 29(1)(b) was an exception to the general practice of filing an application under section 17, according to which the applicant declared that it itself used or intended to use the trade mark. Under section 29(1)(b), by contrast, use of the trade mark was made through the registered user only. An application for registration filed under section 29(1)(b) had to be accompanied by a simultaneous application for registration of a registered user under section 28.[88]

Typical situations in which a trade mark application is made on the basis of use of the mark by the licensee include those where a foreign manufacturer wishes to appoint a licensee to manufacture and market its goods in the U.K., or where the applicant seeks to extend the mark into additional product areas in which it does not currently manufacture. The Trade Marks Act 1994 provides simply that an application for registration of a mark shall state that

---

[85] See para. 4–47.

[86] Trade Marks Act 1994, s. 28(4). The prohibition against sub-licensing under the Trade Marks Act 1938 could be understood in terms of the view that trade mark licensing is only possible where there is direct connection in the control between the proprietor and the user with respect to the trade mark.

[86a] See also, *supra*, paras. 4–07 to 4–12.

[87] See, para. 4–11. See also s. 30(7) of the Trade Marks Act 1994, which puts an exclusive licensee having the rights and remedies of an assignee under s. 31(1) on the same legal footing as a proprietor, in connection with the right of the licensee to call upon the proprietor to take action with respect to an infringement.

[88] See Chap. 3, paras. 3–3 to 3–34. Note that even if no explicit provision is made with respect to a registered user similar to that of s. 29(1)(b), if a bona fide licence relationship can be established, it is possible that the application will be allowed to proceed on the basis of the intended registered user. For example, in India, where the domestic trade mark law does not include a provision similar to s. 29(1)(b), the right solely to apply on the basis of use by the registered user, a minority-owned subsidiary of the applicant, was implied by the Supreme Court of India. *Dristan T.M.* [1986] R.P.C. (S.C.) 1985, rev'g [1984] F.S.R. 215 (1969).

the mark is used by the applicant or with his consent with respect to the goods or services for which the registration is sought, or that the applicant has a bona fide intention to use the mark.[89]

---

[89] Trade Marks Act 1994, s. 31(3).

5. Licensing in the United States: The Concept of a Related Company

There is no provision under U.S. trade mark law for the registration of a   5–01
licensee[1] and licensing is not even explicitly referred to in the Lanham Act.
Nevertheless, the Lanham Act deals with the issue of trade mark licensing as
part of its regulation of federal trade mark rights. In particular, licensing is
addressed in connection with the use of a trade mark by a 'related company',
under sections 5 and 45 of the Lanham Act. Section 5, as amended in 1988,
provides as follows:

'Where a registered mark or a mark sought to be registered is or may be
used legitimately by related companies, such use shall inure to the benefit
of the registrant or applicant for registration, and such use shall not
affect the validity of such mark or of its registration, provided such mark
is not used in a manner to deceive the public. If first use of a mark by a
person is controlled by the registrant or applicant for registration of the
mark with respect to the nature and quality of the goods or services,
such first use shall inure to the benefit of the registrant or applicant, as
the case may be.'[2]

Section 45 provides the definition of a 'related company':

'The term "related company" means any person whose use of a mark is
controlled by the owner of the mark with respect to the nature and
quality of the goods or services on or in connection with which the mark
is used.'[3]

These provisions set out the principles under which trade mark licensing is
recognised in connection with registered trade marks.[4] This chapter will
discuss the development and implementation of these principles.

---

[1] See, Chaps. 3 and 4, respectively, regarding the registered user provisions and the registration
of licences.
[2] 15 U.S.C. 1056.
[3] 15 U.S.C. 1127.
[4] Use of a trade mark is addressed in s. 2.38 of the Trademark Rules of Practice, the regulations
which implement the Lanham Act, and by the U.S. Patent and Trademark Office, in its
Trademark Manual of Examination Procedure, (2nd ed.), May 1993, U.S. Department of
Commerce, Patent and Trademark Office (TMEP), particularly Chap. 12.01.

The Notion of a Related Company: The Historical Background

5–02   The development of the provisions in the Lanham Act regarding use of a trade mark by a related company can be seen to derive from a series of judgments in which U.S. courts had shown a willingness to recognise trade mark licensing under certain circumstances. Unlike the *Bowden Wire* decision in the U.K., there was no judgment in the U.S. which was viewed as prohibiting trade mark licensing.[5] As one commentator noted shortly after the passing of the Lanham Act in 1946, it was sheer fantasy to conclude that prior to its enactment, 'the licensing of trade marks [had been viewed as] improper...'.[6]

Early View Did Not Recognise the Validity of a Trade Mark Licence

5–03   Nevertheless, the judicial recognition of the validity of trade mark licensing under U.S. law occurred only gradually. At one time, it was widely held in the United States, as in the United Kingdom, that the function of a trade mark, being the identification of the actual source of the goods, was incompatible with licensing. Under this view, a trade mark could not be used by someone else, *i.e.* the licensee, who was not in fact the actual source of the goods.

Licence Likened to An Assignment

In effect, licensing was likened to the assignment of a trade mark. In both cases, the transfer of rights in the trade mark was prohibited without the passing of the underlying goodwill. The classic formulation of this position under U.S. law was that '[a] trademark cannot be assigned, or its use licensed, except as incidental to a transfer of the business or property in connection with which it has been used'.[7]

Gradual Recognition of Valid Trade Mark Licensing

5–04   This position began to change as courts in the U.S. came to realise that the source function of trade marks, narrowly construed, no longer kept pace with the use of trade marks in modern commerce. In particular, the courts began to articulate the view that trade marks also served as a guarantor of quality,

---

[5] See Chap. 3, paras. 3–08 to 3–10 for discussion on the *Bowden Wire* case.
[6] Schniderman, 'Trade-Mark Licensing – A Saga of Fantasy and Fact,' *Law & Contemporary Problems*, 248, 252 (1949). See generally, Reynolds, 'Contemporary Problems in Trademark Licensing,' *The Trademark Reporter*, Vol. 49, 1141 (1959), and note, 'Trademark Licensing', *Duke Law Journal*, Vol. 1968, 875.
[7] *Macmahan Pharmacal Co. v. Denver Chemical Co.*, 113F, 468, 474–475 (8th Cir. 1901). See also s. 70 of the English Patent, Designs and Trade Marks Act 1883, which provided that '[a] trade mark, when registered, shall be assigned and transmitted only in connexion with the goodwill of the business concerned in the particular goods or classes of goods for which it has been registered, and shall be determinable with that goodwill.'

irrespective of any consideration of the source of the goods.[8] In the words of one court:

'Keeping pace with industrial and business development the law has advanced a considerable distance from the earlier decisions which were made when small individual businesses, personally owned and personally managed, were the rule rather than the exception.'[9]

There was no provision in the predecessor to the Lanham Act, the Trademark Act of 1905, giving explicit recognition to licensing. Nevertheless, ruling under the 1905 Act, some courts demonstrated a readiness to confer judicial approval on certain forms of trade mark licensing.

Control by the Licensor of Main Ingredient of Further Manufacture

In this situation, the licensor either manufactures or otherwise supplies the 5–05 licensee with the main ingredient of a product, thereby controlling quality. The licensor may also exercise some form of supervision or control over the manufacture of the finished goods. The finished goods are then sold under the licensor's trade mark. Many of the earliest licensing cases involved this type of relationship, the most notable of which were the so-called *Coca-Cola* cases.[10] There, the proprietor arranged for the bottling and distribution of the soft drink under the mark through local bottlers. The proprietor furnished the syrup to the bottler and controlled the bottling process by means of a contract between it and the bottler. The validity of this arrangement was upheld by some courts.[11]

In variations of this arrangement, the proprietor sought to control its trade 5–06 mark in other contexts. They included trade marked flour used in the baking of bread, the use of rayon by a fabric manufacturer, the use of yarn by a clothing manufacturer, and the use of cotton piece goods by a shirt manu-facturer.[12] For example, the purveyor of cotton piece goods sold under its well known U.S. trade mark 'Fruit of the Loom' allowed manufacturers to process the piece goods into shirts which were then sold under the same trade mark. The court concluded that the proprietor had exercised significant control over the manufacture of the shirts, including the 'select[ion of] only reliable manufacturers of high standing, and have required such manufacturers to join with the owner of the trade mark in such warranty and guaranty...'[13]

In these situations, the finished product bore the trade mark of the essential ingredient furnished by the licensor. At issue was whether, in addition to the control that the licensor exercised over the main ingredient, the licensor exercised effective control over the final product. If the licensor did exercise such control, the arrangement was upheld.

---

[8] See, *supra*, Chap. 2, 2–18 to 2–26, on the quality function of a trade mark.
[9] *Keebler Weyl Baking Co. v. J.S. Ivins' Son*, 7 F. Supp. 211, 214 (E.D. Pa. 1934).
[10] See Shniderman, *supra*, n. 6, p. 253.
[11] Taggart, 'Trade-Marks and Related Companies: A New Concept in Statutory Trade-Mark Law,' (1949) 14 *Law & Contemporary Problems*, 234, 238.
[12] See Taggart, *supra*, n. 11, and cases cited therein, p. 237.
[13] *B.B. & R. Knight Inc. v W.L. Milner & Company*, 283 F. 816 (N.D. Ohio 1922); see also Taggart, *supra*, n. 11, at pp. 237–238.

Formula Control and Licensed Manufacture of Patented Goods

5–07   Here, the focus was on the supply by the licensor of the formula by which the licensed product was made. Often the formula was in the context of a licensed patent, but know-how could also be involved. This form of licensing extended to the granting of multiple licences, each of which was the subject of a separate patent for the manufacture and sale of distinct products, but all of which were identified by the same trade mark.[14] The question in these circumstances was whether, in addition to the licensing of the patented formula or know-how, there was distinct control over the manufacture of the product.[15]

In a leading case, the court held that where there was the licensing of patents for instruments and medicines together with a license to use the licensor's trade mark, the licensor could be said to have exercised satisfactory control so as to preserve its rights in the trade mark. There, the court found that the licensor frequently inspected the licensee's plant, and took an active part in the advertising, manufacture and sale of the products.[16]

Control by Share Ownership

5–08   The courts were also prepared to recognise control over the use of the trade mark by virtue of share ownership by the licensor of the licensee. Circumstances ranged from a wholly-owned subsidiary for distribution and sales[17] to 50 per cent ownership by the licensor in a subsidiary which manufactured goods under the trade mark.[18] Where the parent tended to engage in some way in trade in connection with the licensed product, *i.e.* the parent did not merely hold the mark, the degree of actual control, if any, that it exercised over the subsidiary with respect to the trade mark was not usually questioned by the courts.

The Special Case of the Holding Company

5–09   When a holding company was involved, the courts were prepared to recognise the validity of a licence arrangement as well, at least where the parent took some overall control of the use of the mark by all the subsidiaries.

In the *Keebler Weyl Baking* case, the plaintiff was one of a large number of wholly-owned subsidiaries of a holding company which purported to control their general operations and policies, even if it did not specifically use the mark in connection with the goods of interest. The validity of the licence, in respect of the unregistered trade mark *Club Crackers* for soda crackers, was upheld in the following language:

'I can see no imposition upon the public, no abandonment, and no other

---

[14] See Shniderman, *supra*, n. 6, p. 257.

[15] *cf.* the treatment of a trade mark licence as part of a patent licence arrangement under U.K. practice, under the registered user provisions. See, *e.g. Work Manual, supra*, Chap. 3, n. 70, at 27–61 to 27–63.

[16] *Smith v. Dental Products Company*, 140 F.2d, 140 (7th Cir. 1944), cert. denied, 322 U.S. 743 (1944); see also Shniderman, *supra*, n. 6, pp. 254–255.

[17] Shniderman, *supra*, n. 6, n. 46, p. 256.

[18] Shniderman, *supra*, n. 6, p. 256.

element which impairs a trade mark when the corporation which owns it, which in turn is owned by a general control, permits other corporations under the same general control to use the mark upon an identical product which they produce in accordance with the owner's directions and instructions.'[19]

This decision can be viewed both as recognition (a) that financial ownership *per se* may imply general control over the activities of wholly-owned subsidiaries, even where the parent is not the proprietor of the trade mark, and (b) of the function that a house mark serves in creating a corporate identifier for use by the parent's subsidiaries and affiliates. The result of the *Keebler Weyl Baking* case should be compared with that reached by the Comptroller-General in the U.K. in the *Radiation* case, a rare if unique instance prior to the enactment of the Trade Marks Act 1938 in which a form of trade mark licensing, based on the use of a house mark by subsidiaries of the trade mark proprietor, was approved.[20]

Limitations on Recognition of Licensing by a Holding Company

Licensing by a mere holding company was not always recognised. In particular, 5–10 such an arrangement was found to be insufficient for purposes of trade mark registration in the name of the holding company. The leading example was the *U.S. Steel* case. There, registration of the mark 'U.S.S.', being the initials of the United States Steel Corporation, was not allowed because the applicant did not use the mark, and its only assertion of control was via its shareholding in the various subsidiaries.[21] The *Keebler Weyl Baking* case was distinguished on the ground that, in that case, the applicant-subsidiary had used the mark.

These decisions, in which registration was refused when the alleged control was based only on financial ownership, suggested that a licensing arrangement was more likely to be recognised if the proprietor, in addition to being the parent of the licensee, also made actual use of the trade mark, or some form of control was shown.[22]

Licensing for Use of Trade Mark on Related Goods Based on Quality

At least one decision during the period suggested that licensing was proper 5–11 on goods that had not been manufactured by the licensor, but over which the licensor maintained a similar level of quality to that maintained by it over other goods. In the *Finchley* case, the licensor had used its trade mark in respect of clothing. It then licensed use of the mark to a manufacturer of hats. The court held that the licensor had shown that it had passed on the same level of quality regarding the hats as it had ensured with respect to the clothing.[23]

---

[19] *Keebler Weyl Baking, supra,* n. 9, at p. 214.
[20] For further discussion of the *Radiation* case, see Chap. 2, *supra,* para. 2–22.
[21] *Ex p. United States Steel Corp.* 23 U.S.P.Q. 145 (Comr. 1934); see also Shniderman, *supra,* n. 6.
[22] See Taggart, *supra,* n. 11, p. 237.
[23] *Finchley Inc. v. George Hess Company,* 24 F. Supp. 94 (E.D.N.Y. 1938); see also Shniderman, *supra,* n. 6, p. 257.

No Licensing Recognised for a Naked Licence

5–12   Judicial recognition of trade mark licensing did not extend to a naked licence. Where all evidence of control was absent, the licence would be deemed to be ineffective as a 'license in gross'.[24]

In one notable case, it was found that the licensee had granted numerous 'licenses' for the making of baked goods under the mark, without exercising any quality control over the product.[25] The court stated that '[t]here was nothing in the licensing agreements that required that the bread or doughnuts sold by the defendants conform to any fixed standards. The defendant was at liberty to affix the trade mark to any bread or doughnuts that he chose.'[26] The licences were therefore held to be ineffective. In another decision, an early form of a service franchise involving the use of a mark in respect of a putative national 'chain' of teachers' employment agencies was not enforced. Here, the court found that, despite the common use of the mark by the various branches, no genuine licence arrangement had been established since no control could be shown.[27]

The Enactment of the Related Company Provisions

The Legislative process

5–13   It was against this judicial background, which accorded a limited recognition of trade mark licensing based on evidence of control, that the related company provisions of the Lanham Act were enacted in 1946. Three major stages in the legislative history of these provisions can be identified.

Licensing Recognised in Respect of Use by a Subsidiary

5–14   In the earliest form of the proposed legislation, the draft text focused principally on extending the right of registration based on trade mark use only by the applicant's wholly-owned subsidiary company. The provision was intended, in the view of one of the bill's sponsors, to address the problem raised in the *U.S. Steel* case.[28]

This limited recognition of licensing was seen as deriving from the proposal (later abandoned) to allow the assignment of a trade mark without the transfer of the goodwill.[29] It was reasoned that use by a subsidiary could hardly be more objectionable than permitting the assignment of a trade mark without goodwill.[30] Financial control of a wholly-owned subsidiary was seen

---

[24] See Chap. 6, para. 6–43, for the connection between quality control and a naked licence.

[25] *Broeg v. Duchaine*, 67 N.E. 2d 466 (1946); see also Shniderman, *supra*, n. 6, pp. 257–258.

[26] *Broeg v. Duchaine*, at 468; see also, Shniderman, *op. cit.*, n. 6, pp. 257–258.

[27] *Everett O. Fisk & Co. v. Fisk Teachers' Agency*, 3 F.2d 7 (8th Cir. 1924); see also Taggart, *supra*, n. 11, p. 241; see also, Shniderman, *supra*, n. 6, p. 253.

[28] See, *supra*, n. 21.

[29] See Shniderman, *supra*, n. 6, 20, *cf.* with s. 22 of the Trade Marks Act 1938, and s. 24(1) of the Trade Marks Act 1994, where assignment of a trade mark without the transfer of the goodwill is recognised.

[30] But see Shniderman, *supra*, n. 6, at p. 13.

as providing sufficient identity of interest between the licensor and the licensee in the use of the trade mark so as to ensure that no deception of the public would occur.

'Related Company' Defined More Generally

Subsequently, a revised draft of the legislation added a definition of 'related company', which underscored the importance of control more generally, and in which contractual control was expressly mentioned. Here, the quality function of trade marks, and its relevance to licensing, was taken into account. The approach taken in this draft could be viewed as giving recognition to the line of bottling and other main ingredient cases, in which the licensor's control over the incorporation of the main ingredient by a third-party licensee was contractual.[31]

It has been claimed that contractual control of trade mark use is a weaker form of control than financial ownership, because there is an absence of any identity of interest between the parties, except as provided for in the agreement. It was apparently for this reason that the proposed definition of a related company added a specific reference to deception of the public, to make it clear that mere contractual relations between the licensor and licensee would not be sufficient if the licensed use would still result in deception. This provision was seen as giving expression to the interest at common law in protecting the public against deception in the transfer of trade mark rights.[32]

Control Not Dependent Upon Ownership of the Licensee

In the final stage of the legislation, the definition of a related company dropped all reference to ownership of the licensee by the licensor as a requisite for control. This revision meant that there was no further indication in the statute of how control of the licensed use would be effected. As now defined, a 'related company' is any person who 'controls or is controlled by' the registrant. This was also understood to mean that either the parent or a subsidiary could be the trade mark proprietor,[33] although doubts were expressed as to whether a related company could register the trade mark on its own behalf in all instances.[34]

Addition of the Word 'Legitimately'

The word 'legitimately' was also added to the final form of the provision. This was done in response to the concerns expressed by the U.S. Justice Department, which viewed trade mark licensing with suspicion, particularly when it rested on a contractual relationship rather than financial control.[35] It was feared that trade mark licensing 'would be used as colorable legal

5–15

5–16

5–17

---

[31] See *supra*, paras. 5–05 to 5–06, see also Taggart, *supra*, n. 11, p. 242.
[32] See Taggart, *supra*, n. 11, p. 242.
[33] Taggart, *supra*, n. 11, p. 242; Shniderman, *supra*, n. 6, p. 251.
[34] See Taggart, *supra*, n. 11, at 242, Shniderman, *supra*, n. 6, p. 251, n. 32.
[35] See, *infra*, para. 5–28, Chap. 3, para 3–33 and Chap. 6, paras. 6–10 to 6–20, for discussion of the difference between financial and contractual control.

sanctions for contracts directed toward price control, against the production of competitive products, for allocation of markets, division of user, and fixing of channels of distribution.'[36]

In the end, the Justice Department's concerns were assuaged by adding the word 'legitimately'. Trade mark licensing would not *ipso facto* be held to violate the U.S. antitrust laws. However, the use of a trade mark by a related company would not necessarily be shielded from attack under the antitrust and trade regulation laws.

The *Du Pont* Case: The Broad Principles of Trade Mark Licensing Are Affirmed

5–18   Shortly after the enactment of the Lanham Act in 1946, the Court had an opportunity to consider the scope of trade mark licensing in the case of *E.I. Du Pont Nemours & Co. v. Celanese Corp. of America.*[37] This decision was in fact given on the basis of the 1905 U.S. Trade Mark Act, rather than on the 'related company' provisions of the Lanham Act. However, the 'related company' provisions were presumably in the mind of the court, and the decision remains a leading statement on the nature of permissible licensing under U.S. trade mark practice.

The issue was a motion to cancel a registered trade mark on the grounds that the use of the mark by a non-exclusive licensee did not indicate the name of the licensor and that there was insufficient quality control. These arguments were rejected. The *Du Pont* decision laid to rest the likelihood that trade mark licensing would be permitted only under the most stringent requirements of control and identification of source. The reasoning of the Commissioner in the case was based on the distinction between an assignment, where an abandonment of the assignor's rights are intended, and a licence, where the licensor expressly reserves certain rights in the trade mark under the terms of the licence agreement. A judicial forfeiture of the licensor's rights, where no such abandonment was intended, should be avoided.[38]

On appeal, the validity of the licence was upheld, but the court's emphasis was different. The court stated that 'a *proper* license agreement is valid,' thereby laying stress on the fact that the issues of control and lack of deception, and not merely the existence of a licence, are determinative.[39] The court was satisfied that the conditions had been met.

The appellant argued strenuously in favour of a narrow scope for valid trade mark licensing, in which ambiguities in the licence relationship with respect to control and source could be construed against the validity of the licence. In particular, the appellant claimed that there had to be clear proof of actual quality control, no breach of the contract by the licensee, clear identification of the licensor on the product, and no grace period after

[36] Quoted in McCarthy, *Trade Marks and Unfair Competition* (1st ed.), para. 18: 17 (C); see also Taggart, *supra*, n. 11.
[37] 167 F.2d 484 (C.C.P.A. 1948), aff'g 69 U.S.P.Q. 258 (1946).
[38] 69 U.S.P.Q. at 260. *cf.* with the view regarding forfeiture as expressed by the House of Lords in the *Sports International* case, *infra*, Chap. 12, at 12–33 to 12–36.
[39] 167 F.2d at 490 (emphasis added).

termination or notice of termination in which the licensee could continue to use the mark.[40] These arguments were rejected.[41]

The *Dawn Donut* Case: The Basic Principles Under the Lanham Act are Affirmed

As stated, the *Du Pont* case expressed a broad recognition of valid trade mark   5–19
licensing under the Lanham Act, even though the related company provisions were not technically in issue. The approach taken by the *Du Pont* case was subsequently approved under the Lanham Act as well.

The judgment often cited as the leading case in this respect is *Dawn Donut Co. Inc.* v. *Hart's Food Stores Inc.*[42] In that case, the court pointed to multiple trade mark licences between the plaintiff and various licensees, based both on contractual and non-contractual grounds. The question regarding all of these licence arrangements was whether there was sufficient quality control. The court's approach was expressed as follows:

> 'If the licensor is not compelled to take some reasonable steps to prevent the misuses of his trademark in the hands of others the public will be deprived of its most effective protection against misleading uses of a trademark. The public is hardly in a position to uncover deceptive uses of a trademark before they occur and will be at best slow to detect them after they happen. Thus, unless the licensor exercises supervision and control over the operations of its licensees the risk that the public will be unwittingly deceived will be increased and this is precisely what the Act is in part designed to prevent.'[43]

The court's emphasis on the requirement of quality control was predicated on the notion that, in the absence of such control, use of the mark would amount to a naked licence which would result in an abandonment of the proprietor's rights in the mark.[44] The absence of control would lead to a situation in which 'products bearing the same trademark might be of diverse qualities,' whereby the trade mark would lose its significance as an indication of origin, and the mark would be deemed to be abandoned.[45]

Further Aspects of a Related Company Clarified

While the validity of trade mark licensing under U.S. law is no longer in   5–20
question, two issues regarding the application of the related company provisions have received particular clarification by the courts.

---

[40] 167 F.2d at 488–489.
[41] See Chap. 6, for discussion on quality control.
[42] 267 F.2d 358, 121 U.S.P.Q. 430 (2nd Cir. 1959).
[43] 121 U.S.P.Q. 430 at 437.
[44] 121 U.S.P.Q. 430 at 436–437.
[45] 121 U.S.P.Q. 430 at 437. s. 1064 of the Lanham Act provides that a trade mark registration may be cancelled for abandonment, while s. 1127 defines 'abandonment' to include a mark that has lost its significance as an indication of origin. See Chap. 6, paras. 6–43 to 6–47, for discussion on abandonment and naked licensing.

Must the Licensor Also Use the Mark?

5–21   First, the argument has occasionally been put forward that a party cannot acquire rights solely via controlled use by a third-party licensee, in the absence of its own use of the mark. This is to be distinguished from use solely by a subsidiary of a holding company, in relation to which the related company provisions had always been understood to overrule the *U.S. Steel* decision.[46]

5–22   This position had been championed by an Assistant Commissioner in a series of decisions in the 1950s.[47] It rested on the view that the related company provisions do not operate to create any rights of proprietorship in a mark that did not previously exist. Since only the licensee-user used the mark, the Assistant Commissioner attempted to argue that the licensor could not claim any rights by virtue of that use.[48] However, this position was rejected by the courts, most notably in the *Turner* case.[49] There, the court held that the registration of the *Playboy* service mark for night clubs was valid, even though the registrant did not itself operate any clubs, by virtue of the control which the registrant exercised over the use of the mark in the operation of the clubs by and through the licensees/franchisees (and sub-licensees/sub-franchisees). A similar result has been reached even when the applicant, a bank holding company, could not legally render the banking services performed by the affiliated banks, and thus could not itself even use the mark.[50]

The position has been explicitly rejected by the U.S. Trademark Office as well.[51] It is now unequivocally the rule 'that rights to a mark may be acquired and maintained through the use of that mark by a controlled licensee even when the only use of the mark has been, and is being, made by the licensee.'[52]

Must the Licensor Be Identified?

5–23   Secondly, it was claimed that a related company relationship did not exist in circumstances where the licensor was not identified in conjunction with the controlled use of the trade mark by the licensee. The rationale here was that unless the licensor was identified, deception as to the source of the goods indicated by the trade mark would occur, particularly if only the name of the manufacturer licensee appeared on the goods. Under this argument, the quality assurance or guarantee function of a trade mark did not render the source requirement a nullity.

---

[46] See, *supra*, n. 21.

[47] *Re Alexander*, 114 U.S.P.Q. 547 (1957); *A.E. Staley Manufacturing Co. v. Scott*, 118 U.S.P.Q. 312 (1958); *Re C.B. Donald Co.*, 117 U.S.P.Q. 485 (1958); *Re C.B. Donald Co.*, 122 U.S.P.Q. 401 (1959)].

[48] This view was first articulated in *Re Alexander*, *supra*, n. 47, p. 548.

[49] *Turner v. H.M.H. Publishing Company*, 380 F.2d 224, 229 (5th Cir. 1967). See also, *e.g. Alligator Company v. Robert Bruce Inc.*, 176 F. Supp. 377 (E.D. Pa. 1959); *Joseph Bancroft & Sons Co.*, 129 U.S.P.Q. 329 (1961); *Warner Bros. Inc. v. Road Runner Car Wash Inc.*, 189 U.S.P.Q. 430, 431 (T.T.A.B. 1976)]; *Mr. Rooter Corp. v Morris*, 188 USPQ 392 (E.D. La. 1975).]

[50] *Central Fidelity Banks Inc. v. First Bankers Corp. of Florida*, 225 U.S.P.Q. 438 (T.T.A.B. 1984).

[51] *Pneutek Inc. v. Scherr*, 211 U.S.P.Q. 824 (T.T.A.B. 1981).

[52] *supra*, n. 51, p. 833. See also, *ABC Moving Company v. Brown*, 218 U.S.P.Q. 336 (1983) plus the cases therein. *cf.* with the approach taken under the Trade Marks Act 1938, especially s.29. See Chap. 3, paras. 3–30 to 3–34.

This position has also been rejected.[53] '[T]here was nothing in the common law which requires that a trademark be used in connection with the trade name of the owner.'[54] Further, if the applicant or registrant is an individual, his name need not be identified on the product or packaging material of the licensee.[55] It has also also been held that the inclusion of the dealer's name, together with the trade mark of the proprietor/manufacturer, serves no more than to indicate from whom the product was purchased, and no deception could be said to occur.[56] The court in the *Du Pont* case itself held that while the licensee's failure to identify the proprietor in certain advertisements may have breached a provision of the license contract, it did not work a deception on the public.[57]

5–24

1988 Amendments with Respect to the Related Company Provisions

The provisions of sections 5 and 45 of the Lanham Act with respect to the related user provisions remained unchanged until the Trademark Law Revision Act of 1988. At that time, both sections were amended.

5–25

Section 5 Amended

Section 5 was amended by adding a final sentence to the section, which as we have seen now reads as follows:

5–26

> 'If first use of a mark by a person is controlled by the registrant or applicant for registration of the mark with respect to the nature and quality of the goods or services, such first use shall inure to the benefit of the registrant or applicant, as the case may be.'

The sentence was added to section 5 to codify Trademark Rule 2.38(a),[58] and to make it clear that first use by a licensee will inure to the benefit of the applicant or registrant. It also overruled previous authority which had held that a licensee's first use of a trade mark, without clear identification of the licensor/applicant, would not vest rights of proprietorship in the licensor.[59]

---

[53] *Re Telesco*, 149 U.S.P.Q. 309, 310 and cites therein; *Re First National City Bank*, 168 U.S.P.Q. 180, 181 (1970); *Re General Battery & Ceramic Corp.*, 157 U.S.P.Q. 121, 122 (1968) and the cites therein.

[54] *Tetra Pak Company, Inc. v. Schneider*, 125 U.S.P.Q. 460, 461 (1960).

[55] *Re Briggs*, 229 U.S.P.Q. 76, 77 (1986) and the cites therein.

[56] *Re General Battery & Ceramic Corp.*, 157 U.S.P.Q. 121 (1968).

[57] *Du Pont, supra*, para. 5–18.

[58] See *supra*, n. 4.

[59] 'USTA/Trademark Law Revision Act of 1988,' *The Trade Mark Reporter*, Vol. 77, at 448–449; see, *e.g. Re C.B. Donald Co.*, 117 U.S.P.Q. 485 (1958), and the discussion, *supra*, n. 47. *cf*. subs. 28(2) of the Trade Marks Act 1938.

Definition of 'Related Company' Under Section 45 Amended

5–27   The definition of 'related company' was also amended. As noted above,[60] it now reads as follows:

> 'The term 'related company' means any person whose use of a mark is controlled by the owner of the mark with respect to the nature and quality of the goods or services on or in connection with which the mark is used.'

Quality Control and Financial Control between Parent and Subsidiary Clarified

5–28   The amendments addressed two issues. First, they dealt with the apparent anomaly which existed under the definition as enacted in 1946, whereby the licensee could 'control', as well as be 'controlled by' the licensor. The reference to control by the licensee over the licensor has been eliminated from the definition, with the result that a related company is an entity over which trade mark control is exercised, even if the related company is the parent and the controlling company is, for trade mark purposes, the subsidiary.

This is to be distinguished from the financial control that the parent continues to exercise over the subsidiary by virtue of its ownership. The relationship between the two forms of control, trade mark control by the subsidiary and financial control by the parent, has been described thus: 'Obviously, the license can be drawn so that the subsidiary "controls" the nature of the quality of the goods/services. At the same time, it is abundantly clear that the parent company controls the subsidiary in all respects.'[61]

Taken literally, the position that the subsidiary can exercise control over the parent's use of the trade mark appears to be at odds with the notion of financial control by the parent over the subsidiary which, under certain circumstances, is also deemed to imply control of the use of the trade mark.[62] Perhaps the better way to understand the matter is that where financial control is concerned, it is ultimately of minor consequence whether the parent, or the subsidiary, is the proprietor of the trade mark. In such circumstances, the expectation is not that there exists express contractual control by the subsidiary over the parent in connection with use of the trade mark but that there is an identity of interest between them. In such circumstances, trade mark control derives from this identity of interest, whoever, the parent or the subsidiary, is the proprietor of the mark.[63]

---

[60] See above, para. 5–01.

[61] USTA Report, *supra*, n. 59, p. 420.

[62] See *supra*, paras 5–09 and 5–10; Chap. 3, para. 3–33, and *infra*, para. 535 and Chap. 6, paras. 6–17 to 6–18, regarding financial control.

[63] *cf.* the licensed use of the trade in the *Revlon* case in the U.K., when ultimate control was found to be exercised by the U.S. parent, irrespective of the actual proprietorship of the mark in the U.K. by a subsidiary, see, Chap. 7, para. 7–27.

Elimination of the Reference to 'Legitimate' Control

Secondly, the amendments deleted the word 'legitimately' from the definition   5–29
of a 'related company.' The reference to 'legitimate' control was viewed as
superfluous, since control which satisfies the definition of a 'related company'
must 'inherently' be in compliance with all applicable laws.[64]

Nevertheless, the term 'legitimately' remains part of the provisions of
section 5. It was explained that this was done in order to indicate that the
'legitimacy requirement (*i.e.* that there is no violation of the U.S. antitrust
laws) extends to the control over the use of the mark by the trademark
owner.'[65] While this explanation is not entirely clear, the net effect of the
amendment in practice appears to be minor.

Related Company Use and Intent-to-Use Applications

The major change to the Lanham Act by virtue of the 1988 amendments was   5–30
the establishment of an application based on 'intent-to-use' the mark.[66]
Previously, an application under U.S. practice required that the mark be used
in interstate commerce as a prerequisite to filing. Under the amendment, no
use is required as a prerequisite to application, although the registration will
not be issued until proof of actual use is made.

Accordingly, the same principles that govern related company use will also
apply to an intent-to-use situation, subject to the following. An intent-to-use
application requires that there be a 'bona fide intention' to use the mark.[67]
Where the applicant asserts a bona fide intention to use the trade mark
through a related company, the examiner need not inquire at the time of the
application about the status of the related company, the degree of quality
control and the nature of the goods or services. Such an inquiry is made only
later, when the applicant files a statement of use.[68]

The Related Company Provisions under U.S. Trade Mark Practice

The Principles of Valid Trade Mark Licensing under Sections 5 and 45

The provisions regarding a 'related company' under sections 5 and 45 of the   5–31
Lanham Act articulate a series of principles which set out the metes and
bounds of valid trade mark licensing under U.S. law and practice. These
principles can be summarised as follows:

---

[64] USTA Report, *supra*, n. 59, p. 420.
[65] USTA Report, *supra*, n. 59, p. 420.
[66] 15 U.S.C. 1051(b).
[67] 15 U.S.C. 1051(b).
[68] See the Trade Mark Manual of Examining Procedure (TMEP), *supra*, n. 4 above, s.902.01(a)
and subs.1201.03(a)(ii). *cf.* U.K. practice under the Trade Marks Act 1938, where an application
was filed under s.29. See also, Chap. 3, paras. 3–30 to 3–34.

(a) The foundation for licensed use of a trade mark is quality control by the proprietor.

(b) The controlled use of the trade mark by the related company must not otherwise work a deception on the public.

(c) Provided that there is quality control, the licensed use of a trade mark does not adversely affect the validity of an application or of a registration, *i.e.* trade mark licensing is permissible.

(d) The controlled use of the trade mark by a licensee inures to the benefit of the applicant or the proprietor of the mark. Conversely, the controlled use of the trade mark does not inure to the benefit of the licensee.

(e) As the controlled use of the trade mark inures to the benefit of the applicant or proprietor, an applicant may base its application for registration of the trade mark, and a proprietor may assert its continuing right in the registered trade mark, on the use of the trade mark by the related company.

Thus, the provisions regarding a 'related company' rest on the same bedrock as that which determines valid trade mark licensing generally, namely quality control with respect to the use of the trade mark by the licensee.

Examination Practice in Respect of Related Companies

5–32   Despite the absence of any system for the registration of trade mark licenses, the procedures for examination of trade mark applications under U.S. law have developed an extensive set of guidelines in the context of use of the mark by a related company. These guidelines have sought to address the question of when the use of the trade mark by a licensee will be deemed to inure to the benefit of the applicant, and what evidence is required to establish that there is the requisite degree of control.

The Trademark Manual of Examining Procedure

5–33   The Trademark Manual of Examining Procedure is intended to direct the examiners in their examination of an application.[69] In addition, the U.S. Manual is publicly available and is consulted by practitioners. Section 12.01 sets out guidelines in connection with trade mark use by a related company. The guidelines focus on the relationship of the related company to the applicant's claim for registration of the trade mark.

Summary of Guidelines

5–34   The guidelines set out in the TMEP in connection with use of a trade mark by a related company can be summarised as follows:

(a) Section 5 of the Lanham Act does not create any right of proprietorship in the mark that did not previously exist, nor does the related company

---

[69] See *supra*, n. 4. Hereinafter, the Trade Mark Manual of Examining Procedure shall be referred to as either 'U.S. Manual' or 'TMEP'.

acquire any rights in the registered trade mark by virtue of its use.[70] Rather, the provisions merely recognise the fact that when a related company situation exists, use of the mark is deemed to inure to the benefit of the applicant.[71]

(b) The proprietorship of a mark is determined solely by reference to who controls the nature and quality of the goods sold or the services furnished in relation to the mark. Use may be either solely by the related company whose use inures to the benefit of the applicant, or by both the applicant and a related company whose use inures to the benefit of the applicant.[72]

(c) The applicant must disclose use of the mark by a related company if the application is relying on such use.[73] Failure so to disclose in the application will bar the applicant from relying upon such use as the basis for its application.[74]

(d) The applicant may also claim proprietorship by virtue of controlled use of the trade mark by the related company, even if the applicant itself has made no use of the mark.[75]

(e) Reliance on use of the mark by the licensee can be made only if the related company uses the mark in connection with the same goods or services that appear in the application.[76]

(f) If the name of a person other than the applicant appears on the specimens, the applicant may be asked to explain its relationship with that person in order to establish that it is a related company, unless the relationship is clear from the context without the need for any further clarification.[77] If the applicant does not rely on the use of the related company, however, no reference to the use of the related company is needed.[78]

(g) Section 5 of the Lanham Act does not deal with the situation in which rights are claimed by virtue of the registration of a related company, since use, and not registration, of the mark by the related company inures to the benefit of the applicant. Registration of a conflicting mark by a party controlled by the applicant may even bar the later registration.

(h) A later application filed by a party controlled by the registrant of an earlier registration may be refused on the grounds of likelihood of confusion. There is, however, no longer a rule against such a registration *per se*. In some instances, the close relationship between the two parties

---

[70] *Warner Bros. Inc. v. Road Runner Car Wash Inc.*, 189 U.S.P.Q. 430, 432 (T.T.A.B. 1975).

[71] TMEP, s. 1201.03.

[72] TMEP, s. 1201.01(3) and s. 1201.03.

[73] TMEP, s. 1201.03(a).

[74] *Re Silenus Wines, Inc.*, 194 U.S.P.Q. 261, 263 n. 2 (CCPA 1977).

[75] TMEP, s. 1201.01(2); *Pneutek, Inc. v. Scherr, supra*, n. 51.

[76] TMEP, s. 1201.03 see also *Re Admark, Inc.*, 214 U.S.P.Q. 302 (T.T.A.B. 1982) (Application for registration for service mark for advertising agency services cannot rely on purported use of the mark by a related company for retail services).

[77] TMEP, s. 1201.01 and s. 1201.04; *Stagecoach Properties, Inc. v. Wells Fargo & Co.*, 199 U.S.P.Q. 341 (T.T.A.B. 1978). This requirement has been cut back under Examination Guide no. 1–94 (J), issued on January 28, 1994.

[78] TMEP, s. 1201.03(a).

may be deemed to constitute a single source and thereby eliminate any likelihood of confusion.[79]

Contractual Control and Financial Control

5–35   The U.S. Manual provides guidelines on how trade mark control may be evidenced. Controlled use of the trade mark by a related company will typically be found in one of two situations: a parent-subsidiary relationship and a contractual relationship between the licensor and the licensee.[80] In contrast to U.K. practice, the U.S. Manual does not appear to give explicit recognition to control by virtue of a related patent licence, although it does make a distinction between a certification mark and use of a mark in connection with a patent licence.[81] The two situations, contractual control and financial control, need not be mutually exclusive. In particular, financial control may be augmented by a written contract, and this may even be desirable.[82]

Control Based on Use by a Wholly-Owned Subsidiary

5–36   Where the parent's application is evidenced by a specimen which solely identifies the subsidiary, the parent's claim of proprietorship will be accepted upon establishing that the related company is a wholly-owned subsidiary of the applicant.[83] Control over the wholly-owned subsidiary's use of the trade mark is presumed from the applicant's financial ownership of it, and use of the trade mark by the wholly-owned subsidiary inures solely to the benefit of the parent.[84]

Control Based on Use by a Non-Wholly-Owned Subsidiary

5–37   During the hearings on the enactment of the Lanham Act, the idea that a related company relationship should be limited to use of the trade mark by a wholly-owned subsidiary was rejected.[85] However, if the subsidiary is not wholly-owned, further proof of the nature of the controlled use of the trade mark by the subsidiary will probably have to be shown.[86]

Control may be evidenced by submission of a written contract or agreement, evidence of an oral agreement, or even by a statement of facts indicating the nature of control.[87] The licence agreement may also be oral, although problems

---

[79] TMEP, subs. 1201.07(a) and *Re Wells*, 787 F.2d 1549 (Fed. Cir. 1986).

[80] TMEP, subs. 1201.03(b)(iii); *cf.* with U.K. practice Chap. 6, para. 6–06.

[81] TMEP, subs. 1306.09(c). See para. 5–45 regarding use of a mark in connection with a patent, and Chap. 8, paras. 8–18 to 8–30, for further discussion of a certification mark.

[82] See Chap. 10, para. 10–66. *cf.* with the U.K. Trade Marks Act 1994, where the provisions for registration of a licence and the need to maintain quality control may lead to more extensive use of written licence agreements (Cook, 'The Trade Marks Bill 1994', Seminar Paper, June 16, 1994).

[83] TMEP, subs. 1201.03(c).

[84] *Capitol Tie Rack*, 150 U.S.P.Q. 357 (W.D. Ill. 1966). See also *Perry Knitting C. v. Meyers*, 101 U.S.P.Q. 176 (S.D.N.Y. 1954) as cited in Coolley, 'Related Company: The Required Relationship in Trademark Licensing,' *The Trademark Reporter*, vol. 77, p. 306, n. 40.

[85] Coolley, n. 84, p. 306, n. 39.

[86] TMEP, subs. 1201.03(b).

[87] TMEP, subs. 1201.03(b)(iii). See also *Pneutek, Inc. v. Scherr, supra*, n. 51, at 833, 834.

of proof may likely be encountered.[88] The mere recitation that the applicant exercises effective financial control over the related company may not be sufficient to establish the fact of controlled use of the trade mark by the non-wholly-owned subsidiary.[89] One may well ask whether it is not overly formalistic to provide that trade mark control is presumed from use by a wholly-owned subsidiary of the applicant, but not where there is less than complete ownership of the related company.[90]

The Ultimate Issue is Control

However, the ultimate issue before the Examiner is not whether the precise 5–38 terms and conditions of the licence, written or oral, can be proved but whether quality control exists. In proceedings before the Trade Mark Office, the entire record, and not just the alleged terms of the licence, may be relied upon to prove quality control.[91] A similar approach has been taken by the courts.[92]

Indeed, in the absence of a written licence, it is arguable whether examination practice actually distinguishes between proof of control based on the oral licence and proof of adequate control based on the entirety of the record. For example, in one case an applicant alleged the existence of an oral licence, the only terms of which were that the licence be 'royalty free' and that use of the marks be undertaken 'under certain conditions'. The applicant was permitted to set out in its application what it asserted to be the provisions of the oral licence with respect to quality control, and to elaborate on these provisions on the record.[93]

Controlled Use Based on Relationship Between Subsidiaries

One subsidiary cannot serve as the related company for another subsidiary. 5–39 In such circumstances, the presumption of control based on the applicant's financial ownership of the subsidiary does not arise.[94] Thus, use of a mark by one subsidiary does not inure to the benefit of another subsidiary, in the absence of evidence by the applicant that there is independent controlled use of the mark by the second subsidiary.[95] The same principle extends to companies which have the same directors or which occupy the same premises.[96]

---

[88] See, *e.g. Raven Marine, Inc.* 217 U.S.P.Q. 68 (T.T.A.B. 1983) and *Basic Inc. v. Rex*, 167 U.S.P.Q. 696, 697 (T.T.A.B. 1970). See Chap. 11, paras. 11–03 to 11–13 for discussion of oral licences.

[89] *Re Hand*, 231 U.S.P.Q. 487, 488 (T.T.A.B. 1986).

[90] *cf.* with the practice under the Trade Marks Act 1938, Chap. 3, paras. 3–07, 3–11, 3–12, 3–26, 3–27, 3–31, 3–33.

[91] TMEP, subs. 1201.038(b)(iii).

[92] *National Lampoon, Inc. v American Broadcasting Cos.*, 182 U.S.P.Q. 24, 26 (S.D.N.Y. 1974), aff'd *per curiam*, 182 U.S.P.Q. (2d Cir. 1974); *Dawn Donut Co. v. Hart's Food Stores, Inc.*, *supra*, para. 5–19.

[93] *Raven Marine, supra*, n. 88 at 70. In this case, the applicant failed to establish that its relationship with the user had provided for adequate quality control.

[94] TMEP, subs. 1201.03(b)(ii) and s. 1201.03(c).

[95] TMEP, subs. 1201.03(b)(ii); see also *Re Pharmacia, Inc.*, 2 U.S.P.Q. 2d 1883 (T.T.A.B. 1987) and *Greyhound Corp. v. Armour Life Insurance Co.*, 214 U.S.P.Q. 473 (T.T.A.B. 1982).

[96] *Raven Marine, supra*, n. 88, at 69.

Nothing would preclude a parent from claiming that use by more than one wholly-owned subsidiary will each inure to its benefit by virtue of its financial control over them.

Individual Shareholder as Licensor of the Trade Mark

5–40 An individual, like any legal person, can be the licensor of a trade mark. In particular, a shareholder or an officer of the company may claim proprietorship in the trade mark by virtue of use by a related company, although individual applicants have sometimes been afforded different treatment from that given to companies.

A distinction was once drawn between the situation in which a parent-subsidiary relationship exists and both parties are companies, and the situation in which an individual owns some or all of the shares of a company. In the latter circumstances, it was held that controlled use of the trade mark by the company still had to be shown.[97]

This evidence is no longer required, at least with respect to a wholly-owned company. If the application for trade mark registration is supported solely by use by the applicant's wholly-owned subsidiary, it does not matter whether the applicant is a company or an individual; the treatment will be the same. Any requirement that further explanation be given of the control of the mark is, therefore, obviated.[98] However, the requirement that evidence of control be shown in a situation where the applicant is an individual with less than 100 per cent ownership of the related company still appears to be in effect. To establish a right of proprietorship in the trade mark, the individual shareholder will have either to use the mark himself or to demonstrate that he is responsible for the controlled use of the trade mark by the company.[99]

Individual Applicant As Both Shareholder and Officer of the Licensee Company

5–41 It has occasionally been claimed that an individual applicant who also serves as an officer of the licensee company can almost never be deemed to be the proprietor of the mark by virtue of controlled use by the company. The reason advanced is that the applicant exercises quality control in his capacity as an officer rather than as an individual.

This position has been rejected, at least where the individual applicant used the mark prior to the incorporation of the related company; otherwise an individual applicant would find it extremely difficult ever to be a valid registrant if he was also a serving officer of the licensee company.[1]

However, where the individual applies for registration of the mark after the establishment of the company, and claims use solely through the related company, the argument that the individual is exercising quality control in his

---

[97] TMEP (1st ed.), January 1974, as revised January 1986, s.1201.03(c).
[98] Re Hand, supra, n. 89, at 488.
[99] TMEP, subs. 1201.03(b)(i); see also Re Hand, supra, n. 89, and the citations therein.
[1] Re Briggs, 229 U.S.P.Q. 76, 77 (1986).

capacity as an officer of the company, and that no use inures to him by virtue of controlled use by the related company, may be better founded.

Control is the touchstone

The key criterion is always whether there is control by the individual shareholder of the use of the trade mark by the company. No related company relationship is created where it is not established that the shareholder individually, as distinct from the corporation, is ultimately responsible for the controlled use of the trade mark.[2]

A written licence agreement between the individual shareholder and the company may provide conclusive proof of quality control. For example, in a case where the registrant entered into a written agreement whereby it licensed the company in which it owned 50 per cent of the shares to use the registered trade mark subject to express provisions regarding quality control, a related company relationship was found. Use by the company was held to be controlled use which inured to the benefit of the shareholder-registrant.[3] However, the arrangements between an individual shareholder or officer and the related company regarding the use of the trade mark are often not set out formally in a written document. Provided that an oral licence can be established and adequate quality control shown, the claim of use by a related company may be adequately supported.[4]

5–42

Use Inuring to the Applicant or Registrant As the Basis for Suit

Typically, the applicant or registrant of the trade mark will claim that use of the mark by the related company inures to its benefit. It may be possible, however, that a third party will assert this in order to bring in the licensor as a defendant to an action.

In one case, the plaintiff in an infringement action named the licensor as an additional defendant, although the sole use of the mark had been made by its wholly-owned subsidiary. The court held, on the basis of the *Turner* case as well as the related company doctrine, that all use, including any alleged infringing use of the mark by the licensee, inures solely to the 'benefit' of the licensor. The licensor, therefore, had been properly named as a defendant.[5]

This reliance on the notion of a related company relationship and on the *Turner* line of cases can be questioned. Perhaps the key to this judgment simply lay in the fact that since there was financial control, there was a unity

5–43

---

[2] *cf. Smith v. Coahoma Chemical Company Inc.*, 121 U.S.P.Q. 215 (CCPA 1959), where the shareholder's ownership of the company was not sufficiently complete for the shareholder and the corporation to be viewed as 'equitably' consituting a single entity, with *Briggs*, n. 1, where control was found to be exercised by the shareholder/officer.

[3] *Pneutek, Inc. v. Scherr, supra*, n. 51, at 833, 834 (T.T.A.B. 1981).

[4] *Basic Inc. v. Rex*, 167 U.S.P.Q. 696, 697 (T.T.A.B. 1970). *cf.* with *Raven Marine*, n. 88, at 70, where it was held that when the terms of an oral licence provided only that the license be 'royalty free' and that use of the marks be undertaken 'under certain conditions', the record did not support a finding that there was a related company relationship.

[5] *Hester Industries Inc. v. Holly Farms Food Inc.*, 16 U.S.P.Q. 2d 1318, 1319 (S.D.W.V. 1990). The *Turner* case is discussed *supra*, in para. 5–22.

of interest between the parent and subsidiary.[6] Would the same result be reached in the situation where the plaintiff's claim is based on alleged infringing use by a third party licensee rather than a wholly-owned subsidiary? If not, or if the proprietor of the mark successfully argued against the sufficiency of the quality control in order to refute the claim that it had an interest in the mark, the licensee could then conceivably be the sole defendant in an action for infringement.

Use by a Related Company of a Trade Mark or Service Mark Distinguished from Certification Mark Use

5–44   A related company relationship is sometimes mistakenly asserted to support an application for registration of a certification mark.[7] In these situations, the applicant will typically point to a contractual arrangement whereby the licensee itself uses the mark subject to quality control. Such use of the mark does not support certification mark use because it does not satisfy the basic requirement of a certification mark, namely that it represents a certification with respect to some characteristic of the goods or services.[8] This false reliance on a related company in connection with a certification mark has been well-expressed thus, whereby related company use:

> '... involves the right of a licensor to choose the licensees that use its mark against the obligations of the owner of a certification mark to certify the goods or services for **any** person who meets and maintains the standards and conditions which such mark certifies.'[9]

No Certification Mark As Part of a Patent Licence

5–45   The same holds true if the applicant is a patentee, and the mark is being used in connection with a patent licence. Here, similarly, the purpose of the licence and the control that it exercises over the licensee is to identify and distinguish the goods of the applicant rather than to certify the standards of the patented product.[10]

The Identity of the Proprietor of a Mark When a Parent-Subsidiary Relationship is Involved

5–46   The U.S. Manual also sets out guidelines on whether the parent or the subsidiary is the proper applicant for registration. In principle, either party may be the applicant for registration of the trade mark. The decision as to the proprietorship of the trade mark will generally be left to the parties, since the filing of the application will be deemed to reflect the arrangement reached

---

[6] See *supra*, para. 5–28.
[7] See Chap. 8, paras. 8–18 to 8–30, for further discussion of certification marks.
[8] TMEP, s. 1306.09(b).
[9] *Re Monsanto Co.*, 201 U.S.P.Q. 864, 870 (T.T.A.B. 1978).
[10] TMEP, s. 1306.09(c).

between them in the most appropriate way,[11] in accordance with the following:

(a) If the parent is the applicant, and there is no reference in the specimen of use to a related company, the mere fact of financial ownership by the applicant will usually support the parent's application.[12]

(b) Even if both the parent and the related company are identified, the parent's application will generally be deemed to be proper.[13]

(c) When the subsidiary is the applicant, and the specimen identifies only the subsidiary, or the subsidiary and the parent, this will support the application by the subsidiary.[14]

(d) However, if the subsidiary is the applicant, and the specimen identifies only the parent, the Examiner will probably request further evidence, since such circumstances are deemed 'unusual'.[15]

Technically speaking, the issues concerning proprietorship posed here do not address any licensing matter, since there is no question whether the use of the mark by one party inures to the benefit of the other. Rather, the key point is which of two parties is the proper proprietor of the application. A similar issue arises when considering the question of use and proprietorship of a trade mark as between a manufacturer and a distributor.[16]

5–47

---

[11] TMEP, s. 1201.03(c).
[12] TMEP, s. 1201.03(b).
[13] TMEP, s. 1201.03(b).
[14] TMEP, s. 1201.03(b).
[15] This point was well-expressed in the TMEP (1st ed.), January 1974, as revised January 1986, s. 1201.04.
[16] See Chap. 7, paras. 7–39 to 7–43, for discussion of trade mark use by distributors.

6. Quality Control

Introduction

Trade mark licensing is distinguished from other types of intellectual property   6–01
licensing by the requirement for quality control over the licensee's use of the
mark. It was the recognition that quality control is compatible with the source
theory of trade marks that led to the legal recognition of trade mark licensing.[1]

As long as the licensed use of the trade mark is subject to quality control,
the trade mark is deemed to function as the identifier of source, and the mark
serves to distinguish its goods from those of others. This is accomplished by
imputing the licensee's use of the trade mark to the licensor.[2] When this
occurs, there continues to be a connection in the course of trade between the
proprietor of the mark and the goods.

Quality Control and the Risk of Invalidity

Quality control also impacts on the validity of the very trade mark that is   6–02
being licensed. If there is an absence of quality control, the purported licence
fails in its essential function as the identifier of the source of the goods. The
licensee's use of the trade mark is then no longer deeded to be used by the
licensor. In these circumstances, the proprietor's exclusive right to the mark
is liable for revocation.[3]

Seen in this way, all trade mark licensing contains an element of risk,
because, the continuing validity of the trade mark may depend upon how the
licensee uses the mark. Set against the commercial and legal advantages of
trade mark licensing is the danger that unsupervised licensing without quality
control may result in a forfeiture of the proprietor's rights in the trade mark
itself. For this reason, quality control, and the risk that the proprietor's
exclusive rights in a licensed trade mark be lost, are inextricably intertwined.

Quality Control: The Approach Under U.K. Law

Given the central importance of quality control in trade mark licensing, it is   6–03
surprising perhaps that no definition of quality control was found in the
Trade Marks Act 1938. There was no definition even in connection with the

---

[1] See *supra*, Chap. 2, paras. 2–18 to 2–26.
[2] See *supra*, Chap. 2, para. 2–19. See also discussion regarding quality control in connection
   with contract manufacturers and certification marks, *infra*. Chap. 8.
[3] Revocation may occur either because the mark has become misleading or deceptive, or the
   mark has become generic. See *supra*, Chap. 1, para. 1–07.

registered user provisions, which purported to ensure that quality control arrangements are in place. Thus, the Trade Marks Act 1938 provided that, as a condition for the registration of the registered user, the parties should indicate 'the degree of control by the proprietor' over the licensee.[4] The Trade Marks Act 1938 did not specify, however, what is meant by 'degree', or the nature of the 'control.'

No Single Standard of Control Was Specified Under the Trade Marks Act 1938

6–04   Under the Trade Marks Act 1994, the Registry no longer examines the terms of the licence agreement to determine whether there is sufficient provision for quality control. In explaining this change, it has been observed that the public has become much accustomed to the supply of goods and services provided under licence. Thus, the Registry need no longer serve as the public's watchdog in the prevention of deception. Instead, the focus will be on the registered trade mark as a valuable piece of property, both in terms of its ability to attract custom and, concomitantly, to demand and receive royalties or other consideration from a licensee. Under this view, it will now be for the proprietor of the mark, and not the Registry, to ensure that there will not be uncontrolled use that could lead to a loss of distinctiveness, with a resulting devaluation in the mark as a piece of property.[5]

Nevertheless, it remains useful to consider the approach to quality control that was taken by the Registry under the provisions of the Trade Marks Act 1938 for the following reasons:

(a) The Registry's accumulated expertise in this area over the years may serve as a guidepost to practitioners in approaching the issue of quality control, even under the Trade Marks Act 1994.[6]
(b) In those jurisdictions in which the registered user system still calls upon the Registry to conduct a substantive examination of the quality control provisions of a licence, the practice of the Registry can still be expected to be instructive.

6–05   The standard for quality control has been described by the Registry as the 'conditions [that] should ensure that the proprietor is capable of exercising control over the use of his mark.'[7] Thus there is no predetermined set of criteria which sets out what constitutes quality control in all instances. The parties satisfied the Registry that, under the circumstances, adequate provision has been made for quality control.

As noted above, it is presumed that the Registry has particular expertise in making the determination that adequate provision has been made for quality control. When the conditions for quality control were approved by the

[4] s. 28(4)(a). See, *supra*, Chap. 4, paras. 4–32 to 4–39.
[5] See *infra*, paras. 6–29 to 6–30.
[6] See *Actomin Products Application* (1952) 69 R.P.C. 166; (1953) 70 R.P.C. 201.
[7] Trade Marks Registry, *Work Manual*, Registration of Users, Chap. 27, para. 27–37.

Registry, the registered user recordal provided proof that adequate provision for quality control had been made by the parties.[8]

Typical Forms of Control

Nevertheless, generalisations about quality control can be made. Two principal situations have been recognised in which quality control typically is exercised:

    6–06

(a) Contractual control of the user with respect to the quality of the marked goods;

(b) Financial control of the user by the proprietor of the trade mark.

In addition, the proprietor and the licensee may be connected by virtue of a patent licence, whereby the marked goods are made under a licence in accordance with a patent held by the proprietor.[9] The *Bowden Wire* case itself can be understood in part as an example of a trade mark licence which is included in a patent licence.[10]

Financial control and contractual control will apply equally to a licensed service mark, even though the mechanism of control may differ. More than one form of control may exist in connection with a single licence arrangement.[11] In particular, control in accordance with a patent licence may often be evidenced by contractual or financial control as well.

Contractual Control

Contractual control over the licensed trade mark is typically found when the parties are unrelated to each other, although related parties may provide contractually for quality control as well.[12] Contractual control is frequently characterised as less robust than financial control, because it is based merely on agreement between unrelated parties, rather than on a mutuality of interest between related parties.[13]

    6–07

Whether this distinction between contractual control and financial control is always correct can perhaps be challenged, depending on the freedom that

---

[8] This is so, even if the quality control may not by itself have been sufficient in all cases under the Trade Marks Act 1938 to establish a connection in the course of trade between the proprietor of the mark and the goods. Thus, it was observed by Lord Brightman, in the *Hollie Hobbie* decision, that 'I can discern no general rule that the mere ability to control quality is always to be sufficient to establish the required connection,' at least where trafficking in the mark was found. [1984] F.S.R. 209. See the discussion on the *Hollie Hobbie* case and trafficking under the Trade Marks Act 1938, Chap. 3, paras. 3–37 to 3–40.

[9] Davy, *License, Assign, But Don't Endanger Your Trade Mark*, ECTA, no. 4 (1987), p. 45; *Work Manual, supra*, n. 7 para. 27–30.

[10] See discussion of the *Bowden Wire* case, Chap. 3, paras. 3–08 to 3–10

[11] *Work Manual, supra*, para. 27–31.

[12] See, Chap. 10, generally, regarding the nature of a licence agreement.

[13] See, Chap. 6 *infra*, paras. 6–17 to 6–19, for discussion regarding financial control. This view may not be fully apt with respect to the treatment of licences under the Trade Marks Act 1994. Under the Trade Marks Act 1938, a registered user agreement for related companies often took the form of a simple statutory declaration, setting out the relationship between the parties. This may no longer be sufficient under the Trade Marks Act 1994: instead, a more complete form of licence agreement may be required (Cook, 'The Trade Marks Bill 1994', Seminar Paper, June 16, 1994).

a particular subsidiary enjoys. However, there is no doubt that contractual control depends solely on the performance of the terms of the agreement, rather than on the overall fabric of relations between the parties.

Slight Control May be Adequate

6-08   It was said that the Registrar's standards for evidence of quality control under the Trade Marks Act 1938 'are somewhat slight.'[14] This characterisation of quality control may be understood in terms of both the legal and practical context in which a registered user recordal took place.

Under the Trade Marks Act 1938, the registration of a registered user indicated that the reasonable possibility of quality control (including an emphasis on the right of the proprietor to inspect the goods) had been found to exist.[15] However, it did not ensure that quality control was in fact present nor did the registered user registration imply that there was an on going duty to ensure that quality control is sustained. Indeed, as a practical matter, the Registrar was unable to monitor the actual maintenance of quality control for all of the registered user registrations on the Registry. As a result, the extent to which quality control was actually put into effect and maintained could not be taken for granted simply because the quality control provisions had been approved by the Registry.

Basic Contractual Provisions for Quality Control

6-09   Despite these reservations regarding quality control, it is useful to consider what kinds of quality control provisions were likely to be approved by the Registry. The *Work Manual* of the Trade Marks Registry, Chapter 27, entitled 'Registration of Users', contains four examples of conditions and restrictions that provide for quality control. The *Work Manual* was one of a series of such manuals prepared by the Registry on various subjects for the guidance and instruction of the Registry's staff under the Trade Marks Act 1938. It contained four examples of conditions and restrictions that provide quality control via a contractual agreement.[16] While it is recognised that there is no such thing as a standard form of quality control provision, these examples address typical situations in which quality control can be said to exist.

Example 1

6-10   'The trade mark is to be used by the registered user (who is to be the sole registered user while he remains so registered) in relation to the goods only so long as they are manufactured in accordance with standards of quality laid down by the registered proprietor from time to time and only so long as the registered proprietor or his authorised representative has the right and is permitted to inspect the goods and the methods of manufacturing them on the premises of the registered user and is supplied with samples of the goods on request.'

---

[14] *Kerly*, para. 13–31; see also *supra, Hollie Hobbie T.M.*, n. 8, at 208.
[15] *Work Manual, supra*, para. 27–33(b).
[16] *Work Manual, supra*, para. 27–36.

Example 2

> 'The trade mark is to be used by the registered user in relation to the goods only so long as they are manufactured by him in accordance with specification laid down, directions given and information supplied by the registered proprietor from time to time and only so long as the registered proprietor or his authorised representative has the right and is permitted to inspect the goods and the methods of manufacturing them on the premises of the registered user and is supplied with samples of the goods on request.'

Examples 1 and 2 set out terms and conditions for quality control in their most basic form. Quality does not mean luxury, or the highest possible level of quality. Nor must the level of quality remain constant over time. The level of quality may even be changed by the proprietor.[17] What is important is that the change is implemented in a consistent fashion by the licensee, so that the mark continues to identify a single source for the goods.[18]

Three aspects of quality control are identified: (a) specification of the standards to be employed; (b) inspection of goods and methods of manufacture; and (c) supply of samples.[19] It is presumed that attention to these three aspects of quality control, standards, inspection and samples, is likely to ensure that a consistent level of quality is provided for under the licence.

Quality Control Exercised by a Representative of the Proprietor

In addition, these examples give recognition to the fact that, in the modern commercial world, quality control may be carried out by a representative of the proprietor. The proprietor need not itself directly exercise quality control, as long as it remains the ultimate source of control through its representative.[20]   **6–11**

Delegation of Control and Sub-Licensing

Recognition of the proprietor's right to delegate its responsibility for quality control has important implications for 'sub-licensing.' Strictly speaking, sub-licensing was not permitted under the registered user provisions,[21] but an arrangement was sometimes made whereby the proprietor/licensor entered into a separate contractual relationship with both the licensee/sub-licensee and the sub-licensor, respectively. The licensee/sub-licensor was appointed the representative of the proprietor/licensor with responsibility for monitoring   **6–12**

---

[17] *Bostitch*, at 19 *supra*, Chap. 2, n. 21, p. 197.

[18] But see, *supra*, Chap. 2, paras. 2–31 to 2–33, for suggestion that quality *per se* may be relevant in certain instances.

[19] The provision that the registered user be a sole user, if appropriate, was not properly part of the quality control provisions under the Trade Marks Act 1938. Rather, it derives from the requirements of s. 28(4)(a) of the Trade Marks Act 1938, which provided that the fact of a sole licence (*i.e.* there is only one licensee, but the proprietor still enjoys the right to use the trade mark) be recorded.

[20] Recognition of the right of the proprietor to delegate a representative to exercise quality control was given judicial approval under the registered user provisions of the South Africa Trade Marks Act then in effect. *Ritz Hotel Ltd v. Charles of the Ritz* [1988] F.S.R. 549, 566 (S. Ct., App. Div.).

[21] Trade Marks Act 1938, s. 28(11).

the quality control, while the licence was actually granted the sub-licensee by the licensor.[22]

To the contrary, the Trade Marks Act 1994 permits sublicensing.[23] While this provision can be expected to make unnecessary the need for two separate contracts. *i.e.* one between the licensor and licensee, and another between the licensor and sub-licensee, the practical relationship between the licensor and licensee/sub-licensor with respect to inspection and control of the sub-licensee's use of the mark may not change in many circumstances.

Quality Control and the Contract Manufacturer

6–13   No mention is made in these two examples of the right of the licensee to delegate the manufacture of the licensed goods, under the terms and conditions of the licensee, to a contract manufacturer. Such practice is nevertheless well established. This has been described by one court as follows: '[A] registered user may have the components made by one company, assembled by another, the trade mark affixed by a third and the goods marketed by a fourth.'[24] Thus, as long as the goods satisfy the quality control requirements, it does not necessarily matter whether or not the licensee itself actually makes the goods.

Greater Specificity in the Terms of Quality Control

Example 3

6–14   'The trade mark is to be used by the registered user in relation to the goods (a) only so long as they have been prepared in special vehicles supplied by the registered proprietor with equipment and using ice cream mix and ancillary supplies supplied or approved by the registered proprietor and in accordance with recipes, formulae and instructions given by the registered proprietor from time to time and only so long as the registered proprietor or his authorised representative is permitted to enter for inspection of vehicles from which the goods are sold and (b) only so long as the goods are sold in the territory comprised from and including...'

---

[22] See also Art. 1, 2 and 3(b) and (c) of the E.C. Competition Rules on Franchising Agreements, which state that the franchise relationship, including the franchisee's right to use the mark, is a two-party arrangement only and *infra*, Chap. 13, para. 13–24.

[23] Trade Marks Act 1994, s. 28(3).

[24] *Accurist Watches Ltd v. King* [1992] F.S.R. 80, 88 (H.C. 1991). See also *Bostitch, supra*, n. 17, at 197, where the court held that the proprietor may 'procure his supplies from sub-contractors, or arrange for assembly of completed articles by someone of his choice in lieu of doing it himself,' as long as it is not 'calculated to deceive or cause confusion.' See also para. 37 of the recent judgment of the European Court of Justice in *IHT Internationale GmbH v. Ideal–Standard GmbH*, C–9/93 (June 22, 1994), in which the court stated that 'the origin which the trade mark is intended to guarantee is the same: it is not defined by reference to the manufacturer but by reference to the point of control of manufacture.' See, generally, discussion on contract manufacturers, Chap. 8, paras. 8–01 to 8–16.

Example 4

> 'The trade mark is to be used by the registered user in relation to the
> goods only so long as they have been prepared by him from ingredients
> and in accordance with recipes, formulae and instructions supplied by
> the registered proprietor from time to time and only so long as the
> registered proprietor has the right and is permitted to inspect the method
> of preparation, storage and sale of the goods on the premises of the
> registered user, which premises shall have been approved by the registered
> proprietor, and is supplied with samples of the goods on request.'

While the three basic aspects, specification of standards: inspection of manufacture; and provision of samples remain equally applicable here, the terms
and conditions of control prescribed in examples 3 and 4 are more detailed.
This further specification may have been required by the Registry or it may
have been initiated by the proprietor itself.

Requirements Regarding Supply May be Contrary to Competition Law

There is a danger, however, that too much quality control may be present. **6–15**
This is particularly so in connection with the requirement in example 3 that
the licensee use ancillary supplies 'supplied or approved by the registered
proprietor.'

It should be appreciated that these supply requirements might pose a
problem under, for example, both U.S. and E.C. law, especially when a
franchise arrangement is involved. The objection is that the proprietor has
effected a tie-in between the right of the licensee to use the mark and the
terms and conditions under which the licensee is obliged to purchase certain
related supplies.[25] The trade mark proprietor would be well advised to limit
any requirement of direct purchase of supplies by the licensee to those which
are essential to the subject matter of the licence, and for which no substitute
can be obtained from any other source, in case the quality of the goods is
impaired.

For instance in example 3, a distinction can be made between the ice cream
mix, which presumably lies at the heart of the licence arrangement and which
is unique to the licensor, and ancillary supplies, such as napkins and plastic
spoons, for which alternative sources of supply are likely to exist. While
neither arrangement is necessarily free from doubt in the context of restraint
of trade, the latter provisions are certainly less potentially troubling than the
former.[26]

---

[25] *cf.* the E.C. Competition Rules on Franchising Agreements, particularly Art. 3(1)(a) and (b),
Art. 4(a), and Art. 5(b), (c); the Commission Decision of December 23, 1977 regarding
Compari ([1977] O.J. L70/69); and the Commission Decision of March 23, 1990 regarding
Moosehead/Whitbread ([1990] O.J. L100/32), with such U.S. decisions as *Siegel v. Chicken
Delight, Inc.*, 448 F.2d 43 (9th Cir. 1971), and *Principe v. McDonald's Corp.*, 631 F.2d 303 (4th
Cir. 1980). See generally, Chap. 13, paras. 13–23 to 13–24.
[26] See, in this connection, the U.S. case regarding an alleged tie-in involving ice cream speciality
store franchises, *Krehl v. Baskin-Robbins Ice Cream Company* 664 F.2d 1348 (9th Cir. 1982).

Quality Control in Respect of a Service Mark

6–16   With the recognition of service marks under the Trade Marks Act 1938, the licensing of a service mark also became subject to the registered user provisions. While the Registry did not publish sample provisions for quality control of a service mark licence, the following two examples of quality control provisions are instructive:

Example 1

'The User hereby undertakes to use the Trade Marks in relation to the provision of the Services in accordance with the directions given by the Proprietor from time to time and to permit the Proprietor or his authorised representative to inspect the carrying out of the Services.'

This example sets out the basic elements of quality control for a service mark, namely: (a) specification of standards and (b) inspection of the premises at which the services are to be provided. As with trade marks, the quality control may be carried out by a representative of the licensor. Since no goods are involved, no provision can be made for the furnishing of samples to the licensor. This points to the fact that it may be more difficult to specify and to monitor performance under a service mark licence. The parties may include, however, a provision obliging the licensee to furnish the licensor with samples of advertising and promotional materials.

Example 2

'The User hereby undertakes to use the Service Mark in relation to the provision of Services only so long as the materials used in relation to the Services are approved by the Proprietor, and the Services are carried out in accordance with directions given by the Proprietor from time to time, and to permit the Proprietor or his authorised representative on request to inspect the carrying out of the Services. The User shall continue to provide the same Quality of Service in connection with the Service Mark as has hitherto been provided by the User in its capacity as a wholly-owned subsidiary of the Proprietor.'

This example suggests that the standard of quality may derive from the licensee rather than the licensor. This may occur when the licensee is no longer owned by the licensor, where the standard of control had been set by the licensee as the subsidiary of the licensor, and the licensee continues to use the service mark on a licensed basis as an independent entity. In these circumstances, the method of control would change from financial to contractual control.

Financial Control

6–17   Financial control addresses 'the various forms of financial connection between the parties.'[27] Such control does not require that the licensee is the wholly-owned subsidiary of the proprietor. Majority ownership, and perhaps even a minority position of influence over the affairs of the user, may be sufficient. Control may be direct or indirect. Financial control may also be evidenced by control by the user over the proprietor.[28]

Financial control is in effect presumed from the fact that 'there can be no divergence of aims' between a licensor and a licensee which has an ownership interest (or vice versa).[29] Because of this presumed identity of interest, a formal contract may not be required, although such an agreement may be desirable for other reasons (such as taxation).[30] As financial control may be found even in the absence of any formal contractual relationship between the parties, it is considered the stronger form of control. It was sometimes suggested that a registered user registration may not even have been necessary when financial control was involved, although the accuracy of this view is questionable.[31]

Examples of Financial Control

As in the case of contractual control, the *Work Manual* contained a number of examples of financial control which address frequent types of situations.[32]   6–18

Example 1

(Unspecified Degree of Control by the Proprietor Over the Licensee)

'The mark is to be used by the registered user (who is to be the sole registered user while he remains so registered) in relation to the goods/services only so long as the registered user remains controlled by the registered proprietor.'

Example 2

(More Specific Degree of Control by the Proprietor over the Licensee)

'The mark is to be used by the registered user in relation to the goods/services only so long as the registered proprietor owns sufficient share capital of the registered user to enable the registered proprietor to elect or appoint a majority of the directors of the registered user.'

---

[27] *Work Manual, supra,* para. 27–59.
[28] *Work Manual, supra,* para. 27–60. See also, *supra*, Chap. 3, paras. 3–26 to 3–33. A similar set of presumptions regarding financial control can be found under U.S. practice, although in a somewhat different context. See Chap. 5, paras. 5–35 to 5–41.
[29] *Work Manual, supra,* para. 27–30(b).
[30] See, *infra*, Chap. 10, para. 10–06, Chap. 14, paras. 14–33 to 14–65.
[31] *Work Manual, supra,* para. 27–59; see also Chap. 3, paras. 3–31 to 3–34 regarding financial control and an application filed under ss. 29(1)(b) of the Trade Marks Act 1938. But see the contrary view, at least with respect to the Trade Marks Act 1994, *supra*, n. 13.
[32] *Work Manual, supra,* para. 27–60. The captions provided are by the author.

Example 3

(Third Party Control Over Both the Proprietor and the Licensee)

> 'The mark is to be used by the registered user in relation to the goods/services only so long as both the registered proprietor and the registered user are controlled by . . .'

Example 4

(Lesser Degree of Control by the Proprietor Over the Licensee)

> 'The mark is to be used by the registered user in relation to the goods/services only so long as the registered user is controlled either directly or indirectly by the registered proprietor.'

Example 5

(Indirect Control by the Proprietor Over the Licensee)

> 'The mark is to be used by the registered user in relation to the goods/services only so long as the registered user is controlled by [X Company] and only so long as [X Company] is controlled by the registered proprietor.'

Example 6

(Proprietor Must Remain the Sole Owner of the Licensee)

> 'The mark is to be used by the registered user in relation to the goods/services only so long as the registered user is/or remains a wholly owned subsidiary company of the registered proprietor.'

Example 7

(Registered User Must Remain the Statutory Subsidiary of the Licensee)

> 'The mark is to be used by the registered user in relation to the goods/services only so long as the registered user remains a subsidiary company, as defined in . . . the Companies Act 1985, of the registered proprietor.'

The general reference to control in example 1 may be criticised for lack of precision, although approval of the provision reflected the position of the Registry that control may be demonstrated in a number of ways.[33] It is not certain that the various forms of financial control described in these examples would all be recognised under U.S. practice as evidencing quality control, in the absence of other support, such as a formal written licence agreement. This is particularly so when the ultimate financial control over both the

---

[33] *cf.* the concern expressed by the *Work Manual* that the term 'subsidiary' should be defined by precise reference to a statutory definition (Example 7).

proprietor and the licensee is exercised by a third party which has no direct relationship with the trade mark.[34]

Obligation to Pay Royalties Is Not Sufficient

The claim that financial control is present merely because there is an obligation to pay royalties seems incorrect.[35] The financial arrangements between the parties, such as royalties or other payments, 'are seldom relevant to the question of control of the use of the mark.'[36] However, the payment of royalties may be relevant in challenging the position of a putative licensee seeking rectification of the trade mark on the ground of non-use.[37]

6–19

Control Based on a Patent

The presumption of quality control arising as a result of the existence of a British patent will often be based on the terms of the patent licence itself, although there is no requirement under the Patents Act 1977, or its predecessor, that a patent licensor exercise quality control in the trade mark sense.[38]

6–20

The term of the licence (as with the registered user registration) need not be coterminous with that of the registered patent.[39] This is a matter for agreement between the parties. Thus, the parties may by contract provide that use is permitted only for as long as the patent remains valid. Equally, however, the parties may agree on some lesser or greater period for the duration of the trade mark licence.[40]

Quality Control in the Absence of a Registered User Recordal

Under the Trade Marks Act 1938, it was held that a registered user recordal is merely permissive.[41] The result of this position is that licensed use of a registered trade mark which serves to distinguish the licensed goods from those of others will be recognised if there is evidence of quality control and even if there is no recordal of the registered user.[42] In the absence of a registered user recordal, however, sufficient evidence of quality control *must have been* offered. This can be seen in the *Bostitch* case, where the court upheld the validity of the licence arrangement, even in the absence of a registered user recordal, in the following words:

6–21

'The essential (that is to say, specialised) components were to be manufactured and sent to England by the proprietors, and only the non-

---

[34] See, Chap. 5, paras. 5–39 to 5–41.
[35] *McGregor T.M.* [1979] R.P.C. 36, 39.
[36] *Work Manual, supra,* para. 27–35. But see practice under U.S. law, *supra,* Chap. 5, para. 5–38.
[37] *Job T.M., infra,* n. 52.
[38] Kerly, (12th ed., 1986) para. 13–31; *Work Manual, supra,* paras. 27–61—27–63.
[39] *Work Manual, supra,* para. 27–63.
[40] *Work Manual, supra,* para. 27–63. If the trade mark licence extends beyond the period of validity of the British patent, there should be explicit contractual provision for quality control.
[41] *Bostitch, supra,* Chap. 3, n. 24 at p. 195. See also Chap. 3, paras. 3–07 to 3–13.
[42] *Bostitch, supra,* at p. 197.

essential (that is to say, commonly procurable) components supplied from other sources. In supplying all the relevant working drawings, manufacturing and assembly data, and specimen components for reproduction, without which it is not and cannot be said that any manufacture or assembly . . . . would have been initiated, Bostitch Inc. were imposing their identity upon the articles produced therefrom, and thus saving goods made by other hands from being fairly regarded as goods of other makers.'[43]

6–22   The validity of a licence purporting to license an unregistered trade mark remains unresolved.[44] What is more certain, however, is that the principles of quality control expressed by the court in *Bostitch* will apply to such an arrangement, if the licence of the unregistered trade mark is otherwise given legal effect.

Inadequate Quality Control under the Trade Marks Act 1938

6–23   The failure to exercise quality control may, under appropriate circumstances, was sometimes fatal to the licensor's proprietorship of the trade mark, even if the licence arrangement was subject of a registered user registration.[45] In fact, the number of reported cases under U.K. law that have found inadequate quality control in a trade mark licence have been few.[46] This can apparently be explained in part by the registered user provisions themselves.

While it was not mandatory, the recordal of a registered user evidences the existence of quality control, providing a strong incentive for the parties to register a licence. Since the Registry does typically not inquire into whether the provisions will actually be performed, a challenge as to the adequacy of the quality control will probably have to be made by a third party. Such challenges have been infrequent.

6–24   Nevertheless, occasionally, the courts have found that inadequate quality control was being exercised, despite the presence of a registered user registration reciting quality control. Two cases, *McGregor Trade Mark*[47] and *Job Trade Mark*[48], are instructive in this respect.

The McGregor Case: No Actual Control Is Present

6–25   The *McGregor* case considered a situation in where the registered user provisions provided for quality control, but no actual control was found to have taken place. The registered user registration contained a typical set of quality control provisions.[49] The registered user registration stated that the goods were to be made in accordance with directions from the proprietor regarding the materials and methods to be used, and the proprietor or his

---

[43] *Bostitch, supra,* at p. 197.
[44] See, *supra,* Chap. 3, paras. 3–14 to 3–19.
[45] See discussion, *infra,* 6–25 to 6–28.
[46] *cf.* the discussion of the abandonment cases under U.S. law, below, paras. 6–43 to 6–47.
[47] *McGregor T.M.* [1979] R.P.C. 36. [1979] R.P.C. 36.
[48] 1993 (F.S.R.) 118.
[49] See, *supra,* paras. 6–10 to 6–15 for examples of quality control provisions.

authorised representative was permitted to take samples and inspect the goods and methods of manufacture.[50] These requirements had not been complied with at all.

The claim was made (by the registered user) that there was no quality control, as no directions or instructions were given to the licensee. Thus, there was no controlled use of the mark, and the registration was subject to cancellation on grounds of non-use. The argument was accepted. The court pointed out that the function of quality control is to ensure that the source theory of trade marks is preserved ('there is only source controlling the question of quality.')[51] When such control is absent, no one is responsible for the quality of the goods identified by the mark and the central purpose of the trade mark as the identifier of source is deemed to have failed.

It was of no consequence that the licence agreement seemed to provide that the quality control was merely permissive. The terms of the registered user registration were determinative, and they stated that quality control was mandatory. Indeed, it is doubtful whether parties could, by private agreement, ever override the mandatory nature of quality control.[52]

Job Trade Mark: Inadequate Control

A more difficult question arises in relation to the adequacy of the control, when some quality control has taken place. In the recent *Job Trade Mark* case, the registrar found that although there had been some initial acts of control over the manufacture of cigarette paper bearing the mark, there had not been sufficient quality control during the relevant period.[53]   6–26

The facts of this case are complicated. At all times, from the execution of the licence agreement in the 1950s, the licensee appeared to have been a member of a large commercial group embracing the licensor, the licensee and the applicant for rectification. The degree of quality control exercised by the French proprietor of the mark was in dispute.

Taking the position of the proprietor, the most that could be said was that, at one time, the French proprietor had in place a regime for testing the goods manufactured in the United Kingdom, consisting of physical inspection and laboratory analysis. In addition, there had apparently been contact at high managerial level between the parties.[54]

Distinction with the McGregor Case Rejected

The proprietor sought to distinguish its situation from that of the *McGregor*   6–27 case on two grounds:

---

[50] *McGregor T.M., supra,* n. 47, at 52.

[51] *ibid.* at 53. See *supra,* Chap. 2, paras. 2–06 to 2–17, for discussion of source theory of trade marks.

[52] *McGregor T.M., supra,* n. 97, at 53.

[53] Technically, the ruling on quality control was reached by the registrar merely as a matter of caution, as he had already concluded that the applicant for rectification did not have standing as a 'person aggrieved.' *Job T.M., supra,* n. 48 at 138.

[54] *Job T.M., supra,* n. 48, at 146.

(a) Initially, there had been some exercise of quality control through the submission of samples;

(b) The unsophisticated nature of the goods required less extensive quality control.

De Minimis Control Held Not To Be Sufficient

6–28   As far as alleged extent of control was concerned, the Registrar held that the control exercised during the relevant period was too slight to constitute a permitted use of the trade mark within the meaning of the registered user provisions under the Trade Marks Act 1938.[55] Due to the inadequate quality control with respect to manufacture, the goods as identified by the mark in France had become distinguishable from those made and marked in the U.K. In other words, the mark no longer signified a single source for the goods. The Registrar's words are noteworthy in this regard:

> 'I am unable to reach a conclusion that there was continuing effective quality control by Job France. They may have carried out certain analysis work and they may have visually inspected the product but there was apparently no system for follow-up discussions with Job England. I therefore have to assume that quality control as laid down in the Registered User agreement was not effected. In this connection it is relevant to consider the stringent quality control exercised in relation to the Belgium Co....'[56]

Quality Control: The Transition from a Public to a Private Matter

6–29   As noted above, the Trade Marks Act 1994 has eliminated any substantive examination by the Registry of the quality control provisions of the licence as a prerequisite to registration of the licence. Even under the Trade Marks Act 1938, however, the Registry was not the sole arbiter of quality control. Thus, the Registry never comprehensively monitored the actual compliance of the parties with the quality control provisions of a registered user recordal. This was largely left to the parties themselves and to third parties.[57]

Moreover, since the *Bostitch* decision, the prevailing view had been that the registered user provisions were merely permissive. This means that quality control need not have been established to the satisfaction of the Registry in the context of a registered user recordal to have been deemed effective.

Quality Control: Public Protection Against Deception or Property Interest of the Licensor?

6–30   From a slightly different perspective, the question of whether quality control is a matter of public or private enforcement is another way of asking whether

---

[55] *Job T.M., supra,* n. 48, at 146.

[56] *Job T.M.,* n. 48, at 148. The issue of the unsophisticated nature of the goods was apparently not considered to be germane.

[57] This was, at the least, because of the limited resources available at the registry to actually monitor licence agreements.

quality control is ultimately intended to protect the public against deception, or to enhance the property value of the licensor's trade mark. While historically the protection of the public interest was paramount, the current trend appears to favour the latter interest.

This position was forcefully expressed in the White Paper. Arguing against the interventionist role of the Registry in assuring quality control, the following was noted:

> '[T]he strongest guarantee that a proprietor will maintain control over the way in which his trade mark is used is that it is in his own interest to do so. A trade mark is a valuable piece of property, in terms both of its power to attract customers and of the royalties which can be demanded from licensees. Its value is however ultimately dependent on its reputation with the public. If the proprietor tolerates uncontrolled use of his trade mark the value of this property will be diminished. In an extreme case the registration of the mark may become liable to be revoked if it has become deceptive or generic through such use. It is however the responsibility of the proprietor, not the Registrar, to prevent the devaluation of his own property.'[58]

The view of the licenced trade mark as a valuable piece of property has also been expressed in the Trade Marks Act 1994.[59]

Quality Control and Merchandising

When the emphasis is placed on the property interest of the proprietor in the trade mark, quality control may become synonymous with high quality, or at least the absence of inferior quality. Confusion may then become a secondary concern. This is because the mark may no longer primarily be an indicator of source, but may have become a valuable property right in its own right. Where the proprietor enters into merchandising agreements for example in a wide variety of product areas, it is the licensed mark itself which becomes the object of trade.[60]   6–31

Indeed, when character merchandising is involved, the outward manifestations of quality control may no longer apply solely to the licensed trade mark. The same, or similar, quality control provisions may be found in a character merchandising licence agreement involving copyright or design, as well as the trade mark *per se*. This may be the case, even if quality control is not relevant to the validity of the licensed copyright or design.

The concern here is the absolute quality of the licensed product, where control provides the mechanism by which such quality is maintained. In such circumstances, the unique characteristic of quality control, as indicating the

---

[58] White Paper, *Reform of Trade Marks Law*, Cm. 1203 (1990), para. 4.36.
[59] Trade Marks Act 1994, s. 22.
[60] See, *supra*, Chap. 2, paras. 2–31 to 2–33, for discussion on the use of trade marks in merchandising, and Chap. 3, paras. 3–35 to 3–41, for discussion on licensing and trafficking.

source of trade mark, may no longer be relevant.[61] The result is that when the property interest of the proprietor, rather than the public concern against deception, is paramount, the underlying rationale for quality control may undergo a partial shift in emphasis. This does not mean that quality control in trade mark licensing has disappeared, but its function may have changed. This is a development that merits close attention.

QUALITY CONTROL: THE U.S. PERSPECTIVE

Introduction

6–32   In the U.S., the analysis of quality control derives principally from the application of the 'related companies' doctrine to trade mark licensing, rather than from any registration requirements.[62] Under U.S. law, no administrative procedure exists whereby the quality control provisions are reviewed and approved by the Registry as part of the registration of the trade mark licence. As a result, there is no administrative authority for quality control, especially when contractual control is claimed, similar to that which was enjoyed by virtue of the registration of a registered user under the Trade Marks Act 1938.

This does not mean that quality control is not addressed under U.S. practice. On the contrary, quality control remains a fundamental aspect of valid trade mark licensing under U.S. practice, and both the U.S. Trade Mark Office and the courts are called upon to rule on the sufficiency of quality control under specific circumstances. The absence of a registered user registration requirement does however, mean, that the context in which quality control is addressed differs from that in the United Kingdom.[63] Thus, while there is a similarity in the conceptual underpinnings of quality control under the two systems, it is appropriate to consider separately the principal elements of quality control under U.S. law.[64]

---

[61] See, *e.g. supra*, White Paper, n. 58, which observed that 'it is virtually impossible to construct a legal framework that would distinguish between straightforward character merchandising (using for example a popular cartoon character having no independent existence as a trade mark), the practice of decorating goods such as T-shirts or mugs with a trade mark having a reputation in connection with quite different goods, and cases where a trade mark simultaneously decorates the goods and distinguishes their source.'

[62] See, *supra*, Chap. 5, for discussion of the development and application of the 'related companies' doctrine, and *infra*, below, paras. 6–33 to 6–47, for discussion of the development of quality control in terms of the 'related companies' doctrine as set out in s. 5 and s. 45 of the Lanham Act. See generally, Comment, 'Trademark Licensing: The Problem of Adequate Control', 50 Trade Mark Rep. 820 (1969); Borchard & Osman, *Trademark Licensing and Quality Control*, 70 Trade Mark Rep. 99 (1980); Rudnick, 'Franchising and Licensing in the U.S.' 115th Annual Meeting of the U.S. Trademark Association 1993, vol. 2, 527–536.

[63] See, *e.g. supra*, Chap 5, paras. 5–34 to 5–43, for the treatment of quality control under U.S. examination practice, particularly in relation to control by financially related companies.

[64] See, Chap. 2, paras. 2–18 to 2–26, for a discussion of the development of the relationship between quality control and trade mark licensing under the U.K. and U.S. law.

Right to Exercise Control or Actual Control?

It is not settled whether actual control, or the mere contractual right to 6–33
exercise control, is sufficient. While the majority of U.S. courts appear to
have held that actual control is required, there has from time to time been
the suggestion that adequate contractual provision for quality control may be
sufficient.[65] The emphasis on actual control reflects the view that no formal
written agreement is necessary for quality control to be established.[66] Indeed,
the licensor's supervision and monitoring of the licensee's use of the mark, in
the absence of any express contract right, may be sufficient.[67] What is
ultimately important is whether there is factual evidence of quality control.

No Agreement On The Quantum of Control Required

Even if a mere contractual right to exercise quality control is not deemed 6–34
sufficient, the courts are not in agreement about how much actual control is
required. There is little doubt that where comprehensive quality control is
found, including 'actual licensor supervision, inspections, product specifications, operating manuals, licensee training, and express contractual provisions,' the quality control requirements will be satisfied.[68] The question is
whether less comprehensive quality control may also be sufficient and, if so,
what type of control is satisfactory.

Quality Control By the Licensee

There is an established readiness by U.S. courts to give recognition to quality 6–35
control on the basis of the exercise of control by the licensee. In a leading
case, the court emphasised the long time use of the trade mark by the licensee
without receipt of any complaints from customers.[69] The court also relied on
the licensor's inspection of the licensee's facilities during the period of
negotiations and on the familiarity with the licensor in the licensee's expertise
in the product area, in finding that there had been sufficient quality control.
The integrity of the licensee was also deemed significant.[70]

It is questionable, however, to what extent reliance can be placed on the
exercise of quality control by the licensee if the licensor is far removed in

---

[65] cf. *Alligator Co. v. Robert Bruce, Inc.*, 176 F. Supp. 377, 379 (E.D. Pa. 1959) with *Visa U.S.A. Inc. v. Birmingham Trust National Bank*, 216 U.S.P.Q. 649, 653 (Fed. Cir. 1982), cert. denied sub nom. *SouthTrust Bank of Alabama v. Visa U.S.A., Inc.*, 464 U.S. 826 (1983).

[66] *National Lampoon, Inc. v. American Broadcasting Companies, Inc.*, 376 F. Supp. 733, 737 (S.D.N.Y.), aff'd, 497 F.2d 1343 (2d Cir. 1974) *(per curiam)*.

[67] *Dawn Donut Co. v. Hart's Food Stores, Inc.*, 276 F.2d 358, 367 (2d Cir. 1959). See also the recent judgment of the European Court of Justice in the *Ideal–Standard* case, *supra*, n. 24, in which it was stated in para. 38 that 'the decisive factor is the possibility of control over the quality of the goods, not actual exercise of that control.'

[68] Rudnick, *supra*, n. 64 at 536. See also, *Turner v. HMH Publishing Co.*, 380 F.2d 224 (5th Cir.), cert. denied, 369 F.2d 1006 (1967).

[69] *Land O'Lakes Creameries, Inc. v. Oconomowoc Canning Co.*, 221 F. Supp. 576 (E.D. Wis. 1963), aff'd, 330 F.2d 667 (7th Cir. 1964). See also *Transgo, Inc. v. Ajac Transmission Parts Corp.*, 768 F.2d 1001 (9th Cir. 1985), cert. denied, 106 S. Ct. 802 (1986).

[70] *Syntex Laboratories Inc. v. Norwich Pharmacal Co.*, 315 F. Supp. 45 (S.D.N.Y. 1970), aff'd, 437 F.2d 566 (2d Cir. 1971).

terms of expertise from the licensed product, particularly when collateral licensing or character merchandising is involved.

Licensee Control over Services

6–36   In a case involving restaurant services, sufficient quality control was found where the licensor maintained certain rights of control by virtue of the lease, had general knowledge of the restaurant's operations and had previously enjoyed a close relationship with the licensee, and where the licensee used similar menus and served similar fare.[71]

In an earlier case involving dancing school services, adequate control was found where the licensee took measures to ensure that it continued to provide instruction in accordance with the standards and methods of the licensor. The fact that the licensor did not actively interfere with internal management, and even failed to exercise its right of control, did not mean that quality control was absent.[72]

Degree of Actual Inspection

6–37   Actual inspection is frequently held to be sufficient evidence of quality control.[73] Every item need not be inspected to satisfy this requirement, provided that a representative number of items are examined.[74] The mere fact than an inspection has been carried out may not be sufficient in all instances. In particular, the inspectors may be unqualified to carry out a meaningful examination. If this is the case, and there is no other evidence of control, the court may find that no quality control has been exercised.[75] In one case, the licensor's duty to furnish the licensee with written standards of quality, even in the absence of actual inspection, appears to have been sufficient evidence of quality control.[76]

Control by a Third Party

6–38   Quality control may be carried out by a third party representative, or by an agent, of the trade mark proprietor.[77] Such third party control may in particular form the basis for valid trade mark use by a sub-licensee.[78] Such control may also, although not necessarily, support a claim of quality control in an assignment and licence back situation.[79]

---

[71] *Stock Pot Restaurant, Inc. v. Stockpot, Inc.*, 222 U.S.P.Q. 665, 668 (Fed. Cir. 1984).

[72] *Arthur Murray, Inc. v. Horst*, 96 U.S.P.Q. 363, 364 (D. Mass. 1953).

[73] See, *e.g. supra*, National Lampoon, n. 65, at 737.

[74] *Carl Zeiss Stiftung v. V.E.B. Carl Zeiss, Jena*, 293 F. Supp. 892, 918 (S.D.N.Y. 1968), modified on different grounds and aff'd, 433 F.2d 686 (2d Cir. 1970), cert. denied, 403 U.S. 905 (1971).

[75] *Dawn Donut*, n. 67, Lumbard J. (dissenting).

[76] *Hormel & Co. v. Hereford Heaven Brands, Inc.*, 138 U.S.P.Q. 325, 326 (Trademark Trial and Appeal Board 1963).

[77] *Accurate Merchandising, Inc. v. American Pacific, Inc.*, 186 U.S.P.Q. 197 (S.D.N.Y. 1979).

[78] See, *supra*, Turner, n. 68.

[79] See *Haymarket Sports, Inc. v. Turian*, 198 U.S.P.Q. 610 (CCPA 1978), for a frequently cited example in which no quality control was found in an assignment and licence back arrangement. See also, *infra*, paras. 6–48 to 6–63.

Note, however, that in a case where the applicant for trade mark registration merely made arrangements with potential suppliers to process pickles for a third party, which actually sold the product and controlled the specifications as well as the quality of the goods, the applicant was held to obtain no benefit from such control and use.[80]

Quality Control by Competing Licensees: Is There Infringement?

An interesting question in connection with the relationship between quality control and infringement was raised in *Ballet Makers v. United States Shoe Corp.*, namely, can one licensee sue another licensee for infringement?[81] The court emphasised that no claim against the genuineness of the product manufactured by the second licensee could be raised, since there was sufficient quality control over the two licensees to ensure that the proprietor maintained responsibility for the goods.[82]

6–39

Quality Control and Common Law Expansion of the Licensor's Territory

Particularly thorny questions arise under U.S. law where the territorial scope of the mark's protection is claimed on the basis of the actual extent of the mark's use by the licensee.[83] The key is the exercise of quality control by the licensor.

6–40

In one case, the extension of use by the licensee beyond the territory specified in the licence agreement was deemed to inure solely to the benefit of the licensor. The court noted that the licensor's control over the activities of the licensee was apparent.[84] The fact that the licensor had acquiesced in the licensee's expansion of activities beyond the territory specified in the agreement was of no consequence, in the light of the quality control exercised in the additional territory.

On the other hand, the trade mark owner's rights in the trade mark in territories in which it exercises quality control is not adversely affected by failing to exercise quality control over the use of the mark by licensees in other territories. In such circumstances, the erstwhile licensee may claim rights in the mark in the abandoned territory, without affecting the rights of licensor

---

[80] *Ex P. Jongleux & Lundquist, Inc.*, 101 U.S.P.Q. 77, 82 (Com. Pat. 1954).

[81] *Ballet Makers v. United States Shoe Corp.*, 633 F. Supp. 1328 (S.D.N.Y. 1986).

[82] The court's view of quality control in this context should be compared with the understanding of the term in the *El Greco* case, Chap. 8, paras. 8–12 to 8–16. The court also questioned the correctness of the result reached in a previous case, *Burma-Bibas, Inc.*, which held that one licensee could sue another for infringement, where the custom of the industry was that there was only one source of the designer goods. *Burma-Bibas, Inc. v. Excelled Leather Coat Corporation*, 584 F. Supp. 1214 (S.D.N.Y. 1984).

[83] *cf.* with discussion, *supra*, Chap. 3, paras. 3–28 to 3–34, regarding s.29 of the Trade Marks Act 1938.

[84] *Cotton Ginny Ltd v. Cotton Gin Inc.*, 10 U.S.P.Q. 2d 1108, 1110, 1111 (S.D. Fla. 1988). See also *Dennison Mattress Factory v. Spring-Air Co.* 308 F.2d 403, 409 (5th Cir. 1962) ('A trademark owner ... may introduce his trademark and create a demand for his variety of goods in new territory, by licences subject to his control.')

in those territories in which it still exercises sufficient quality control over the mark.[85]

No Discernible Quality Control

6–41   The courts have, on occasion, upheld the existence of sufficient quality control in circumstances where virtually no discernible quality control appears to have been exercised.[86] One should be wary, however, when considering these cases, because the facts do not always point unequivocally to the existence of a trade mark licence. For example, the oft-cited case of *Union Tank Car Co. v. Lindsay Soft Water Corp.* can perhaps be better understood as an instance of a distribution relationship where the issue of quality control should not really have ever been considered.

Forfeiture of Trade Mark Rights Due to Absence of Quality Control

6–42   U.S. courts seem reluctant to find that no actual quality control has taken place, if the result would be the forfeiture of the licensor's rights in the trade mark.[87] The U.S. Trademark Office may be less reluctant to find an absence of quality control, perhaps because of the public interest in extending protection only to marks which identify a distinct source for the goods or services.[88]

Thus, a trade mark owner may enjoy a grace period before it is required to exercise quality control or face abandonment and forfeiture. The length of the grace period depends upon the circumstances. In one case, a six-year period was allowed, until the licensor learned of the licensee's unsupervised use of the mark.[89] Similarly, a licensee cannot fail to comply with bona fide quality control provisions, and then claim abandonment of the trade mark on the grounds of an absence of quality control.[90]

Abandonment Due to Lack of Quality Control

6–43   Perhaps because of this tendency on the part of the courts against the forfeiture of trade mark rights, the instances in which no quality control has been found

---

[85] *Shiela's Shine Products, Inc. v. Shiela Shine, Inc.*, 179 U.S.P.Q. 577, 584 (5th Cir. 1973).

[86] See most notably *Union Tank Car Co. v. Lindsay Soft Water Corp.*, 257 S. Supp. 510 (D. Neb. 1966), aff'd *sub nom. Heaton Distribution Co. v. Union Tank Car. Co.*, 387 F. 2d 477 (8th Cir. 1967) and *Hurricane Fence Co. v. A-1 Hurricane Fence Co.*, 468 F. Supp. 975 (S.D. Ala. 1979) ('The fencing business is unique and only minimal quality controls ought to be required'. 468 F. Supp at 989.)

[87] See, *e.g. supra, Transgo, Inc.*, n. 69, holding that the party asserting insufficient control must meet a high burden of proof; accord, *Edwin K. Williams & Co., Inc. v. Edwin K. Williams & Co.-East*, 542 F.2d 1053, 1059 (9th Cir. 1976), cert. denied, 433 U.S. 908 (1977); *United States Jaycees v. Philadelphia Jaycees*, 209 U.S.P.Q. 457, 463 (3rd Cir. 1981). See also *Kentucky Fried Chicken Corp. v. Diversified Packaging Corp.*, 549 F.2d 368, 387 (5th Cir. 1977) ('Retention of a trademark requires only minimal quality control.'). *cf.* with the U.K. approach to the licensee's forfeiture of rights under the licence, Chap. 12, paras. 12–31 to 12–42.

[88] See, *supra*, Chap. 2, paras. 2–06 to 2–17, for discussion of source theory of trade marks..

[89] *Shiela's Shine Products*, *supra*, n. 85, at 585.

[90] *Edwin K. Williams & Co., Inc.*, *supra*, n. 87, at 568; *cf.* with *McGregor T.M.*, *supra*, para. 6–25.

are relatively infrequent. Nevertheless, U.S. courts and tribunals do sometimes find a 'naked licence' due to an absence of quality control. In such situations, the mark is deemed to have lost its trade mark significance, *i.e.* its ability to serve as an indicator of source.[91]

Lack of Sufficient Control over Goods

(a) In one case, the sale of goods labelled and sold by a third party under 6–44 the applicant's trade mark, in the absence of any quality control, was held to justify the denial of registration. The reasoning was that such use of the trade mark was likely to lead to public confusion regarding the source of the goods.[92]
(b) In another case, it was found that the grant to third parties of unrestricted rights to employ a trade mark on goods of the same class and which were sold to the same group of purchasers through the same channels of trade, without any provision for quality control, constituted a naked licence.[93]
(c) In another, there was ambiguity over whether the agreement for the transfer of the trade mark was an assignment or a licence. Viewed as a trade mark licence, abandonment of the trade mark was held to have taken place, on the grounds that there was no licensing of a clearly identifiable product, the licensee was permitted to use the mark on other products, and the licensor had no control over the nature and quality of the product.[94]
(d) A provision in a licence agreement stating that the licensee covenants to maintain the same standards as those of the licensor have been found not to be evidence of quality control, where the licensee was given the freedom to manufacture the product under the mark in any manner that it chose.[95]
(e) Finally, the unsupervised and uncontrolled use of the *King Kong* name, character and story by multiple licensees over a 45-year period has been held to be abandonment of the mark.[96]

Royalties and Quality Control

(a) In the absence of any quality control, the existence of a written licence 6–45 agreement, which provided for the payment of royalties, was held to

[91] *Haymarket Sports, Inc., supra,* n. 79; *Yocum v. Covington,* 216 U.S.P.Q. 21 (Trademark Trial and Appeal Board 1982).
[92] *Circus Foods, Inc. v. Frank Herfort Canning Co., Inc.,* 110 U.S.P.Q. 501 (Com. of Patents 1956).
[93] *Poole v. Kit Mfg. Co.,* 184 U.S.P.Q. 302, 303 (N.D. Texas 1974).
[94] *Clairol Inc. v. Holland Hall Products, Inc.,* 165 U.S.P.Q. 215, 221 (Trademark Trial and Appeal Board 1970).
[95] *Cartier, Inc. v. The Three Sheaves Co., Inc.,* 204 U.S.P.Q. 377, 382 (S.D.N.Y. 1979).
[96] *Universal City Studios, Inc. v. Nintendo Co., Ltd.,* 578 F. Supp. 911, 929 (S.D.N.Y. 1983).

be a naked licence. The payment of royalties was deemed insufficient to support a claim of quality control.[97]

(b) The converse has also been held not to apply; the failure to make royalty payments does not in itself constitute an absence of quality control, giving rise to a naked licence.[98]

(c) In another case, unsupervised consent given to third parties to use trade mark on pelts in exchange for payment of royalties was held to be an abandonment.[99]

Absence of Quality Control Over a Service Mark

6–46   (a) In one case, the rights to a service mark for restaurant services were deemed abandoned when the purported licence agreements were silent on quality control and there was no evidence of actual control.[1]

(b) In another case, a mere consent to allow a bank to use a service mark for certain banking services was held to be a naked licence when the agreement did not set any quality control standards or make any arrangements to ensure that quality control standards were being met.[2]

(c) An alleged transfer of real estate services which did not restrict the broker's operation of business or quality of work, together with a lack of evidence of any significant attempt to control the quality of the licensee's services, has been held to be abandonment.[3] The court recognised that the quality control required for services is more difficult to describe than that required for goods, but found that no significant exercise of quality control had occurred.

The Risk of Insufficient Quality Control

6–47   As may be seen from these examples, a trade mark proprietor which enters into a licence arrangement may put the validity of the mark at risk if insufficient quality control is found.

ASSIGNMENT AND LICENCE BACK

6–48   An arrangement is sometimes reached whereby proprietorship of a trade mark is transferred, or assigned, from one party to another, and the use of the

---

[97] *Ritz Associates, Inc. v. Ritz-Carlton Co., Inc.*, 134 U.S.P.Q. 86, 88 (S.D.N.Y. 1962). But see *W.R. Grace & Co. v. Wrap-On Co., Inc.*, 165 U.S.P.Q. 473, 474 (Trademark Trial and Appeal Board 1970), where the continuing payment of royalties was deemed sufficient to establish the licensor as the proprietor of the mark, at least where quality control had been exercised for at least part of the relevant period.

[98] *Berkshire Fashions Inc. v. Sara Lee Corp.*, 14 U.S.P.Q. 2d 1124, 1127–1128 (S.D.N.Y. 1990).

[99] *Midwest Fur Producers Ass'n v. Mutation Mink Breeders Ass'n*, 127 F. Supp. 217 (W.D. Wis. 1954).

[1] *Heaton Enterprises of Nevada, Inc. v. Lang*, 7 U.S.P.Q. 1843, 1847 (Trademark Trial and Appeal Board (1988)).

[2] *First National Bank of Omaha v. Autoteller Systems Service Corp.*, 9 U.S.P.Q. 1740, 1743 (Trademark Trial and Appeal Board (1988)).

[3] *First Interstate Bankcorp. v. Stenquist*, 16 U.S.P.Q. 2d 1704, 1707 (N.D. Cal. 1990).

trade mark is immediately licensed back to the assignor (the former proprietor of the mark). This is referred to as the 'assignment and licence back' of the trade mark. On the granting of the licence, the assignee of the trade mark becomes the licensor, and the assignor of the mark becomes the licensee.

An assignment and licence back arrangement has been described by the U.S. court in the *E.J. Gallo Winery* case as an 'apparently well-settled commercial practice.'[4] It occurs typically in two situations: a) the transfer of the trade mark rights between entities for commercial reasons; and b) in settlement of a trade mark dispute,[5] and raises questions in connection with the transfer of goodwill and presence of quality control.

Transfer of Trade Mark Rights for Commercial Reasons

In the first situation described above, the assignment and licence back may derive from a corporate decision to shift the proprietorship of the trade mark from one member of the corporate family to another, for example from the parent to a subsidiary, or vice versa, while the use of the mark continues to be made by the assigning entity.[6] Of course, the transfer of the proprietorship of the trade mark between corporate entities need not involve a licence back to the assignor, if the use of the trade mark is also taken up by the new proprietor. An assignment and licence back may result from the sale of the trade rights to an independent entity, which may do no more than hold title to the trade mark. The new proprietor then licenses the trade mark back to the assignor-licensee, which continues to use the mark on its goods or services.   **6–49**

Settlement

The assignment and licence back arrangement is also sometimes employed as part of a settlement of a trade mark dispute. One party gives up proprietorship of the trade mark, subject to a continued right to use the mark as a licensee. This arrangement should be distinguished from a consent agreement, in which both parties maintain proprietorship of their respective trade marks.[7]   **6–50**

Benefits of an Assignment and Licence Back

No Split in the Goodwill

The main benefit of an assignment and licence back arrangement is that it enables the assignee to become the proprietor of the trade mark, while the assignor continues to use the trade mark as a licensee with a minimum of commercial interruption. The arrangement may solve a problem which arises   **6–51**

---

[4] *E. & J. Gallo Winery v. Gallo Cattle Co.*, 955 F.2d 1327, 1338 (9th Cir. 1992); see also, *Sands, Taylor & Wood v. Quaker Oats*, 24 U.S.P.Q. 2d 1001, 1009 (7th Cir. 1992).

[5] See, *supra*, Chap. 9, paras. 9–05 to 9–06, regarding consent agreements.

[6] See, *e.g. Portakabin Ltd v. Powerblast Ltd* [1990] R.P.C. 471 (H.C. 1990); *Browne-Vinters Co. Inc. v. National Distillers and Chemical Corporation*, 114 U.S.P.Q. 483; *J. Atkins Holdings Ltd v. English Discounts Inc.*, 14 U.S.P.Q. 1301, 1305, n. 5.

[7] See, generally Chap. 9, for discussion regarding consent agreements.

when the assignor assigns the mark but continues to use it. The splitting of goodwill, whereby the trade mark identifies two distinct sources for the goods, is contrary to the basic principle of trade mark law, namely, that a trade mark identifies a single source, and has been held to render the assignment ineffective.[8]

A properly structured assignment and licence back, however, will overcome the problem. As one U.S. Court noted, 'an assignment may be valid even in cases where the assignor reserves some rights of use of the mark. This can happen where there is an assignment of the mark with the good will of the business followed by a license back to the assignor.'[9] It has also been stated by the *Visa, U.S.A.* court that '[s]ince the license back is valid, it follows concomitantly that there is no split of goodwill from the mark. The mark is used for precisely the same services as before the assignment with use by the licensee inuring to the benefit of the licensor as a related company.'[10]

Priority of Rights May Be Established

6–52 Another benefit occurs in relation to the priority of rights. If the assignor's (licensee's) trade mark is earlier in time than the assignee's (licensor's) trade mark, an assignment and licence back arrangement will enable the assignee to enjoy the legal benefits of the earlier date of the assignor's mark. This could be crucial, if there is a conflicting third party claim regarding priority, and the assignor's trade mark is earlier in right than the third party's trade mark.[11] The assignee can then assert the priority of the assignor's trade mark by virtue of the assignment.

Assignment and Licence Back in Contrast to a Cancellation and Licence

6–53 An assignment and licence back is only one form of arrangement for the resolution of a trade mark dispute. A party may prefer to have the trade mark of the other party cancelled, and to grant the cancelling party a licence, thereby bringing all uses under the protective umbrella of its own trade mark. However, there may be a disadvantage in agreeing to the cancellation of a trade mark, as opposed to an assignment and license back arrangement. This is particularly so if the validity of the trade mark of the assignee is in doubt. If the licensee cancels its trade mark, and the licensor's trade mark is subsequently invalidated, the licensee may find itself without any registered trade mark on its own behalf (because of the assignment) or any right to use the licensor's trade mark (by virtue of the cancellation). If, however, an

---

[8] See, *Greenlon, Inc. of Cincinnati v. Greenlawn, Inc.*, 217 U.S.P.Q. 790 (S.D. Ohio 1982). See also *Macleans v. Lightbrown* (1937) 54 R.P.C. 230, where the fact that the assignor purported to assign its mark, which it had never used, while the assignor continued to operate it's chemist shop under the mark, was held to render the assignment ineffective since no goodwill was transferred.

[9] *Heaton Enterprises of Nevada Inc. v. Lang*, 7 U.S.P.Q. 2d 1842, 1847, n. 16 (Trademark Trial and Appeal Board (1988)).

[10] *Visa, U.S.A., Inc. v. Birmingham Trust National Bank*, 696 F.2d 1371, 1377 (Fed. Cir. 1982).

[11] See, *e.g. supra*, *Visa, U.S.A., Inc. v. Birmingham Trust National Bank*, at 1377; *Geo. A. Hormel & Co. v. Hereford Heaven Brands, Inc.*, 144 U.S.P.Q. 493, 494–495 (1965).

assignment and licence back takes place, the licensee will still enjoy the right to use the trade mark.

Phase Out Period

The period of an assignment and licence back arrangement may be for a fixed period, without any renewal or extension. When duration is fixed, the purpose is often to allow for a period of transition during which the licensee is permitted to phase out its use of the mark, while being given sufficient opportunity to develop goodwill in the other trade mark. For example, a dispute before the European Commission between the *Hershey* and *Herschi* trade marks, for chocolate bars and soft drinks respectively, was resolved by the assignment and licence back of the *Herschi* trade mark for a fixed period.[12]   6–54

Is An Assignment and Licence Back Valid and Enforceable?

The key legal issue in connection with an assignment and licence back is whether the validity of the arrangement can be challenged. Two grounds have been raised, particularly in the context of U.S. law: the validity of the assignment and the validity of the licence.   6–55

Validity of the Assignment

Occasionally, the validity of the assignment of trade mark rights is successfully challenged, particularly under U.S. law. The leading case is *Pepsi Co., Inc. v. Grapette Co.*[13] There, the claim was made that the transfer was invalid, or a mere naked assignment took place, because no tangible assets or goodwill were transferred, and the result of the transaction was to leave the parties effectively in the same position, as far as the trade mark was concerned, as they were prior to the transaction.[14]   6–56

Difficulty in Challenging the Validity of the Assignment

The modern tendency, even in the U.S., is to relax the requirement for the transfer of goodwill in an assignment, even in an assignment and licence back situation. The test is whether the assignment and licence back 'does not disrupt continuity of the products or services associated with a given mark.' If no disruption is found, the assignment will be held to be valid.[15]   6–57

A good illustration of the difficulty of in challenging an assignment and licence back on the grounds of invalidity of the assignment is the *E. & J. Gallo Winery* case.[16] In settlement of a dispute, the Gallo Winery received an

---

[12] 'Hershey/Herschi', Twentieth Report of Commission Policy of the EC Commission (1990), point 111.

[13] 416 F.2d 285 (8th Cir. 1969).

[14] Under U.K. law, the question may not be raised in this form. Trade Marks Act 1938, ss. 22(1), (7); Kerly, para. 13–11; *Reuter v. Mulhens* (1953) 70 R.P.C. 23 and Trade Marks Act 1994, ss. 24(1).

[15] *E. & J. Gallo Winery, supra*, n. 4, 955 F.2d at 1337.

[16] See, *supra*, n. 4.

assignment of the other party's mark for Gallo Salame and then licensed back the right to use that mark on meat and cheese packages. The court rejected a claim that the assignment was invalid. It held that it is not necessary for tangible assets to be transferred; it is sufficient that the goodwill of the business accompanies the mark. Goodwill passed in the circumstances of this case for two reasons:

(a) The Gallo Winery had received sufficient information from Gallo Salame to enable Gallo Winery 'to continue to attract the business which Gallo Salame had been conducting under the Gallo mark.'

(b) The mark was assigned in settlement of a bona fide infringement action. According to the court, the assignor had unfairly capitalised on the goodwill of the *Gallo* mark. By virtue of the assignment, the public perception, namely that the Gallo Salame mark belonged to the Gallo Winery, became consistent with commercial reality. The 'return' of the goodwill to the Gallo Winery was deemed to support the assignment.[17]

Assignment Upheld Regarding Ancillary Service

6–58   A further illustration is the decision in the *Visa, U.S.A.* case, involving the assignment and licence back of a service mark.[18] The court held that a valid assignment had occurred when the assignor transferred to the Visa credit card company the service mark *Check-O.K.* in connection with the cheque cashing service of its business.[19] This was so, despite the fact that the court acknowledged that the assignor's service was only 'ancillary' to its main grocery business.[20]

Assignment Invalidated When Assignor Continued to Use the Mark

6–59   Nevertheless, a U.S. court will now and again disallow an assignment and licence back on the grounds that the assignment is invalid. For example, in one case, the court ruled that the assignor had not transferred any assets connected with the trade mark, or the right to do business under the mark. As a result, 'the assignor relinquished nothing,' and the assignment was invalidated.[21]

Challenge to Validity of Licence Back Based on Lack of Quality Control

6–60   It has been alleged that a licence back is invalid because it is a naked licence without any quality control.[22] In the main, this argument has been rejected. For example, in the *E. & J. Gallo Winery* case, the court rejected the claim

---

[17] *supra*, n. 4, at 1337.

[18] *Visa, U.S.A.*, *supra*, n. 10, at 1377.

[19] *Visa, U.S.A.*, *supra*, n. 10, at 1376.

[20] *cf.* the treatment of the services provided under the *VISA* mark under U.K. practice. *VISA* T.M. [1985] R.P.C. 323. There, the court overturned the decision of the Registrar, holding that the Visa provided both financial services as well as trading in cheques as a separate and distinct good.

[21] *Greenlon, Inc.*, *supra*, n. 8, at 794.

[22] See, generally, above, regarding invalidation of a licence due to the absence of quality control.

that there was no adequate quality control over the licensee. The court noted the following:

'[A] simultaneous assignment and license back is valid, where, as in this case, it does not disrupt continuity of the products or services associated with a given mark. ... The assignment/license back had the beneficial effect of bringing commercial reality into congruence with customer perception that [the Winery] was controlling [Gallo Salame's] use.'[23]

Adequate quality control has also been found in the context of the assignment and licence back of a service mark.[24]

Licence Back Not Necessarily a Naked Licence

It has been held that the failure to make royalty payments as part of an assignment and licence back does not amount to a naked licence.[25] Even control by the licensee itself has been found sufficient to defeat a claim alleging the invalidity of an assignment and licence back arrangement.   6–61

'[R]eliance upon the integrity of a licensee is sufficient to fulfill the control requirement where a history of trouble-free manufacture provides a basis for such reliance.'[26]

There is nothing invalid *per se* about the licensing of a trade mark as part of an assignment and licence back arrangement. The question is whether the arrangement fails to meet the requirements for adequate quality control, or otherwise gives rise to a naked licence.[27] Thus, the general principles which govern quality control generally apply equally to an assignment and licence back arrangement.

Examples of the Licence being Held to be Invalid

Reported instances of such a licence being invalid on the grounds of inadequate quality control are rare. In one U.S. case, the court held, on unusual facts, that the assignment and licence back of a service mark in the banking industry contributed to the abandonment of the mark when the assignee holding company failed to show any interest in the mark.[28] In the main, however, the fact that the assignor/licensee continues to use the mark as before will overcome a claim of insufficient quality control.   6–62

Right to Sue

Under the Trade Marks Act 1938, an assignment and licence back arrangement could give rise to a problem in connection with the right to sue. This is because the registered user provisions set out the circumstances under which   6–63

---

[23] *Gallo, supra*, n. 10, at 1337–1338, quoting 1 J. McCarthy, para. 18:1 (I).
[24] *Visa, supra*, n. 10, at 1377.
[25] *Berkshire Fashions Inc. v. Sara Lee Corp.*, 14 U.S.P.Q. 2d 1124, 1127 (S.D.N.Y. 1990).
[26] *Syntex Laboratories, Inc. v. Norwich Pharmacal Co.*, 166 U.S.P.Q. 312, 320 (S.D.N.Y. 1970), affirmed on other grounds, 169 U.S.P.Q. 1 (2nd Cir. 1971).
[27] See, *supra*, paras. 6–43 to 6–47.
[28] *Intrawest Financial Corp. v. Western Nat. Bank*, 610 F. Supp. 950, 957 (D. Col. 1985).

either the proprietor, or the registered user, but not both, could sue for infringement.[29] Construing this section, it was held that a registered user could not be joined with the proprietor as a plaintiff.[30]

Suppose, however, that an assignment and licence back arrangement had been put in place, but that neither the assignment nor the registered user recordal had been entered onto the Register. In this situation, the beneficial and legal ownership of the trade mark may have been split. In one such case, the court apparently allowed the parties to the assignment and licence back agreement (both members of the same corporate family) to sue jointly for infringement. No challenge to the right of both parties to sue was made by the defendant.[31] It is arguable whether the result would have been different if the parties had been unrelated.

Under section 30(4) of the Trade Marks Act 1994, where the licensee brings infringement proceedings, the licensee may not proceed with the action, without the leave of court, unless the proprietor is either joined as a plaintiff or added as a defendant. A similar provision is contained in section 31(4) with respect to an action brought by the proprietor or the exclusive licensee for an infringement in respect of which the moving party has a concurrent right of action with the other.[32]

---

[29] Trade Marks Act 1938, s.28(3).
[30] See, *Levi Strauss, supra*, Chap. 4, para. 4–19.
[31] *Portakabin Ltd, supra*, n. 6. See also Chap. 4, paras. 4–07 to 4–18, for discussion of the licensee's right to sue under the Trade Marks Act 1994. The need to register the assignor as the licensee in an assignment and licence back situation still remains under the Trade Marks Act 1994.
[32] Trade Marks Act 1994, ss. 30(4), 31(4).

7. Trade Mark Rights and Distribution

INTRODUCTION

This chapter will discuss the nature of trade mark use by distributors. Not   **7–01**
every non-infringing use of a trade mark by a third party is by way of a
licence. The most common situation in which a non-licensed party may use
the mark is in connection with the distribution of the goods by a person,
such as a wholesaler, agent, importer, dealer or retailer, where the goods bear
the manufacturer's trade mark.[1] The distributor, as part of the chain of
distribution, may use the mark, or otherwise associate himself with it,
particularly in the advertising and promotion of the goods.[2]

DISTINGUISHING BETWEEN TRADE MARK LICENSING AND OTHER FORMS OF DISTRIBUTION

Trade mark licensing is only one form of distribution. From the point of view   **7–02**
of trade mark use, the distinction between licensing and other forms of
distribution may not be sharply drawn because of the variety of ways in
which the distribution of goods may be carried out. In one notable decision
of the European Commission, a manufacturer of shoes employed 'company
owned shops, franchisees, franchise-corner retailers, and tradition retailers'
to distribute its goods.[3] In each of the arrangements, there was use of the
trade mark in connection with the distribution of the goods.

The choice of which particular form of distribution to adopt will depend   **7–03**
upon a series of factors. The overriding concern is to find the arrangement
which allows the most effective distribution of the goods in the given
circumstances. Provided that the trade mark appears on the goods and is used
in the advertising and promotion of the goods in accordance with the
manufacturer's guidelines, the manufacturer may well not attribute much
importance to the legal question of how the use of the trade mark is
characterised.

---

[1] These various functions will be collectively referred to as 'distribution', and the person carrying
them out as a 'distributor,' unless a further distinction is required. This does not preclude the
distributor from applying his mark on the goods, if appropriate, to designate the source of
the distribution services. See, *infra*, para. 7–22.

[2] There are other third party uses of a mark, most notably by a contract manufacturer and
pursuant to a certification mark. These additional uses are discussed in Chap. 8.

[3] Korah, 'Franchising and the EEC Competition Rules,' p. 37, citing *Charles Jourdon* ([1989]
E.C. 94); [1989] 4 C.M.L.R. 591.

A Trade Mark Licence May Reflect Changes in the Distribution Relationship

7–04   The way in which the goods are distributed under the trade mark may also reflect changes in the relationship between the parties over time. The manufacturer may initially view the person solely as a distributor of goods supplied to it for sale under the manufacturer's mark. Later, the manufacturer's need for increased production capacity, which it may be unable to meet from its own resources, or which can be achieved more efficiently by encouraging production by third parties, may lead to the granting of a trade mark licence to the same person.

In a variation of this situation, a foreign manufacturer may intend to establish a local licensee to manufacture and distribute its goods, but the licensee will require a period of time in which to develop its manufacturing capacity. Until such capacity is established, the manufacturer will therefore make the goods available to the licensee for distribution, and the licensee will in effect function as a distributor for the goods in the territory.[4] The move to local production by means of licensing may not necessarily be voluntary. War-time conditions, or local manufacturing regulations, may require a foreign manufacture to authorise the person to manufacture and market the goods locally.[5]

Licensing as the First Option

7–05   Of course, the manufacturer may enter into a licence arrangement straightaway in order to expand production and marketing by taking advantage of the licensee's manufacturing and marketing capacity and capability, without having established any prior distribution relationship with the licensee. In such a situation, loyalties may not always be clear and unambiguous, due to the balance of commercial power between the licensor and licensee.

Judicial Uncertainty in Distinguishing between Distribution and a Licence Arrangement

7–06   This variety of circumstances underscores the fact that it is sometimes difficult clearly to identify and characterise the nature of trade mark use in the context of the distribution function. Occasionally, even the courts have not clearly recognised the difference between trade mark licensing and the use of the trade mark by a distributor.[6]

---

[4] In one case, the licensee's failure to commence manufacture following a period of distribution led to the termination of the licence agreement. As a result, the person could no longer serve as either a distributor or a licensee, despite having built up the market for the trade mark in the territory. *Mitchelstown Co-op v. Nestle* [1989] F.S.R. 353 (S. Ct. of Ireland).

[5] The *Bostrich* and *Manus* cases provide examples of situations where the war-time conditions forced the foreign manufacturer to change the relationship with its U.K. distributor. The respective courts differed in their understanding of whether the change of relationship in respect of the use of the trade mark gave rise to a licence. See *supra*, Chap. 3, paras. 3–08, 3–32.

[6] See, *e.g. Hurricane Fence Co. v. A–1 Hurricane Fence Co*, 208 U.S.P.Q. *314*, (S.D.Ala., 1979).

Licensing versus Distribution: The E.C. Dimension

The distinction between licensing and distribution also arises under the competition laws of the European Community. The presence of a trade mark licence determines whether the general competition laws, or a specific block exemption, apply to the arrangement, since only one characterisation may apply to a given agreement. This is because there is a block exemption to cover distribution arrangements, but no block exemption for a trade mark licence which makes up the major part of that agreement.[7]

7–07

Two Issues Raised in Distinguishing Between Licensing and Distribution

As a result the trade mark licensing may be inextricably intertwined with the distribution function, and the demarcation line between them may well be blurred. In distinguishing between licensing and other forms of distribution in respect of trade mark use, two main issues have arisen:

7–08

(a) What is the nature of distributor's use of the trade mark?
(b) If no licence relationship is created by the use of the trade mark by the distributor, can the distributor claim a right of proprietorship in the mark?

THE NATURE OF THE DISTRIBUTOR'S USE OF THE TRADE MARK

General Rule: Use of the Trade Mark by a Distributor is Permitted Without Licence

The general rule is that use of the trade mark by a distributor does not require the permission of the proprietor. A distributor will typically move goods bearing the trade mark of the manufacturer along the chain of distribution. The trade mark will have been applied to the goods by the manufacturer or by a third party under the manufacturer's control or instruction. The goods being distributed are the genuine goods of the manufacturer and bear a valid trade mark. No licence is required for the use of the mark by the distributor under such circumstances, and the lack of presence of quality control is therefore not relevant.[8]

7–09

---

[7] See, *infra*, Chap. 13, paras. 13–12 to 13–57 for further discussion of licensing under the E.C. competition law.

[8] This position was well-expressed under English law in the case of *Champagne Heidsieck v. Buxton* [1930] 1 Ch. 330. It was codified under s. 4(3)(a) of the Trade Marks Act 1938. See, *infra*, paras. 7–11 to 7–15 for further discussion. The same rule applies under U.S. law. See, *e.g. Star-Kist Foods, Inc. v. P.J. Rhodes & Co*, 227 U.S.P.Q. 44 (9th Cir. 1985).

Use of the Trade Mark by a Distributor was Permitted under Section 4(3)(a) of the Trade Marks Act 1938

7–10   The general rule was set out in section 4(3)(a) of the Trade Marks Act 1938, which provided that:

> '[t]he right to the use of a trade mark given by registration as aforesaid shall not be deemed to be infringed by the use of any such mark as aforesaid by any person – (a) in relation to goods connected in the course of trade with the proprietor or a registered user of the trade mark if, as to those goods or a bulk of which they form part, the proprietor or the registered user conforming to the permitted use had applied the trade mark and has not subsequently removed or obliterated it, or has at any time expressly or impliedly consented to the use of the trade mark.'

The effect of section 4(3)(a) was that use of a trade mark in the ordinary course of the distribution of goods, where the trade mark has been applied by the proprietor, was not an infringement.[9] In the words of Templeman L.J.:

> '... [B]y section 4(3)(a) of the Trade Marks Act 1938 there is no infringement where the trade mark is applied by the proprietor. The object of the section is to prevent the owner of the trade mark claiming infringement in respect of a product which he has produced and to which he has attached the trade mark.'[10]

7–11   This has also been explained in terms of the 'genuine articles' exception as follows:

> 'It has never been an infringement to use a registered trade mark in connection with what may for convenience be described as "the genuine article"; such use is not deceptive. Section 4(3)(a), which had no counterpart in the 1905 Act, now provides the relevant defence.'[11]

The Rationale for Section 4(3)(a)

7–12   The route by which section 4(3)(a) was included in the Trade Marks Act 1938 is noteworthy. Section 4(1) of the Trade Marks Act 1938 provides broadly that the proprietor of a trade mark enjoys the 'exclusive right to the use of a trade mark.' A trade mark is defined under section 68 of the Trade Marks Acts 1938 as a 'mark used or proposed to be used in relation to goods for the purpose of indicating, or so as to indicate, a connection in the course of trade between the goods and some other person.'

Construed literally, this might be understood to mean that *any* use of the trade mark by a distributor would be an act of infringement, since it could be deemed to indicate a connection in the course of trade between the distributor and the goods, rather than between the proprietor and the goods.

---

[9] *Work Manual* of the Trade Marks Registry, Chap. 27, Restriction of users, para. 27–4; Kerly, *Law of Trade Marks and Trade Names* (12th ed., 1986), para. 14–34.

[10] *Revlon, infra,* n. 37, at p. 116.

[11] *Accurist Watches Ltd v. King* [1992] F.S.R. 80, 85 (H.C.)

Section 4(3)(a) made it clear, however, that the distributor's use of a mark which has been applied by the proprietor is not an act of infringement.

Treatment under the Trades Marks Act 1994

The Trade Marks Act 1994 appears to address the issue of distributor's use   7–13
of a trade mark somewhat differently. After setting out the grounds for infringement in section 10, the new Act then states in subsection 10(8) as follows:

> 'Nothing in the preceding provisions of this section shall be construed as preventing the use of a registered trade mark by a person for the purpose of identifying goods or services as those of the proprietor. But any such use otherwise than in accordance with honest practices in industrial or commercial matters shall be treated as infringing the registered trade mark if the use without due cause takes unfair advantage of, or is detrimental to, the distinctive character or repute of the trade mark.'[12]

The provisions of this subsection would appear to include bona fide use of the mark by a distributor. The grant to this distributor is not, however, a blanket permission to use the mark in a way that exploits or does harm to the character or reputation of the mark. Like section 4(3)(a) of the Trade Marks Act 1938, section 10(6) of the Trade Marks Act 1994 can be understood as permitting the distributor to use a registered mark in carrying out its distribution function, and no infringement of the mark will be deemed to occur.

The Exclusion Applied to Advertising

The exclusion under section 4(3)(a) of Trade Marks Act 1938 also applied to   7–14
the distributor's use of the trade mark in advertising. Under section 4(1)(b) of the Trade Marks Act 1938, infringement would occur if the mark were used 'in an advertising circular or other advertisement', because such use is deemed to 'import a reference' to the proprietor of the trade mark.[13]

This prohibition against importing a reference could conceivably apply to use of a trade mark by a distributor in its advertising and promotion of the goods, even in the absence of any likelihood of deception. Under section 4(3)(a), however, there was no infringement when the distributor advertises the goods in the course of its normal distribution function.

Under the Trade Marks Act 1994, unauthorised use of a mark in advertising may give rise to infringement. Presumably, therefore, comparative advertising may be deemed an infringement under the Trade Marks Act 1944 in appropriate circumstances.[14]

---

[12] Trade Marks Act 1994, s.10(1).
[13] s.4(1)(b); Kerly, para. 14–27.
[14] See s.9(4)(d) of the Trade Marks Act 1994, which provides that use of a mark 'on business papers or in advertising' shall be subject to the infringement provisions of the Act. Unlike the Trade Marks Act 1938, however, it does not appear that there exists a separate test for infringement by way of use of the mark in advertising.

Express or Implied Consent

7–15   As noted above, section 4(3)(a) provided that use of a trade mark pursuant to the express or implied consent of the proprietor shall not be deemed an infringement.[15] Thus, consent also provides the basis for use of the trade mark by a distributor. Under different statutory language, at least one Canadian court has reached a similar result, suggesting that the distributor's use of the mark is sanctioned by virtue of the manufacturer's consent.[16] The claim has been raised particularly in connection with the matter of parallel importation.

ALTERATION OF THE GOODS BY THE DISTRIBUTOR

Acts of Alteration May Be Prohibited

7–16   The right of a distributor to use the trade mark may be restricted, particularly if the distributor can be said to have physically altered the goods in the process of distribution. Difficult questions will arise concerning whether such alteration is deemed to have severed the trade link between the goods and the manufacturer and the mark no longer serves the purpose of identifying the source of the goods or services as those of the proprietor or licensee.

Section 6 of the Trade Marks Act 1938 enables a claim of infringement to be brought against the distributor of goods for certain specified acts of alteration of the goods bearing the trade mark, or the alteration, obliteration or addition of marks or other writing to the goods.[17] The prohibited acts were set out in section 6(2)(a) of the Trade Marks Act 1938[18] and can be summarised as follows:

(a) Application of the trade mark to the goods after the goods have been altered.

(b) Alteration, partial removal or partial obliteration of the trade mark that is on the goods.

---

[15] See paras. 7–26 *et seq.*, which discuss the issue of exhaustion in connection with the use of the mark by a distributor, particularly in the context of parallel importation. See *infra*, Chap. 9, for discussion of consents more generally, and *infra*, paras. 10–04 and 10–05, for discussion of the contrast between a consent and formal licensing.

[16] *All Canada Vac Ltd v. Lindsay Manufacturing Inc.* (1990) 2 C.P.R. (3d) 385, 396; (upheld on appeal) 33 C.P.R. (3d) 285, where the court recognised 'the continuity of the transaction from manufacturer through distributor to ultimate consumer under the *sanctioned* use of the trade mark ...' (emphasis added). Under s.9(1) of the Trade Marks Act 1994, '[t]he proprietor of a registered trade mark has exclusive rights in the trade mark which are infringed by use of the trade mark in the United Kingdom *without his consent*' (emphasis added). See also section 10(5) of the Trade Marks Act 1994, which provides that the use of the trade mark in labelling, packaging, or on business papers, without authorisation, shall be deemed an infringement. Query whether the proprietor's consent may be implied as well as express, as provided in s.4(3)(a) of the Trade Marks Act 1938. See also, discussion, Chap. 9, regarding consents, and Chap. 11, regarding oral, implied and constructive licenses.

[17] There was no parallel s.6, including the prohibitions contained in s.6(2), with respect to service marks.

[18] These prohibitions have been criticised as contemplating infringement in circumstances where 'there may be no possibility of deception.' Kerly, para. 14–42.

(c) Removal or obliteration of the trade mark, in whole or in part, without also removing or obliterating completely any additional matter on the goods that serves to connect the proprietor with the goods.

(d) Application of any other trade mark to the goods.

(e) The addition of any other matter that is likely to injure the reputation of the trade mark.

The prohibitions provided under section 6(2) were subject to an important limitation, namely that infringement could not be alleged unless there was 'a contract in writing' explicitly imposing such restrictions on the user.[19] This requirement was seen by some as unduly restrictive of the manufacturer's rights under the section.[20]

Prohibition Against Alteration as an Exception to Exhaustion

It has been suggested that the adoption of Article 7(2) of the E.C. Trade   7–17
Marks Directive in connection with the exhaustion of rights will overcome the limitations of section 6 of the Trade Marks Act 1938.[21] That Article states as follows:

(1) The trade mark shall not entitle the proprietor to prohibit its use in relation to goods which have been put on the market in the Community under the trade mark by the proprietor or with his consent.

(2) Paragraph 1 shall not apply where there exist legitimate reasons for the proprietor to oppose further commercialisation of the goods, especially where the condition of the goods is changed or impaired after they have been put on the market.

With several slight changes, the text of Article 7 has been adopted in full in section 12 the Trade Marks Act 1994.[22] It can be expected that the courts will be called upon to interpret the meaning and scope of paragraph 2 of Article 7, as adopted in the Trade Marks Act 1994 with respect to the distributor's right of alteration. In this regard, the approach under U.S. law, as described below, may be instructive.

---

[19] Trade Marks Act 1938, s.6(1).

[20] See the White Paper, *supra*, Chap. 4, n. 1, para. 3–34 thereof, citing the view of the Mathys Committee, *British Trade Mark Law and Practice*, Cmnd. 5601 (1974), which suggested the easing of the requirement of a written contract to require only that written notice of the restriction be given.

[21] See the White Paper, *supra*, Chap. 4, n. 1, para. 3.36 thereof, which states that '[i]mplementation of paragraph (2) [of Article 7] will overcome the shortcomings of s.6 of the 1938 Act...'

[22] s.12 of the Trade Marks Act 1994 provides as follows:
   '(a) A registered trade mark is not infringed by the use of the trade mark in relation to goods which have been put on the market in the European Economic Area under that trade mark by the proprietor or with his consent.
   (b) Subsection (1) does not apply where there exist legitimate reasons for the proprietor to oppose further dealings in the goods (in particular, where the condition of the goods has been changed or impaired after they have been put on the market).'
   See paras. 7–26 to 7–29, for a further discussion of the application of the principle of exhaustion under the Trade Marks Act 1938.

The Approach Under U.S. Law

7–18 There is no specific provision under the Lanham Act that directly provides for infringement upon the occurrence of the acts described in section 6 of the Trade Marks Act 1938. The test applied under the Lanham Act is the general test for infringement, namely whether there is a likelihood of confusion in connection with the use of the trade mark by the distributor under such circumstances.[23]

The Right to Recondition

7–19 In the U.S. Supreme Court case of *Champion Spark Plug*,[24] it was held that reconditioned spark plugs sold under the original trade mark did not infringe, even if the product sold was inferior to the original product. The Court reasoned that:

> 'Inferiority is immaterial so long as the article is clearly and distinctively sold as repaired or reconditioned rather than as new ... [T]hat is wholly permissible so long as the manufacturer is not identified with the inferior qualities of the product resulting from the wear and tear or the reconditioning by the dealer. Full disclosure gives the manufacturer all the protection to which he is entitled.'[25]

Various lower court decisions have distinguished themselves from this judgment, and have found the sale of the altered goods bearing the trade mark of the plaintiff to constitute infringement when it would be a 'misnomer' to continue to call the goods by the original name.[26] For example, in one case, altered watches bearing the *Bulova* name were viewed as a 'new construction', so that they could no longer be deemed to be *Bulova* watches.[27]

Use of a Trade Mark in Advertising

7–20 Under U.S. law, an independent dealer may refer to the trade mark of the manufacturer in the promotion and sale of the goods. However, use of the trade mark must not represent that he is the authorised representative of the manufacturer, or is in any other way connected with the proprietor of the trade mark.[28]

Addition of Distributor's or Licensee's Trade Mark in Conjunction with the Proprietor's Trade Mark

7–21 The circumstances contemplated by sections 6(2)(d) and (e) of the Trade

---

[23] s. 32 and 43(a).

[24] *Champion Spark Plug Co. v. Sanders*, 331 U.S. 125 (1947).

[25] 331 U.S. 125 (1947) at 130. The Court relied on the basic rule, as expressed in the case of *Prestonettes, Inc. v. Coty*, 264 U.S. 359, 368 (1922) as follows: 'When the mark is used in a way that does not deceive the public we see no such sanctity in the word as to prevent its being used to tell the truth. It is not taboo.'

[26] The *Champion Spark Plug* case itself recognised this possibility. See 331 U.S. at 129.

[27] *Bulova Watch Co. v. Allerton Co.*, 328 F.2d 20 (7th Cir. 1964).

[28] *e.g. Bandag v. Al Bolser's Tire Stores, Inc.*, 750 F.2d 903 (Fed. Cir. 1984).

Marks Act 1938 raise the possibility that an additional mark to that of the licensed mark may be applied to the goods. There are two principal situations in which this may occur (a) the distributor applies its own mark; and (b) the licensee applies its own mark. The question is whether, under the infringement provisions of the Trade Marks Act 1994, such application of a third-party mark is prohibited.[29]

Distributor's Trade Mark

There is nothing to prevent the distributor from applying its own mark to the goods, particularly if the mark identifies the distribution service, as distinct from the goods being sold. The only restriction is that the distributor's mark must not infringe the manufacturer's mark. It is preferable that this issue be dealt with by contract in the distribution agreement.

7–22

The manufacturer should also take care that the distributor's trade name or company name does not include the manufacturer's mark, in whole or in a material part. For example, if the manufacturer's trade mark for the goods is *Fair Lady*, it should make certain that the distributor does not incorporate *Fair Lady* as part of its trade name or company name (such as 'Fair Lady Trading and Distribution'). The failure to adhere to this rule may lead to an undesirable dispute over the rights to the trade mark on termination of the distribution agreement, when the distributor may seek to continue to use a form of the mark as part of its company name or trade name.

Licensee's Trade Mark

This should be distinguished from the application of the licensee's mark on the licensed goods. The issue here is the simultaneous use of two marks of different ownership, belonging to the licensor and the licensee respectively, but where the licensee's use of the licensor's mark is subject to the quality control provisions of the licence. The test focuses on the likelihood of confusion, based on the form and manner in which the two marks are presented, as well as on any terms in the licence agreement.[30]

7–23

The GE Trade Mark Case

The leading judgment in this regard is the *GE T.M.* case.[31] There, a U.S. company licensed its housemark *GE* in rondel form to two subsidiaries in the United Kingdom. One subsidiary used the licensed mark in combination with its own trade mark (*Simplex*), while the other subsidiary used the licensed mark in a composite form (*Mono-GE-Gram*). The general rule regarding such side-by-side use of the marks was stated by Graham J. as follows:

7–24

'There is nothing inherently wrong in two trade marks having different

---

[29] Trade Marks Act 1994, s.10.
[30] See generally, Gault, 'A Reappraisal of the GE Trade Mark Case – Simultaneous Use of Trade Marks of Different Ownership' [1980] E.I.P.R. 343.
[31] See, *supra*, Chap. 3, n. 33.

connotations being used along side each other either under the Trade marks Act, or, it may be added, at common law, ... provided of course and so long as there is a proper connection in the course of trade between the proprietor or proprietors and the goods.'[32]

It could be argued that use of the mark in composite form (*Mono-GE-Gram*), is more problematic than use in combination with another mark (*Simplex GE*).[33] The precise nature of the relationship between the parties, the degree of quality control with respect to the licensed mark and the accompanying marking will all be relevant to the question of confusion when two such marks are used.[34]

7–25   Two examples of labelling may be instructive:

(a) Where Company X acquires Company Y, and Company Y applies the mark of Company X in addition to its own mark, the following labelling has been suggested:

'Manufactured by Company Y, proprietor of mark ABC and sold under licence from Company X, proprietor of mark DEF.'

(b) Where Company X licenses Company Y to manufacture and sell a product under a mark of Company X, and Company Y applies its own mark as well, the following labelling has been suggested:

'Manufactured under licence from Company X, proprietor of mark DEF, and sold by Company Y, proprietor of mark ABC.'[35]

THE DISTRIBUTOR'S RIGHT OF TRADE MARK USE UNDER THE EXHAUSTION PRINCIPLE

Exhaustion Principle Applied to Use of Mark by Parallel Importer-Distributor

7–26   It has already been noted that section 12(1) of the Trade Marks Act 1994 provides for the exhaustion of rights in the use of the mark in relation to goods put onto the market in the European Economic Area either by the proprietor or with his consent.[36] Even in the absence of any explicit statutory provisions under the Trade Marks Act 1938, the exhaustion principle has been recognised under domestic U.K. law.

A claim of exhaustion typically arises in a situation involving parallel importation from abroad outside the European Economic Area. The defendant

---

[32] *GE, supra*, Chap. 3, n. 33, at p. 463.

[33] This possible distinction was put forward *obiter* by Winn L.J. in *GE, supra*, Chap. 3, n. 33, at 384.

[34] If space does not permit explanatory marking on the product, a similar explanation of the ownership and use of the two marks might be included in the advertising and promotional literature. Care should be taken in all such markings and explanations.

[35] Adapted from Gault, *supra*, n. 39, at p. 345.

[36] See, *supra*, para. 7–17.

engaging in the parallel importation into the United Kingdom of the goods bearing the trade mark argues, in defence to a claim of infringement, that the proprietor or licensee (or the registered user under the Trade Marks Act 1938) has exhausted its rights in the mark.

Under the Trade Marks Act 1938, both limbs of section 4(3)(a) were held as supporting a claim of exhaustion, namely that (i) the proprietor had applied the goods in the course of trade, or (ii) there had been express or implied consent to the use of the mark. Unlike the application of section 4(3)(a) in connection with use of the trade mark by a domestic distributor in the normal course of trade, there was less unanimity on the application of section 4(3)(a) to the use of the mark by an importer engaging in parallel importation.

The Revlon Case: Section 4(3)(a) Given Broad Application Regarding Exhaustion

In the case of *Revlon Inc. v. Cripps & Lee Ltd*,[37] the Court of Appeal relied   7–27
on section 4(3)(a) in allowing the parallel importation of shampoo marked and manufactured abroad by the U.S. parent of the proprietor of the trade mark in the U.K. Buckley and Bridge L.JJ. concluded that while neither the proprietor of the U.K. trade mark nor, indeed, any of the affiliates involved in the manufacture and sale of the product, had applied the trade mark to the goods in question, the proprietor was deemed to have consented to use of the mark by virtue of the control exercised over the proprietor (and all other subsidiaries holding the mark in other countries) by the parent.

Templeman L.J. also held that due to the parent's control, the proprietor could be deemed to have applied the mark by virtue of the action of the parent. The mark had become an international housemark. In such a circumstance, '... section 4(3)(a) cannot be evaded by substituting the monkey for the organ-grinder'.[38]

Consent Disproved by Clear Marking to the Contrary on Imported Product

In a subsequent case involving a challenge to parallel importation, consent   7–28
under section 4(3)(a) of the Trade Marks Act 1938 was rejected in the face of marking to the contrary.[39] In particular, the court pointed to the terms of the licence agreement under which the Canadian licensee manufactured the products in Canada. The agreement unequivocally refused to extend the licensee's rights in the trade mark outside the territory of Canada. In addition, the containers of the motor oil product carried the following language:

'Manufactured in Canada under license from Castrol Limited. No license is granted or is to be implied by the sale or supply of this container under or in relation to any patent [,] trade mark or copyright of or

---

[37] [1980] F.S.R. 85.
[38] *Revlon* at 116. The result of the *Revlon* case, although not necessarily its reasoning, was followed in other jurisdictions. See, *e.g. Protective Mining & Industrial Equipment Systems (Pty.) v. Audiolens (Cape) (Pty) Ltd*, App. Ct., S.A., 1987(2) 961 (1987); *Winthrop Products Inc. v. Sun Ocean (M) SCN. BHD.* [1988] F.S.R. 430, H.C. Malaysia.
[39] In *Castrol Ltd v. Automobile Oil Supplies Ltd*, [1983] F.S.R. 315.

owned by Castrol Limited anywhere in the world outside Canada. Castrol, Castrol GTX and GTX are Canadian Registered Trade Marks Number 68/16,714, 170,225 and 172,326 respectively.'[40]

While this language was held to be effective in respect of imports from Canada, the potential efficacy of such a measure within the European Community must be evaluated under applicable E.C. law, which prohibits the use of licences to divide up various national markets within the Community.[41]

The Colgate Case: The Scope of Exhaustion is Narrowed

7–29   The broad scope accorded a distributor to engage in parallel importation under the Trade Marks Act 1938 was subsequently narrowed in the case of *Colgate Palmolive v. Markwell.*[42] The court in *Colgate* found that the parallel importation of toothpaste bearing the plaintiff's trade mark did not fall within the scope of section 4(3)(a) of the Trade Marks Act 1938. Both limbs of section 4(3)(a) were considered.

The court rejected a blanket conclusion that application of a trade mark to goods by the subsidiary is imputed to be an act of the parent. The court further concluded that consent could not be implied where the quality of the imported toothpaste differed materially from that of the domestic product.[43]

The Status of Parallel Importation Under U.S. Law

7–30   It is worthwhile to consider the issue of parallel imports under U.S. law. The status under U.S. law of a party engaging in parallel importation must be divided into two parts, customs law and trade mark law. The U.S. Supreme Court has ruled on the issue of parallel imports in connection with customs law. The status of parallel importation under the Lanham Act, however, has not been resolved by the Supreme Court.[44]

Parallel Importation Under the Customs Regulations

7–31   Under section 526 of the Tariff Act 1930, the U.S. Treasury Department implemented regulations regarding the importation of goods bearing a valid U.S. trade mark. Section 526 prohibited the importation into the U.S. of merchandise bearing a trade mark registered in the U.S. and owned by a U.S. entity, unless the importer had written consent from the trade mark proprietor.[45]

However, the Treasury Department promulgated regulations which carved

---

[40] [1983] F.S.R. at 321.

[41] See, *infra*, Chap. 13, para. 13–07. See generally, W. Rothnie, *Parallel Imports* (1993).

[42] (1989) R.P. (49).

[43] Such differences in quality could also be viewed as disproving the claim that the imported goods are genuine goods.

[44] *Infra*, Chap. 13, paras. 13–08 to 13–11, for application of the exhaustion doctrine regarding trade marks under the rules of the European Community.

[45] The section was enacted by Congress in response to an opinion by the Second Circuit Court of Appeal, which had denied a right of enforcement to a domestic distributor against the parallel importation of wine. *A. Bourjois & Co. v. Katzel*, 275 F. 53 (2nd Cir. 1921), rev'd, 260 U.S. 689 (1923).

out several exceptions to this provision. These exceptions sanctioned the parallel importation of goods bearing the same mark where: (a) the U.S. and foreign marks were owned by the same entity, or both trade mark proprietors were subject to common ownership or control, or (b) the foreign manufacturer applied the mark to the goods under the authorisation of the U.S. proprietor.

The Variety of Situations Involving Parallel Imports: The K Mart Case

The issue before the U.S. Supreme Court in the *K Mart* case[46] was whether   7–32 these exceptions were consistent with section 526. Three different basic factual situations which involved parallel importation were described by the court:

A The U.S. distributor, which is unrelated to the foreign manufacturer, obtains the right to register the trade mark in the U.S. and to distribute the manufacturer's goods there.

B The proprietor of the U.S. mark is an affiliate of the foreign manufacturer in one of three different circumstances:

  (1) The proprietor is a subsidiary of the foreign manufacturer and is established in order to distribute the manufacturer's goods in the U.S.

  (2) The proprietor of the U.S. mark establishes a foreign subsidiary to manufacture abroad for import back into the U.S. bearing the registered U.S. trade mark.

  (3) The proprietor of the U.S. mark establishes an unincorporated manufacturing division abroad for import back into the U.S. bearing the registered U.S. trade mark.

C The proprietor of the U.S. trade mark allows a foreign licensee to use the mark abroad, but the grant of the licence is conditional on the goods not being imported into the U.S.

Cases A and B(1) involve a U.S. distributor and a separate foreign manufacturer; Cases B(2) and B(3) concern a U.S. distributor where the goods are manufactured abroad by a related manufacturer.[47] Case C involves an arrangement where the goods are manufactured and marked by a foreign licensee, and are then distributed into the U.S. in an unauthorised fashion.

What is common to all of these situations is that there is a challenge by the parallel importer to the exclusive right of the U.S. trade mark proprietor to control distribution of the goods in the United States under the trade mark.

Prohibition of Parallel Import of Licensed Product Struck Down

The Supreme Court struck down the regulation which prohibited the pro-   7–33 prietor-licensor from preventing the import of the licensed goods by an unauthorised distributor (Case C). However, it upheld the regulations which permit the entry of goods manufactured abroad by the trade mark proprietor

---

[46] *K Mart v. Cartier Inc.*, 486 U.S. 281, 1988.
[47] Presumably manufacture could also be done by an unrelated third party.

or its affiliate, where both the U.S. and foreign trade marks are owned by the same person, or the respective trade mark proprietors are parent-subsidiary or are otherwise subject to common ownership or control (Cases B(1), (2) and (3)). The right of the distributor to prevent parallel importation in the circumstances in Case A when the parties are unrelated, which had originally given rise to the enactment of section 528, remains unchanged.

The result is that, under the Tariff Act 1930, the importation of goods manufactured abroad and bearing the same mark as a mark registered in the U.S., either in the name of a third party distributor or a licensor, may be prohibited. If, however, the domestic distributor is substantially related to the foreign manufacturer, the parallel importation may be permitted.[48]

Parallel Importation Under the Lanham Act

7–34   Under section 42 of the Lanham Act, the importation of merchandise which copies or simulates a registered trade mark is prohibited. In addition, section 32 of the Lanham Act prohibits a 'reproduction, counterfeit, or colorable imitation' of a trade mark that is likely to cause confusion of deception.

It has generally been held that neither provision applies to the parallel importation and sale of genuine goods bearing the genuine mark.[49] Thus, the test has become whether the goods being imported differ in a material or physical way from the goods being sold by the U.S. proprietor of the mark.[50] One court held that the importation of goods in a common control situation does not contravene the Lanham Act. Other courts, however, have included this test in the general question of whether the goods are genuine.[51]

Material differences in the goods include different warranties or ingredients for the local foreign market. In one case, the mere fact the 'adoption papers' of the imported Cabbage Patch dolls were in Spanish rather than in English was held to be sufficient.[52] The open ended nature of the test puts a burden on the parallel importer to be certain that the goods are identical in every respect. Otherwise, the importation could be prohibited, even if it might be construed to fall within an exception under the Customs regulations.

---

[48] More recently, in the case of *Lever Bros. Co. v. U.S.*, 796 F. Supp. 1 (D.D.C. 1992), the court ordered the Customs Service to prohibit foreign goods from entering the U.S. if they differed in a material way from those that are usually sold in the U.S. under the mark. In response, the Customs Service has proposed a new regulation that would implement this decision in a situation in which the U.S. and foreign trade mark proprietors are under common ownership or control. If the regulation is made final, it will not apply when the mark is owned both in the U.S. and abroad by the same party. 57 F.R. 28608.

[49] *Weil Cermaics and Glass Inc. v. Dash*, 11 U.S.P.Q. 2d 1001 (3rd Cir. 1989).

[50] See, *e.g.* Lever Bros. Co. v. U.S., 11 U.S.P.Q. 2d 1117, 1123 (D.C. Cir. 1989); *Original Appalachian Artworks, Inc. v. Granada Electronics, Inc.*, 2 U.S.P.Q. 2d 1343 (2nd Cir. 1987).

[51] *cf. NEC Electronics v. Cal Circuit ABCO*, 810 F.2d 1506 (9th Cir.), cert. denied, 481 U.S. 851 (1987) with *Lever Bros., supra*, n. 48.

[52] *Original Appalachian Artworks, supra*, at n. 50.

TREATMENT OF DISTRIBUTORS BEFORE THE REGISTRY

No Registration of Distributor as a Registered User Was Required

The status of trade mark use by a distributor arose in the context of the   7–35
registered user requirements. The approach of the Registry under the Trade
Marks Act 1938 was that the distributor should not normally have been
recorded as a registered user of a trade mark, because (a) use by the distributor
does not constitute use within the meaning of the Trade Marks Act 1938 and
(b) section 4(3)(a) of the Trade Marks Act 1938 provides that such use does
not infringe the trade mark rights of the manufacturer.[53]

Problems Raised in Registering a Distributor as a Registered User

Nevertheless, the Registry received applications from proprietors who, due to   7–36
an overabundance of caution, wished to record a distributor as a registered
user, and such applications were sometimes accepted.[54] There were, however,
several problems with sanctioning the recordal of a distributor as a registered
user.

Burden on the Registry

Such applications burden both the proprietor of the trade mark and the   7–37
Registry with the expense and effort of the unnecessary registration of a
distributor as a registered user.

Registration of Distributor May Be Construed as Necessary for Validity of the Mark

The registration of a distributor as a registered user might erroneously have   7–38
implied that a proprietor which did not register its distributors could put the
validity of its trade mark in jeopardy.[55] This was so, even though it became
generally accepted that the registered user requirements were permissive and
not mandatory.[56]

STATUS OF DISTRIBUTORS AS RELATED COMPANIES UNDER U.S. REGISTRATION PRACTICE

Under the practice of the U.S. Patent and Trademark Office, an applicant for   7–39
registration of a trade mark in the U.S. can base its claim of ownership either
on its own use of the mark, or on use by a related company.[57] Use by a

---

[53] Trade Marks Registry, *Work Manual*, Chap. 27, Registration of Users, para. 27–4.
[54] *Work Manual* s.27–4.
[55] *Work Manual* s.27–4.
[56] *Work Manual*, s.27–3. See also, *supra*, Chap. 3, paras. 3–04 to 3–13, for discussion on the permissive nature of registered user registration under the Trade Marks Act 1938. See also discussion *supra*, Chap. 4, paras. 4–41 to 4–42.
[57] See, *supra*, Chap. 5, for discussion of a related company under the Lanham Act.

related company includes both a parent-subsidiary relationship and a licence arrangement with a third party. It does not, however, include use of the mark by a distributor. 'A party that distributes goods bearing the mark of a manufacturer or producer [the goods being owned by that manufacturer or producer] . . . is neither the owner of the manufacturer's or producer's mark nor a related-company user.'[58]

Accordingly, for the use of the mark by the distributor to be viewed as consistent with the applicant's claim of proprietorship in the mark, it must be deemed as direct use by the applicant. This result is not affected by the addition onto the goods of wording such as 'Sold by . . .,' or 'Distributed by . . .' or 'Imported by'. All these additions are seen as being merely informative.[59] They do not change the fact that the use of the mark by the distributor is deemed to be direct use by the applicant.

CAN THE DISTRIBUTOR CLAIM PROPRIETORSHIP OF THE TRADE MARK?

Distinction Between Licensee and Distributor

7–40   The discussion above has focused on the nature of the distributor's rights of use of the trade mark. The other aspect of this issue is whether a distributor can obtain any right of proprietorship in the mark.

There is a sharp distinction between a licensee and a distributor with respect to the right of proprietorship of the trade mark. A licensee has no right to assert proprietorship in the trade mark.[60] In exchange for the right to use the trade mark free from threat of suit, and subject to the exercise of quality control, proprietorship of the mark belongs to the licensor. In the words of one court, '[c]ertainly, use of the trade name by the licensee builds no right in the licensee as against the licensor.'[61]

Manufacturer May Not Be Identified as the Source of the Goods

7–41   In a distribution situation, however, the matter of the proprietorship of the mark is not so simple drawn. Typically, despite the distributor's use of the trade mark, the distributor enjoys no claim of proprietorship thereof.[62] However, a distributor may, under appropriate circumstances, claim that it,

---

[58] *Trademark Manual of Examining Procedure* (2nd ed.) May 1993, U.S. Department of State, Patent and Trademarks Office ('TMEP'), para. 1201.05. See also para. 1201.06(a) ('Applicant is Merely Distributor or Importer') ('A distributor, importer or other distributing agent of the goods of a manufacturer or producer does not acquire right of ownership in the manufacturer's or producer's mark merely by moving the goods in trade.')
The TMEP is relied upon by trade mark examiners in the U.S. in examining applications, and indicates the current practice under U.S. trade mark registration practice.
[59] TMEP, para. 1201.05.
[60] *Sidewinder Trade Mark*, [1988] R.P.C. 261 at 269.
[61] *Pike v. Ruby Foo's Den, Inc.*, 232 F.2d 683, 685 (D.C. Cir. 1956).
[62] See, *supra*, paras. 7–10 to 7–25, for discussion of distributor's use of a trade mark in the normal course of distribution.

and not the manufacturer, is the proprietor of the mark. This occurs in a situation in which the distributor, in carrying out the distribution function, uses the trade mark in such a way that the public comes to identify the goods with it rather than with the manufacturer.

The distributor's claim of proprietorship may be particularly apt when the product is a new one, or the manufacturer is a foreign entity attempting to break into the domestic market, but it applies more generally whenever the commercial identity of a product can be attributed, at least in large part, to the efforts of the distributor. The trade mark might then be said to represent the sum total of the goodwill that the trade mark has acquired within the territory with respect to the goods. In such circumstances, the issue of the proprietorship of the mark may not be straightforward.

Circumstances in Which Distributor's Claim of Proprietorship May Be Raised

The question of the distributor's right of proprietorship of the trade mark will typically be raised in one of three situations: 7–42

(a) The manufacturer challenges the distributor's claim of proprietorship of the trade mark. This claim by the manufacturer occurs more often when a foreign manufacturer is involved, but it may also happen as well when both parties are local as in the *Hurricane Fence* and *Wrist Rocket* cases.[63] Here, the manufacturer does not apply for registration of the trade mark straightaway, and only later discovers that the distributor has, in the meantime, applied for registration of the trade mark in its own name.[64]

(b) The distributor may challenge the application for registration of the mark on behalf of the manufacturer.[65] Under both situations (a) and (b), the manufacturer-proprietor may seek to assert the existence of a licence arrangement in order to defeat the distributor's claim of proprietorship.

(c) A third party may challenge the distributor's proprietorship of the trade mark. The third party will typically be either a rival applicant for registration or an alleged infringer.[66]

---

[63] See, *e.g. Hurricane Fence, supra*, n. 6.; *Wrist-Rocket Mfg. Co., Inc. v. Saunders Archery Co.*, 183 U.S.P.Q. 17 C.D. Ncb. 1974.

[64] See, *e.g. Gynomin Trade Mark* [1961] R.P.C. 408. In that connection, s.60 of the Trade Marks Act 1994 adopted Art. 6 *septies* of the Paris Convention, which enables the overseas proprietor of a trade mark to take action (including refusal, cancellation or assignment) against a domestic agent or representative who attempts to register the mark in the U.K., within three years of becoming aware of the activity.

[65] *E.G. Omega Nutrition U.S.A. Inc. v. Spectrum Marketing Inc.*, 18 U.S.P.Q. 2d 1373 (N.D. Cal. 1991).

[66] *cf., e.g.* the results in *Implex Electrical Ltd v. Weinbaum*, 46 R.P.C. 13 (1928) with *Re Inescourt* 44 R.P.C. 405 (1927) decision. See generally, Lane, *The Status of Licensing Common Law Marks* (1991).

Foreign Manufacturer Can Obtain Goodwill through Domestic Distribution of the Product

7–43   In considering the possibility that the distributor may assert the right of proprietorship of the trade mark, it should be appreciated that a foreign manufacturer can acquire domestic goodwill in the trade mark, in addition to any foreign goodwill that it might enjoy, provided that the trade mark serves to identify the manufacturer as the source of the goods within the domestic territory. Thus, the import of foreign goods is no bar to the manufacturer's claim of proprietorship in the trade mark.[67] However, it is in this situation that the distributor may have the strongest claim of proprietorship in the mark, on the grounds that the trade mark has come to be identified with it, rather than with the manufacturer.

GENERAL GUIDELINES IN DETERMINING PROPRIETORSHIP OF TRADE MARKS BY DISTRIBUTORS

7–44   The question of proprietorship of a trade mark, as between a manufacturer and a distributor, will depend upon the particular facts of each case.[68] However, several general guidelines under U.K. law can be identified.

A Manufacturer Popularly Associated With The Goods

7–45   If one trader has become known to the public as the manufacturer of the goods, only slight evidence will be required to establish that the goodwill in the trade mark belongs to the manufacturer rather than the distributor.[69] Thus, in the *Gynomin* case, a former sales agent could not claim any right of proprietorship in the trade mark for registration purposes, when the pharmaceutical goods had clearly borne the house mark and name of the manufacturer for some time. The court went so far as to find that the former agent's application for trade mark registration amounted to fraud.[70]

In another case, *In re Warschauer*, the dealer-applicant had previously registered the same mark for the same goods, but had allowed the previous registration to lapse. The evidence indicated that the foreign manufacturer, and not the dealer, was identified with the goods, despite the lapsed registration in favour of the dealer.[71]

Exclusive Distributorship

7–46   A distributor's claim of proprietorship will lie only if the distributorship is

---

[67] *Implex Electrical, supra*, n. 66; *J. Lesquendieu's T.M.* [1934] 51 R.P.C. 273, 277; *Manus v. Fullwood & Bland* [1948] 65 R.P.C. 329, 338 (trial court).
[68] *In the Matter of Application No. 1253070 by Danish Specialities Ltd. to register Lady of Denmark* (Opposition No. 18417), 1989, p. 9 (unreported).
[69] See, Kerly, para. 2–21.
[70] *Gynomin Trade Mark, supra.*, n. 64.
[71] *Re Warschauer*, 43 R.P.C. 46 (1925).

exclusive. Firm evidence of an exclusive appointment is preferred.[72] However, the fact that an exclusive distributorship exists does not in itself confer proprietorship of the trade mark upon the distributor.[73]

Promptness in the Filing of the Application

Prompt measures by the manufacturer in seeking registration or in taking   7–47
other steps to protect the trade mark will support the manufacturer's claim of proprietorship. On the other hand, the manufacturer's failure to do so may support the distributor's claim of proprietorship.

In the *Karo Step*[74] decision, the distributor had used the trade mark for only four months prior to filing an application for registration. In contrast, in the *Diehl*[75] case, the court emphasised that the distributor had promoted the trade mark for seven years before the foreign manufacturer applied for application of the mark, and that the manufacturer had expressed no interest in the trade mark prior to that time. Even more remotely, the failure of the foreign manufacturer to apply for registration of the trade mark, despite over 50 years of use by the local entity, was held to amount to either an assignment or abandonment of its rights in the trade mark in the United Kingdom.[76]

Cumulative Efforts of the Distributor to Develop Local Goodwill

The cumulative efforts made by the distributor or importer to develop the   7–48
local goodwill of the trade mark will support the distributor's claim of proprietorship.

In the *Diehl* case, the importer had invested heavily in advertising, without any apparent participation or co-operation of the foreign manufacturer. In addition, the importer gave a year's guarantee, provided an after-sales service for the goods and was also the sole source of spare parts.[77] Furthermore, in the *Boot Tree* case, the court held, on a motion for an interlocutory injunction, that the promotional activities of the importer had raised a serious question regarding the importer's claim that it had acquired local reputation and goodwill in the trade mark.[78]

Identification of the Manufacturer on the Promotional Materials

The extent to which the promotional materials and the goods prominently   7–49
identify the foreign manufacturer will be considered in evaluating the manufacturer's claim of proprietorship.

In one case, the product was promoted with an emphasis upon the German

---

[72] *Diehl T.M.* [1970] R.P.C. 435, 443.
[73] *Inescourt, supra*, n. 66, at 19; *Karo Step T.M.* [1977] R.P.C. 255, 264 (Examiner).
[74] *Supra*, n. 83.
[75] *Supra*, n. 72, at 440–441.
[76] *Weston T.M.* [1968] R.P.C. 167.
[77] *Supra*, n. 72, at 438, 443.
[78] *Boot Tree Ltd v. Robinson* [1984] F.S.R. 545, 549–550.

manufacturer rather than the trade mark.[79] There were similar circumstances in the *Warschauer* case, where the primary identification indicated on the goods was of the German manufacturer.[80] More recently, in the *Danish Specialists* case, clear identification of both the manufacturer and the importer on the product label refuted the importer's claim that the trade mark did not serve as a manufacturer's mark.[81]

By contrast, in the *Diehl* case, while purchasers may have been aware that the goods were of German origin, the promotional materials did not specifically identify the German manufacturer.[82]

Consent to the Development of Reputation by the Distributor

7–50   Actions taken by the distributor or importer with the explicit or tacit consent of the manufacturer in connection with the development of the local reputation of the trade mark are more likely to contribute to the benefit of the distributor or importer.

Explicit Consent

7–51   Explicit consent, typically in the form of a written distribution agreement, may refer to a variety of activities to be carried out by the distributor or importer in connection with the trade mark. Most notably, provision may be made for the appointment of the distributor as the exclusive distributor, and there may be an undertaking to promote the marketing and sale of the goods without identifying the manufacturer. There are also instances in which the manufacturer assigns the registered trade mark to the distributor, and executes a simultaneous conditional reassignment document which will come into effect on termination of the distribution agreement.[83]

Tacit Consent

7–52   Tacit consent may be no more than another way of expressing the fact that the manufacturer has, due to inaction or silence, waived or acquiesced in favour of the distributor, or has abandoned its rights. The scope of the reliance on tacit consent to refute a manufacturer's claim of proprietorship is potentially broad.

In the *Weston* case, abandonment of the manufacturer's rights in the mark was found where the manufacturer had asserted no local rights in the mark over a 50-year period.[84] As a further example, it was held in the *Diehl* decision that the trade mark had been registered by the United Kingdom importer with the tacit consent of the manufacturer.[85] The complete lack of attention paid by the manufacturer to the importer's use of the trade mark in advertising

---

[79] *Karo Step, supra* n. 73, at 264, 270.
[80] *Supra,* n. 71.
[81] *Supra,* n. 68, at 13–14.
[82] *Supra,* n. 72, at 438–439.
[83] See, *infra,* para. 7–56, for conditional assignments under U.S. practice.
[84] *Supra,* n. 76.
[85] *Supra,* n. 72, at 444.

and promotion was construed as consent to the importer's acquisition of the local goodwill.[86] In a Canadian case, the court found that the U.S. company had allowed the local distributor to become identified as the source of the goods. Thus, whatever rights the manufacturer had once enjoyed in the mark had been lost to the distributor.[87]

Tacit Consent Refuted

However, an express provision to the contrary is likely to refute a claim of tacit consent. Thus, a distribution agreement which expressly states that (a) proprietorship in the mark belongs solely to the manufacturer, (b) the distributor shall acquire no right of proprietorship in the mark, (c) the distributor shall make no application for registration of the mark and that any such application shall be for the benefit of the manufacturer and (d) upon termination, the distributor or importer will cease all use of the mark except in accordance with the termination provisions of the agreement, will all support the manufacturer's claim of proprietorship.[88]   **7–53**

Further, an explicit provision prohibiting an importer from including the trade mark as part of its company name will strengthen the manufacturer's position, should the importer seek to claim proprietorship in the trade mark.

ADDITIONAL ASPECTS OF PROPRIETORSHIP UNDER U.S. PRACTICE

Additional aspects of the question of proprietorship of the trade mark in connection with use of the mark by a distributor can be identified under U.S. practice.   **7–54**

Proprietorship Is a Matter for Agreement Between the Parties

The question of proprietorship of a trade mark as between the manufacturer and an exclusive distributor is first and foremost a matter of agreement between the parties.[89] It has been stated that the agreement can either be in the form of an acknowledgement or of an assignment.[90]   **7–55**

The cases are not unanimous, however, on whether the assignment or acknowledgement is conclusive of the issue of proprietorship.[91] At least one court has found that the agreement of the parties is not conclusive, and that

---

[86] *Supra*, n. 72.

[87] *White Consolidated Industries, Inc. v. Beam of Canada* (Fed. Ct. 1991).

[88] See, *e.g. Diehl, supra,* n. 72, at 437.

[89] See, *e.g. Re George Ball, Inc.,* 153 U.S.P.Q. 2d 426 (TTAB 1967); *Omega Nutrition U.S.A.,* above; *International Armament Corporation v. Matra Manhurin International, Inc.,* 630 F. Supp. 741 (E.D. Va. 1986); *J. Atkins Holdings Ltd v. English Discounts Inc.,* 14 U.S.P.Q. 2d 1301 (S.D.N.Y.) (1990); *Premier Dental Products v. Darby Dental Supply Co.,* 794 F.2d 850 (3rd Cir. 1986); *Model Rectifier Corp. v. Takachito International, Inc.,* 220 U.S.P.Q. 508 (C.D. Cal.). aff'd 221 U.S.P.Q. 502 (9th Cir. 1983); *Far-Best Corp. v. Die Casting 'ID' Corp.,* 165 U.S.P.Q. 277 (TTAB 1970).

[90] *George Ball, supra,* n. 89, at 427.

[91] *cf. George Ball, supra,* n. 89, with *Premier Dental, supra,* n. 89.

evidence concerning public perception of which entity stands behind the trade mark may also be relevant.[92]

Conditional Assignment May Be Valid

7–56   A conditional assignment of the trade mark to the distributor, with a reassignment of rights to the manufacturer upon the termination of the distribution agreement, is valid.[93] The period of the assignment to the distributor does not have to be coterminous with the duration of the trade mark registration.[94]

Presumption in Favour of the Manufacturer in the Absence of Assignment of Acknowledgement

7–57   In the absence of an assignment or acknowledgement of the distributor's proprietorship of the trade mark, there is a presumption in favour of the manufacturer.[95] Under the practice of the U.S. Trademark Office, a distributor cannot claim proprietorship in the trade mark of the manufacturer if the distributor is 'merely ... moving the goods in trade', and the mark is assumed to belong to the manufacturer.[96] Notation on a product, to the effect that the goods have been produced by a foreign manufacturer, will tend to indicate that the local applicant is a mere importer or distributor.[97]

Presumption of Proprietorship by the Manufacturer May be Rebutted

7–58   The presumption of proprietorship in favour of the manufacturer may, however, be rebutted by the distributor. Various factors will be considered in determining whether the distributor's claim is valid.

In a leading case, *Wrist-Rocket*, the court identified two sets of circumstances under which a distributor might be able to claim the right of proprietorship in the trade mark.[98] In the one, the distributor orders the manufacture of the goods or controls their production. In the other, the goods pass through the distributor in the course of trade and the distributor gives the goods the benefit of his reputation.[99]

---

[92] *Premier Dental, supra*, n. 89, at 854.
[93] See, *e.g. Scandanavia Belting Co. v. Asbestos & Rubber Works*, 257 F. 937 (2d Cir, 1919); *George J. Ball, supra*, n. 89; *Premier Dental Products, supra*, n. 89; *International Armament, supra*, n. 89.
[94] *George Ball, supra*, n. 89.
[95] See, *e.g. Ilapak* BNA (42) 97 (1991); *Far-Best Corp. v. Die Casting 'ID' Corp., supra*, n. 89; *Spencer v. VDO Instruments Ltd*, 142 U.S.P.Q. 72 (DC Mich. 1964); *Shaver v. Heller & Merz Co.*, 108 F. 821 (8th Cir. 1901); *Paul v. Woods*, 40 F.2d 668 (DC NY 1930).
[96] TMEP, para. 1201.06(a).
[97] TMEP, para. 1201.06(b).
[98] *Wrist-Rocket, supra*, n. 63, at 22.
[99] *Wrist Rocket, supra*, n. 63, citing *Electronic Communications Inc. v. Electronic Components for Industry Co.*, 443 F.2d 487, 492, 170 U.S.P.Q. 118, 122 (8th Cir.), cert. denied, 404 US 833.

Factors to be Considered in Determining Proprietorship

The court in the *Wrist-Rocket* case identified the following questions as   7–59
relevant to a determination of the issue of proprietorship.

(a)Which party invented and first affixed the trade mark on the product?
(b) Which party designed and adopted the label?
(c) Which party's name appeared together with the trade mark?
(d) Which party maintained the quality and uniformity of the product?
(e) With whom does the public identify the goods and to whom does it
    turn for warranty work and complaints?[1]

Application of the Test for Proprietorship

There is no single formula for the application of these elements. For example,   7–60
in the *Omega* case, the court found *all* of the factors to be in favour of the
distributor's claim of proprietorship. There, the distributor had created the
mark (although mere invention of the mark, without use, is not likely to be
significant), had used the mark for the life of the distribution agreement solely
in conjunction with its own name and had exercised a major role in
maintaining the quality control of the product. The court noted that none of
these factors was on its own conclusive but found in favour of the distributor
overall.[2]

Compare that with the situation in the *Ilapak* case in which the manufacturer
produces a 'core' machine, and then further modifies it in accordance with
customer specifications furnished by the distributor. In such a situation, the
court found that the public identified the product with the manufacturer and
the distributor's claim of proprietorship of the mark was accordingly rejected.[3]

CONTRACTUAL UNDERTAKINGS BY THE DISTRIBUTOR

As we have seen, trade mark rights in a distribution situation can give rise to   7–61
various trade mark issues, both in connection with the use of the trade mark
and with its ownership. Because of this, a distribution agreement will typically
contain provisions relating to the trade mark which will affect both the
manufacturer and the distributor.

Contractual Undertakings of the Distributor

The distributor may make one or more of the following undertakings in the   7–62
distribution agreement with respect to its use of the trade mark:

(a) To acknowledge the manufacturer's exclusive ownership of the trade
    mark and all the rights thereunder, and to declare that it shall acquire

---

[1] *Wrist-Rocket, supra,* n. 63, at 26. These factors were cited with approval by the *Omega Nutrition* court, *supra,* n. 89, at 1376.
[2] *Omega, supra,* n. 89, at 1376.
[3] *Ilapak, supra,* n. 95.

no rights in the mark by virtue of its use in connection with the distribution of the goods.

(b) Not to file an application for the registration of the same or a similar trade mark, and to undertake to assign to the manufacturer any such rights if an application for registration is filed.

(c) To co-operate with the manufacturer in obtaining registration of the trade mark.

(d) Not to challenge the exclusive rights of the manufacturer in the trade mark.

(e) Except as otherwise permitted in connection with the distributor's own mark, to sell the manufacturer's goods only under the trade mark.

(f) Not to use any other identical or similar trade mark in connection with the distribution of the goods.

(g) Not to incorporate the trade mark in whole or in material part in its company name or trade name.

(h) Not to materially alter the goods bearing the trade mark, unless otherwise specifically permitted under the distribution agreement.

(i) To submit for the review of the manufacturer the distributor's advertising and promotional material.

(j) To report any infringing third party use of the trade mark and to co-operate with the proprietor in prosecuting any such infringer.

Contractual Undertakings by the Manufacturer

7–63 The manufacturer, for its part, may undertake the following with respect to use of the trade mark by the distributor.

(a) To seek registration of the trade mark and to maintain the registration in effect.

(b) To defend the trade mark against third party infringement.

(c) To defend and hold the distributor harmless in connection with any action brought against the distributor by a third party in connection with the use of trade mark.

(d) To provide for the sell-off, repurchase or transfer of remaining goods bearing the trade mark on termination of the distribution agreement.

7–64 The extent to which these provisions will be included in the particular distribution agreement will depend on all the circumstances of the arrangement, including in particular the relative commercial strengths of the parties involved.

8. Other Authorised Third Party Uses of a Trade Mark

TRADE MARK USE BY A CONTRACT MANUFACTURER

The Contract Manufacturer's Position in the Product Cycle

Trade mark use by a distributor represents the end of the product and **8–01**
marketing cycle. As we have seen, such use does not usually give rise to a
licence relationship between the manufacturer and distributor.[1] There may
also be use of the trade mark by a third party at the outset of the product
cycle, namely when the product is manufactured in accordance with the
specifications of the trade mark owner. It has long been accepted that a trade
mark need not designate the actual physical source of manufacture of the
goods. It is sufficient that the proprietor has merely selected or ordered the
goods manufactured by a third party, which affixes the proprietor's mark to
them. Here, as well, such authorised third-party use of the trade mark,
popularly known as 'contract manufacturing,' does not give rise to a trade
mark licence.

Contract Manufacturing Not a New Phenomenon

The contract manufacturer is hardly a new phenomenon. By the turn of the **8–02**
last century, goods were commonly being made to order for sale under the
trade mark or name of a party other than the manufacturer.[2]

In finding that a dealer in flour had the right of proprietorship of a trade
mark, the United States Supreme Court stated more than a century ago that:

> 'The brand did not indicate by whom the flour was manufactured, but
> it did indicate the origin of its selection and classification.'[3]

More recently, the court in the *Bostitch* case described the possibilities
available to a trade mark proprietor with respect to the manufacture of the
goods as follows:

---

[1] See, Chap. 7, paras. 7–10 to 7–39.
[2] See, *e.g. J. Defries*, 23 R.P.C. 341, 343 (1906). 'You would revolutionise the whole state of
trade if a man who made anything to special order would be entitled to stop another man
selling goods under his own name.' See also the Trade Marks Act 1905, s. 1, where a trade
mark was defined as a 'mark used or proposed to be used upon or in connection with goods
for the purpose of indicating that they are the goods of the proprietor of such mark by virtue
of manufacture, selection, certification, dealing with, or offering for sale.'
[3] *Menendez v. Holt*, 128 U.S. 514, 52 (1888). See also the discussion on the anonymous source
function of trade marks, *supra*, Chap. 2, para. 2–16.

153

'There is nothing in the Trade Marks Act, or in the principles of trade mark law which have been developed thereunder, which requires a proprietor of a registered trade mark to refrain from introducing modifications or variations in the goods to which he applies his mark or in the manner in which they reach the market. If he should find it convenient to transfer manufacture from one locality to another, to procure his supplies from sub-contractors, or arrange for assembly of completed articles by someone of his choice in lieu of doing it himself, these and a vast number of other changes in procedure are his sole concern.'[4]

Scope of Contract Manufacturing

8–03 The diversity of contract manufacturing can be seen by considering the following situations.

The development of modern mass retailing has witnessed the rise of the house mark on goods manufactured by third parties. Indeed, the trade mark proprietor may not be involved in the manufacture of the goods at all; all of its goods may be manufactured for it by third party manufacturers. Here, the trade mark comes to be identified with a certain level of quality for a variety of goods emanating from a single retail source, despite the fact that the goods are made by outside manufacturers.

It is also possible that goods made by the same manufacturer will be sold under several trade marks, each of which is owned by a different proprietor. As has been observed, 'western consumers do not care where the insides of their latest gadget are made as long as there is a nice familiar name, like IBM, on the case.'[5] The contract manufacturer may well be located in a foreign country. Indeed, the international dimension of contract manufacturing has become the norm for certain industries.[6] As a result contract manufacturing has become a frequently encountered relationship in which one party manufactures goods for another.

The Contract Manufacturer's Rights with Respect to the Trade Mark

8–04 In each of the situations outlined above, the question may be asked: What right, if any, does the contract manufacturer gain in connection with the use of the trade mark?

The contract manufacturer does not act as a licensee of the mark. It is not engaged in the trading of the goods in such a way that a connection is created by the mark between the contract manufacturer and the goods. The contract manufacturer's relationship with the goods is limited to their manufacturer.

---

[4] [1963] R.P.C. at 197.
[5] *The Economist*, 'Survey: Asia's Emerging Economies' 321, No. 7733, p. 20, November 16–22, 1991.
[6] For example, 'four-fifths of the pocket calculators bearing [a well-known] brand are made by ... a Taiwanese company which is the world's biggest maker of pocket calculators.' *The Economist, supra,* n. 5.

Thus, no connection in the course of trade warranting the registration of the contract manufacture as a registered user is created.[7]

The first edition of the U.S. Trademark Examination Manual well-expressed the principle that a contract manufacturer is not a 'related company.' It stated that when the applicant for trade mark registration 'contracts with another party to have goods produced for applicant by the other party and instructs said party to place a mark on the goods for applicant, that is the equivalent of applicant itself applying the mark on its own goods ...'[8] In such circumstances, the contract manufacturer will not come to be identified by the public with the mark in the course of trade.

The Contract Manufacturer Mistakenly Described as a Licensee

Nevertheless, courts have on occasion mistakenly characterised a contract manufacturer as a licensee. Thus, one court has held that '[w]hen a dealer buys goods from a manufacturer and orders the manufacturer to place its mark on the product prior to delivery, then the manufacturer is at best acting as a licensee of the dealer.'[9] In another decision, the *Wrist-Rocket* case, it was held that the use of the trade mark by a manufacturer amounted to the grant of a licence, even if only an implied licence, where the dealer directed both the production of the goods and the application of the mark.[10]

8–05

This mischaracterisation of a contract manufacturer as a licensee is not surprising. The contract manufacturer appears to apply the mark to the goods, and the proprietor of the mark will probably exercise some sort of quality control with respect to the goods. In the eyes of some courts, this is apparently sufficient to create a licence relationship.[11]

The Nature of Trade Mark Use by a Contract Manufacturer: The Accurist Watches Case

However, the characterisation of the contract manufacturer as a licensee is almost certainly incorrect. As the contract manufacturer does not use the trade mark in a way that identifies it with the goods in the course of trade, the conditions which give rise to a licensing relationship are not present, despite the fact that the contract manufacturer may affix the mark to the goods and be subject to quality control with respect to the goods.

8–06

This can be seen from a consideration of the case of *Accurist Watches Ltd*

---

[7] See *Accurist Watches Ltd. v. King*, (1992) F.S.R. 80, holding that the sale of goods by the contract manufacturer marked pursuant to the instructions of the registered user under the provisions of the Trade Marks Act 1938 does not constitute infringement.

[8] U.S. Trademark Manual, U.S. Department of Commerce, Patent and Trademark Office (1st ed.), s. 1201.08(c). See also the observation made in para. 37 of the recent judgment of the European Court of Justice in *IHT Internationale GmbH v. Ideal-Standard GmbH*. C–9/93 (June 22, 1994), that 'the origin which the trade mark is intended to guarantee is the same: it is not defined by reference to the manufacturer but by reference to the point of control of manufacture.'

[9] *Aveda Corp. v. Evita Marketing Inc.* 12 U.S.P.Q. 2d 1902, 1097 (D. Minn. 1989).

[10] *Wrist-Rocket Mfg. Co. Inc. v. Saunders Archery Co.*, 183 U.S.P.Q. 16, 25 (D. Neb. 1974).

[11] See *supra*, Chap. 3, para. 3–23, regarding the confusion that sometimes has arisen in distinguishing between direct and licensed use of a mark.

v. King[12]. The issue was whether infringement occurred when the contract manufacturer (i) made watches to the order and subject to the specifications of the registered user of the mark, (ii) affixed the mark to the watches, (iii) shipped the goods to the registered user subject to a reservation of title provision, (iv) repossessed the goods when the registered user failed to make payment, and (v) then sold the watches bearing the registered mark.

The defendants argued that, under section 4(3)(a) of the Trade Marks Act 1938, their actions did not constitute infringement.[13] In ruling in favour of the defendants that no infringement had taken place, the court addressed two major questions.

Was the Representation Made by the Trade Mark True?

8–07 First, was the sale of the watches by the contract manufacturer bearing the trade mark of the proprietor a true representation? The court held that it was. The use of the mark on the watches indicated a connection in the course of trade between the goods and the registered user, and the goods were genuine. In the words of the court, the trade mark '... represented to the public that they were genuine *Bueche-Girod* watches, that is to say they were the goods of the English company by reason of their manufacture or selection.'[14]

The court rejected the argument that because of the retention of title clause (or other form of security), the registered user never legally obtained title to the goods, and therefore, no connection in the course of trade had been established. The court noted that if this position were correct, it would do great harm to commercial life by destroying the effectiveness of retention of title clauses and other forms of security.[15] By accepting the watches from the contract manufacturer, the registered user had obtained a right to market the goods, which was a sufficient connection in the course of trade.

The court emphasised that the parties had acted in accordance with the terms of the contractual arrangements between them. Thus, it was noted that '... a registered user may have the components made by one company, assembled by another, the trade mark affixed by a third and the goods marketed by a fourth.'[16] The court also observed that the acceptance of the goods by the registered user satisfied the 'purchase' requirement, whereby the goods could be distributed in the U.K. under the trade mark only if they were 'purchased' by the registered user.[17]

---

[12] [1992] F.S.R. 80. The action was brought under R.S.C., Ord. 14A for the determination of the point of law as to whether the defendants had a statutory defence to the action.
[13] See, *supra*, Chap. 7, paras. 7–11 to 7–15, for discussion of s. 4(3)(a) of the Trade Marks Act 1938 to a claim of infringement.
[14] *Accurist Watches, supra*, n. 7, at 86.
[15] *Accurist Watches, supra*, n. 7, at 87.
[16] *Accurist Watches, supra*, n. 7, at 88.
[17] *Accurist Watches, supra*, n. 7, at 89–90.

Was the Mark Applied in Accordance with the Permitted Use?

Secondly, the court held that the mark had been applied by the contract 8–08
manufacturer in accordance with the terms of the registered user registration.
The court's words are also instructive on this issue:

> 'In most cases a trade mark is applied not by the registered proprietor
> or the registered user but by a packager, printer, bottler or canner. In
> my judgment, that is enough. This is an obvious situation where the
> Latin tag *qui facit per alium facit per se* applies.'[18]

Consent to Use of the Mark by the Contract Manufacturer

Alternatively, the registered user was deemed to have consented to the use of 8–09
the trade mark by the contract manufacturer when it entered into the supply
contract. The court reasoned that the right of the contract manufacturer to
sell the goods bearing the trade mark under, in general, and the reservation
of title provision, in particular, was expressly authorised under the contract.
Under such circumstances, the consent of the registered user would be
implied.[19]

Compare this result with the situation in which the contract manufacturer
seeks to sell-off the remaining goods which it had manufactured pursuant to
an agreement. At least one court in the U.S. has held that under the
circumstances, a contractual term in favour of such a right of sale by the
contract manufacturer would be implied.[20] Of course, if the sale of the goods
by the contract manufacturer breached the agreement between the parties, no
consent could successfully be asserted.

*Application of these Principals to a Direct Relationship Between the Proprietor
and the Contract Manufacturer*

While the *Accurist Watches* case involved the manufacture of the goods 8–10
pursuant to the instructions of a registered user, the principles in the case
apply equally where there is a direct relationship between the proprietor of
the trade mark and the contract manufacturer. The key is that the mark
identifies a connection in the course of trade between the proprietor and the
goods, and the contract manufacturer has affixed the mark in accordance
with the instructions of the registered proprietor of the mark, or an authorised
licensee. Thus, as long as the mark identifies a connection in the course of
trade between the proprietor and the goods, and the contract manufacturer
affixed the mark pursuant to the agreement or with the consent of the
proprietor, the sale of the goods by the contract manufacturer under circumstances such as those described in the *Accurist Watches* case will be
permitted.

---

[18] *Accurist Watches*, *supra*, n. 7, at 89.
[19] *Accurist Watches*, *supra*, n. 7, at 90. See *infra*, Chap. 9, regarding consents.
[20] *Woodcutters Manufacturing, Inc. v. Eagle Picher Industries*, 215 U.S.P.Q. 1033, 1043 (W.D.
Mich. 1982).

Contract Manufacturer as Proprietor of the Trade Mark

8–11   Unlike the situation involving the use of a trade mark by a distributor,[21] it is difficult to imagine a set of circumstances under which the contract manufacturer will be in a position to use the mark in a manner that will create an identification in the course of trade between it and the goods. This is the case even if the name of the manufacturer appears on the goods, since the goods will have been selected by the proprietor and the mark will be affixed upon the goods on his instructions.

This can be seen in the decision reached in the U.S. case of *Avakoff v. Southern Pacific Co.*[22] There, the court held that the mere transportation of goods by the manufacturer to the applicant was not a bona fide use of the trade mark. The court reasoned that the shipment:

> '... was purely a delivery of the goods to the applicant from the manufacturer ... That is, it was a shipment of the goods in preparation for offering the goods for sale. It did not make the goods available to the purchasing public.'[23]

This underlines once again that trade mark rights are concerned with commercial identity rather than with the actual source of manufacture of the goods. The fact that a contract manufacturer makes the goods, applies the trade mark to them on the instructions of the trade mark proprietor and then transports the goods, is insufficient, even taken together, to bring a successful claim that the mark has come to indicate a connection in the course of trade between the contract manufacturers and the goods.

Sale by the Manufacturer: The El Greco Problem

8–12   What about the situation in which the trade mark proprietor rejects delivery of trade marked goods from the manufacturer, perhaps because of late delivery or because of a change of plan by the trade mark proprietor, and the manufacturer then sells the goods without authorisation? In the event that the contract between the parties is silent on the matter, the question that has been considered by several U.S. courts is under what circumstances the goods sold by the manufacturer will not be deemed 'genuine', thereby giving rise to a claim of infringement.

The El Greco Case

8–13   The leading decision in favour of a narrow definition of genuine goods, *i.e.* that an infringement has occurred when the goods are subsequently sold, is the *El Greco Leather Products* case.[24] The contract manufacturer in that case produced shoes for the trade mark proprietor. Shipment of the shoes by the manufacturer was subject to inspection to ensure that the goods satisfied

---

[21] See Chap. 7, para. 7–42 *et seq.*
[22] 226 U.S.P.Q. 435 (Fed. Cir. 1985).
[23] Avakoff, *supra*, n. 22, at 436.
[24] 1 U.S.P.Q. 2d 1016 (2d Cir. 1986), reversing 224 U.S.P.Q. 921 (E.D.N.Y. 1984).

the proprietor's specifications and quality control standards. The contract manufacturer apparently received a fixed price per pair of shoes upon approval and delivery. Two lots of shoes were cancelled without any inspection having taken place. Those shoes, bearing the trade mark, were subsequently distributed through intermediaries.

Goods Found Not To Be Genuine

The majority of the U.S. court of appeal, overruling the lower court, found that the failure to obtain approval upon inspection meant that the shoes were not genuine. The inspection and approval of the shoes 'were an integral part of the appellant's effort at quality control.'[25] Accordingly, the subsequent sale of the shoes constituted trade mark infringement.

Burden on Contract Manufacturer to Prove Genuine Goods

The court of appeal emphasised that the burden was on the contract manufacturer to ensure that the sale of the rejected lots did not infringe the proprietor's rights in the trade mark. In so ruling, the court of appeal rejected the position of the trial court that the proprietor of the trade mark had a duty to expressly provide for how such rejected goods are to be disposed by the contract manufacturer. In particular, the contract manufacturer, in order to avoid an infringement action, should have taken the following steps:

(a) Removed the trade mark from the goods (as was customary in the industry);
(b) Afforded the proprietor an opportunity to inspect the goods and certify their quality, or sought instructions from the proprietor on how to dispose of the goods.[26]

A Broader Notion of Genuine Goods

The dissent took issue with the conclusion of the majority. It found that: 8–14

'[a]s long as the goods are manufactured under the direction of the trademark owner, bear the trademark registered and issued by the trademark owner, and are not of an inferior quality, the products are considered genuine. It is not necessary to a finding of genuineness that the goods be distributed with the trademark holder's express authorisation.'[27]

The Line is Not Easily Drawn

This minority view in the *El Greco* case has been echoed in other decisions.[28]   8–15

---

[25] 1 U.S.P.Q. at 1018.
[26] 1 U.S.P.Q. 2d at 1018. *cf.* with *Diamond Supply Co. v. Prudential Paper Products Co.*, 223 U.S.P.Q. 869 (S.D.N.Y. 1984), where the trade mark proprietor waived its right by explicitly instructing the contract manufacturer that it 'did not care' how the goods were disposed of.
[27] 1 U.S.P.Q. 2d at 1020.
[28] *Diamond Supply, supra*, n. 26, *Monte Carlo Shirt Co., Inc. v. Daewoo International (America) Corp.*, 707 F.2d 1054 (9th Cir. 1982).

Indeed, the line between the majority and minority views in the *El Greco* case is not easily drawn. The same court of appeal in a later case held that 'the unauthorised sale of a trademarked article does not, without more, constitute a Lanham Act violation.'[29] The test is always likelihood of confusion, although how confusion is defined under the circumstances is not always consistent.

The El Greco Problem – Pay Attention to Contractual Provisions

8–16   Given the uncertainty of these decisions, the lesson to be learned from the *El Greco* case is that a prudent manufacturer should consider providing in the manufacturing contract for the conditions under which the contract manufacturer may dispose of trademarked goods which are supplied to the proprietor. At the very least, the contract manufacturer should seek to obtain a waiver from the proprietor regarding the disposal of goods which have not been delivered.

A Different Role for Quality Control?

8–17   The role of quality control in the *El Greco* court's analysis should be carefully noted. There was no claim that the manufacturer was a trade mark licensee. Nevertheless, the court found support for its view of quality control in the case law on licensing.[30] Quality control, in the sense of precise adherence to the manufacturing guidelines of the trade mark proprietor, was deemed to be crucial. The failure to adhere to the quality control requirements resulted in a likelihood of confusion over the source of the goods sold by the manufacturer.

Quality Control in Distribution

Quality control in the sense suggested by the *El Greco* court has also been relied upon to prevent the sale of goods where the product requires strict quality control during the distribution process. In one case, the fact that the distributor sold the beer without keeping it refrigerated during the 2,000 mile shipment gave rise to a claim of infringement. The beer was no longer genuine.[31] A similar result was reached in another case where oil was resold, without providing for proper storage.[32]

---

[29] *H.L. Haydon Co. of N.Y. v. Siemens Medical Systems*, 879 F.2d 1005, 1029 (2d Cir. 1989). In this case, the unauthorised sale of x-ray equipment by a terminated distributor did not amount to infringement under the Lanham Act, so long as the distributor did not hold itself to be part of the plaintiff's authorised sales network.

[30] 1 U.S.P.Q. 2d at 1019.

[31] *Adolf Coors Co. v. A. Genderson & Sons, Inc.*, 486 F. Supp 131 (D. Col. 1980).

[32] *Shell Oil Co. v. Commercial Petroleum, Inc.*, 928 F.2d 104 (4th Cir. 1991).

CERTIFICATION MARKS

Certification Mark Certifies Quality of the Goods

Certification Mark Under U.K. Law

Another instance in which there is third party use of a trade mark is in **8–18**
relation to a certification mark. A certification mark is used to indicate that
the goods have been certified by the proprietor of the mark in respect
of origin, material, method of manufacture, quality, accuracy or other
characteristics. A certification mark must be adapted to distinguish the goods
which it certifies.

Under the Trade Marks Act 1938, an application for registration of a
certification mark was principally governed by section 37 and Schedule 1. In
particular, subparagraph 1(4) of the Schedule 1 required that regulations
governing the use of the mark by the certified party be submitted to the
Registrar. Certain matters were reserved for consideration by the Board of
Trade, namely whether the proprietor is competent to certify the goods;
whether such registration is to the public advantage; and whether the regulations governing the use of the mark are satisfactory. Also, there was a
provision for application to the Board of Trade with respect to expungement
or variation of the registration. Application for registration of a certification
mark was apparently rarely made under the Trade Marks Act 1938.[33] There
was no corresponding provision for certification of services.

A certification mark is defined under subsection 50(1) of the Trade Marks **8–19**
Act 1994 in a manner similar to the definition contained in subsection 37(1)
of the Trade Marks Act 1938.[34] Registration of certification marks extends to
both trade marks and service marks.

The registration of certification marks is regulated by Schedule 2 of the
Trade Marks Act 1994. The basic framework for the registration of certification marks under the Trade Marks Act 1938 remains in place. In
particular, the applicant for registration is required to file regulations governing
the use of the mark, and the use of the mark by a certified user should be in
accordance with these regulations.[35] The certification mark may designate the
geographic origin of the goods or service.[36] Unlike the Trade Marks Act 1938,
there is no delegation of authority to the Board of Trade or other body.

---

[33] s.37(1) of the Trade Marks Act 1938 defined a certification mark as a 'mark adapted in relation
to any goods to distinguish in the course of trade goods certified by a person in respect of
origin, material, mode of manufacture, quality, accuracy or other characteristic, from goods
not so certified ...' It has been stated that s.37, together with the definitions in s.68, Sched. I
and para. 7 of Sched. III, in effect provided for a separate code in connection with certification
marks. It was estimated that about one dozen applications were filed each year. Kerly, *Law of
Trade Marks and Trade Names* (12th ed., 1986), para. 8–79.

[34] s.50(1) provides as follows:
   '(1) A certification mark is a mark indicating that the goods or services in connection with
   which it is used are certified by the proprietor of the mark in respect of origin, material, mode
   of manufacture of goods or performance of services, quality, accuracy or other characteristics.'

[35] Sched. 2, s.6–11.

[36] Sched. 2, s.3. This provision is consistent with Article 15(2) of the EC Trademark Directive.

Registration of a certification mark under the Trade Marks Act 1994 is stated to be the responsibility of the registrar.[37]

An authorised user of a certification is expressly likened to a licensee of a trade mark in specified circumstances, namely, unauthorised application of the mark to certain material, prohibition of importation of infringing goods, and order as to disposal of infringing goods.[38] The registered certification mark may be assigned, subject to the consent of the registrar.[39]

Certification Mark Under U.S. Law

8–20   Provision for registration of a certification mark is also possible under U.S. law, where a certification mark may apply to both goods and services.[40] The key point about a certification mark is that the certifying organisation or association must not trade in the goods that it is certifying. Thus, the certification is undertaken by the proprietor of the mark, but the mark is applied to the goods by a person other than the proprietor. This is in contrast to a normal trade mark or service mark, where the mark must signify a connection in the course of trade between the proprietor and the goods or services.

No Licence is Created

8–21   Although a certification mark is used by a third party with the authority of the proprietor, no licence arrangement is created.[41] The certification mark is 'applied by other persons, to their goods or services, with authorisation from the owner of the mark.'[42] For this reason, the provisions governing the registration of a licensee (and, under the Trade Marks Act 1938, the registration of a registered user), do not apply to a certification mark.

No Licensee Estoppel

In addition, at least under U.S. law, a party using the certification mark is not estopped on the grounds of licensee estoppel from challenging the validity

---

[37] It is noted that under the earlier draft of the Bill (HL Bill 5), provision was made in s.17 for the Secretary of State to perform certain of the functions with respect to certification marks.
[38] Sched. 2, s.13(1).
[39] Sched. 2, s.12.
[40] See ss.4 and 45 of the Lanham Act. s.45 defines a certification mark as 'any word, name, symbol, or device, or any combination thereof:
(1) used by a person other than its owner, or
(2) which its owner has a bona fide intent to permit a person other than its owner...
to certify regional or other origin, material, mode of manufacture, quality, accuracy, or other characteristics of such person's goods or services or that the work or labor on the goods or services was performed by members of a union or other organization.'
[41] *Midwest Plastic Fabricators v. Underwriters Laboratories*, 12 U.S.P.Q. 2d 1267, 1269, n. 3 (TTAB 1989)
[42] TMEP, para. 1306.01. See generally, Holtzman, 'Certification Marks: An Overview,' 81 *The Trademark Reporter* 180 (1991).

of the mark. Since no licence is created, it has been held that the doctrine of licensee estoppel cannot apply.[43]

The Relevance of Quality Control to Certification Marks

It would, however, be inaccurate to say that quality control is not relevant   8–22
to a certification mark. When a party is permitted to affix the certification mark on its goods, the mark denotes that the goods have satisfied certain quality control standards. The question that arises is what is the nature of quality control in connection with a certification mark.

The Sea Island Cotton Case

The nature of control in the context of a certification mark was considered   8–23
in detail in the case of 'Sea Island Cotton' Certification Trade Marks.[44] Expungement was sought of a certification mark registered on behalf of an organisation named the West Indian Sea Cotton Association Inc. (referred to as WISICA) in three classes in respect of cotton goods and the clothing containing cotton of a certain description grown in the West Indies.

The focus of the expungement was over the right to use the words 'Sea Island Cotton', which formed a principal part of the certification mark. The applicant for expungement had sought to register its own similar trade mark, but its application had been blocked by the earlier registrations of the certification mark on behalf of WISICA. Citing paragraph 4, Schedule 1 of the Trade Marks Act 1938, the applicant sought expungement on the grounds that: (i) WISICA was no longer competent to certify the goods in question; (ii) WISICA had failed to observe a portion of the regulations to be observed in carrying out the certification; and (iii) it was no longer in the public advantage for the mark to be registered, since little cotton of the proper description was actually grown in the West Indies.

Competence to Certify Does Not Require Actual Examination

The Board of Trade ruled that the requirement that the proprietor of a   8–24
certification mark be competent to certify did not mean that the proprietor had to carry out an actual examination or investigation of the goods in question. Tracing the legislative history of the provision, it ruled that it was sufficient that the 'proprietor must have the practical ability to certify.'[45]

The role of the proprietor of the certification mark was more likened to a committee of a club that evaluates the qualifications of a candidate for membership than to a policeman that enforces the law. This view 'is consistent

---

[43] Midwest Plastic Fabricators, supra, n. 35. See, infra, Chap. 9, paras. 9–51 to 9–59, for discussion regarding licensee estoppel.

[44] [1989] R.P.C. 87 (Board of Trade).

[45] The Board of Trade cited the case of Application by Union Nationale Inter-Syndicate des Marques Collectives (1922) 39 R.P.C. 97 and 346. There, Lord Sterndale M.R. observed at p. 359 that on the basis of the amendment of the Act of 1919 to s.62 of the 1905 Act (the predecessor to s.37 of the Trade Marks Act 1938), 'the wording of the statute was intended to do away with that necessary investigation.'

with the regulations which require the proprietor to satisfy himself that an authorised user is of good standing and agrees to use the mark only upon 'proper' goods, but does not impose an obligation upon the proprietor to ensure that the authorised user acts in accordance with the agreement.'[46]

Did The Registrant Exercise Control?

8–25   Even if the proprietor is not required to carry out an actual examination of the goods, the issue of control is still relevant to a consideration of competence. The issue is two-fold: First, the proprietor must be able to exercise control necessary to ensure compliance with the regulations; second, such control must in fact have been exercised. The Board of Trade noted that 'an isolated instance of failure does not necessarily demonstrate a lack of competence, but continued and persistent failure would probably do so.'[47]

The Board of Trade reviewed the various regulations regarding the use of the certification mark. It noted that the Advisory Committee of WISICA had been lax in performing certain of the regulations, particularly in the issuance of certificates of use of the mark and in monitoring such use. Prima facie, such failure to adhere to the regulations would appear to warrant expungement.

Expungement Was Denied

8–26   Nevertheless, the application for expungement was denied, due to 'extenuating circumstances.' The Board of Trade pointed to the following points as amounting to such extenuating circumstances:

(a) It was not established that any certificate holder was unfit and would have been denied a certificate.

(b) It was not established that any certificate holder applied the mark in a manner inconsistent with the regulations.

(c) Even if the mark was expunged, it still was adapted to distinguish and was not deceptive. The past failure of the Advisory Committee had in the meantime been remedied by the appointment of two new members. The regulations would be varied to reflect these changes.

(d) While the West Indies cotton industry had declined, there was evidence of a likely revival.

(e) The public advantage argued in favour of permitting use of the mark by all persons who qualify in accordance with the regulations.

(f) There is no public advantage in allowing the applicants to register its similar trade mark. No useful purpose would be served in treating the expungement as a lesson for other proprietors of certification marks in similar circumstances.'[48]

---

[46] [1989] R.P.C. 87 at 103.
[47] *supra*, n. 38, at 104. The Board of Trade rejected the claim that WISICA engaged in trade in the goods which, as noted, is inconsistent with the notion of a certification mark and would, if true, have warranted expungement.
[48] *supra*, n. 38, at 109.

Quality Control: A U.S. View

The issue of control in the contest of a certification mark has also been   8–27
considered under U.S. law. In the *Midwest Plastic Fabricators v. Underwriters
Laboratories* case, the claim was made the 'UL' certification mark should be
cancelled because the proprietor of the mark did not control or police its
mark.[49]

This mark is widely used in the U.S. to certify that the product in question
has been inspected by the Underwriters Laboratories and has been deemed to
meet the safety standards set by Underwriters Laboratories for that product.
In effect, the argument was that due to a lack of quality control, the
certification mark failed in its essential purpose, namely to certify the goods
as being of a certain quality. This argument was rejected. Interestingly, the
court cited several leading cases in the area of trade mark licensing generally
in support of its position regarding the nature of quality control in the context
of a certification mark. The Federal Circuit observed that there is no 'hard
and fast' rule regarding what degree of quality control is necessary to overcome
a petition for cancellation of a certification mark. On the one hand, it noted
that

> '[t]he purpose of requiring a certification mark registrant to control use
> of its mark is the same as for a trademark registrant; to protect the
> public from being misled ... In the case of a certification mark registrant,
> the risk of misleading the public may even be greater because a cer-
> tification mark registration sets forth specific representations about the
> manufacture and characteristics of the goods to which the mark is
> applied.'[50]

The Trademark Trial and Appeal Board, in the first ruling on the case,
had described the degree of inspection and examination as not requiring a
fool-proof system. 'There is no requirement for such a 100 per cent effective
system and indeed, such would be a practical impossibility.'[51] Rather, the test
laid down by the Federal Circuit Court of Appeals for control of a certification
mark is that 'the owner must take reasonable steps, under all the circumstances
of the case, to prevent the public from being misled.'[52]

In connection with deception of the public, the Trademark Trial and
Appeal Board had noted that it was not significant that the manufacturer of
the certified goods, rather than the proprietor of the certification mark, makes
the declaration regarding certification.[53] Indeed, it is the manufacturer of the
goods that perhaps has the greatest interest in seeing the certification mark
be applied to the product. What is important is that the use of the certification

---

[49] *Midwest Plastic Fabricators v. Underwriters Laboratories*, 12 U.S.P.Q. 2d 1267 (Trademark
Trial and Appeal Board 1989), aff'd, 15 U.S.P.Q. 2d 1359 (Fed. Cir. 1990). s.14(5) of the
Lanham Act provides that a certification mark may be cancelled due to the failure of the
proprietor of the mark to exercise control.

[50] *Midwest Plastic Fabricators v. Underwriters Laboratories*, 15 U.S.P.Q. 1359, 1362 (Fed. Cir.
1990).

[51] *supra,* n. 43, 12 U.S.P.Q. 2d at 1273.

[52] *supra,* n. 43, 15 U.S.P.Q. 2d at 1363.

[53] *Midwest Plastic Fabricators, supra,* n. 43, 12 U.S.P.Q. 2d at 1275, n. 9.

mark is in accordance with the terms and conditions of the proprietor of the mark.

Provisions Governing Use of a Certification Mark

8–28   As noted, few marks have apparently been registered as certification marks under U.K. practice. However, it is conceivable that there will be increased interest in the registration of such marks, particularly in the computer and telecommunications fields, where the certification of universal standards may well take on greater importance. For this reason, it is worthwhile considering in board outline some of the most important provisions of the regulations governing use of a certification mark. The *Sea Island Cotton* case contains a useful guide. It notes the following provisions:

(a) The designation of whom within the proprietor's organisation is responsible for the issuing, renewing and withdrawing of certification of use by the authorised user.

(b) The keeping of a register which contains the names, addresses, and other information about the authorised user, and the goods or services for which use of the mark is authorised.

(c) The terms and conditions under which the certification of use is granted, including the standard which the goods or services must meet in order to use the mark.

(d) Proof that each authorised user is of good repute and sound financial standing, and evidence that he intends to carry out bona fide activity in respect of the goods or services that are the subject of the certification.

(e) The terms and conditions by which use of the mark by the authorised user may be monitored by the proprietor or his representative, including reporting requirements by the authorised user and the right of the proprietor to examine the relevant books and records.

(f) The terms and conditions by which the authorised user may be withdrawn or cancelled.[54]

The inclusion of these or similar provisions would appear to address the issue that the proprietor has a reasonable opportunity to exercise control over the use of the mark in the certification of the pertinent standard.

Collective Marks in the Trade Marks Act 1994

8–29   The Trade Marks Act 1994 provides for registration of collective marks. The explicit recognition of collective marks under U.K. trade mark law is new. A collective mark is defined in section 49(1) of the Trade Marks Act 1994 as a 'mark distinguishing the goods or services of members of the association which is the proprietor of the mark from those of other undertakings.'

The essence of the collective mark is that it indicates who is entitled to use the mark, principally by members of an association. Unlike a certification mark, however, which establishes criteria that the goods or services must

---

[54] [1989] R.P.C. at 92.

meet in order that the certification mark may be applied to them,[55] a collective mark designates a direct connection between the collective association and the members of the association ('authorised users') that use the mark.

Collective marks are regulated by Schedule 1 of the Trade Marks Act 1994. Despite the difference in purpose between certification marks and collective marks, the provisions of Schedule 1 that regulate collective marks are similar in many respects to those of Schedule 2 that regulate certification marks. In particular, the use of the respective marks is by a person other than its proprietor in accordance with the provisions of the regulations governing such use. Collective marks are also recognised under the U.S. trade mark laws. The definition of a collective mark under the Lanham Act is similar to that set forth in the 1994 Trade Marks Act.[56]

8–30

---

[55] See *Reform of Trade Marks Law*, Cm. 1203 (1990), p.29.
[56] s.45 of the Lanham Act defines a collective mark as:
'... a trademark or service mark:
(1) used by the members of a cooperative, an association, or other collective organisation'. See *Sebastian International Inc. v. Longs Drug Stores Corp.*, D.C. Cal., No. CV 93–2891, March 11, 1994. In that case, the unauthorised sale of genuine hair care products bearing a collective mark, made by a non-member of the collective, was enjoined on the ground that confusion could be caused among consumers who had come to expect certain ancillary functions from the collective, including quality control. The court reasoned that the collective mark connoted a closer connection with the proprietor of the mark than did a trade mark to the manufacturer of the goods identified by the mark. *cf.* with the cases discussed in connection with the *El Greco* case, *supra*, paras. 8–12 to 8–16.

9. Consent and Delimitation Agreements, No Challenge Clauses and Licensee Estoppel

Agreements are frequently entered into under which the parties mutually consent to the use, and/or the registration, of their respective trade marks, subject to specified terms and conditions. Such arrangements are called consent or delimitation agreements. Consent agreements are typically found in several distinct situations: **9–01**

- (a) Consents are granted by rival applicants in connection with two or more pending applications of arguably similar trade marks.
- (b) The proprietor of a registered trade mark consents to the registration of a pending application.
- (c) A consent agreement is reached by the parties prior to the filing by either party of an application for registration of its particular trade mark.
- (d) A consent agreement is entered into to bring to a conclusion opposition or cancellation proceedings, an infringement action, or other dispute.

These situations are not mutually exclusive. This is particularly so when registrations and applications in more than one country are involved, so that the status of the respective trade marks may differ, depending upon the country. In such circumstances, the consent agreement could well contain a combination of provisions which involve both the mutual recognition of trade mark rights in some and the recognition of superior rights of registration in others. Thus, consent agreements can be complex in content.

A Consent Agreement is Neither an Assignment Nor a Licence

A consent agreement is often confused with an assignment or a licence. In truth it is neither, but a separate and distinct arrangement by which the parties agree to co-exist in connection with their respective trade marks. **9–02**

A Consent is Not an Assignment

A consent agreement is not an assignment because neither party to the agreement is transferring the proprietorship of its trade mark to the other.[1] The purpose of a consent agreement is to define the terms and conditions by which each party may use and assert rights in its trade mark. The trade marks themselves, however, remain the exclusive property of their respective proprietors.

A Consent Is Not a Licence

A consent agreement is not a licence because neither party is granting permission to the other to use its trade mark. Rather, the basis of a consent agreement is that the parties seek to distinguish the use of their *respective* marks. The distinction may be on the basis of the marks themselves, the goods or services, the territory, or a combination of such factors.[2]

This is dissimilar to a licence, which is predicated on the notion that the commercial identity of the licensee is submerged into the licensor, and therefore that the licensor must ensure quality control in the use of the trade mark by the licensee.[3] The consent agreement, by contrast, seeks to define and highlight the separate and distinct identities of the two parties. Thus, quality control, in the sense required by a licence, is not directly relevant to a consent agreement. In effect, '[a] licence integrates, while a consent differentiates.'[4]

Consent as Part and Parcel of a Trade Mark Licence

9-03 While a consent agreement may be distinguished from a licence agreement, it must be appreciated that a form of consent still plays a role in trade mark licensing.

Licensing derives from the idea that a trade mark is a negative right, which entitles the proprietor to prevent third parties from the trade mark. A party which uses a trade mark without the consent of the proprietor may well be liable in an action for infringement.[5] The corollary is that use of the trade mark by a third party with the consent of the proprietor is a defence to a claim of infringement.[6] It follows that consent in this sense is part and parcel of a valid trade mark licence. There will be no licence unless the proprietor can be said to have consented, either expressly or implicitly, to the other

---

[1] *Waukesha Hygeia Mineral Springs Co. v. Hygeia Sparkling Distilled Water Co.*, 63 F. 438 (7th Cir. 1894); *T & T Mfg. Co. v. A.T. Cross Co.*, 197 U.S.P.Q. 763, aff'd 201 U.S.P.Q. 561, cert. denied, 441 U.S. 60 (1978). It has been held that a consent agreement is not recordable as an assignment. *Waukesha Hygeia Mineral Springs, supra*, at 440.

[2] See, *infra*, paras. 9–26 to 9–31, and Chap. 15, 'Sample Consent Agreement,' for sample provisions of a consent agreement.

[3] See Chap. 6, and Chap. 8, for discussion on quality control.

[4] McCarthy, *Trademarks and Unfair Competition*, 2nd ed., para. 18.25, p. 866. But see discussion on quality control, *infra*, paras. 9–07 to 9–10.

[5] This is specifically provided for in the Lanham Act, which defines infringement as use of the trade mark by a person 'without the consent of the registrant.' 15 U.S.C. 1114 (1). Note also s. 9(1) of the Trade Marks Act 1994, which provides that '[t]he proprietor of a registered trade mark has exclusive rights in the trade mark which are infringed by use of the trade mark in the United Kingdom without his consent.'

[6] Trade Marks Act 1938, s.4(3)(a); see the discussion in connection with the *Accurist Watches* case, *supra*, Chap. 8, paras. 8–06 to 8–10.

party's use of the trade mark. The interrelationship between consent and licensing was stated by one U.S. court as follows:

> 'It is beyond doubt that an owner of a mark can consent to or license the use of that mark. It is also clear, however, that such consent can be withdrawn, it can be subject to limitations, or the consent can expire under the terms of the agreement between the parties.'[7]

The court's observation is notable only in the sense that the proprietor's consent to the use of the trade mark is so fundamental to a licence that it is rarely expressed separately from the fact of the licence itself.

Licence Versus Consent: The Likelihood of Confusion

It may be argued that the distinction between a licence and a consent can be understood in terms of the issue of likelihood of confusion. Under this view, a licence seeks to eliminate confusion, whereby the controlled use of the trade mark by the licensee will be deemed use by the licensor, while a consent rests on the notion that there is no confusion so long as each of the parties uses its respective trade mark in accordance with the consent agreement.   9–04

Whether this view is completely accurate can be better appreciated by comparing two possible resolutions of a dispute involving the trade marks of the respective parties by way of licence and consent, respectively.

Resolution by Licence: Assignment and Licence Back or Cancellation and Licence

A dispute over the trade marks of the respective parties may be resolved by one party granting to the other party a licence. There are two principal ways by which such a licence is provided: 9–05

(a) The parties provide for an assignment of the trade mark by one party to the other, so that the trade marks are all owned by one party, with a licensing back to the assignor by the assignee of the right to use one or more of the assigned trade marks. The assignment and licence back provides that proprietorship of the marks shall be held by a single owner, while at the same time, it permits the licensee to continue to use its mark.[8]

(b) One of the parties cancels its registrations and pending applications. It then enters into a licence arrangement for the use of the trade marks belonging to the other party.

The common denominator in both of these licence arrangements in settlement of a dispute is that they purport to resolve the issue of confusion by concentrating proprietorship in a single party, which then licences use of the mark to the other party.

---

[7] *Burger King Corp. v. Metro Club, Inc.*, 208 U.S.P.Q. 293, 299 (E.D. Mich. 1980).

[8] See, *supra*, Chap. 6, paras. 6–48 to 6–63, for further discussion on assignment and licence back arrangements.

Resolution by Consent

9–06   Alternatively, the dispute may be resolved by means of a consent agreement. Here, the underlying assumption is that the two marks are not confusingly similar, at least for so long as the parties abide by the terms of the consent. Each party remains the proprietor of its trade mark and each party continues to use its own mark. As one court noted: '[I]n essence, [a consent is] an admission that the subsequent party's use of the mark for its goods is not likely to cause confusion.'[9]

Confusion As a Factor in a Consent Agreement

9–07   The question raised by these examples is how both a licence and a consent agreement can be appropriate, if one is based on preventing confusion, while the other is not. The answer is that the simple distinction between a licence and a consent, based on quality control, may be more apparent than real.[10]

It has long been recognised that a consent agreement may also be concerned with preventing confusion between two trade marks. Thus, it was held by a U.S. court in a case decided in the last century that a consent agreement

'is not an attempt to transfer or license the use of a trademark, or any rights therein, or any word thereof, but fixes and defines the existing trade mark of each, [in order] that confusion and infringement may be prevented.'[11]

Indeed, if no element of confusion is involved, the motives of the parties in entering into the consent agreement may be questioned. For example, there may be coercion by one of the parties, or the intent illegally to divide territories or otherwise to use the marks in an anti-competitive manner. These kinds of situations have been described by the European Court of Justice as a mere 'fictitious agreement,' where 'the proprietor of an earlier mark institutes manifestly unfounded proceedings against a new mark in order to induce a badly advised, often economically weaker, applicant to settle an artificial dispute by entering into a delimitation agreement.'[12]

A Consent Agreement Prevents Future Confusion

9–08   The confusion which is to be prevented by virtue of a consent agreement may be different, however, from that addressed by a licence. The consent agreement seeks to minimise, if not eliminate, the possibility that the use of the mark by one party can spill over into the area of use of the other's mark and cause confusion. If the parties enter into a consent agreement, it is assumed that

---

[9] *Richdel, Inc. v. Matthews Co.*, 190 U.S.P.Q. 37 (Trademark Trial and Appeal Board 1976).
[10] When resolution of a dispute involves numerous national jurisdictions, it is not unusual for the final form of the agreement to be a hybrid arrangement which contains both consent agreements and licences, depending upon the particular country. Such a hybrid arrangement may be employed, despite the fact that the underlying use and commercial effect of the respective marks may differ little between the countries of interest.
[11] *Waukesha Hygeia Mineral Springs Co. v. Hygeia Sparkling Distilled Water Co.*, *supra*, n. 1.
[12] *BAT v. Commission*, *infra*, n. 64, at 491, para. 31.

there is no confusion in connection with the *current* use of the parties' respective trade marks.[13] Adherence to the terms of the consent agreement will then prevent future confusion by delimiting each party's use of its trade mark in a non-confusing manner.[14]

Failure to Adhere to Terms of Consent May Result in Infringement

For example, in the *Hygeia* mineral water case, the parties sought to resolve their dispute over use of the Hygeia mark by distinguishing the formats and products in connection with their respective uses of the mark. When an assignee of one party later began to use the trade mark other than as set out in the consent, the other party sought to prohibit such use of Hygeia on the grounds that it was confusing and not as permitted by the agreement.   9–09

The court gave full effect to the consent agreement, and enjoined the assignee-defendant from using the mark other than as provided for in the consent. The court further noted that the 'contract operates by way of estoppel upon each of the contracting parties...'[15]

Indeed, it has been held under U.S. law that a consent may have an estoppel-like effect in favour of third parties whose use of a trade mark falls within the scope of use permitted under the consent agreement. The reasoning is that since there is no confusion between the respective trade marks of the parties under the consent agreement, there can be no confusion with respect to third party use of a mark which also falls within the scope of the agreement.[16]

A Consent Agreement and the Existing Likelihood of Confusion

While a consent agreement may be viewed in terms of preventing future confusion, there are circumstances in which a court has acknowledged the validity of a consent agreement, despite an existing likelihood of confusion between the respective marks.   9–10

For example, in the *T & T Mfg.* case, the U.S. court reasoned that the consent agreement was not drafted with an intent to deceive the public, that the goods of the respective parties were of similar quality, and that as a matter of public policy private contracts should be enforced. These factors were held to outweigh the concern that the consent agreement did not eliminate the likelihood of confusion with respect to the two trade marks.[17]

---

[13] Indeed, the division of use between the parties to the consent agreement may well be broader than that required to prevent confusion. See, *e.g. Frito-Lay, Inc. v. So Good Potato Chip Co.*, 191 U.S.P.Q. 560 (8th Cir. 1976); McCarthy, *supra*, n. 4, 2nd ed., para. 18:25, p.869.

[14] It is understandable, therefore, why the parties to a consent agreement may include a provision obligating one other to take all reasonable steps to prevent future infringement.

[15] *Waukesha Hygeia Mineral Springs, supra*, n. 1.

[16] See, *e.g. California Fruit Growers Exchange v. Sunkist Baking Co.*, 76 U.S.P.Q. 85 (7th Cir. 1947). Another way to understand the effect of a consent in these circumstances is that it is an admission against interest with respect to a party to the consent that seeks to allege infringement against a third-party use of the mark. McCarthy, *supra*, n. 1, 2nd Ed., para. 18:25.

[17] *T & T Mfg., supra*, n. 1.

This result may be particularly apt when the consent agreement constitutes a settlement.[18]

Policy Considerations Regarding Consents: Private and Public Interests

9–11   As the preceding paragraph regarding the *T & T Mfg.* case suggests, a consent agreement may involve both private and public interests.

First, there is the interest of the parties themselves. An agreement is reached by the parties in order to enable them to use and/or to obtain the registration of their respective trade marks, and thereby to protect their rights in such marks. Secondly, the registration and protection of deceptive or confusing trade marks is against the public interest.

The Interests May Not Be Compatible

9–12   While there is a presumption that the parties to the consent agreement are concerned with guarding against public confusion in connection with the use of the respective trade marks, there is no certainty that this is the case. A consent agreement reached under the threat of legal action or in exchange of payment cannot necessarily be expected to take into consideration the public interest. Even in a more typical situation, the interests of the parties in ensuring mutual registration or use of their respective marks does not guarantee that there will be no confusion. The possible divergence of interests was well-expressed by one court in the following words:

> 'The practice [of consents] must necessarily lead to bargaining, and there is, it seems to me, a risk that, while the owner of the trade mark may be satisfied, the public may continue to be confused because the consent of the registered proprietors cannot prevent confusion arising.'[19]

CONSENTS IN THE CONTEXT OF REGISTRATION PRACTICE

Approach Under the Trade Marks Act 1938

9–13   The interplay between private and public interests was seen in the treatment accorded to consent agreements in the registration practice under the Trade Marks Act 1938.

Under the Trade Marks Act 1938, mutual consents were permitted when concurrently pending applications for identical or similar trade marks were cross-cited. The use of mutual consents in this manner derived from section 12(3) of the Trade Marks Act 1938. That section authorised the Registrar to resolve conflicting applications for registration where the 'marks are identical or nearly resemble each other.' In such a case, mutual consents may have

---

[18] But see *infra*, para. 9–35, regarding the position of the European Court of Justice in applying Art. 85 to the lawfulness of a consent agreement, even in the context of a settlement.
[19] *In the Matter of an Application by Hans Emmanuel Neumann Enoch*, 64 R.P.C. 118, 121 (1945). But see, *infra*, para. 9–17, regarding the primacy of the intent of the parties to a consent under the Trade Marks Act 1994.

been sufficient to obtain registration, when the respective marks were deemed to have been too close to rely merely on cross-notice to the respective applicants, but were not deemed to be so similar that their co-existence on the Registry would have been likely to cause confusion.[20]

The Registry Guidelines for section 12(3) procedure in connection with the granting of mutual consents essentially provided that:

> 'Where the marks are too close for cross-notice and the Registrar decides that mutual consents would suffice the procedure depends upon whether or not such consents are obtained. If they are, both applications will be accepted and consents are obtained. If they are not, both applications will be advertised *before* acceptance on cross-notice and the matter left to opposition.'[21]

When the two applications were cross-cited, and mutual consents were obtained, neither applicant necessarily enjoyed a superior position over the other with respect to the terms and conditions of the consent agreement. Accordingly, each party had to carefully weigh up whether it was desirable or possible to reach an accommodation with the conflicting applicant.

Consent by the Proprietor to the Registration of a Trade Mark

Here, a valid and subsisting registration was cited against an application on the ground that the application is likely to cause confusion with the registered mark.[22] A consent was viewed as a workable solution to the problem posed by the requirements of section 12(1) of the Trade Marks Act 1938, namely that no mark was to be registered if it was likely to deceive or cause confusion with a previously registered trade mark.[23] However, a query arose over the effect of the consent in overcoming the statutory objection to registration based on the previously registered trade mark.

9–14

A Consent Agreement Need Not Be Conclusive

The key point under the Trade Marks Act 1938 is that a consent agreement need not have been given conclusive weight by the Registrar in deciding whether or not to register the mark or marks at issue.[24] The key is whether the consent may have 'tended to satisfy' the Registrar about certain matters in respect of the registration of the trade mark.[25]

9–15

In this connection, the Registrar was prepared to assume that the parties themselves are in a position to decide whether there is a likelihood of confusion between the two trade marks.[26] Moreover,

> '... [i]f the applicants are able to obtain the written consent of the owner

---

[20] 'Guidelines for s.12(3) Procedure' (issued 1978), paras. 3, 4.
[21] Guidelines, *supra*, n. 20, at para. 3.
[22] s.12(1).
[23] *Re John Crowther*, 65 R.P.C. 369, 371.
[24] *Dewhurst's Application* (1896) 13 R.P.C. 288; *In the Matter of British Lead Mills Ltd* [1958] R.P.C. 425.
[25] *Consarc Trade Mark* [1969] R.P.C. 179; *Velvo Glo Trade Marks* [1961] R.P.C. 255, 261, 262.
[26] *Linpac Trade Marks* [1973] R.P.C. 661, 663, 664.

of some already registered mark to the registration of their proposed mark, that fact in itself serves as evidence which will or may legitimately influence the mind of the Registrar...'[27]

However, the mere fact that the parties consented to mutual use of the respective marks did not prevent the Registrar from rejecting the mutual registration of the marks on the ground that the likelihood of confusion is contrary to the public interest. This has been succinctly stated as follows:

'At most [a consent] is evidence bearing on the likelihood of confusion and need not be accepted by the Registrar if he takes the view that the conflicting marks are so close that deception or confusion of the public are bound to arise.'[28]

Failure to Obtain Consent Will Lead to Rejection of the Application

9–16 Conversely, if an applicant failed to obtain consent from the registrant upon being so requested by the Registrar, the application would probably have been rejected.[29]

In one case, the applicant failed to provide a consent as requested, and the application was subsequently rejected. On appeal, the court noted that the consent was not requested as a condition for acceptance, but in order to assist the Registrar in 'reconsidering' whether to withdraw his objection based on the likelihood of confusion. Thus, reliance on the consent served to expand the ability of the applicant to overcome the Registrar's objection.

Public Interest May No Longer Be Relevant

9–17 Under the Trade Marks Act 1994, a dramatic shift has occurred in the weight accorded to a consent agreement. The registrar apparently no longer need take into consideration the likelihood of confusion in assessing whether or not to register a mark on the basis of the consent. Subsection 5(5) simply provides that 'nothing in this section [dealing with refusal of registration based on the prior rights of third parties] prevents the registration of a trade mark where the proprietor of the earlier mark or earlier right consents to the registration'.[30]

The approach reflected in this subsection is consistent with the view that a trade mark is a right of property, and the proprietor of the mark is deemed to be the party best situated to protect the value of his mark. The registrar is no longer called upon to protect the public interest, at least with respect to likelihood of confusion, in giving effect to the consent agreement.[31] The question can be raised whether, under such a provision, the registrar will ever

---

[27] *Velva Glo Trade Marks, supra,* n. 25, at 261, 262.

[28] *Benji Trade Mark,* [1988] R.P.C. 251, 255.

[29] *Consarc Trade Mark, supra,* n. 25; *Linpac Trade Mark, supra,* n. 26, at 666; *Velva Glo Trade Marks, supra,* n. 25, at 261, 262.

[30] The original draft of this subsection was followed by the phrase, 'unless it appears to the registrar that there is a likelihood of confusion.' The phrase was omitted in the final form of the bill.

[31] See, *supra,* Chap. 4, para. 4–03 for a discussion of the emphasis in the Trade Marks Act 1994 on the proprietary nature of a trade mark.

be able to refuse a consent on the ground of the public interest, even if the agreement has anti-competitive effect or otherwise results from collusion between the parties.

Registrar Need Not Enquire into the Background of the Consent

It has been no defence to a failure by the applicant to submit a consent that the Registrar failed to enquire about the reasons why the consent was not granted. The Registry had no such obligation.[32] **9–18**

A Consent May be Withdrawn

A written consent has not prevented the registrant from subsequently withdrawing its consent and challenging the registration in an opposition, since a consent 'is a discretionary matter.'[33] **9–19**

Registrant's Motivations in Granting a Consent

It might appear that the proprietor of a registered trade mark has no great motivation to provide a consent to an applicant. There are several reasons why this may not be so, and why the granting of a consent may be advisable. **9–20**

(a) A consent agreement can ensure that the applicant will limit its use of its trade mark in a manner that will not extend into the registrant's sphere of operations. It may be desirable, therefore, to reach agreement on the terms of a mutual consent at the outset, rather than to rely on more cumbersome and uncertain procedures, such as a cancellation or an infringement action, to sort out such rights in the future.[34]

(b) The refusal of the registrant to grant a consent to the applicant is not without risk in relation to regarding the continuing validity of the registrant's own trade mark. The applicant, faced with the prospect of rejection of the application because of the failure to obtain a consent, may then seek to expunge the registered mark from the Register.

This is what happened in the *Kodak Trade Mark* case; after a consent was not granted, the applicant successfully sought expungement of the registered

---

[32] *Linpac Trade Marks*, *supra*, n. 26, at 666.

[33] *Benji Trade Mark* [1988] R.P.C. 251, 255. Query whether this result is consistent with the principle that the terms of a consent agreement are to be enforced in the same way as any other contract. It was recognised early on under U.S. law that a consent agreement is viewed as giving rise to working an estoppel between the parties with respect to the contractual undertakings therein. *Waukesha Hygeia Mineral Springs Co.*, *supra*, n. 1, at 440.

[34] A related matter is how to ensure that a mutual consent does not leave a grey area land in which a third party can use the mark in a manner that does harm to both parties. It has been suggested under the Trade Marks Act 1938, that the parties should perhaps secure complementary registrations whose respective specifications collectively exhaust the goods of a single class, and then work out between them how the mark is to be used by each of them in a manner that is not likely to cause confusion. Kerly, *Law of Trade Marks and Trade Names* (12th ed., 1986), para. 10–50, p.150, n.48. Such a result is more easily described than carried out. It is probably unworkable in the U.S., where the specification of goods is limited to the goods of actual use.

trade mark on the ground that the mark had not been used to identify the source of the goods, but merely as part of an advertisement.[35] In such circumstances, perhaps it would have been preferable for the registrant to have granted the consent at the outset.

Consents Under U.S. Registration Practice

9–21 The weight accorded to a consent agreement in connection with *ex parte* proceedings for registration of a trade mark under U.S. practice has changed over time, reflecting differing views of the proper accommodation between public and private interests.

Public Interest Paramount

9–22 At one time, public interest was paramount. It was held that the existence of a consent agreement regarding use of a trade mark could not supplant the role of the U.S. Patent Office in protecting the public against confusion by denying registration to such a mark.[36] As a result, consent agreements were accorded little or no weight in determining the registrability of a trade mark.

This reluctance to accord weight to a consent agreement also reflected the clear distinction between the right to use a mark, which lay within the power of the parties to the consent agreement to decide, and the right to register the mark, which was viewed as falling within the purview of the Patent Office as the guardian of the public interest.[37]

Increased Recognition of Private Interests

9–23 However, more recently, emphasis has been placed on respecting the judgment of the parties to a consent agreement regarding the likelihood of confusion for purposes of registration as well as use. The leading case is *re Du Pont de Nemours & Co.*,[38] in which Judge Markey stated as follows:

> 'Thus when those most familiar with use in the marketplace and most interested in precluding confusion enter agreements designed to avoid it, the scales of evidence are clearly tilted. It is at least difficult to maintain a subjective view that confusion will occur when those directly concerned say it won't.'[39]

Judge Markey went on to state that 'citation of "the public interest" as a basis for refusal of registration is a bootless cry.'[40]

---

[35] [1990] F.S.R. 49.
[36] See, generally, Van Santen and Claessens, 'Consents to Register in Ex Parte Cases Under Section 2(d) of the Lanham Act: A Forty Year Debate,' 79 T.M.R. 89 (1989).
[37] See Van Santen and Claessens, *supra*, n. 36.
[38] 177 U.S.P.Q. 562 (CCPA) 1973.
[39] *Du Pont, supra*, n. 38, at 568.
[40] *Id.*, footnote omitted.

Is A 'Naked' Consent Sufficient?

As a result of the *Du Pont* decision, consent agreements under U.S. practice   9–24
have been accorded greater weight in determining registrability.[41] Nevertheless,
the issue is not free from doubt.

Frequently, the question of the weight to be accorded is expressed by
reference to whether the consent is a 'naked' consent, which will be accorded
little or no weight, or whether the consent contains 'provisions designed to
preclude confusion, *i.e.* limitations on continued use by each party.'[42] In such
cases, a consent will be accorded weight only if it specifies the conditions of
use of the respective marks, including format and product line, as well as any
territorial restrictions, in a way that ensures that no confusion will result.[43]

The Four Seasons Decision

Others have maintained that this is a misreading of the *Du Pont* decision,   9–25
which only found that a consent, naked or otherwise, may be taken into
consideration in assessing likelihood of confusion.[44] On this view, to hold
otherwise would be to return to the discredited position that the U.S. Patent
and Trademark Office is better placed than the parties to the consent
agreement to determine when use of the marks is deceptive or confusing.

This view was strongly reinforced by a recent decision, *Re Four Seasons
Ltd*,[45] given by the Court of Appeal for the Federal Circuit. This court serves
as the court of appeal from decisions of the U.S. Patent and Trademark Office
on matters of trade mark registration.

The applicant and the registrant had reached a consent agreement regarding
registration of the mark 'Four Seasons Biltmore', but the Examiner and the
Trademark Trial and Appeal Board had both rejected the application on the
ground that there was a likelihood of confusion between that mark and the
previously registered mark 'The Biltmore Los Angeles'. The court of appeal
reversed and granted the registration. It admonished the Patent and Trademark
Office not to 'second-guess the conclusions of those most familiar with the
marketplace.' It went on to state that '[h]ere the self-interests of applicant
and registrant have caused them to enter into a consent agreement determining
that confusion of their marks is likely.' The agreement should therefore be
accorded great weight.

The court of appeal also reiterated the position that the refusal to register
does not deny the owner of the unregistered mark the right of use under U.S.
law. Accordingly, the refusal to register would not serve to protect the public
from confusion with respect to use. Such policing is left to the self-interest of

---

[41] See, *supra*, para. 9–23.
[42] *Du Pont, supra*, n. 38, at 567–568.
[43] See, *e.g. Re Permagrain Products, Inc.*, 223 U.S.P.Q. 147 (Trade Mark Trial and Appeal Board
1984); *Re M. Seman & Co., Inc.* 223 U.S.P.Q. 52 (1984); *Re Riddle*, 225 U.S.P.Q. 630 (Trade
Mark Trial and Appeal Board 1985).
[44] See, *e.g. Re N.A.D., Inc.*, 224 U.S.P.Q. 969 (CAFC 1985); *Bongrain International (America) v.
Delice de France*, 1 U.S.P.Q 2d 1775 (CAFC 1987).
[45] 26 U.S.P.Q 2d (1993). *cf.* with the approach adopted under the U.K. Trade Marks Act 1994,
supra, para. 9–16.

the parties. The existence of the consent agreement indicates that no such danger was perceived.'[46]

Still, the prudent course of action when relying on a consent agreement in *ex parte* proceedings is to avoid the charge that a naked consent is involved by specifying in writing the grounds which support the claim that no confusion is likely to arise.

A CONSENT AGREEMENT AS AN ENFORCEABLE CONTRACT

9–26 It has been held that a consent agreement is an enforceable contract, subject of course to applicable contract law.[47] Several different provisions typically contained in a consent agreement are of particular interest.

Declaration of No Likelihood of Confusion

9–27 The parties declare that their respective marks do not infringe each other and that there is no likelihood of confusion between them. This declaration gives recognition to the supposed basis of a consent agreement, namely the absence of present confusion between the marks since, if confusion exists, doubt can be cast, at least prior to the Trade Marks Act 1994, on the bona fides of the agreement. It has been held, under U.S. law, that in the absence of an express declaration, such a declaration may be implied.[48]

The absence of confusion is limited to the use of the respective marks in accordance with the provisions of the consent agreement. There are numerous cases in which one party has sued for infringement on the ground that the use of the other party's trade mark has deviated from the terms of the agreement.[49] In such circumstances, the declaration that the marks are not confusingly similar cannot be used to bar a claim of infringement (or breach of contract).

Co-operation Between the Parties

9–28 A consent agreement will sometimes contain a term providing for specified forms of co-operation between the parties. In such a case, not only do the parties agree to delimit the use of their respective trade marks, but they make further affirmative undertakings to support the terms of delimitation.

The co-operation may be limited to mutual assistance to enable the other party to obtain and protect the registration of its trade mark (including the filing of a statement of consent), or it may extend to on-going measures

---

[46] 26 U.S.P.Q 2d, *supra*, n. 44, at 1071, 1072.

[47] *Apple Corps. Ltd v. Apple Computer Inc.* [1992] F.S.R. 431. See the discussion in para. 9–09 above, and the *Hygeia Mineral Water* case, *supra*, n. 7. See also *Visa International Service Association v. Bankcard Holders of America*, 784, F.2d 1472, 1473 (a party to a settlement 'will be held to his consent unless enforcement of the contract would result in injury to the public through confusion.') See generally, *infra*, Chap. 10.

[48] *Croton Watch Co. v. Laughlin*, 208 F.2d 93, 96, 99; 99 U.S.P.Q. 229 (2d Cir. 1953).

[49] The leading U.S. case is the *Hygeia Mineral Water* case, *supra*, n. 1. For examples of U.K. cases in this regard, see the authorities cited in footnotes 52 to 54 below.

designed to ensure that the parties do not use their respective marks in a manner contrary to the spirit of the consent agreement. In so far as such undertakings are enforceable in law, the parties should consider carefully to which degree they wish to commit themselves to such co-operation.

'Field of Use' Restrictions

The parties will define the scope of use of their respective trade marks, including the format of the marks, the goods and services for which the respective marks will be used and territorial limitations, if any, in connection with the use of the marks.[50]

9–29

Borrowing from the law of patent licensing, this provision has sometimes been called a field of use restriction.[51] It is presumed that so long as these delimitations are adhered to by the parties, no likelihood of confusion regarding the use of the respective trade marks will occur. However, where one of the parties uses its trade mark beyond the scope set out in the consent agreement, there may be a breach of contract.[52] A consent agreement has also been held to have been breached when the trade mark was used in a form which was not specified in the agreement.[53]

Breach May Also Give Rise to Infringement

Breach of a consent agreement may also give rise to a claim for infringement.[54] An infringement occurs when the use of the trade mark, other than in accordance with the terms of the consent, infringes the other party's trade mark. This points to the fact that the purpose of a consent agreement is to delineate clearly the boundaries for the use of the respective trade marks in order to prevent possibly confusing overlap in the future.

9–30

However, not every breach of the agreement will constitute infringement. For example, it is possible that the scope of the consent may be broader than would be required to prevent confusion.[55] Here, a breach of the contract may not give rise to an infringement, as long as the use of the respective marks does not actually create confusion.

Scope of Breach of Contract and Infringement May Depend Upon Form of the Consent Agreement

It is not always clear whether breach of a consent agreement has occurred and, if so, whether there is also infringement. Much may depend upon the

9–31

---

[50] Territorial limitations tend to take on more importance when multiple national jurisdictions are involved and the parties appear to partition their respective marks on a national basis. See *infra*, paras. 9–36 to 9–38.

[51] *Apple Corps.*, *supra*, n. 47.

[52] *Peck (John) & Co. Ltd v. Zelker (R.) Ltd* [1963] R.P.C. 85 (1963).

[53] *English Rose Ltd v. Daintifyt Brassiere Co. Ltd* [1957] R.P.C. 335; *Frito-Lay, Inc. v. So Good Potato Chip Co.*, 191 U.S.P.Q. 560 (8th Cir. 1976).

[54] *Inde Coope Limited v. Paine & Co.* [1983] R.P.C. 326.

[55] See, *supra*, para. 9–08, regarding consent agreements and the likelihood of future confusion.

precise inter-relationship between the mutual undertakings. Several possible forms of consent agreement are worth mentioning here:

(a) A and B both undertake to limit themselves to prescribed uses of the mark, which are apparently distinct from each other.[56] While an unauthorised use of the mark by one of the parties in the grey area between the respective delimitations on use will be a breach of the consent agreement, it does not follow that infringement has occurred. It will depend, in part, upon how different and distinct the two sets of goods are.

(b) The same as (a), except that A and B undertake not to use the mark on specified goods of the other party.[57] Here again a breach of the agreement need not also amount to an infringement.

(c) A is granted all possible uses of the mark, except for a narrowly defined prescribed use by B. If B expands its use of the mark beyond the scope specified in the agreement, it is more likely to be liable for infringement as well as for breach of contract.

(d) A undertakes to use the mark on specified goods (*e.g.*, coffee and tea), and B undertakes not to use the mark on a broader class of goods (*e.g.* beverages). If, *e.g.* B uses the mark on fruit juice, the issues of both breach and infringement are subject to the interpretation of the consent agreement regarding the scope of the respective undertakings.[58] Here, ambiguity in the description of the scope of the prohibited goods will make A's task of proving both breach and infringement more difficult.[59]

(e) A undertakes to limit the use of the mark to specified goods and for a set period of time, and B undertakes to use the mark on all other goods of interest. During that time, A attempts to establish goodwill in a new trade mark. After the time period has elapsed, B alone will have exclusive rights to the use of the trade mark which is the subject of the agreement.[60]

DELIMITATION AGREEMENTS UNDER THE TREATY OF ROME

Delimitation Agreements Are Not Unlawful *Per Se*

9–32   Consent agreements (more commonly known in the context of E.C. law as delimitation agreements) are subject to Article 85 of the Treaty of Rome.[61] Article 85 prohibits agreements between undertakings that have as their object

---

[56] *e.g.* records versus computers, both traded under the *Apple* trade mark. See *Apple Corps. Ltd, supra,* n. 47.

[57] This appears to have been the arrangement in the *Apple* case, *supra,* n. 47.

[58] *General Foods Corp. v. Louis Ender, Inc.*, 327 NYS 2d 572 (1971); *Louis Ender, Inc. v. General Foods Corp.*, 175 U.S.P.Q. 449 (2nd Cir. 1972), cert. denied, 410 US 930.

[59] See, *e.g. Champale, Inc. v. Joseph S. Picket & Sons, Inc.*, 671 F.2d 289 (8th Cir. 1982).

[60] See, *e.g.* the E.C. Commission Decision regarding the *Penney's* mark [1978] 2 C.M.L.R. 100.

[61] See generally, Fawlk, 'Trademark Delimitation Agreements Under Article 85 of the Treaty of Rome,' The Trademark Reporter, Vol. 82, no.2 (1992), at 223; 'Guidelines for Trademark Licensing in the Foreign Community,' U.S. Trademark Association, 1992.

or effect the prevention, restriction or distortion of competition within the E.C. and which affect trade between Member States.[62]

There is nothing in a delimitation agreement that renders such an arrange- 9–33 ment unlawful *per se* under the Treaty of Rome. This applies to where both registered and unregistered trade marks are involved.[63] The Court of Justice has given express recognition to this point as follows:

> '... [A]greements known as "delimitation agreements" are lawful and useful if they serve to delimit, in the mutual interest of the parties, the spheres within which their respective trademarks may be used, and are intended to avoid confusion or conflict between them. That is not to say, however, that such agreements are excluded from the application of Article 85 of the Treaty if they also have the aim of dividing up the market or restricting competition in other ways.'[64]

It can be seen that the Court of Justice recognises that a delimitation agreement may serve to avoid conflict or confusion between the trade marks of the respective parties. The issue is whether such an agreement violates the prohibitions of Article 85.

Common Law Restraint of Trade Likened to Article 85

Lord Justice Nicholls has observed that the same common law principles that 9–34 determine an unlawful restraint of trade are also embodied in the test for legality of a delimitation agreement under Article 85. He emphasised three elements:

(a) A contract that has the mere effect of restricting competition is unenforceable.

(b) To enforce a restraint of trade, there must be identified a legitimate interest of the party in whose favour the restraint has been made.

(c) The restraint must go no further than is necessary in the protection of that interest.[65]

Purpose of the Delimitation Agreement Is Not Relevant

The purpose for which a delimitation agreement is made will not usually 9–35 affect the inquiry as to whether or not the agreement violates Article 85. Thus, it should be immaterial whether it is intended to settle a dispute, or to reach a business accommodation between the parties in connection with their

---

[62] See, *supra*, Chap. 13 for further discussion on Art. 85.

[63] See the comments of Lord Justice Nicholls to the Statement of Objections of the Commission in the Apple matter, as reported in *Apple Corps Ltd v. Apple Computer, Inc.* [1991] 3 C.M.L.R. 49, 83; Fawlk, *supra*, n. 81, pp. 236.

[64] *BAT v. Commission* 35/83 [1985] 2 C.M.L.R. 470, 491 (para. 33). See also Statement of Objections of the Commission, at p.14, as reported in Fawlk, *supra*, n. 61, at pp. 236–237. *cf.* the statement of the Commission that '[a] no challenge clause would normally restrict competition ...' *Re Penney's Trade Mark* [1978] 2 C.M.L.R. 100, 111, para. 53.

[65] *Apple Corps Ltd v. Apple Computer, Inc.* [1991] 3 C.M.L.R. 49; Fawlk, *supra*, n. 61, p. 235.

respective trade marks.[66] This should be compared with the view in the U.S. where, on occasion, the fact that a settlement is involved has tipped the scales in favour of giving effect to the consent agreement.[67]

Delimitation Agreements Which Partition National Markets Are Unlawful

9–36   When the effect of the delimitation agreement is to partition the market on the basis of the respective trade marks, the agreement has been held unlawful. Partitioning of markets can be accomplished by providing that each of the parties will undertake not to use its mark in specified jurisdictions, leaving the other party free to use its mark in those jurisdictions without challenge. Unlawful partitioning by means of a delimitation agreement has been found in a number of situations.

BAT v. Commission

In the case of *BAT v. Commission*, the Court of Justice upheld the Commission's decision that a delimitation agreement which effectively kept one of the parties out of the German market in respect of certain tobacco products was unlawful.[68] Here, the delimitation agreement had the effect of excluding one of the parties from a key market of the other.

Sirdar/Phildar Decision

The partitioning of markets was also considered by the Commission in the *Sirdar/Phildar* decision. The Commission ruled in a preliminary decision that when one party undertook not to sell its goods in France, and the other undertook not to sell identical goods in the U.K., the delimitation agreement was unlawful under Article 85. The marks were similar and the goods were identical, and the agreement had the effect of partitioning the market.[69]

A Territorial Restriction Is Not Necessarily Unlawful

9–37   This does not mean that all delimitation agreements which contain a territorial restriction will be prohibited under Article 85. A notable example is the Commission's *Penneys* decision.

An Irish textile company trading under the *Penney's* mark agreed to discontinue its use of that mark in various countries and to limit its use of the word as a trade name to Ireland only. The Commission ruled that the restriction was not appreciable because the Irish company had not acquired significant goodwill in the mark, if any, except in Ireland.[70]

---

[66] *Bayer AG. Heinz Sullhofer* [1990] 4 C.M.L.R. 182 (ECJ), involving a patent matter. See also Fawlk, *supra*, n. 61 at p. 226.
[67] See, above, para. 9–10, regarding the *T&T Mfg.* case.
[68] *BAT v. Commission, supra*, n. 64.
[69] *Sirdar/Phildar* [1975] 1 C.M.L.R. D 93.
[70] *Penney's* Decision, *supra*, n. 64.

The Search for Less Restrictive Solutions

The Commission will look with disfavour on territorial restrictions when less   9–38
restrictive solutions to the delimitation agreement are available. This principle
was recognised by the Commission in the *Penney's* decision. It stated in that
case that parties in such a situation 'must seek the least restrictive solution
possible, such as incorporating distinguishing marks, shapes or colours to
differentiate the products...'[71]

The principle was also applied in the Syntex/Synthelabo investigation. Both
parties traded in health care products under similar marks, which were in
part comprised of the prefix 'Syn'. Under the terms of delimitation agreement,
Synthelabo (France) agreed not to use its marks for its products in the
U.K. and in certain non-E.C. countries. The Commission commenced an
investigation of the agreement.

In a release, the Commission indicated that it found that the agreement
had the effect of partitioning the market. In particular, it noted that 'less
restrictive solutions should be examined to determine if, for example, an
agreement on how a trade mark should be used would succeed in eliminating
the risk of confusion.'[72] In fact, the marks of the respective companies had
co-existed in several Community countries. As a result, the parties amended
the agreement to allow full co-existence of all their respective marks throughout the Common Market.

Sufficient Distinctions Between the Marks

In another informal proceeding, the Commission terminated its investigation   9–39
of a delimitation agreement under which the parties had divided their use of
the mark *Persil*, only after the parties added distinctive get-ups to their
respective products and a territorial limitation was abandoned.[73]

No Challenge Clauses

A no challenge clause is frequently included in a consent agreement. This   9–40
provision typically provides that each of the parties undertakes not to lodge
any applications or other objections, or seek cancellation of any application
for or registration of the other party's trade mark.

Further Points Noted Regarding a No Challenge Clause

As a matter of contract law, at least when such a provision is included as   9–41
part of a settlement agreement, a no challenge clause has been held to be
enforceable under English law (subject to a claim of restraint of trade and
the requirements of Article 85 of the Treaty of Rome).[74] Taking guidance

---

[71] *Penney's, supra*, n. 64.
[72] 'Nineteenth Report on Competition Policy' of the E.C. Commission (1989) (point 59).
[73] *Re the Persil Trademark* [1978] 1 C.M.L.R. 395.
[74] *Apple Corps. Ltd v. Apple Computer Inc.* [1992] F.S.R. 431.

from several U.S. decisions, the court held that the U.S. authorities –

> '... strike a correct balance between the three public interests which arise
> in relation to no-challenge agreements made as part of a settlement of a
> dispute, namely the public interest in the due performance of contracts,
> the public interest in the settlement of disputes and the public interest in
> trade mark matters.'[75]

In upholding the enforceability of a no challenge clause, the High Court in
the *Apple Corps*[76] case made several further observations:

(a) The Trade Marks Act 1938 does not prevent a party from surrendering
its right to challenge a trade mark. If this were otherwise, parties could
virtually never resolve trade mark disputes on the basis of a delimitation
of use.

(b) A no challenge clause is enforceable *in personam* as a personal obligation
deriving solely from contract, even if the consent agreement covers
trade mark applications and registrations in other national jurisdictions.
The no challenge obligation is not a proprietary right attaching to the
trade mark itself.

(c) An injunction preventing the challenge of trade mark rights by a party
to the consent agreement, contrary to the provisions of the no challenge
clause, does not require evidence of foreign law, even if the injunction
applies to proceedings in foreign jurisdictions.

No Challenge Clauses: The Problem of Non-Use

9–42   No challenge clauses have also been considered under E.C. law in the context
of delimitation agreements. In the *BAT v. Commission* case, the Court of
Justice, in affirming the ruling of the Commission, held that a no challenge
clause was a restriction on competition where there had been no use of the
mark for more than five years after its registration in Germany.[77]

In this case, it was noted that under German law, non-use of a mark for
more than five years leaves the mark open to cancellation. The delimitation
agreement in issue had been signed one day after the expiry of the five year
period. The result was that the agreement restricted the freedom of the owner
of the *Toltec* mark to use the mark in Germany and to challenge the validity
of the *Dorcet* mark there, despite the dormancy of it.[78]

9–43   The opposite situation, where the no challenge clause only applied to the
five year period running from the date of application, was addressed by the

---

[75] *Apple Corps.*, *supra*, n. 74, at 468. The U.S. cases are *Beer Nuts*, 477 F.2d 326 (6th Cir. 1973);
Danskin, Inc. v. Dan River, Inc., 498 F.2d 1386 (C.C.P.A. 1974); and *MWS Wire Industries Inc.
v. California Fine Wire Co., Inc.*, 797 F.2d 799 (9th Cir. 1986).
[76] *Apple Corps.*, *supra*, n. 74.
[77] *BAT Cigaretten-Fabriken Gmbh v. E.C. Commission* [1985] F.S.R. 533.
[78] *BAT v. Commission*, *supra*, n. 64, at 492, para. 35. More generally, the Court's ruling in the
BAT v. Commission case can be said to establish the principle that an unused mark cannot
serve as the basis for imposing restrictions via a delimitation agreement. See Statement of
Objections of the Commission in the Apple matter, as reported in *Apple Corps, supra*, n. 63;
Fawlk, *supra*, n. 61, at 235.

Commission in the *Penney's* case. There, no appreciable restriction was found.[79] The Commission reasoned that the no challenge clause was in effect only for five years, the period of time in which trade mark use may be established under most national trade mark laws. It was very likely that use would be made of the trade mark during that period. Thereafter, the mark could be challenged if no use had been made.[80]

When is a No Challenge Clause Enforceable?

No general statement about the enforceability of a no challenge clause can be derived from these rulings. Nevertheless, the fact that delimitation agreements have been recognised as 'useful' and 'legal' by the Court of Justice in *BAT v. Commission*, so long as they satisfy the requirements of E.C. competition law, suggests that such a clause will be evaluated under the traditional approach of Article 85.[81]   **9–44**

No Challenge Clauses in Licences

There is no certainty that the same considerations apply to a no challenge clause in a trade mark licence. In particular, the importance of achieving finality as a part of a settlement delimitation agreement appears less relevant to a commercial licence arrangement.[82]   **9–45**

Challenge by the Licensee to Registration of the Licensor's Trade Marks

It is sometimes provided as part of a settlement that the licensee will assist the licensor in securing registration of the trade marks which are the subject of the licence. Can the licensee subsequently challenge these applications, on the grounds that: (a) the licence agreement does not expressly prevent the licensee from filing such an opposition, (b) no such negative term can be implied, and (c) the right to oppose is granted under the Trade Marks Act?   **9–46**

It has been held that there is no need to imply such a term in order to prevent the licensee from filing an opposition, because the very fact of the filing of the opposition is 'contrary to the [explicit] terms of the agreement'.[83] Such conduct is contrary both to the licensee's obligation to assist the licensor in applying for registration and to the licensee's acknowledgement that the licensor is the sole proprietor of the trade marks.[84] No argument in relation to licensee estoppel was raised by the licensee in that case. This result suggests that the court may view a no challenge clause with favour.

---

[79] *supra*, n. 64, at 111, para. 53.
[80] *supra*, n. 64, at 111–112, paras. 54, 55.
[81] See, *infra*, Chap. 13, paras. 13–05 to 13–11, for discussion on Art. 85.
[82] See, *e.g.* Bayer v. Sulhofer, *supra*, n. 66, where the Court of Justice permitted a no challenge clause in connection with a royalty free patent licence in settlement of a patent dispute. It also has been suggested that a no challenge clause as part of a purely domestic U.K. agreement might be contrary to the *Statute of Monopolies*. Robertson, *infra*, n. 98, at 377.
[83] *Sport International B.V. v. Hi-Tec Sports Ltd* [1990] F.S.R. 312, 313–31.
[84] *Sport International*, above, at 312, 313–315. But *cf.* with the result reached in the *Windsurfing* case, *supra*, n. 85.

The Status of No Challenge Clauses in Trade Mark Licences under E.C. Law

9–47   The status of a no challenge clause in a trade mark licence has been upheld by the Commission in the *Moosehead/Whitbread* decision.

Earlier, in the case of *Windsurfing International Inc. v. E.C. Commission*, the Court of Justice had held that a clause requiring the licensee to acknowledge the validity of the licensor's trade marks was tantamount to a no challenge clause which was caught by Article 85 because it was restrictive of competition. The Court intimated that the imposition of the clause was an unwarranted extension of the subject matter of the patent licence.[85] However, the precise question of the enforceability of a no challenge clause in a trade mark licence was not answered.

The Moosehead/Whitbread Decision

9–48   The issue was subsequently considered by the Commission in the *Moosehead/Whitbread* decision.[86] The Canadian brewer Moosehead entered into a licence agreement to enable the licensee to enter the U.K. market.[87] The agreement contained a no challenge clause with respect to the *Moosehead* trade mark. The Commission evaluated the enforceability of the no challenge provision under general principles of EC competition law.

Challenges to Ownership and Validity Distinguished

9–49   The Commission distinguished between challenges to the ownership of the trade mark and its validity.

Regarding the ownership of the trade mark, the Commission was of the opinion that the undertaking did not amount to a restriction on competition, whether the challenge could have been brought on the basis of prior use or prior registration. It did not matter who the proprietor of the trade mark was. In the words of the Commission: 'Whether or not the licensor or licensee has the ownership of the trademark, the use of it by any party is prevented in any event, and competition would thus not be effected.'[88]

An undertaking not to challenge the validity of the trade mark, however, was more problematic. here, the continued existence of an invalid mark could serve as a barrier to entry into the market. The commission described the barrier to entry as follows:

'Only where the use of a well-known mark would be an important advantage to a company entering or competing in any given market and the absence of which therefore constitutes a significant barrier to entry,

[85] *Windsurfing International Inc. v. E.C. Commission* [1988] F.S.R. 154, paras. 75–81.
[86] O.J. [1990] L100/32. See generally, Subiotto, 'Moosehead/Whitbread: Industrial Franchises and No-Challenge Clauses Relating to Licenced Trade Marks Under EEC Competition Law', E.I.P.R. 12(9), 1990, 334.
[87] An oddity of the factual background to this matter is that the parties were apparently also joint proprietors of the trade mark.
[88] *supra*, n. 86, L 100/36.

would this clause ... constitute an appreciable restriction of competition...'[89]

Thus, a traditional analysis under Article 85 would be employed to determine whether the no challenge clause could have an appreciable effect on competition.

Reviewing the facts, the Commission reached the conclusion that any anticompetitive effects from maintaining the mark would be negligible, because the mark had only recently been introduced into the U.K. market. Accordingly, the barrier to entry, if any, would be slight.[90]

No Challenge Clauses Under the Block Exemptions

The result of the *Moosehead/Whitbread* decision appears to be that a no   9–50
challenge clause in a trade mark licence may well be enforceable, unless, perhaps, the undertaking involves a well known mark. This is true unless a block exemption applies to the agreement and provides otherwise.

The Commission of the European Community has, by issuing regulations (to so-called 'block exemptions'), sought to clarify under what circumstances Article 85(1) of the Treaty of Rome, which prohibits certain types of anticompetitive conduct, does not apply to specified types of provisions in licensing agreements of intellectual property rights, including patents, know-how and franchising. Conversely, the block exemptions also indicate which types of provisions do not fall within the scope of the exemption and which, therefore, remain subject to Article 85(1).

The block exemptions in the context of trade mark licensing are discussed in Chapter 13. It is worth noting at this point that the certain of the block exemptions that govern the licensing of intellectual property rights appear to prohibit the licensor from imposing a no challenge clause on the licensee. None of these provisions refers, however, explicitly to a trade mark licence. Thus, Article 3(1) of the patent Block Exemption Regulation prohibits a no challenge clause in respect of 'industrial or commercial property rights',[91] while Article 5(f) of the Franchise Block Exemption Regulation refers to a similar prohibition with respect to 'industrial or intellectual property rights'.[92] In both cases, this prohibition is without prejudice to the licensor to terminate the licence should a challenge be made. It is arguable that the scope of these prohibitions includes a trade mark licence.

On the other hand, Article 3(4) of the Know-How Regulation only prohibits a no challenge clause regarding licenced know-how or licensed patents.[93] A no challenge clause in connection with a related trade mark might be valid

---

[89] *supra*, n. 88, at L 100/36.
[90] *id.* The question has been raised how 'well-known' a mark must be to constitute a barrier to entry. Rothnie, 'EC Competition Policy, the Commission and Trade Marks', *International Business Lawyer*, November 1991, p. 497.
[91] Regulation 2349/84 on the Application of Art. 85(3) of the Treaty is Certain Categories of Patent Licencing Agreement [1984] O.J. 1219/15 as amended [1993] O.J. L21/8.
[92] Regulation 4087/88 on the Application of Art. 85(3) of the Treaty to Categories of Franchise Agreements [1988] O.J. L359/46.
[93] Regulation 556/89 on the Application of Art. 85(30) of the Treaty of Certain Categories of know-how Licensing Agreements [1989] O.J. L61/1 as amended [1993] O.J. L21/8.

under such circumstances.[94] Taken as a whole, the question of whether the block exemptions prohibit a no challenge clause in the licence agreement must be viewed as not fully settled.

LICENSEE ESTOPPEL

Introduction

9–51   A trade mark is a negative right which empowers its proprietor to prevent other parties from using the mark without the proprietor's permission. By granting a licence and entering into an agreement with the licensee, the proprietor elects not to exercise its negative right with respect to the licensee.

The issue that arises is whether the license relationship creates a correlative obligation on the part of the licensee, not to attack the validity of the trade mark. The argument in favour of such an obligation on the part of the licensee has been expressed by one U.S. court as follows:

> '[A] licensee should not be permitted to enjoy the benefit afforded by the agreement while simultaneously urging that the [trade mark] which forms the basis of the agreement is void.'[95]

The U.K. Situation

9–52   It is frequently stated that the licensee of an intellectual property right is estopped from denying the validity of that right. This position is based on the following passage of Lord Westbury:

> 'Now with the first contention on the part of the Respondent is this, that, notwithstanding that relation continues, he is at liberty to deny the title of the Appellants to the ownership of the inventions, for the use of which he is thus paying a royalty. We are all very well aware that that is a proposition inconsistent with the law, as it would be equally inconsistent with ordinary reason and good sense of mankind.'[96]

The principle has most often been applied to patent licenses,[97] but its general applicability has been questioned.[98] If the principle applies to a trade mark licence, it has the effect of denying the licensee certain statutory rights of challenge.[99]

---

[94] Subiotto, *supra*, n. 86, at p. 339. For further discussion on the block exemptions, see *infra*, Chap 13, paras. 13–12 to 13–43.

[95] *Lear, Inc. v. Adkins*, 435 P.2d 321, 325–326 (1967).

[96] *Crossley v. Dixon*, 11 All E.R. 1039 at 1043.

[97] See *Terrel on the Law of Patents* (13th ed., 1982) at para. 9.21.

[98] Robertson, 'Is the Licensee Estoppel Law Still Good Law? Was it Ever?' [1991] 10 E.I.P.R. 375.

[99] *e.g.* opposition to registration removal for non-use and the general power to expunge a registration (s.32). *Apple Corps. Ltd v. Apple Computer, Inc.* [1992 F.S.R.] 431, 461.

Has the Issue of Licensee Estoppel Been Resolved?

It has been stated that no judgment has squarely recognised the applicability   **9–53**
of licensee estoppel to a trade mark licence.[1] However, two judgments have
been cited in support of this position.

In *Re Silexine Paint's Ltd Application*, the hearing officer concluded that
'the Law of Estoppel does not operate to prevent Counsel for the Applicants
from making submissions to the effect of the Agreement in partial support of
the contention that the mark in suit wrongly remains upon the Register . . .'[2]

In the other case, *McGregor Trade Mark*,[3] Judge Whitford affirmed the
decision of the hearing officer, allowing the registered user to challenge the
registration of the trade mark on the ground that no quality control had been
exercised.[4] There was a suggestion that the public interest in expunging invalid
marks from the Registry should take precedence over any estoppel owing to
the conduct of the two parties.[5]

The court in the *Apple Corps* case, in reviewing these judgments, was of
the opposite view, namely, that the issue of licensee estoppel had not even
been raised in either judgment, much less that the principle had been given
judicial recognition.[6]

The Job Case: Has Licensee Estoppel Finally Been Recognised?

However, the recent decision in the *Job* case[7] suggests that licensee estoppel   **9–54**
will bar a licensee from seeking rectification of the registration of the licenced
trade mark. In that case, the Registrar held that the licensee could not bring
an action for rectification since it was not a 'person aggrieved.' Under the
Trade Marks Act 1938, only a person aggrieved has *locus standi* to bring a
rectification action. The Registrar reasoned as follows:

> 'Thus in my view there is no doubt whatsoever that the royalty payment
> related to use of the [registered] marks in the United Kingdom. Proceeding
> from this, I accept [the] arguments in relation to the impossibility of
> simultaneous approbation and reprobation, and in relation to estoppel,
> in that the applicants on the one hand claim that the 1958 [licence]
> agreement is extant and they intend to pay the royalty and continue
> using the *JOB* mark under that agreement, and at the same time argue
> that the marks should be removed from the register. I, therefore, find
> formally that by reason of estoppel the applicants cannot be "persons
> aggrieved" . . .'[8]

---

[1] Robertson, *supra*, n. 88, at 60. The issue was considered in detail, albeit in *obiter* only, in the
Apple Corps. case, *supra*, n. 99.

[2] 71 R.P.C. 91, 93 (1954).

[3] [1979] R.P.C. 36.

[4] *Supra*, n. 2, at 52–53.

[5] *Supra*, n. 2, at 54.

[6] *Supra*, n. 99, at 461–465.

[7] *Job T.M.* [1993] F.S.R. 118, see also discussion in Chap. 6, paras. 6–16 to 6–18.

[8] *Supra*, n. 7. It is noted that the case of *Crossley v. Dixon*, which is considered the leading
judgment in favour of the doctrine of licensee estoppel under U.K. law, was referred to in the
Job decision. However, the various U.K. and U.S. cases cited in the *Apple Corps.* decision
regarding the applicability of the doctrine in connection with trade mark licences, were not
mentioned in the *Job* decision.

Licensee Estoppel under U.S. Law

9–55   U.S. law has clearly distinguished between the validity of licensee estoppel for a patent licensee and a trade mark licensee.

Estoppel and Patent Licences

9–56   Regarding patent licenses, the landmark U.S. Supreme Court decision of *Lear, Inc. v. Adkins* held that licensee estoppel does not apply to a patent licence.[9] The court reasoned that the interest in holding parties to their contractual promises must give way to the public interest in ensuring that all ideas should be freely available unless protected by a valid patent.

Estoppel Applies to Trade Mark Licences

9–57   The situation is different regarding trade marks, where *Lear v. Adkins* has been held not to apply.[10] The prevailing law is that a licensee is estopped from challenging the trade mark during the course of the license agreement. The licensee has given recognition to the proprietor's title in the mark by virtue of the licence.[11] This estoppel has been held not to apply when the licenced mark was registered after the expiry of the licence agreement.[12]

Applicability of Estoppel After Expiry of the Licence Agreement

9–58   There is a difference of opinion on whether the licensee is estopped from challenging the trade mark after the expiry of the licence agreement. Some courts have held that the estoppel is effective even after expiry of the agreement.[13] Others have held that the estoppel comes to an end with the termination of the agreement.[14]

More recently, an intermediate position has come into favour: '[A]fter expiration of the license, a former trademark licensee may challenge the licensor's title on facts that arose *after* the contract has expired.'[15] This approach is seen as affirming the licensee's recognition of the trade mark by virtue of entering into the agreement, while not preventing the licensee from ever challenging the trade mark after expiration of the licence.

---

[9] 395 U.S. 653 (1969).

[10] *Beer Nuts, Inc. v. King Nut Co.*, 477 F2d 326 (6th Cir. 1973); *Danskin, Inc. v. Dan River, Inc.*, 182 U.S.P.Q. 370 (CCPA 1974).

[11] *Professional Golfers Association v. Bankers L. & C. Co.*, 514 F.2d 665, 671 (5th Cir. 1975).

[12] *National Council, YMCA v. Columbia YMCA*, 8 U.S.P.Q. 2d 1682, 1686 (D.C.S.C. 1988).

[13] *Professional Golfers Association*, *supra*, n. 11, p. 671; *Heaton Distributing Co. v. Union Tank Car Co.*, 387 F.2d 477 (8th Cir. 1967).

[14] See *e.g. Professional Golfers Association*, above, at 671; *Donald F. Duncan, Inc. v. Royal Tops Mfg. Co., Inc.*, 141 U.S.P.Q. 567 (N.D. Ill. 1964).

[15] *Professional Golfers Association*, *supra*, n. 11, p. 671, emphasis in original, *Chrysler Motors Corp. v. Alloy Automotive Co. Inc.*, 661 F. Supp. 191, 193 (N.D. Ill. 1987); *Garri Publication Associates Inc. v. Dabora*, 10 U.S.P.Q. 2d 1694, 1697 (Trademark Trial and Appeal Board (1988).

Estoppel Only Applies to A Licence Arrangement

The doctrine of licensee estoppel is applicable only when a licence relationship   9–59
exists, whether by way of a formal agreement, an oral licence, or by virtue
of an affiliation relationship between a national organisation and its local
branch. It does not apply when the putative licensees are merely a sub-group
of a group's general membership[16], nor in relation to a certification mark.[17]

---

[16] *Opticians Association v. Independent Opticians of America*, 14 U.S.P.Q. 2d 2021, 2026 (D.C.N.J.
1990); rev'd on other grounds, 17 U.S.P.Q. 2d 1117 (3rd Cir. 1990).
[17] *Midwest Plastic Fabricators*, 12 U.S.P.Q. 2d 1267, 1269, n. 3 (Trademark Trial and Appeal
Board 1989), aff'd on other grounds, 15 U.S.P.Q. 2d 1359 (Fed Cir. 1990).

10. The Trade Mark Licence Agreement: The Interrelationship Between the Proprietary and the Contractual

INTRODUCTION

A trade mark licence is typically part of a broader commercial relationship **10–01** between the licensor and licensee. As such, the parties seek to ensure that the terms and conditions of the agreement are set out in a valid and enforceable contract. This means that a trade mark licence agreement will address both proprietary and contractual rights.

The licensor grants the licensee permission to use the trade mark. The rights and duties of the respective parties under the grant derive from the licensor's proprietary rights in the trade mark. In addition, the parties will specify the commercial and financial arrangements between them in connection with the grant of licence and the law of contract will therefore come into play. This chapter will discuss the nature of the interrelationship between the proprietary and contractual aspects of a trade mark licence.

The Trade Mark Licence and the Proprietary Right

A Trade Mark as a Negative Right

It is frequently said that a trade mark licence is the grant of permission by **10–02** the proprietor for the use of the trade mark by a third party. In the absence of this permission, such third party use would be an infringement.[1]

This characterisation of a trade mark licence is based on the view that an **10–03** intellectual property right is a negative right, that is to say it confers upon the proprietor of the trade mark the power to prevent others from using the mark without permission. When such permission is granted, it provides the licensee with a defense against a claim of infringement.

The idea of a trade mark as a negative right could be seen in section 4(3)(a) of the Trade Mark Act 1938, which provided that use of a registered trade mark by a third party should not be deemed an infringement if the proprietor of the mark '... has at any time expressly or impliedly consented to the use of the trade mark.' Conversely, in the absence of consent, use of the trade mark by a third party was deemed an infringement.[2] The Trade Marks Act

---

[1] *T&T Manufacturing Co. v. A.T. Cross Co.*, 201 U.S.P.Q. 561, 565 (1st Cir. 1978).
[2] See also s.32(a) of the Lanham Act, which states that infringement of a registered trade mark occurs when any person uses the trade mark 'without the consent of the registrant.'

1994 reads as follows: 'The proprietor of a registered trade mark has exclusive rights in the trade mark which are infringed by use of the trade mark in the United Kingdom without his consent.'[3]

A Licence is More Than a Consent to Use the Trade Mark

10–04   However, the proprietary interest in a trade mark licence extends beyond the notion of a consent. The focus of licensing under the Trade Marks Act is not merely to consent to the use of the trade mark by the licensee, but also to set out the terms and conditions of the licensee's use of the trade mark.

Under the approach taken under the Trade Marks Act 1938, the key to valid licensing was that the licensee's use of the mark indicated a connection in the course of trade between the proprietor and the goods.[4] Under the Trade Marks Act 1994, the focus is on the trade mark 'as a valuable piece of property, in terms both of its power to attract customers and of the royalties which can be demanded from licensee.'[5] Despite this difference in approach, the linchpin to successful licensing is the controlled use of the mark by the licensee. This is principally accomplished by the exercise of quality control by the licensor over the licensee.[6]

A similar conception of trade mark licensing is seen under U.S. law, in the idea of a 'related company' under the Lanham Act.[7] Here, also, quality control provides the means for ensuring that the licensee's use is consistent with the licensor's interest in the mark.

As a result, a trade mark licence does not merely provide the licensee with a defense to a claim of infringement. Rather, trade mark licensing extends to specifying the circumstances by which an authorised third party use of the trade mark does not, depending upon the view taken, either deceive the public or otherwise impair the licensor's rights in the mark. Further, when these conditions are met, use of the trade mark by the licensee will inure to the benefit of the licensor.[8]

Thus, a trade mark which is used by the licensee in a manner consistent with the terms and conditions of the licence thereby protects the proprietary interest of the licensor in the mark.

---

[3] Trade Marks Act 1994, s.9(1). This view is also incorporated within the E.C. Trade Marks Directive, especially Arts. 3(2)(c), 4(5), 5(1),(2) and 10(3). See, *supra*, Chap. 9, for discussion on consent more generally. It is conceivable that a trade mark licence could be compelled by operation of law rather than freely consented to by the licensor. In the 1970's, the U.S. Federal Trade Commission did not rule out the possibility that a compulsory licence might be an appropriate remedy for monopolistic behavior, even if it was not imposed under the circumstances (*Re Borden, Inc.*, 3 CCH Trade Reg. Reporter, para. 21490. aff'd on other grounds, 674 F.2d 498 (6th Cir. 1982)). But see Art. 21 of the Agreement on TRIPS, part of the GAAT Agreement 1994, which provides that 'compulsory licensing shall not be permitted.'
[4] Trade Marks Act 1938, s.68.
[5] Reform of Trade Marks Law, Department of Trade and Industry, Cm. 1203 (1990) ('White paper'), para. 4.32.
[6] See, *supra*, Chap. 6, regarding quality control.
[7] ss.5 and 45. See, *supra*, Chap. 5, for a discussion of the 'related companies' provisions under the Lanham Act.
[8] See, *supra*, Chap. 4, at paras. 4–33 and 4–34; and Chap. 5, para. 5–34.

The Licence as a Commercial Arrangement

In addition to the proprietary aspect, there is also a significant commercial **10–05** aspect to a trade mark licence. Here, the relationship between the licensor and the licensee is governed principally by the law of contract. As such, there are many forms that the commercial aspects of the licence agreement can take. The commercial terms will reflect the relative commercial power which each party brings to the licence arrangement.

Thus, the licensor may be the proprietor of a well known trade mark, for which competition between prospective licensees for the right to use the mark is keen, and to a large extent the licensor will be able to dictate the terms of the transaction. On the other hand, the trade mark may be obscure or newly adopted, while the prospective licensee has proven manufacturing and distribution capabilities in a given territory. Here, it may be the licensee who will drive the commercial terms.

Three Reasons Why a Licence is Embodied in a Written Agreement

Whatever the commercial basis for the licence agreement, the parties, par- **10–06** ticularly when they are unrelated, will typically enter into a written agreement.[9] There are three principal reasons, which reflect the fact that the licence addresses both proprietary and contract rights of the parties:

Evidence of the licence: A written document will ease the evidential burden of establishing the basic terms, such as the grant of consent, the identification of the trade marks covered by the licence, the duration, the goods or services involved and the scope of the permitted territory. It may also serve to exclude a right which would otherwise be conferred by statute.[10]

Commercial terms: The parties to a trade mark licence will primarily view the licence as a commercial arrangement in commercial terms, particularly in connection with the payment of royalties and other financial terms. The parties will therefore look to the agreement to establish their respective commercial rights and duties.[11]

Quality control: A written document will make it easier to establish quality control, either for the purpose of recording the licensee if relevant in the jurisdiction, or for otherwise substantiating the presence of adequate quality control.[12] Detailed quality control provisions may be relied upon to counter a claim that the exercise of quality control is inadequate or insufficient, as well as to clarify the contractual obligations of the parties in that respect.

---

[9] Even when the parties are related, such as in a parent-subsidiary relationship, a formal written contract is to be recommended, if only to establish a foundation for the issue of royalty payments and the like in connection with the tax authorities. See, below, Chap. 14, at paras. 14–33 to 14–65.

[10] For example, the licensee's right to sue for infringement under sections of the Trade Marks Act 1994. See generally, Chap. 4 at paras. 4–07 to 4–25.

[11] See, *infra*, paras. 10–11 to 10–23.

[12] See, *infra*, paras. 10–14 to 10–23.

THE TYPES OF PROVISION THAT ADDRESS THE RIGHTS IN A LICENCE AGREEMENT

Are the Rights in a Written Licence Agreement Overlapping or Complementary?

10–07　In recognising that a written trade mark licence agreement addresses both the proprietary and contractual rights of the parties, it is necessary to distinguish between three types of provision which are contained in the agreement.

(a) Some provisions refer directly to the licensor's proprietary rights under the trade mark licence. To the extent that these rights are included in the licence agreement, the licensor will have a contractual right in them as well.[13]

(b) Some provisions refer to contractual rights of the licensor in the licence agreement. Depending upon the construction given to the subject matter of the provision, the provision may also be deemed to relate to a proprietary interest of the licensor.[14]

(c) Some provisions refer to a mere contractual right in favour of the licensee.[15]

Each of these categories is discussed more fully below.

The Licensor's Proprietary Rights Under the Trade Mark Licence

10–08　The basic right of the licensor with respect to the trade mark is proprietary, namely, to permit the use of the trade mark by the licensee in accordance with the terms and conditions specified in the licence.[16] Any use of the trade mark by the licensee, other than as authorised by the licensor, will be an infringement of the licensor's proprietary rights in the trade mark.

Generally speaking, the licensor's proprietory rights in the trade mark licence can reasonably be said to be comprised of the following provisions:

(a) The form, covered by the registration, in which the trade mark may be used;

(b) The scope of the goods or services for which the licence is granted;

(c) The territory in which the trade mark may be affixed;

(d) The quality of the goods manufactured or the services provided;

(e) The duration of the licence.[17]

Both Proprietary and Contractual Rights in the Subject Matter

10–09　The various aspects of the proprietary rights of the licensor set out above may or may not be included in a written agreement. To the extent that they are included in the agreement, they are protected under the law of contract

---

[13] See, *infra*, paras. 10–08 to 10–10.
[14] See, *infra*, paras. 10–11 to 10–14.
[15] See, *infra*, paras. 10–15 to 10–17.
[16] See, *supra*, paras. 10–02 to 10–03.
[17] These provisions are expressly identified in Art. 8(2) of the E.C. Trade Marks Directive.

as well. While the general subject matter of the proprietary and contract rights in the licence may even be identical or virtually so, there is no reason to limit a licensor to only one set of rights.

In an English judgment, the *Sport International* case, the court stated that the plaintiff could press forward on its claim for infringement, 'not withstanding that it succeeds on the contract claim because, as we understand it, the measure of damages may be more favorable to it.'[18]

In another example, it has been held, under U.S. law, that the awarding of both damages for infringement, and liquidated damages as provided for under the licence agreement, in each case on account of post-termination use of the trade mark, did not amount to a double recovery. Liquidated damages were awarded for breach of the licence agreement, while infringement damages were awarded for unauthorised use of the trade mark after termination of the agreement.[19]

It is not necessary that the contractual provision be expressly stated in the agreement. In the *Sport International* case, the court held that an enforceable provision may be implied in the agreement. In that case, the court implied a term that the defendant will not sue any of the marks without a licence from the plaintiff.[20] Moreover, in a subsequent proceeding in this matter, the court held that an undertaking by the licensee to offer reasonable assistance to the licensor in connection with the prosecution of applications carried with it the obligation by the licensee not to oppose any such registration, despite the absence of any explicit undertaking to that effect.[21] The result is that, depending upon the particular provisions of the agreement, the licensor may enjoy both proprietary and contractual rights in the same subject matter. **10–10**

The foregoing applies unequivocally only in the case of a registered trade mark. With an unregistered trade mark it is uncertain, particularly under United Kingdom law, to what extent, if any, the licensor has any proprietary right in the trade mark *vis-à-vis* the licensee.[22] However the judgment in the so-called *Ninja Turtles* case seems to have recognised the possibility of a proprietary right in a licence of an unregistered mark.[23]

Contractual Rights of the Licensor Which May or May Not also Be Deemed Proprietary

There are certain aspects of a trade mark licence agreement in which the licensor's proprietary right in the subject matter of the provision is less certain. **10–11**

---

[18] *Sport International Bossum B.V. v. Hi-Tec Sports Ltd* [1988] R.P.C. 329, 337.
[19] *Ramada Inns Inc. v. Gadsden Motel Co.*, 1 U.S.P.Q 2d 1011 (11th Cir. 1986]. Query, however, whether such a result would be rejected under U.K. law as amounting to a double recovery, which is highly disfavoured. See, *infra*, para. 10–31.
[20] *Sport International*, *supra*, n. 18, at 334.
[21] *Sport International Bossum B.V. v. Hi-Tec Sports Ltd* [1990] F.S.R. 312, 314, 315 (H.C. 1987].
[22] See Lane, *The Status of Licensing of Common Law Marks*, 1991.
[23] *Mirage Studios v. Counter-Feat Clothing Company Ltd* [1991] F.S.R. 145.

No Proprietary Right

10–12 In a leading United Kingdom case under the Trade Marks Act 1938, *Actomin Products Ltd's Application*,[24] the court held that a dispute over the alleged breach of a provision in the licence agreement, under which the licensee was obliged to spend no less than twelve hundred pounds twice a year on advertising, was not a matter 'relating to trade mark registration, or ... questions of deception or confusion in the use of trade marks in the course of trade.'[25]

Similarly, in a U.S. case,[26] the court recognised a claim for breach of contract, where the licensee was required to obtain written approval from the licensor for the sale of certain food items not directly covered by the licence. However, the court held that the sale of unauthorised food items did not amount to infringement, since it found that no proprietary right in the mark was involved.

Proprietary Right Recognised

10–13 In contrast, in another U.S. case,[27] the licensee's conduct was viewed as a breach of its duty to maintain quality control. Where the licensee used the licensor's trade mark on frozen dairy products other than those specified by the licensor under the licence agreement, the court found that there was both a breach of contract and infringement of trade mark, even in the absence of termination.[28]

Occasionally, the court has sought to distinguish between a licence to distribute the goods and the right of the licensee to use the trade mark itself. In one U.S. case, the court ruled that under the terms of the agreement, the exclusive distributor had received a licence to sell the defendant's goods, but not to affix the trade mark on goods of its own manufacture. The court held that such manufacture and use of the trade mark beyond the scope of the licence was an infringement, even if the distribution licence remained valid.[29]

Quality Control Provisions

10–14 It is arguable that the licensor enjoys a proprietary right in relation to the licensee's performance of the quality control provisions.[30] In addition, to the extent that the quality control obligations are based on contractual provisions, the licensor will also have contractual rights with respect to those provisions.

---

[24] (1953) 70 R.P.C. 201.
[25] *Supra*, n. 24, at 203.
[26] *Terry v. International Dairy Queen Inc.*, 218 U.S.P.Q. 905, 911, 912 (N.D. Indiana 1983).
[27] *Franchised Stores of New York Inc. v. Winter*, 159 U.S.P.Q. 221 (E.D.N.Y. 1965).
[28] See, also, *Carvel Farms Corporation v. Nathan*, 159 U.S.P.Q. 225 (S.D.N.Y. 1966).
[29] *Jordan Rand*, 217 U.S.P.Q. 795, 799–800 (D.C.P.R. 1982), citing *Franchised Stores of New York Inc.*, *supra*, n. 27.
[30] See Art. 8(2) of the E.C. Trade Marks Directive.

However, it is then fare from clear precisely what constitutes the quality control provisions of a given licence.[31]

The Licensee's Contractual Rights Under the Trade Mark Licence

No Proprietary Right in the Licence

It has been held by the House of Lords in the *Sports International* case that 10–15 the licensee has no proprietary interest in the trade mark licence. The licence simply serves as a defence to an infringement claim by the licensor.[32] Under this judgment, the licensee's rights in the trade mark licence are merely contractual in nature.

However, one can ask whether this characterisation of the licensee's rights in the licence as merely contractual is fully consistent with the Trade Marks Act 1994. This is particularly seen in the right of certain exclusive licensees to bring action for infringement.[33] These provisions underwent material change during the legislative development of the Trade Marks Act 1994. In its initial form, a clear distinction was made between the rights of action of exclusive and non-exclusive licensees, respectively, whereby the right of action of an exclusive licensee was likened to that of an assignee as a matter of law.[34]

Apparently in response to objections in respect of this characterisation, the final form of the bill eliminated the provision that likened the exclusive licensee to an assignee as a matter law. In its place, the Trade Marks Act 1994 contains general provisions governing the right of action of a licensee, whether exclusive or non-exclusive.[35] These general provisions are then made subject to an exception in the situation where the licence agreement itself provides that the exclusive licensee shall have the same rights and remedies as if the grant of the licence had been an assignment. The exclusive licensee may in such cases bring an action in his own name.[36]

The rights conferred upon such exclusive licensees thus seem to call into 10–16 question the continued applicability of the *Sports International* decision.[37] In accordance with the view that the licensee has no proprietary right in the licence, there are a variety of circumstances in which the licensee may assert its contractual rights against the licensor.

---

[31] A similar question is raised in connection with the construction of a best endeavours obligation. See, *infra*, Chap. 12, paras. 12–48 to 12–58. The parties might consider detailing the terms in the licence agreement which relate to the quality control requirements. On the other hand, it is conceivable that one or both of the parties may prefer to address the quality control provisions in a more general manner. Regarding quality control generally, see Chap. 6.

[32] *Sport International, Bursam v. Inter-Footwear*, (1984) All E.R. 321. See also, *infra*. Chap. 12, para. 12–34.

[33] Trade Marks Act 1994, s. 31. See generally, above, Chap. 4, paras. 4–07 to 4–25.

[34] *Supra*, Chap. 4, at para. 4–08.

[35] Trade Marks Act 1994, s. 30.

[36] Trade Marks Act 1994, s. 31.

[37] On occasion, U.S. courts have found a proprietary right in favour of a licensee. For example, in *Burma-Bibas, Inc. v. Excelled Leather Coat Corp.*, 223 U.S.P.Q. 969, 970 (S.D.N.Y. 1984), the court held that the licensee may have a claim against the licensor and second licensee for infringement of the first licensee's proprietary rights in the unregistered trade mark. Whether this result is correct has been questioned.

Financial Obligations of the Licensor

10–17 Perhaps the most likely situation is when the licensor owes the licensee monies, or the licensor does not fulfill its obligations regarding the expenditure of funds for advertising or promotion.[38] In such circumstances, the licensee will either cease to pay royalties or attempt to set-off royalty payments against the amount owed to it by the licensor.[39]

Non-Financial Obligations of the Licensor

10–18 Of course, the licensor's obligation need not be financial. In one case, the licensee successfully enforced provisions in the agreement relating to a right of first option and a covenant of non-competition, in order to prevent the licensor from licensing an additional product to a third party.[40]

The licensee's right may also be based on the breach of a warranty given by the licensor. The most typical such warranty is that the licensor has good title to the trade mark, and that it has the right to enter into the licence. The warranty may be expressly contained in the licence agreement or it may be based on statute.[41] Here, again, the licensor's breach of a warranty may give the licensee a right of set-off or counterclaim.[42]

No Proprietary Right in Respect of Termination

10–19 The licensee's contractual right may relate to a matter which, if breached by the licensee, would infringe the licensor's proprietary rights. Thus, if the licensee continues to use the trade mark after the duration specified in the licence agreement, the licensee will be in breach of the licensor's proprietary right in the trade mark. However, if the licensor seeks to terminate the licence before the end of the period specified in the agreement, the licensee will have only a contractual claim against the licensor.

It has also been held under U.S. law that where the licensor terminated the licence on the ground that the licensee did not follow the provisions of the agreement, the licensee did not have an action for infringement or false description under the Lanham Act. The former licensee was left to enforce its rights by means of the alleged breach of contract by the licensor.[43]

---

[38] Durie and Manson, 'The Licensor in Breach: Set-offs, Counterclaims and Outstanding Royalties' [1991] 3 E.I.P.R. 95; *Actomin Products, supra*, n. 24.

[39] Durie and Manson, *supra*, n.38, at 38.

[40] *Pantone Inc. v. Letraset*, 11 U.S.P.Q. 2d 1454 (2nd Cir. 1989).

[41] Thus the Uniform Commercial Code in the U.S., which forms the basis for the law of contract in 49 of the 50 U.S. states, provides in Art. 2–312 for a warranty of title in connection with the sale of intellectual property. However, the National Conference of Commissioners on Uniform State Laws is currently drafting a proposed addition to the Uniform Commercial Code that will cover the contractual aspects of licences, including warranties. If and when the draft is adopted, and it is incorporated as part of the law of contract of the several states, it may have a material effect on the way that the contractual aspects of trade mark licensing are treated under U.S. law.

[42] Durie and Manson, *supra*, n. 38.

[43] *Silverstar Enterprises. Inc. v. Aday*, 218 U.S.P.Q. 142 (S.D.N.Y. 1982).

Exclusivity

As noted above, depending upon the jurisdiction involved, an exclusive **10–20** licensee may enjoy certain rights, particularly with respect to the right to bring suit. As well, the exclusive licensee may enjoy the right to use the mark even to the exclusion of the licensor itself.[44] This is in fact the definition of an exclusive licence under the Trade Marks Act 1994.

The Shoney Case: How Far Does the Exclusivity Provision Limit the Licensor?

The scope of the licensee's right of exclusivity was given a broad interpretation **10–21** in the controversial U.S. case of *Shoney's Inc. v. Shoenbaun.*[45] An exclusive licence typically prevents the licensor from using the mark in the territory (as compared with a sole licence, which limits the number of licensees to one but does not prevent the licensor from competing with the licensee in the territory).

The issue in this case was the construction of the exclusive grant to the licensee 'to use the Shoney's System, Trade Names and Marks within the licensed Territory'. The subject matter of the use was the operation of a restaurant, but the grant did not explicitly limit itself to that use. The Court of Appeal held that the proper construction of the grant was that it prohibited the licensor from *any* use of the trade marks in the territory, not merely from the operation of restaurants. As a result, while the licensee was limited to the use of the mark in relation to restaurants, the licensor was itself otherwise prohibited from using the mark in the territory.[46]

The dissenting view took strong issue with the majority decision. It pointed out that the grant of the licence could only be as broad as the scope of the registered marks, *i.e.* for restaurant services. The majority result was described as a 'dog in the manger' construction, whereby one was permitted to selfishly to withhold from another something which it did not need or could not use. In this case, the licensee succeeded in preventing the licensor from operating motels in the territory, while the licensee itself was limited to the operation of restaurants.[47]

The result reached in the *Shoney* case counsels a licensor to exercise care in drafting the terms of the exclusivity provision. If the licensor wishes to use the mark with respect to goods or services other than those which are subject to the licence, it should consider making that point clear in the agreement.

Can An Exclusivity Provision Be Implied?

It has been argued that in the absence of a provision expressly providing for **10–22** exclusivity, no exclusivity will be implied. While this is the general rule,[48] it may not be a principle set in stone, at least under U.S. law. In one example, the court implied exclusivity based on all the circumstances of the case. In particular, the court pointed to a prior grant of exclusivity to the licensee.[49]

---

[44] s.29(1).
[45] 13 U.S.P.Q. 2d 1643 (4th Cir. 1990).
[46] 13 U.S.P.Q. 2d at 1646–47.
[47] 13 U.S.P.Q. 2d at 1649.
[48] *Pacific Supply Cooperative v. Farmers Exchange*, 137 U.S.P.Q. 835, 845 (9th Cir. 1963).
[49] *Huber Baking Co. v. Stroehmann Bros. Co.*, 116 U.S.P.Q. 348, 355 (2nd Cir. 1958).

Quality Control

10–23 Where it is the licensor which breaches the quality control provisions, the licensee has a contractual right against the licensor. The licensee's rights may be based on the quality control provisions themselves, or other provisions in the licence agreement which relate to the quality control obligations of the licensor.

The Relationship between Proprietary and Contractual Rights in the Payment of Royalties: The *Dairy Queen* Case

10–24 The interrelationship between proprietary and contractual rights in a trade mark licence is perhaps most striking when the licensee allegedly fails to make payment of royalties under the agreement. The licence agreement is then terminated on the ground of breach of a material term, but the licensee continues to use the licensed trade mark. Here, the issue is the interrelationship between the licensor's claim for a debt upon a contract based upon the licensee's failure to pay royalties, and the claim of infringement due to the licensee's unauthorised use of the mark.

The United States Supreme Court, in the case of *Dairy Queen v. Wood*,[50] has identified three alternative understandings of the interrelationship between proprietary and contractual rights in the circumstances described above. These understandings are as follows:

(a) There is no overlap between the rights and they are cumulative. The licensor is entitled to recover the debt due under the contract for the payment of the royalties until the termination of the licence agreement, and to recover damages for trade mark infringement for continued use of the trade mark by the licensee after termination.[51]

(b) The licensor is entitled to base its relief upon a combination of the recovery of the debt due under the contract and pecuniary damages for infringement of the trade mark for the entire period of the infringement, *i.e.* from the moment of the breach for failure to pay royalties, rather than only from the termination of the licence agreement.[52]

(c) The licensor is entitled to recover completely on the basis of either breach of contract or trade mark infringement, as follows:
  (i) the licensor can recover completely under the contract for the period both before and after the attempted termination. As the termination has been ignored, and the licensee has continued to use the trade mark, the termination was of no consequence.
  (ii) Alternatively, the licensor could recover completely on the basis of trade mark infringement, reasoning that because the contract had been breached, the existence of the contract could not serve

---

[50] 133 U.S.P.Q. 294, 297 (1962).
[51] 133 U.S.P.Q. at 297.
[52] 133 U.S.P.Q. at 297, n. 12, citing *McCullough v. Dairy Queen, Inc.*, 129 U.S.P.Q. 400, 401 (E.D. Pa. 1961). Query in the U.K. whether this understanding would amount to a double recovery, which is highly disfavoured.

as the basis for a defence against infringement, even for the period prior to the termination.[53]

While the Supreme Court did not decide which was the proper under- **10–25** standing, it did express the tentative view that the first alternative 'is the most natural construction.'[54] The failure to make a royalty payment gives rise to a contractual claim and may provide the basis for termination of the agreement. Failing or until termination of the licence agreement, the licensee may continue to use the trade mark, since the non-payment of a royalty does not constitute trade mark infringement, nor does it necessarily give rise to termination of the licence agreement.[55]

Other Rights of the Licensee in a Trade Mark License?

Although it is currently understood that the licensee acquires no proprietary **10–26** rights by virtue of the trade mark licence, there may still be circumstances in which the licensee is not limited to its contractual rights under the licence agreement.

Statutory Provision under the U.K. Trade Marks Act 1994 Regarding Apportionment of Settlement

Under the Trade Marks Act 1994, in an infringement action brought by the **10–27** proprietor of a registered trade mark, the court is required 'to take into account' any damage that a licensee has either suffered or is likely to suffer in respect of the infringement. The court may give such directions to the proprietor as the court deems appropriate to hold the proceeds of such monetary recovery on behalf of the licensees.[56]

Where an action for infringement is brought by either the proprietor or the exclusive licensee that is deemed as assignee, and the proprietor and the exclusive licensee have or had concurrent rights of action, the Act provides further instructions regarding the awarding and apportionment of monetary relief.[57]

Court-Awarded Apportionment under U.S. Law

No similar provision regarding the apportionment of recovery is found in the **10–28** Lanham Act. On occasion, however, the courts have found an extra-statutory basis to recognise the licensee's right of recovery in the absence of any contractual provisions.

The most notable decision is *Original Appalachian Artworks*,[58] where the court held that the licensee enjoyed rights to a portion of the proceeds received

---

[53] 133 U.S.P.Q. at 297 n.13, 298.
[54] 133 U.S.P.Q. at 297.
[55] See *McCleod v. Crawford*, 141 U.S.P.Q. 45 (S.C. Neb. 1964). See also, *infra*, Chap. 10, para. 12–54.
[56] Trade Marks Act 1994, at subs. 30(6).
[57] Trade Marks Act 1994, at subs. 30(6).
[58] *Original Appalachian Artworks, Inc. v. S. Diamond Associates, Inc.*, 911 F.2d 1548 (11th Cir. 1990).

by the licensor from a settlement action against an infringer in connection with alleged copyright and trade mark infringement.[59] No mention was made in the licence agreement of any sharing of settlement proceeds between the licensor and licensee proceeds. Nevertheless, the exclusive licensee sought to receive a proportion of the proceeds received from the alleged infringer.

On appeal, the court held that the licensee had a right to such proceeds, despite the absence of any proprietary or contractual right. It ruled that by virtue of the exclusive licence, (a) the licensee had the right to prove whether the acts of the infringer amounted to a misappropriation of the licensee's exclusive licence, and (b) the licensor had a fiduciary duty not to allow the intellectual property right to be used to the detriment of the licensee, the measure of injury being a proportion of the amount of the settlement recovery.[60] Here, the absence of a provision in the agreement regarding the sharing of proceeds did not preclude the recognition of the licensee's right to a proportion of the proceeds on other grounds.

10–29   It is presumed that if the licence agreement had contained an express provision regarding the sharing of proceeds obtained from a settlement or action, it would have governed the situation, and the non-contractual grounds relied upon by the court to reward the licensee would not have come into play. If no pro-rata apportionment is intended, however, the result in this case suggests that the licence agreement should explicitly provide that the grant of the exclusive licence does not confer on the licensee any right to monies recovered or awarded as a result of any proceedings.

Not All Courts Recognise a Fiduciary Relationship

10–30   However, it should be noted that not all courts have recognised that a fiduciary relationship is owing to a licensee under the circumstances of a trade mark licence.[61] In addition, it is questionable whether the court in the *Original Appalachian Artworks* decision would have ruled similarly in the case of a non-exclusive licence.

WHICH SET OF RIGHTS, PROPRIETARY OR CONTRACTUAL TAKES PRECEDENCE?

10–31   Given that the trade mark licence arrangement involves both proprietary and contractual rights, it can be asked whether, in the event of an irreconcilable conflict, one set of rights is to be preferred over the other. Obviously, as far as possible, effect should be given to both sets of rights.

Thus, in one U.S. case both liquidated damages and infringement damages were awarded on account of the licensee's use of the trade mark after termination, even though the infringement damages were calculated in almost

---

[59] The trade mark at issue does not appear to have been registered, but that point does not affect the general thrust of the court's reasoning.

[60] 911 F.2d at 1552–53.

[61] *Weight Watchers of Quebec v. Weight Watchers International*, 188 U.S.P.Q. 17, 21 (E.D.N.Y. 1975).

the same way as the liquidated damages. The court was willing to entertain the risk of some overlap in order to give full effect to the purpose of trade mark law and to ensure that both wrongs were remedied.[62]

In a United Kingdom case, the court implied a contractual provision prohibiting a former licensee from using the trade marks upon termination of the current agreement. The court was aware that the licensee's use of the trade marks already infringed the licensor's proprietary rights, but it held that the contractual provision was necessary to give commercial effect to the agreement in accordance with the intention of the parties.[63]

Contractual Rights may take Precedence

Nevertheless, on occasion, one set of rights may take precedence. One U.S. **10–32** court expressed a policy in favour of enforcing trade mark licences in accordance with the bargain reached by the parties, even if it could do some harm to the trade mark rights of the licensor with respect to possible confusion between marks.[64] In such circumstances, the public interest against the confusing use of a trade mark was secondary to the contractual will of the parties.

Although the decision dealt with the licensed use of a trade mark under a settlement agreement, the policy expressed by the court does not appear to be so limited.[65] Nothing in the rationale would suggest such a limitation. The policy may simply be another way of stating that if the licensor freely enters into agreement with the licensee on the basis of a term or condition that may be inconsistent with the licensor's proprietary rights in the trade mark, the contractual provision may take precedence.[66]

Implications for Licence Drafting

This possibility that the contractual provisions of a licence agreement may **10–33** take precedence underscores the importance of paying careful attention to the

---

[62] *Ramada Inns Inc. v. Gadsden Motel Co.*, 1 U.S.P.Q. 2d 1011 (11th Cir. 1986). Note, however, that such a double recovery is not favoured under English law.

[63] *Sport International, supra,* n. 18, at 334.

[64] *T&T Manufacturing Co. v. A.T. Cross Co.*, 201 U.S.P.Q. 561, 565, 566 (1st Cir. 1978). See also, *supra,* Chap. 9, paras. 9–10 to 9–12.

[65] 201 U.S.P.Q. at 565.

[66] But see the decision of the European Court of Justice in *Bayer v. Sulhofer*, [1990] 4 C.M.L.R. 182, where a no challenge clause was upheld in the context of a royalty-free licence in settlement of a patent dispute and was accorded special treatment.

Note as well that the distinction between proprietary and contractual rights may also be relevant in connection with the question of jurisdiction under U.S. law. There, a claim based upon proprietary rights will be adjudicated in the federal court system, while a claim based principally on a contract issue under the licence agreement will be heard in the appropriate state court.

Thus, the licensor could choose to focus solely on the licensee's failure to pay the royalties, which would be a contract claim properly adjudicated in a state court. Alternatively, it could allege infringement of the trade mark based upon the licensee's post-termination use of the trade mark, which would be adjudicated in a federal court. (*Foxrun Workshop Ltd v. Klone Manufacturing Inc.*, 7 U.S.P.Q. 2d 1655 (S.D.N.Y. 1988)). When both claims are alleged, however, difficult issues of jurisdiction can arise. *Foxrun Workshop Ltd,* above; *T.B. Harms v. Eliscu,* 339 F.2d 823 (2nd Cir. 1964), cert. denied, 381 U.S. 915 (1965).

agreed terms and conditions, in light of the particular concerns of each of the parties.

Licensor's Perspective

10–34 From the perspective of the licensor, care should be taken to ensure that the agreement expressly provides for all of the terms and conditions of the trade mark licence. The licensor should not rely on a vague claim that the licensee is using the trade mark in a manner outside the scope of the license, but should specify what the scope of that use is. Doing so will both reduce any uncertainty over whether or not infringement of a proprietary right has taken place, as well as entitle the licensor to a contractual right in the subject matter. This may be particularly important in the event that no infringement is found to have occurred, but the provision of the agreement has nevertheless covered the issue.

Licensee's Perspective

10–35 From the licensee's perspective, the absence of any proprietary right in the trade mark licence makes it all the more important that the contractual provisions be clearly specified and that the implications of those provisions, especially regarding termination, be understood. Even if the licensee enjoys substantial commercial power, it remains at the mercy of the licensor with respect to the right to use the licensed trade mark, subject only to the provisions of the agreement. This creates a certain lack of symmetry from the point of view of the legal relationship between the parties. It does not, however, prevent the licensee from entering into an agreement which is commercially attractive.

11. Oral, Implied and Constructive Trade Mark Licences

INTRODUCTION

A trade mark licence is usually embodied in a written agreement, particularly **11–01** when the parties to the agreement are unrelated. Not all licence arrangements, however, are evidenced in writing. This chapter will consider the circumstances in which a trade mark licence arrangement may be said to exist, but where there is no written contract, namely: (a) an oral trade mark licence, (b) an implied trade mark licence, and (c) a constructive trade mark licence or a constructive trust.

It will be argued that an oral licence and an implied licence contain many similar features, despite the difference in terminology, while a constructive licence or a constructive trust fits less well within the framework of unwritten agreements.

Applicable Principles of Contract Law

In approaching the issue of oral and implied licence agreements, the basic **11–02** principles of the general law of contract should be kept in mind. A contract may be written, oral, or implied. No writing is required to form a binding contract, unless it is the intention of the parties that there should be no binding contract until the completion of a written agreement, or unless a written agreement is required by law. Otherwise, an oral contract is perfectly valid, provided that its terms can be established with certainty.

When the parties fail expressly to provide that the contract is conditional upon the completion of an agreement in writing, the written agreement may be viewed as a record of the contract, rather than as constituting the contract itself. In this situation, there is no separate written contract, and the document merely evidences the oral agreement reached between the parties. A valid subsequent written agreement may, however, explicitly provide that its purpose is to modify, renew, extend, or even replace the existing oral contract. There is a distinction between an express and an implied contract. Even if there is no clear expression of contractual intent between the parties, an implied contract may still be recognised from the conduct and actions of the parties.

THE ORAL LICENCE

11–03 The question of the existence of an oral trade mark licence arises in the absence of a written licence agreement. In such circumstances, the court may be asked to consider whether a valid and enforceable oral licence exists.[1]

The Approach in the U.K.

11–04 There are strong incentives to enter into a written licence agreement. First, the written agreement establishes the fact of the licence, and significantly eases the evidentiary burden of proving the terms and conditions of the agreement.[2] Secondly, the existence of the registered user provisions under the Trade Marks Act 1938 and the registration of licensees under the Trade Marks Act 1994 has meant that a trade mark licence needs to be in writing in order to satisfy the registration requirements. A written agreement must be submitted in order to record the licence arrangement and to benefit from the statutory rights that derive from registration; evidence of an oral agreement is not acceptable.[3]

Unwritten Licence Agreements Have Been Recognised

11–05 Nevertheless, it is possible for a trade mark licence to subsist in the absence of a written agreement. The leading case under the Trade Marks Act 1938 was *Bostitch*, in which the court held that the registered user requirements are permissive rather than mandatory.[4] In that case, the court found that on the basis of the course of dealing between the parties – including the exchange of correspondence and information, the payment or royalties, and use of the trade marks in advertisements – the licensor had 'impos[ed its] identity upon the articles produced' by the licensee.[5]

The *Bostitch* court did not clearly specify whether, under these circumstances, an oral or implied license had been created. Whatever form of licence had been created, it was held by the court to be valid. The absence of writing was not found to be a fatal bar.

Oral Licence Defeats a Licensee's Claim of Proprietorship

11–06 An unwritten trade mark licence may be relied upon to defeat a licensee's claim of proprietorship in a trade mark. The licensor will argue that the existence of the licence bars the licensee from alleging proprietorship in the mark, on the ground that a licensee can assert no right of proprietorship.

In one case, a manufacturing licence was silent on the issue of the use of

---

[1] *Optician Association v. Independent Opticians of America*, 14 U.S.P.Q. 2d (D.N.J. 1990), 2021, 2026, rev'd on other grounds, 17 U.S.P.Q. 2d 1117 (2nd Cir. 1990).
[2] See, *supra*, Chap. 10, para. 10–06. Under the registration requirements of the Trade Marks Act 1994, s. 28(2) provides that '[a] licence is not effective unless it is a writing signed by or on behalf of the grantor.' See, *supra*, Chap. 4, paras. 4–07 to 4–25.
[3] The same result was reached under the Trade Marks Act 1938. See Trade Mark Manual, at para. 27–47.
[4] *Bostitch Trade Mark* [1963] R.P.C. 183.
[5] *Bostitch*, above, at 197.

the trade mark. The manufacturing licensee then claimed that it was the proprietor of the mark. It was held that even without the formal provision of a trade mark licence (in particular, the absence of any provision for quality control), there was sufficient oral evidence that a trade mark licence had been intended. The licensee's claim of proprietorship in the mark was accordingly rejected.[6]

The Approach in the U.S.

Under U.S. practice, there is no system for the registration of a trade mark **11–07**
licence, and it has been held that no written licence is required to establish a valid trade mark licence.[7] It is not surprising, therefore, that an oral trade mark licence has been recognised as valid in various contexts.

Validity

An oral licence may support a trade mark application, where the licensor- **11–08**
applicant seeks to rely on the use of the mark by the licensee. For example, an oral licence will be accepted by the Trademark Trial and Appeal Board as evidence of use by the applicant-licensor, provided that there is clear evidence of quality control.[8] This should be compared with section 29 of the Trade Marks Act 1938, where an application for registration could have relied on intended use by a licensee rather than the applicant, provided that the application for registration of the trade mark is accompanied by an application for the recordal of the licensee as a registered user.[9]

Under the Trade Marks Act 1994, however, an application for registration need only 'state that the trade mark is being used, by the applicant or with his consent, in relation to these goods or services, or that he has a bona fide intention that it should be so used.' This provision suggests that no written licence is required.[10]

Oral Licence When Written Agreement is Silent

An oral trade mark licence has also been found to exist where there is a **11–09**
written agreement between the parties, but the agreement does not explicitly address the issue of trade mark use.

In one case, use of the mark by a member of the licensor's association, in accordance with the written guidelines of that organisation, was deemed to be evidence of an oral licence.[11] In another case, the Trademark Trial and Appeal Board pointed to the basis of quality control that had been created

---

[6] *Sidewinder* Trade Mark [1988] R.P.C. 261.
[7] *National Lampoon, Inc. v. American Broadcasting Company, Inc.*, 182 U.S.P.Q. 24 (S.D.N.Y. 1974). See generally, *supra*, Chap. 5.
[8] *Basic Inc. v. Rex*, 167 U.S.P.Q. 696 (TTAB 1970); *Re Briggs*, 229 U.S.P.Q. 76 (1976).
[9] See, *supra*, Chap. 3, paras. 3–30 to 3–32.
[10] Trade Marks Act 1994, s. 32(3).
[11] *Council of Better Business Bureau v. Better Business Bureau*, 200 U.S.P.Q. 282 (S.D. Fla. 1978); *cf. Sidewinder T.M.*, *supra*, n. 6.

by virtue of the general contractual arrangement between the parties, in holding that a valid oral trade mark licence existed.[12]

Oral Licence Establishes the Commercial Terms of the Licence

11–10 An oral licence can be relied upon to establish the commercial terms of the agreement. For example, an oral licence agreement has been used to provide a binding obligation on the licensee to pay royalties.[13]

Oral Testimony of a Written Licence Agreement

11–11 The existence of an oral licence should be distinguished from oral evidence that is relied upon to establish the existence of a written licence agreement. This was the result reached by one U.S. Court of Appeal. It relied upon oral testimony in the record to establish the existence of a written trade mark licence, although the exclusive licensee-plaintiff had neglected to introduce the written licence agreement into evidence.[14]

Licensee Estoppel under U.S. and U.K. Law

11–12 U.S. law has given broad recognition to the principle of licensee estoppel, whereby a trade mark licensee is barred from challenging the validity of the trade mark, at least for as long as the licence is in effect.[15] Either a written or oral licence may serve as the contractual basis for estoppel. When estoppel is claimed by the licensor on the basis of an oral licence, it can be expected that the licensee will challenge the existence of the oral licence in order to prevent the operation of the estoppel.

In one case, the licensor failed to establish the existence of an oral licence which would have served to prevent the licensee from challenging the validity of the licensor's mark.[16] Mere membership of a professional organisation was found not to constitute the basis for a licence agreement. On the other hand, in another case recognition was given to an oral licence and the licensee was accordingly estopped from challenging the validity of the mark.[17] The court rejected the licensee's argument that licensee estoppel could only be based on a written licence agreement.

11–13 The application of licensee estoppel to a trade mark licence under U.K. law is less certain.[18] To the extent that licensee estoppel is recognised under

---

[12] *Nestle Co. v. Nash-Finch Co.*, 4 U.S.P.Q. 2d 1085, 1089 (TTAB 1987). *cf.* the *Sidewinder T.M.* case, *supra*, n. 6.

[13] *Yamamoto & Co. (America), Inc. v. Victor United, Inc.*, 219 U.S.P.Q. 969, 970, 978 (C.D. Cal. 1982). Note that the oral licence was ratified by the licensee corporation and reduced to writing in the form of corporate minutes approved in writing by the corporate principals, one of whom was the licensor of the mark. Royalties were due and owing to the licensor from the date that the oral contract became effective.

[14] *Wynn Oil Co. v. Thomas* 5 U.S.P.Q. 2d 1944, 1949 (6th Cir. 1988).

[15] See, *supra*, Chap. 9, paras. 9–55 to 9–59.

[16] *Optician Association v. Independent Opticians of America*, 14 U.S.P.Q. 2d (D.N.J. 1990), 2021, 2026, rev'd on other grounds, 17 U.S.P.Q. 2d 1117 (2nd Cir. 1990).

[17] *Council of Better Business Bureau v. Better Business Bureau*, 200 U.S.P.Q. 282 (S.D. Fla. 1978).

[18] See, *supra*, Chap. 9, paras. 9–52 to 9–54.

U.K. law, the principle stated above regarding an oral licence and licensee estoppel under U.S. law is likely to be equally valid.

THE IMPLIED LICENSEE

Occasionally, an implied trade mark licence has also been found to exist. **11–14** There appear to be two main circumstances in which this has occurred. In the one, an implied licence is seen as a form of defence against a claim of infringement. In the other, the implied licence seems to be virtually indistinguishable from an oral licence.

The Implied Licence as a Defence to Infringement

Under Patent and Copyright Law

An implied licence has been recognised under both patent and copyright law **11–15** as a defence to infringement. A licence is implied by the court in certain situations when the use of the patent or copyright by a third party in connection with an article or work in the regular course might otherwise constitute infringement. The recognition of an implied licence in such circumstances is another way of recognising that not every use of an intellectual property right without the express permission of the rights-holder constitutes an infringement.

For example, an implied right of repair of a patented product has been **11–16** recognised, provided that a new article is not created.[19] In the *Karo Step* case,[20] it was suggested that a trade mark consisting of a device attracted copyright protection in the device as well, and that there was an implied copyright licence to reproduce the device.

Consent and Acquiescence under Trade Mark Law

Although the Trade Marks Act 1938 did not expressly refer to an 'implied **11–17** licence', certain provisions under the Act may be seen as having served a similar function by providing a defence to a claim of infringement. Section 4(3)(a) provided that it shall not be an infringement for a third party either to use a trade mark that has been applied to the goods by the proprietor and has not been removed, or to use it by virtue of the express or implied consent of the proprietor. Section 4(3)(b) went on to provide a defence against the use of the mark in connection with components, accessories or ancillary services.[21]

The Trade Marks Act 1994 provides that the acts defined as infringement

---

[19] *Dellareed Ltd v. Delkim Developments* [1988] F.S.R. 329, 342, 343, 345, citing *Solar Thompson Engineering Co. Ltd v. Barton* [1977] R.P.C. 537; *British Leyland Motor Corp. v. Armstrong Patents Co. Ltd* [1986] R.P.C. 279, H.L.

[20] [1977] R.P.C. 257, 272–274.

[21] See, *supra*, Chap. 7, at paras. 7–11 to 7–15 for discussion of these provisions.

of a trade mark under section 10 shall not be deemed to infringe if done with the consent of the proprietor.[22]

In each of these situations, no trade mark licence in the sense of a permitted use under the registered user legislation, or a registered licence under the Trade Marks Act 1994, is intended. Rather, these provisions are designed to provide a statutory defence against infringement in certain defined circumstances.

Implied Licence as a Separate Defence

11–18   An implied licence has occasionally been cited as a separate ground of defence to trade mark infringement. In the *News Group* case,[23] the claim was made that the use of the plaintiff's masthead on a hoarding was either an implied trade mark licence or a consent. In another example, the *Compaq Computer* case,[24] use of the plaintiff's mark in advertising was alleged to be an implied licence because it was usual practice in the trade.[25]

Course of Dealing

11–19   The key to whether an implied licence will be recognised in these circumstances is the extent to which a course of dealing exists in support of such a finding. The *Bostitch* case may be interpreted this way.[26]

Implied Licence Between Employer and Employee

11–20   Perhaps the most frequent situation in which such a course of dealing has been found under U.S. law is use of a trade mark by an employer or a partnership, where the employee or partner with whom the mark originated subsequently claims proprietorship in the mark.

The case of *Re Sottile* is instructive.[27] The applicant had created and used a service mark in connection with financial services. Subsequently, the applicant became an employee-manager for two companies. In each company, he continued to use the service mark only at the particular branch in which he worked. The Trademark Trial and Appeal Board, in recognising the employee's right of proprietorship in the trade mark, explained the key principle as follows:

'The situation here is not one where an employee creates a mark for use in his employer's business but one where an individual accepting employment offers the use of his personal property to his employer.'[28]

---

[22] Trade Marks Act 1994, ss.9(1). See also, *supra*, para. 9–03.
[23] *News Group Newspapers Ltd v. The Mirror Group Newspapers (1986) Ltd* [1989] F.S.R. 126, 130.
[24] *Company Computer Corp. v. Dell Computer Corp.* [1992] 19 F.S.R. 93 at 97.
[25] In neither of these cases, however, was an implied licence found by the court.
[26] See, *supra*, para. 11–05.
[27] 156 U.S.P.Q. 654 (T.T.A.B. 1968).
[28] *ibid.*, at 656.

As a result, each of the applicant's previous employers was deemed to have used the service mark as an implied licensee. Such use had inured to the benefit of the employee. While the Board did not directly refer to the exercise of quality control, it did point out that the employee had been a branch manager in each situation, and that the mark had been used only at that branch. These circumstances supported the finding of an implied licence.

Subsequent Writing

Some courts have found an implied licence to exist for the period prior to **11–21** the making of a written agreement.

In one case, the trade mark applicant had joined the licensee corporation as president, and the corporation commenced use of the trade mark previously used by the applicant in his personal capacity. Several years thereafter, a formal written licence agreement was entered into between the applicant and the corporation. In addition, the applicant, as president, had actively maintained personal control over the use of the mark by the corporation during the time that the implied licence was deemed to be in effect. The court found that an implied licence existed prior to the written agreement being put in place.[29]

An implied licence has been found to exist even where the subsequent **11–22** writing was silent on the issue of the licence. In the *Hornay v. Hays* case,[30] it was held that the trade mark had been the subject of an implied licence to the corporation from the employee, who had created and previously used the mark in his individual capacity. The implied licence was effective for the duration of the licensor-employee's tenure with the corporation. The applicant's control over the manufacture of the barbecue sauce in accordance with the secret formula ensured that there was quality control.

Course of Dealing in Lieu of the Formal Renewal of the Licence Agreement

It has been held in the *Hurricane Fence* case that a continuation of the course **11–23** of dealing is sufficient to establish the continuing existence of the licence agreement and to overcome a claim that the mark has been abandoned by its proprietor, even when no new written licence agreement has been executed.[31] No attempt was made by the court to characterise the use of the trade mark for the period after the expiry of the written agreement as either an oral renewal or a new oral agreement.

Evidence of Control is Necessary

The existence of an implied licence will be rejected if no evidence of actual **11–24** quality control is offered. Where there was no written or oral licence agreement between a professional association and a defined group of its sub-members, and

---

[29] In *McCormick & Co. Inc. v. Summers*, 141 U.S.P.Q. 258 (T.T.A.B. 1964). A similar result was reached in *Clarke v. Sanderson Films, Inc.*, 139 U.S.P.Q. 130 (1963).
[30] *Hornay v. Hays*, 176 U.S.P.Q. 316 (T.T.A.B. 1972).
[31] *Hurricane Fence Co. v. A-1 Hurricane Fence Co.*, 208 U.S.P.Q. 314, 327 (S.D. Ala. 1979).

no tacit or implied licence agreement between them, no licensing relationship between the parties could be deemed to exist, when the sub-group was merely composed of members of the organisation.[32]

Implied Licence Negates Manufacturer's Claim of Proprietorship

11–25 An implied licence has even been relied upon to invalidate the manufacturer's registration of the trade mark in favour of a registration by the distributor. In the *Wrist-Rocket* case,[33] the court found that the manufacturer used the mark not as the proprietor, but as an implied licensee of the proprietor, subject to the consent and even the control of the distributor. The court emphasised that the public had come to think of the distributor as the source of the goods.[34]

Oral and Implied Licenses – Is There a Difference?

11–26 The characterisation by the courts of these arrangements as 'implied', rather than oral, licences may not connote any substantial difference between these two forms of unwritten licence. In all of these license situations discussed above in which an implied licence was found, there was some form of quality control, even if the control was exercised by an individual or employee over the corporate licensee. These circumstances are similar to those in which an oral licence has been found to exist.

One can question, therefore, whether reliance on a finding of an implied licence is necessary. Proof of quality control is the best evidence that a bona fide trade mark license arrangement exists. At the end of the day, there may not be anything 'implied' about these licences.

THE CONSTRUCTIVE LICENCE

11–27 A constructive licence has occasionally been recognised under U.S. law. It is distinguished from an oral or implied licence on the basis that it has been recognised in situations in which it would appear to be inequitable to allow the constructive licensee to claim superior rights in the mark. The imposition of the constructive licence prevents the constructive licensee from claiming any right of proprietorship, since a licensee cannot assert proprietorship in the trade mark.[35]

---

[32] *Optician Association, supra*, n. 16.

[33] *Wrist-Rocket Mfg. Co., Inc. v. Saunders Archery Co.*, 183 U.S.P.Q. 17, 25–27 (D.Neb. 1974). See *supra*, Chap. 7, paras. 7–40 to 7–60.

[34] *cf.* the result reached here with the constructive licence found in *Far-Best* case, *infra*, n. 37, and the constructive trust imposed in the *Nastri and Tillamook Creamerie* case, *infra*, n. 43. See generally, *supra*, Chap. 7, at paras. 7–40 to 7–60 for discussion of the circumstances under which a distributor may obtain proprietorship in a trade mark.

[35] This approach was particularly favoured by one former member of the Trademark Trial and Appeal Board in the U.S.

Previous Commercial Relationship

One type of situation in which a constructive licence has been found involved **11–28** a dispute over the proprietorship of a trade mark in respect of which there existed a previous commercial relationship between the parties. The applicant or registrant was deemed to be the constructive licensee of the opposing party.

In another case, the applicant for service mark registration had been a **11–29** licensee of the opposer in connection with a different service mark for temporary employment services. Subsequently, the opposer assisted the applicant use the opposer's service mark for permanent employment services. This latter service mark had apparently been the subject of a previous oral licence with several licensees. However, the applicant declined to enter into a licence agreement with the opponent, and instead filed for registration of the service mark in its own name.[36] The applicant was held to be a constructive licensee of the opponent. The Trademark Trial and Appeal Board reasoned that given the background relationship between the applicant and the opponent, any adoption and use of the service mark by the applicant derogated from the opponent's previous rights in the mark.

The Constructive Licence and the Distributor

Another case involved the registration of a trade mark by an exclusive **11–30** distributor without the knowledge of the manufacturer. The manufacturer succeeded in cancelling the registration on the ground that the distributor had been a mere constructive licensee and could acquire no rights of proprietorship without the consent of the manufacturer.[37]

Summary

The conceptual foundation for the imposition of a constructive trade mark **11–31** licence is questionable, and reliance on this doctrine appears to have been limited to a single member of the U.S. Trademark Trial and Appeal Board during the 1960s. The cases in which an implied or oral licence has been recognised can be understood on the basis of quality control in connection with the use of the trade mark. However, quality control does not appear to have been present in the constructive licence situations. It is not surprising perhaps that the doctrine has been relied upon only infrequently.

THE CONSTRUCTIVE TRUST

A constructive trust with respect to use of a trade mark has also been imposed. **11–32** The constructive trust is a well known equitable remedy. The underlying idea is that the constructive trustee is holding something which properly belongs to another, and that it would amount to unjust enrichment to allow him to

---

[36] *Manpower, Inc. v. Affiliated Personal Services, Inc.*, 158 U.S.P.Q. 154 (1968).
[37] *Far-Best Corp. v. Die Casting 'ID' Corp.*, 165 U.S.P.Q. 277 (1970).

retain it. Occasionally, a constructive trust has been imposed upon the party holding the trade mark registration in favour of a third party.

The Constructive Trust and U.K. Practice

11–33 Under U.K. practice, there appears to have been scant reliance on the constructive trust in connection with trade marks. Section 64 of the Trade Marks Act 1938 expressly provided that no trust, implied or constructive, shall be entered on the Registry nor shall any notice of any such trust be received by the registrar. However, the section further provides that any such equitable rights in the trade mark may be enforced against the proprietor personally.[38] A similar provision with respect to implied and constructive trusts is contained in the Trade Marks Act 1994.[39]

Thus, while a constructive trust is not a registrable right, it may be enforceable in court. It is doubtful, however, whether this provision extends to the idea of the constructive trust as embodied in the case law.

It was suggested in argument in the *Bostitch* case that the licensee should be viewed as a constructive trustee of the licensor.[40] This claim was made on the basis of the case of *Aktiebolaget Manus R.J. Fullwood and Bland Ltd,*[41] although that case did not explicitly refer to the doctrine of a constructive trust in reaching its result. The judgment in the *Bostitch* case did not adopt the suggestion.

The Constructive Trust and U.S. Practice

11–34 The imposition of a constructive trust in connection with trade mark use has been more frequent under U.S. practice. An excellent example is the case of *Tillamook Creamery Association v. Tillamook Cheese Association.*[42] In that case, a constructive trust was imposed on a cooperative marketing agent which had registered the trade mark in its own name, rather than on behalf of the dairy cooperative for which it was an agent. The effect of the constructive trust was to invalidate the registration of the trade mark by the marketing agent in favour of the cooperative.

11–35 Perhaps the boldest judicial reliance on a constructive trust with respect to trade marks can be found in the case of *Columbia Nastri, SpA v. Columbia Ribbon Mfg. Co.*[43] In that case, the court imposed a constructive trust to enforce royalty payments by an Italian company to its former U.S. parent and to order the return of the trade marks upon termination of the contract.

The court so held, even though the Italian company had been registered in Italy as the proprietor of the trade marks in question with the consent of the

---

[38] ss. 64(1), 64(2).
[39] Kerly, *Law of Trade Marks & Trade Names* (12th Ed., 1986), p. 250, Trade Marks Act 1994, s.26.
[40] *Bostitch T.M.,* at 185.
[41] 56 R.P.C. 71 (C.A. 1948).
[42] 143 U.S.P.Q. 12 (D. Or. 1964).
[43] 151 U.S.P.Q. 362 (2nd Cir. 1966), aff'g *Columbia Nastri, SpA v. Columbia Ribbon Mfg. Co.,* 147 U.S.P.Q. 205 (S.D.N.Y. 1965)].

U.S. parent, and despite silence in the written agreement on the issue of reversion of proprietorship of the trade marks upon termination of the agreement. The court reasoned that the proprietorship by the Italian company was merely nominal. The real interest in the trade marks belonged to the constructive trustee.

Limitations to the Constructive Trust

More recently, courts appear to have ignored or rejected the imposition of a **11–36** constructive trust with respect to trade marks. It has been held that the imposition of a constructive trust for copyright purposes did not establish common law trade mark rights, where there was a transfer of those trade mark rights without passing any goodwill or exercising any supervision over the subsequent use of the mark by the transferee.[44] Even where equity gives recognition to trade mark rights by virtue of a constructive trust, it is therefore clear that the basic principles of trade mark law will still apply.

---

[44] *Universal City Studios v. Nintendo Co.*, 578 F. Supp. 911 (S.D.N.Y. 1983).

12. Termination and Best Endeavours

INTRODUCTION

Termination of a trade mark licence agreement poses various problems for **12–01** the parties. As long as the licence agreement remains in effect, the use of the trade mark by the licensee is not deemed to infringe the trade mark. And during the term of the licence, all use of the trade mark by the licensee in accordance with the licence inures solely to the benefit of the licensor.

At the moment that the licence is terminated, the relationship between the licensor and the licensee theoretically comes to an end. Termination may come about prematurely, due to a breach of the agreement or other infringing activity in connection with the trade mark by one of the parties, or it may occur by mutual agreement of the parties in accordance with the terms of the agreement. Whatever the reason for termination, any further use of the trade mark by the licensee is, in principle, unauthorised.

The Problem of Post-Termination Use of the Trade Mark

Often, however, it may not be practicable for the licensee immediately to **12–02** cease all activity that is connected with its use of the trade mark. There may be an inventory to be disposed of, orders to be fulfilled, and promotional and advertising material on hand bearing the trade mark. In addition, the licensee may find it difficult to disassociate itself completely from the licensed mark.

Of course, the parties can set out in the licence agreement the terms and conditions by which the licensee will be permitted to wind-down its use of the trade mark after termination. When the licence agreement specifically contains such post-termination provisions, the main question will be whether the parties have complied with these terms.

A more difficult question arises when the agreement is silent on the matter. Even in the absence of specific provisions governing post-termination use of the mark, the licensee may well continue to use the mark to dispose of inventory and the like. The court may then be called upon to decide is such use of the trade mark by the licensee constitutes infringement of the trade mark or a breach of the terms of the licence agreement.[1]

This section will discuss the issues connected with various aspects relating

---

[1] *Sport International Bossum BV v. Hi-Tec Sports Ltd* [1988] R.P.C. 329 (C.A. 1987); *Baskin-Robbins Ice Cream Co. v. D & L Ice Cream Co., Inc.*, 222 U.S.P.Q. 225, 228 (E.D.N.Y. 1983). See also, *supra*, Chap. 10, paras. 10–09, 10–19, 10–24 and 10–25.

to the termination of the licence and the consequences of that termination.

POST-TERMINATION USE AND INFRINGEMENT

12–03 Termination of the agreement involves both trade mark and contract issues. The trade mark question focuses on whether the licensee continues post-termination to use the trade mark in a manner that infringes the rights of the licensor. As a matter of contract, the focus is on whether either of the parties has breached the contract in the post-termination period.

Post-Termination Use of the Trade Mark Must Be Deceptive

12–04 Post-termination use of the trade mark by the licensee is subject to the same test that applies to any unauthorised use of a trade mark by a third party. Not all post-termination use by the former licensee necessarily amounts to infringement. The question is whether the continued use is likely to deceive or cause confusion.[2] In the words of one court, 'A former licensee cannot mislead the public into believing that its affiliation continues once the licensing arrangement has ceased.'[3]

In one case, a franchisee continued to use the licensor's trade mark for at least a year after termination on various items, including ash trays, key rings, receipts and credit application forms. In addition, it continued to display the licensor's mark prominently both inside and outside the hotel. Such continued use was held to be deceptive.[4]

Duty of Former Licensee Compared With Former Distributor

12–05 The former licensee may even be under a greater obligation than other third parties to ensure that the identification of its goods or services is not confusingly similar to those of the former licensor.[5]

There is a difference of opinion as to whether the duty of the distributor with respect to post-termination use of the trade mark is identical to that of a licensee. Some courts that have held that both the distributor and the licensee have an identical duty to distinguish their respective goods upon termination of their right to use the trade mark under the agreement.[6]

---

[2] *Burger King v. Mason*, 710 F.2d 1480, 1492, 219 U.S.P.Q. 225, 228–229 (11th Cir. 1983), rehearing denied, 718 F.2d 1115, cert. denied, 465 U.S. 1102 (1983).
[3] *Professional Golfers Ass'n v. Bankers Life & Casualty Co.*, 514 F.2d 665, 670; 186 U.S.P.Q. 447, 451 (5th Cir. 1975).
[4] *Downtowner/Passport International Hotel Corp. v. Norlew Inc.*, 6 U.S.P.Q. 2d 1646, 1649 (8th Cir. 1988).
[5] *Professional Golfers Association*, above, n. 3; *Holiday Inns, Inc. v. Alberding*, 203 U.S.P.Q. 273, 275 (N.D. Texas 1978).
[6] *Liquid Glass Enterprises v. Liquid Glass Industries*, 14 U.S.P.Q. 2d 1976, 1980 (E.D. Mich. 1989).

Moreover, on both, the obligation to prevent the likelihood of confusion is greater than with a random infringer.[7]

Other courts have distinguished between a licensee and a distributor, holding that a terminated distributor cannot be held to the same standard as a former licensee. In the words of one court, there is no rule that 'a former distributor has a greater duty than others in the market to distinguish its product from that of its prior manufacturer.'[8]

No Special Duty If the Trade Mark Is Abandoned

A former licensee is under no special obligation if the trade mark is sub- **12–06** sequently deemed to be abandoned. Upon abandonment, the licensee, like any other person, may adopt, use and claim proprietorship in the trade mark.[9]

No Right Inures to Former Licensee

It is a fundamental feature of a trade mark licence that all use of the mark **12–07** by the licensee inures to the benefit of the licensor.[10] Thus, a former licensee has no right to any goodwill in the trade mark that was acquired during the period of the licence and it does not acquire any equitable rights in the mark by virtue of the licence.[11]

This principle applies equally to a situation in which the licensee initially serves as the distributor of the goods, and only later becomes a licensee. While a distributor may, under appropriate circumstances, claim proprietorship in the trade mark, a licensee can assert no such right.[12] Once the distributor enters into a licence relationship, its use of the trade mark inures solely to the benefit of the licensor. No claim of proprietorship in the mark can be made upon termination of the licence in respect of any rights that may have accumulated previously as part of the distribution arrangement.[13]

A Trade Mark Licence Does Not Terminate With the Expiry of a Related Patent Licence

A trade mark licence does not come to an end with the termination of any **12–08** related patent licence.[14] At one time, it was held that a trade mark that

---

[7] *Church of Scientology International v. Elmira Mission*, 230 U.S.P.Q. 325, 329 (2nd Cir. 1986). See also *Tavaro v. Jolson*, 223 U.S.P.Q. 950, 955 (S.D.N.Y. 1984), ruling that a former distributor has an added obligation to stay clear of the manufacturer's trade mark.

[8] *Blue Bell Bio-Medical v. Cin-Bad*, 9 U.S.P.Q. 2d 1870, 1873 (5th Cir. 1989), ruling in regard to trade dress.

[9] *Bellanca Aircraft Corp v. Bellanca Aircraft Engineering, Inc.*, 190 U.S.P.Q. 159, 168 (TTAB 1976).

[10] See, *supra*, Chap. 2, paras. 2–18 to 2–21.

[11] *Pacific Supply Cooperative v. Farmers Exchange*, 137 U.S.P.Q. 835, 847 (9th Cir. 1963).

[12] See, *supra*, Chap. 7, para. 7–40.

[13] *Distillerie Flli Ramazzotti v. Banfi Products Corp.*, 151 U.S.P.Q. 551, 555 (N.Y.S.C. 1966).

[14] *Wilbert H. Haase Co. v. Sultz*, 97 U.S.P.Q. 258, 262 (W.D.N.Y. 1953); *Koolvent Metal Awning Corporation of America v. Kool-Vent Awning Corporation of America*, 105 U.S.P.Q. 361, 368 (E.D. Mo. 1955).

described a patented product fell into the public domain upon the termination of the patent licence. This doctrine is no longer valid.

Termination: The Contract Dimension

The Contract May Address the Same Subject as Infringement

12–09 The parties to the licence agreement may expressly prohibit post-termination use of the trade mark by the licensee. If this is the case, the licensor may enforce its contract rights in addition to whatever claim it might enjoy for infringement of the trade mark in respect of the same or similar conduct.[15]

The most common contractual prohibition of this kind is an express obligation by the former licensee not to use the trade mark. A breach of this provision will probably both infringe the licensor's trade mark and be a breach of the licensee's contractual undertaking.

Implied Contractual Prohibition Against Use of the Trade Mark After Termination of the Licence

12–10 Even when the licence agreement is silent on the issue of post-termination use by the licensee, the licensor may claim that the obligation should be implied in the agreement. Such a term prohibiting post-termination use by the licensee was implied by the Court of Appeal in the *Sport International* case, overturning the decision of the High Court, which had refused to imply such a term.[16] In this case, the licensee had continued to use the licenced trade marks after the licence had been terminated for breach of the settlement agreement. The agreement was silent on the licensee's right to use the trade marks after termination.

The licensor argued that a contractual term should be implied, prohibiting the licensee from using the trade marks after the termination of the licence agreement. The Court of Appeal agreed, pointing to the particular circumstances and overall commercial realities that gave rise to the settlement agreement.[17] The Court of Appeal emphasised that the licence agreement contained an explicit provision whereby the licensee acknowledged the proprietary right of the licensor to the licensed marks.

In the Court's view, any use by the licensee after termination of the agreement would render this acknowledgement of the licensor's proprietorship of the trade marks a nullity, unless a term prohibiting post-termination use was implied. The implied term was held to apply equally to post-termination

---

[15] *Sport International*, *supra*, n. 1, at 337. A licensor may seek relief under the law of contract, in addition to a claim for trade mark infringement, because the measure of damages for breach of contract may be more favourable. Furthermore, in respect of the unauthorised use of an unregistered mark, a claim for breach of contract may be preferable to an action for passing off. See Chap. 10, paras. 10–07 to 10–31.

[16] [1988] R.P.C., *supra*, n. 1 at 337.

[17] *ibid*. at 337.

use of unregistered trade marks that were also subject to the agreement.[18]

When Should Such a Term be Implied?

The Sport International Case

Nevertheless, the conditions under which a contractual prohibition against 12–11
post-termination use of the trade mark by the licensee will be implied cannot
be regarded as settled. This may be seen from the *Sport International* case,
where the High Court and the Court of Appeal differed on the point. The
particular facts and circumstances surrounding the agreement will in each
case be crucial to the court's willingness to imply such a term.

Post-Termination Issues Not Directly Related to Trade Mark Use

In addition, the parties may seek to regulate post-termination conduct regard- 12–12
ing matters that do not relate to unauthorised use of the licensor's mark.
Performance of these provisions will be governed solely by the applicable law
of contract.

DURATION AND TERMINATION

Termination occurs either due to the expiry of the duration fixed in the 12–13
licence agreement or by the exercise of a right of termination.

Licence Agreement With an Express Duration

A licence agreement may be for either a fixed or unlimited duration, subject 12–14
to the continuing validity of the trade mark that is the subject of the licence.
If the licence agreement contains explicit provisions regarding duration, no
issue of an implied term arises. The duration of the licence agreement will be
in accordance with those provisions, subject to whatever additional provisions
the agreement may contain regarding prior termination.

No Duration Stated But Provisions for Termination Are Included

If the licence agreement is silent regarding duration but contains specific 12–15
provisions regarding termination, the licence agreement will be terminable in
accordance with these provisions.[19] Again, no implied term regarding the

---

[18] [1988] R.P.C., *supra*, n. 1. *cf.* with *Unistrut Corp. v. Power*, 126 U.S.P.Q. 83, 86 (1st Cir. 1960),
affirming 121 U.S.P.Q. 381, 386 (D. Mass. 1958), where the court held that a modified
agreement that added an explicit prohibition against post-termination use of the trade marks
was valid, with no claim made that there was an implied prohibition under the prior agreement.
[19] One U.S. court has characterised this as an 'indefinite' contract, whereby the '... contract runs
without a fixed end but contains provisions under which the contract might terminate at any
time.' *Nicholas Laboratories Ltd v. Almay, Inc.*, 723 F. Supp. 1015, 1018, citing *Payroll Express
Corp. v. Aetna Casualty and Surety Company*, 659 F.2d (2nd Cir. 1981).

duration would appear to be necessary to give effect to the ultimate duration of the agreement.

Agreement is Silent Regarding Both Duration and Termination

12–16 However, if the licence agreement is silent regarding duration and also contains no provisions for termination, a term may be implied whereby either party may terminate the agreement on reasonable notice to the other.[20]

In the *Bostitch* case, the court suggested that an implied termination provision, whereby the licence would have been revocable upon the provision of reasonable notice by the licensor to the licensee, was appropriate, even if subsequent developments between the parties made the question of the implied term irrelevant.[21] In that case, the licensee had claimed that the grant of licence was irrevocable, but the court rejected the argument.[22]

An Implied Right of Termination When a Period of Time is Specified in the Agreement

12–17 What about the situation in which the licence agreement explicitly provides for termination in the event of specified occurrences, but is unclear whether the period of time expressly mentioned in the agreement establishes a right of termination on expiry? The question is whether a fixed duration for the licence may be implied.

It has been held that reference to consecutive five year periods in a trade mark licence agreement did not provide the basis for an implied right of termination at the end of each such five year period.[23] The reference to the five year period was intended solely to allow the parties to re-calculate the royalties owed under the agreement. The court suggested, however, that had the agreement referred to the five year periods for additional reasons, a right of termination at the conclusion of each five year period might have been implied.[24]

Termination Determined from the Circumstances

12–18 In the event there is no written licence agreement setting out the terms and conditions of termination, the court may be called upon to determine when termination of the trade mark licence took place. For instance, it has been held that termination took place as of the date on which royalty payments

---

[20] *Chitty on Contracts* (26th ed., 1989), p. 565; *First Flight Associates v. Professional Golf Co.*, 189 U.S.P.Q. 497, 500 (6th Cir. 1975), citing *Corbin on Contracts* (26th ed., 1989). See also *Nicholas Laboratories*, and *Payroll Express*, *supra*, n. 19, noting that under New York law, there is a policy against the enforcement of a perpetual contract, in which there is no provision for either a definite end or for termination.

[21] [1963] R.P.C., 183, at 202, 203.

[22] This result has also been cited as an example of withdrawn consent under s. 4(3)(a) of the Trade Marks Act 1938; Kerly, para. 15–44, p. 310, n. 1.

[23] *Nicholas Laboratories*, *supra*, n. 19, at 1017.

[24] *Nicholas Laboratories*, *supra*, n. 19, 1017, 1018.

were discontinued, where this was followed by failed negotiations in respect of a new agreement.[25]

Post-Termination Negotiations for a New Licence

Sometimes the licensor and licensee continue to negotiate following the **12–19** termination of the licence. The licensee in such a situation must ensure either that any post-termination use of the trade mark is subject to a specific provision in the licence agreement allowing use of the trade mark while the negotiations are pending, or that the termination has been suspended conditionally. In the absence of either of these conditions, continued use of the trade mark after termination may be deemed an infringement, despite the existence of bona fide negotiations.[26]

The courts will examine all surrounding circumstances to determine whether an agreement to allow post-termination use of the trade mark pending the outcome of negotiations exists.

In one case, the court found that there was a triable issue on the question of whether the licensor had asked the licensee to continue business as usual during the negotiations for the renewal of the licence agreement. Furthermore, assurance was given by the licensor that if the negotiations failed, the licensee would be given a reasonable amount of time to dispose of its inventory.[27]

The willingness of the court to permit the licensee to prove that it had been authorised to use the mark during the period of negotiations is no substitute for an explicit provision to that effect. The onus falls upon the licensee to make sure that such a provision is included.

EXERCISE OF THE RIGHT OF TERMINATION

The Right to Terminate Is Not Automatic

A termination clause makes clear what is implied in many contracts, namely, **12–20** that a party may terminate an agreement upon a material breach by the other party. However, the right to terminate may be lost if it is not exercised. It is a power of election, even if it is anchored in an explicit termination provision.[28]

Notice of Termination: Oral Notice May Not Be Sufficient

The provision governing termination will often require that notice of ter- **12–21** mination be given in writing. In such a situation, the provisions calling for

---

[25] *First Flight Associates v. Professional Golf* Co., 19 U.S.P.Q. 497, 500 (6th Cir. 1975).
[26] *Bowmar Instrument Corp. v. Continental Microsystems, Inc.*, 208 U.S.P.Q. 496, 506 (S.D.N.Y. 1980); see also *Oleg Cassini Inc. v. Couture Coordinates, Inc.*, 161 U.S.P.Q. 716, 719–720 (S.D.N.Y. 1969).
[27] *Christian Dior-New York, Inc. v. Koret, Inc.*, 229 U.S.P.Q. 997, 998 (1st Cir. 1986).
[28] *Kaiser-Roth Corp. v. Fruit of the Loom, Inc.*, 219 U.S.P.Q. 736 (S.D.N.Y. 1983).

written notice must be carefully followed, and mere oral notice may well not be effective.

In one case, a settlement agreement was voided when it was found that the licensor had never provided written notice of termination, as required under the terms of an earlier licence agreement. Since the licence was still valid, the licensor could not enter into an exclusive licence arrangement as settlement with another party.[29]

A particularly instructive example of the interplay of notice and termination of a licence agreement is found in the *Kaiser-Roth Corp.* decision.[30] There, the licensee successfully challenged the termination of the licence. It argued that the licensor had neither provided reasonable notice to the licensee demanding the submission of certified annual sales reports as required by the agreement (even though royalties had been paid at the time of the submission of an internal sales report) not given express warning to the licensee that failure to comply would result in termination of the agreement.[31]

Liquidated Damages

12–22   Parties sometimes provide that if there is a breach of the contract, the breaching party shall pay a specified amount, in lieu of assessing damages under the principles of contract law. Such a provision is called a liquidated, or agreed, damages clause.

If the liquidated damages provision is found to be merely a convenient way in which to pre-determine the amount of a certain breach, and it is not intended as a penalty or to coerce the party in breach, it will be enforceable.[32] However, the party seeking to rely on a liquidated damages provision must be certain that it has complied with the provisions of the agreement giving rise to the right. For example, in the *Frisch's Restaurants* case, a licence agreement provided that liquidated damages in the amount of $100 per day would be assessed if the former licensee continued to use the trade mark after termination. The licence agreement described what kinds of use of the trade mark would bring the clause into effect.[33] In order to exercise its right under this clause, the licensor had to furnish the former licensee with written notice demanding cessation of the acts prohibited in the agreement, and the terminated licensee then had 15 days to comply, or be liable for payment of the liquidated damages.

The enforceability of this clause was not challenged. However, the court held that the letter furnished to the former licensee with respect to the subject matter of the liquidated damages clause did not comply with the notice requirements of the licence agreement. Reference was only made in passing to the allegedly breaching conduct of the former licensee. The licensor should have made explicit reference to those acts specified in the liquidated damages clause. Liquidated damages were accordingly denied.[34]

---

[29] *Donald F. Duncan Inc. v. Royal Tops Manufacturing Co.*, 343 F.2d 655, 659 (7th Cir. 1965).
[30] *Kaiser-Roth, supra,* n. 28, at 736.
[31] *ibid.* 28, at 751.
[32] *Chitty, supra,* n. 20, pp. 1170 to 1186; *Murray on Contracts* (1974), para. 234.
[33] *Frisch's Restaurants v. Elby's Big Boy*, 849 F.2d 1012, 1016, 1017 (6th Cir. 1988).
[34] *Frisch's Restaurants, supra,* at 1017.

BASIC PROVISIONS GIVING RISE TO TERMINATION

Certain provisions are often relied upon as giving ground for termination.   **12–23**

Termination and the Non-Payment of Royalties

Failure to pay royalties will usually be deemed a material breach unless, **12–24** perhaps, the licence to use the trade mark is only a collateral aspect of the agreement. In the typical situation, the payment of royalties is the principal consideration, and the sole source of income, for the licensor.[35]

Non-payment of a royalty, however, does not necessarily give rise to a right of termination, even when it is expressly mentioned in the termination provisions of a written agreement. When the agreement provides that the licensor may terminate the licence for non-payment after having given notice and following the expiry of a 30-day period in which to remedy the breach, the licensor does not exercise its right if it fails affirmatively to terminate the agreement after the 30-day period.[36]

If the licensor fails to object to the non-payment of royalties within the stipulated time, the licensor can put the licensee into default only by demanding performance, thereby restoring timely performance as an element of the contract.[37] In addition, failure to make royalty payments may give rise *per se* to termination, in the absence of a written licence agreement.[38]

Duty to Submit Annual Sales Reports

A licence agreement will often call upon the licensee to submit periodic **12–25** reports of the amount of goods sold in accordance with the licence. The licensor should pay careful attention to whether such a report must be certified by an independent auditor, or whether a report completed by internal staff of the licensee is sufficient.[39] From the licensee's point of view, the key is to comply with whatever reporting requirements are called for under the licence agreement.

Failure to Exercise Best Efforts

A provision calling upon a party, usually the licensee, to exercise its best **12–26** efforts in regard to the performance of its obligations under the licence agreement generally, or in respect of specific matters, is sometimes included in a licence agreement. The breach of this provision may provide the basis for termination. The question is whether such a provision is enforceable and if so, whether it has been breached.[40]

---

[35] *Kaiser-Roth Corp., supra*, n. 28, at 748.
[36] *McCleod v. Crawford*, 141 U.S.P.Q. 45, 53 (S.C. Neb. 1964).
[37] *Oleg Cassini Inc. v. Couture Coordinates, Inc.*, 161 U.S.P.Q. 716, 722–723 (S.D.N.Y. 1969).
[38] *First Flight Associates v. Professional Golf Co.*, 19 U.S.P.Q. 497, 500 (6th Cir. 1975).
[39] *Kaiser-Roth, supra*, n. 28.
[40] See, below paras. 12–48 to 12–58, for further discussion on best efforts clauses.

WINDING-DOWN THE USE OF THE TRADE MARKS

12–27 Perhaps the principal issue raised by termination is how the licensee is to wind-down its use of the trade mark. At one extreme, the parties may explicitly provide that all use of the mark is to cease on termination of the agreement, in which case any post-termination use would, as noted above, probably constitute infringement.[41]

Alternatively, the parties may seek to provide in the agreement for a winding-down of the use of the mark, in accordance with specified terms and conditions. There is no single formula for accomplishing this.[42]

One way is to designate the channels in which the inventory may be sold, and to limit the period of time for carrying it out. In addition, if a lengthy notice period is possible, the licensor may be able to limit the amount of inventory available during the last month or quarter prior to termination.[43]

Another example is taken from the *Kaiser-Roth* case.[44] The termination provision in that case provided as follows:

> 'After the termination of this licensee agreement, the licensee will not use [the trade mark] or trade name for any purpose whatsoever, including use to designate the origin of constituent materials, except in such instances as written permission to do shall have been granted by licensor subsequent to termination and all rights to the [trade mark] or trade name, whether or not accrued by virtue of use hereunder in connection with Finished Articles, shall revert to licensor. For a period of 90 days following the termination of this agreement, licensee may sell and ship Finished Articles which have been manufactured, labelled and packaged prior to said termination.'[45]

An Implied Provision for Winding-Down

12–28 Occasionally, the court has implied a provision, in the absence of an express term to the contrary, providing for a winding-down period during which the licensee is permitted to sell off the inventory without being liable for infringement or breach of contract.

In the *Bostitch* case, the court was prepared, upon the provision of proper notice by the licensor, to grant the licensee a period of 12 months in which to run down the existing inventory and to unwind a commercial relationship between the parties that had been in effect for over thirty years.[46]

In a U.S. case, the court granted to the contract manufacturer the right to sell off its inventory of stoves and parts which it had manufactured under an agreement with the licensee up to the date of the termination of the licence

---

[41] *Supra*, paras. 12–03 to 12–08.
[42] If the agreement terminates prematurely due to a breach by the licensee, the provisions for winding-down may well be different. *cf.* the discussion of the *El Greco* problem, Chap. 8, paras. 8–12 to 8–16.
[43] See *Christian Dior-New York, Inc. v. Koret, Inc.*, 229 U.S.P.Q. 997, 998 (1st Cir. 1986).
[44] *Kaiser-Roth, supra*, n. 28.
[45] 219 U.S.P.Q. at 738.
[46] [1963] R.P.C., *supra*, n. 21.

between the licensor and licensee.[47] The post-termination grace period granted to the contract manufacturer was implied from all the circumstances among the licensor, licensee and contract manufacturer. It is arguable that this result would also apply to a licensee under similar circumstances.

Implied Provision For Winding-Down Is Unusual

The majority of courts, however, have been unequivocal in their view that **12–29** no grace period should be implied. Representative are the words of Falconer J. in the *Sport International* case:

> '... [T]he fact that there is a licence to use the marks for the sale of particular goods ... does not mean and could not possibly mean that a licensee in those circumstances could avoid having to stop selling under the mark after termination of the licence by building up a stock marked with the goods during the subsistence of the licence for the express purpose of selling them after the licence. In my view, that cannot be seriously argued.'[48]

Time Given for Disposition of the Inventory May Be Crucial

A crucial factor in determining whether the court will imply a post-termination **12–30** grace period is the amount of time that the licensee is given under the agreement to dispose of the inventory after the notice of termination has been furnished. A court may be more likely to imply a grace period when the time between the furnishing of notice and the termination of the agreement is short and unreasonable, and the licensee is deemed to have acted in good faith in the accumulation of inventory prior to the termination.[49]

RELIEF FROM FORFEITURE

Introduction

Even where a licence is terminated in accordance with the provisions of the **12–31** agreement, an issue has sometimes arisen as to whether the licensee may seek relief from forfeiture of the licence under the court's equitable jurisdiction. If the court has authority to grant relief from forfeiture, the effectiveness of the licensor's contractual right to terminate the agreement and revoke the licence will be subject to that equitable jurisdiction.

If such relief from forfeiture is possible, from the point of view of the licensor, it may lead to less certainty regarding whether the licensor can

---

[47] *Woodcutters Manufacturing, Inc. v. Eagle-Picher Industries*, 215 U.S.P.Q. 1033, 1043 (W.D. Mich. 1982).

[48] *Sport International Bussum BV v. Hi-Tec Sports Ltd* (H.C. 1986, unreported, at p. 39.)

[49] See *N.S.W. Company v. Wholesale Lumber & Millwork*, 51 U.S.P.Q. 241, 246 (6th Cir. 1941), where the court permitted the licensee to sell off products for the remainder of the year in light of the 'abruptness with which the contract was terminated' and the fact that the licensee 'had built up stocks of frames in anticipation of obtaining [parts] indefinitely.'

prevent the licensee from any further use of the trade mark, and, with respect to an exclusive licence, whether the licensor is free to grant a new licence or to use the mark in the licensed territory itself.[50]

From the point of view of the licensee, relief from forfeiture, particularly where there has been a breach of a commercial term of the agreement that is not directly related to the grant of the trade mark licence itself, would enable the licensee to cure the breach and to continue to enjoy the right to the licensed use of the mark.

The General Rule in the United Kingdom – No Relief from Forfeiture

12–32 It has been held by the House of Lords that the court has no equitable jurisdiction to grant relief from forfeiture of a trade mark licence. It does not matter what kind of provision in the licence agreement, whether related to the use of the trade mark or to a commercial term, is breached. If the breach gives rise to termination of the licence, no equitable relief in favour of the licensee is available.[51]

The Sport International Case

12–33 The leading case is *Sport International*.[52] The forfeiture clause in question was contained in Tomlin Order that had purported to settle a long standing dispute between the parties involving distribution and trade mark rights. As part of the order, the licensee was granted a licence for a limited period of time for the use of certain trade marks. The licensee further agreed to pay a fixed sum in three instalments and to furnish two bank guarantees.

The termination clause provided that if the licensee failed to furnish the guarantee in a timely fashion, the licensor was entitled to demand the payment in full of all outstanding balances owed, and to terminate the license immediately. The court found that the first bank guarantee had not been provided in a timely manner. The respondent was accordingly entitled under the forfeiture clause to seek judgment on the outstanding balance and to terminate the trade mark licences.

The licensee sought relief from forfeiture of the trade mark licence. The court denied the request. It held that the equitable jurisdiction of the court to grant relief from forfeiture did not apply to a trade mark licence because the equitable jurisdiction applied only to proprietary rights, and rights created by a trade mark licence are merely contractual in nature.[53]

---

[50] *Sport International Bussum BV v. Inter-Footwear Ltd* [1984] 1 All E.R. 376, C.A.; aff'd [1984] 2 All E.R., 321, H.L.
[51] *Sport International Bussum BV v. Inter-Footwear Ltd* [1984] 2 All E.R., 321, H.L.
[52] *Sport International* case, *supra*, n. 50.
[53] [1984] 2 All E.R. 324–325. The issue of whether relief from forfeiture is limited to rights in real property, or may be granted in connection with intellectual property as well, was not resolved. See *BICC v. Burndy Corp. and BICC-Burndy Ltd* [1985] R.P.C. 273 (H.C. 1983).

A Trade Mark Licence is a Mere Contract Right

In the view of the court in *Sport International*, the licence to use the mark **12–34**
created no legal estate in favour of the licensee. A trade mark licence could
not be likened to a commercial lease or to security for the payment of the
instalments, either of which arguably could be said to involve a proprietary
interest. The rights conferred by virtue of the licence were merely contractual,
and the role of the court was to hold the parties to their freely negotiated
bargain. At best, in the words of the Court of Appeal, the trade mark licence
'... enables the licensee to obtain an injunction if the licensor, in breach of
contract, seeks to use the mark in competition with him.'[54]

The Need for Commercial Certainty

The need for commercial certainty in the termination of a trade mark licence **12–35**
was emphasised in the case. This may be seen from the following passage
from the judgment of Oliver L.J., quoted with approval by the House of
Lords:

> 'Here were two commercial concerns, locked in litigation, advised by
> counsel and solicitors. They could not be more at arm's length. One can
> hardly conceive of a case in which certainty is more important than in a
> contract putting an end to litigation. The fact that part of the subject
> matter was the use of a trade mark underlines the need both for certainty
> and for the avoidance of delay, for, if a licence is determined, the licensor
> will wish to know at once, particularly in the case of an exclusive licence,
> whether he is entitled to preserve or to build up his goodwill by entering
> on the territory himself or granting licences to others.'[55]

How Broad is the Scope of the Sport International Case?

However it is still open to doubt whether the *Sport International* decision has **12–36**
closed the door on relief from forfeiture of a trade mark licence.[56]

In *Crittal Windows Ltd v. Stormseal (UPVC) Window Systems Ltd*, the
licence agreement provided broadly for forfeiture of the licence on the breach
of any term of the agreement.[57] The only limitation on the licensor's right to
terminate the licence agreement was that the breaching party was allowed to
remedy a breach that was 'capable of cure', upon receipt of notice of the
breach.

---

[54] [1984] 1 All E.R., at 385. The Court of Appeal also observed that it was difficult to understand
how the court could grant specific performance in favour of a party that had breached an
essential term of the contract. This appears too broad a statement, since the foundation of
relief from forfeiture would appear always to be a material breach of the agreement by the
licensee. The comment in the House of Lords by Lord Templeton on this point is probably
more accurate; he observed that the operative principle is 'that equity will not grant specific
performance where time is of the essence and default is made and not waived.' [1984] 2 All
E.R. at 324.
[55] [1984] 1 All E.R. at 384, C.A.; [1984] 2 All E.R. at 325.
[56] The House of Lords noted that the case involved 'an unusual contract'. [1984] 2 All E.R. at
325.
[57] [1991] R.P.C. 265.

The licensee in this case used certain trade marks in a form contrary to the provisions of the agreement, and the licensor sought to terminate the agreement without providing notice. The breach was held by the court not to be capable of cure, and that no notice was necessary. The licensee then claimed that it was entitled to relief from forfeiture. Relying on the *Sport International* decision, the court in *Crittal Windows* held that it did not have equitable jurisdiction to grant relief from forfeiture.

The licensee in the *Crittal Windows* case had sought to argue that the court had equitable jurisdiction over a trade mark licence, relying on the intervening case of *BICC v. BICC-Burndy Limited*.[58] It was held in that case that the joint owner of patent rights was entitled to relief from forfeiture where there had been a failure to reimburse the other joint owner for certain expenses. The court there stated that a patent assignment gives rise to a proprietary right which is no less entitled to relief from forfeiture than an interest in real property.[59]

The court in *Crittal Windows* was unwilling to apply this result to a trade mark licence. It treated the *Sport International* judgment as binding authority for the principle that a trade mark licence is a mere contractual right, for which there is no relief from forfeiture. The judgment in *Crittal Windows* emphasised that relief from forfeiture appears to have applied only when there is a breach of a promise to pay money in connection with a proprietary right.[60] However, the distinction between a breach of a monetary, as opposed to a non-monetary matter, is not relevant to the issue of relief from forfeiture as long as the rule remains that a trade mark licence is merely a contractual right.

Does the 1994 Trade Marks Act Suggest a Different Result?

12–37 It can be asked whether the rule stated in the *Sport International* case is consistent with the Trade Marks Act 1994. Several points are noteworthy.

Section 31 provides that '[a]n exclusive license may provide that the licensee shall have, to such extent as may be provided by the license, the same rights and remedies in respect of matters occurring after the grant of the licence as if the licence had been an assignment.'[61] The likening of an exclusive trade mark license to an assignment suggests that the reasoning in the *BICC* case, where a patent licence was found to be a proprietary right, may apply to an exclusive trade mark licensee as well. On the other hand, it should be noted that the provision depends upon an agreement between the parties to the licence. Parliament did not adopt an earlier version of this section, whereby any exclusive licensee would be deemed as if it were an assignee as a matter of law.[62]

Moreover, section 25 of the Trade Marks Act 1994 specifies several types of transactions, including a licence, an assignment, and a security interest, as

---

[58] *Supra*, n. 53.
[59] *BICC, supra*, n. 53, at 316.
[60] [1991] R.P.C. at 277–78.
[61] Trade Marks Act 1994, s.31(1).
[62] See discussion of this point in Chap. 4, paras. 4–07 and 4–08.

all being registrable on the registry as 'an interest in or under a registered trade mark.'[63]

At the least, these provisions invite a reconsideration of the scope of the principle stated in the *Sport International* case that relief from forfeiture is not available because of the contractual nature of a trade mark licence.

Relief from Forfeiture and Unclean Hands

A Canadian decision, *Kochhar v. Ruffage Food*, involving the termination of **12–38** a franchise agreement, underscores the relationship between relief from forfeiture and unclean hands. There, the franchisee had been running 'an open till', whereby a portion of the gross sales was not taken into account in calculating the royalty due and owing to the franchisor. The franchisor terminated the franchise, but the franchisee sought relief from forfeiture.

The request was denied, on the ground that the prima facie evidence supported the claim that the franchise had failed to disclose a portion of its gross revenues. Relying on the doctrine that a party seeking an equitable remedy, such as relief from forfeiture, must come to the court with 'clean hands', the court held that such relief was unavailable to the breaching franchisee.[64]

Relief from Penalty

Related to the court's equitable jurisdiction to grant relief from forfeiture is **12–39** its equitable jurisdiction to grant relief from a penalty, the payment of which is provided for in a commercial agreement.[65] Even if a trade mark licence is treated as a mere contract, it has been suggested that a former licensee might be able to rely on this alternative basis for relief. The test for relief from a penalty has been expressed as follows:

'(a) It will be held to be a penalty if the sum stipulated for is extravagant and unconscionable in amount in comparison with the greatest loss that could conceivably be proved to have followed from the breach . . .

(b) It will be held to be a penalty if the breach consists only in not paying a sum of money, and the sum stipulated is a sum greater than the sum which ought to have been paid . . .'[66]

No Penalty Found in Connection with a Trade Mark Licence

There is no reported case where relief from a penalty has been found in the **12–40** context of a trade mark licence. The claim was raised and rejected in the

---

[63] Trade Marks Act 1994, s.25. Note also the words of Lord Templeton in the *Sport International* case: 'I do not believe that the present is a suitable case in which to define the boundaries of the equitable doctrine of relief against forfeiture.' [1984] All E.R. at 325.
[64] Reported in *Blakes's Report*, July/August 1992.
[65] *Sport International* [1984], *supra*, 1 All E.R., at 380.
[66] *BICC*, *supra*, n. 53, at 291–292, quoting from *Dunlop Pneumatic Tyre Co. Ltd v. New Garage & Motor Co. Ltd* [1915] A.C. 79 (L. Dundein).

Sport International case, where the contractual obligation to pay £105,000 was deemed not to be a penalty.[67]

The *BICC* case is instructive in this regard. In rejecting the claim that the assignment of the patent amounted to a penalty, where one co-owner did not reimburse the other for certain expenses, Dillon L.J. stated:

> '[T]he clause is no more a penalty clause than is the ordinary power of re-entry in a lease or the ordinary provision in a patent license to enable the patentee to determine the licence, however valuable, in the event of non-payment of royalties by the licensee.'[68]

Set-Off

12–41　Suppose that the licensee is in breach of a clause calling for the payment of money and that the breach entitles the licensor to terminate the trade mark licence, but the licensee also has a claim against the licensor for monies owed.

A set-off has been defined as a 'defence because the nature and quality of the sum so relied upon are such that it is a sum which is proper to be dealt with as diminishing the claim which is made, and against which the sum so demanded can be set off.'[69] The idea is that when the two claims are related, it is more efficient to dispose of them at one time by reducing the larger claim. The question is whether the claim of set-off can serve as a defence by the licensee to the forfeiture of the licence.

In the *BICC* case, the majority held that the claim by one co-owner of the patent against the other for monies owed for the supply of goods was a valid and complete defence to the specific performance of the assignment of the patent rights due to the failure to reimburse expenses.[70] Kerr J., dissenting, held that the set-off would be effective only if it gave rise to some independent ground for equity to deny the forfeiture of the patent rights.[71]

Set-Off in the Context of a Trade Mark Licence

12–42　It is conceivable that the issue of set-off might arise in the context of the trade mark licensee's non-payment of royalties or, as in the *Sport International* case, in resect of some other monetary obligation under the agreement which triggers termination.

The claim of set-off against the licensor would probably be based on the breach of a provision such as the grant of an additional licence in exclusive territory, the failure to supply the licensee with certain items (particularly in connection with its duty of quality control), the failure to reimburse the licensee for expenses made in connection with the maintenance of a trade mark application or registration, or breach of the licensor's warranty of title,

---

[67] *Sport International, supra* [1984] 2 All E.R. at 324.
[68] *Supra*, n. 53, at p. 312.
[69] *Hanak v. Green* [1958] 2 Q.B. 9.
[70] [1985] R.P.C., *supra*, at 314 (Dillon, J.).
[71] [1985] R.P.C., *supra*, at 317–322.

all of which could give rise to a money claim by the licensee.[72]

In line with the *BICC* case, it is arguable that where the licensee is in a position to claim a set-off against the licensor, it might be able to prevent forfeiture.

CONSTRUCTION OF A TERMINATION CLAUSE: LICENSEE BEWARE!

Apart from the courts' refusal to provide relief from forfeiture of a trade **12–43** mark licence, it can be said generally that courts tend to construe termination provisions strictly. While one should be wary of generalising, strict construction of the termination clause will be more likely to operate to the detriment of the licensee.

Rectification of the Termination Provision Is Unlikely

It is presumed that the provisions of a licence agreement reflect the intention **12–44** of the parties. For example, the termination provision in the *Sport International* case was viewed as expressing an arm's length commercial arrangement.[73] The test there for whether a breach had occurred, the failure to furnish the guarantee immediately upon payment of the instalment, was for all intents and purposes objective. Furthermore, the provision permitting the licensor to enter judgment and terminate the trade mark licence in the event of a breach was construed as giving effect to the intention of the parties to bring the settlement to an immediate end. As such, in the words of Lord Templeton, there was nothing to 'justify rewriting the consent order in the present case so that time ceases to be of the essence.'[74]

A similar request to rectify the agreement in the *Crittal Windows* case was **12–45** summarily dismissed by the court. It ruled that the licence agreement 'was an important commercial agreement' that had been 'negotiated at arm's length by experienced businessmen and their lawyers.'[75]

The Exceptions to Termination Must Be Clearly Specified

If the licensee is to be given an opportunity to avoid termination by correcting **12–46** the breach, this provision should be clearly stated.

In the *Crittal Windows* case, the agreement contained a termination clause which often appears in a licence agreement in one form or another:

> 'Either party may terminate this Agreement without prejudice to its other remedies forthwith by notice in writing to the other if that other either: commits a breach of this agreement; provided that if the breach is capable

---

[72] Durie and Manson, 'The Licensor in Breach': Set-Offs, "Counterclaims and Outstanding Royalties," [1991] E.I.P.R. 95
[73] [1984] 2 All E.R. at 325. See also, *supra*, para. 12–35 and accompanying note.
[74] [1984] 2 All E.R. at 325.
[75] [1991] R.P.C. at 272–273.

of remedy, the notice shall only be given if the party in breach shall not have remedied the same within one month of having been given notice in writing specifying the breach and requiring it to be remedied.'[76]

The court, in construing this provision, held that the alleged breach in question, the use of the trade marks in a manner and form other than as specified in the agreement, was not 'capable of remedy', because it was a continuing breach of a negative obligation not to use the marks except in the prescribed manner.[77] If the licensee had intended that the licensor be required to furnish the licensee with prior notice of the breach in question, together with an opportunity to remedy the breach, it should have so specified, rather than have attempted to rely on the construction of the phrase 'capable of remedy'.

Strict Construction of a Renewal Clause

12–47 Closely related to a termination provision is a provision providing for renewal of the licence agreement. It is the licensee's responsibility to observe the terms of such a provision to the letter.

In one case involving the renewal of a trade mark licence, the agreement specified that notice of the renewal be sent to designated persons and that an advance royalty be paid to the licensor by a certain date. The licensee claimed that it had substantially complied with the procedure set out in the agreement. The court held, however, that the failure strictly to comply with the provisions of the renewal brought about a termination of the licence as a matter of law.[78]

BEST ENDEAVOURS

Introduction

12–48 A particularly thorny issue is the extent to which a party can rely on a so-called 'best endeavours' clause to terminate the agreement. The provision obligates a party, usually the licensee, to use its best endeavours in connection with its performance of the agreement. It comes in different forms, ranging from an obligation on the part of the licensee to use its best endeavours generally in connection with the performance of the licence agreement, to an obligation to use its best endeavours with respect to the performance of a specific provision of the agreement.

At one time, the prevailing view was that a best endeavours provision was

---

[76] [1991] R.P.C. at 269.
[77] [1991] R.P.C. at 275.
[78] *MTV Networks v. Creative Associates and Frank Natale*, 91 Civ. 3609 (S.D.N.Y. 1991) (unpublished). The responsibility for compliance with the provisions of the renewal was apparently assumed by the attorney for the licensee, who then failed to perform the terms strictly as provided in the agreement. See also, *supra*, paras. 12–13 to 12–19.

too indefinite to be enforceable.[79] Today, no such hard and fast rule exists. However, it would be misleading to conclude that a best endeavours provision will always be upheld by the court. Two interrelated questions can be asked in relation to a best endeavours provision:

(a) What is the meaning of 'best endeavours'?
(b) Does an obligation to use 'best endeavours' create an enforceable obligation?

Meaning of 'Best Endeavours': General Principles under U.K. Law

No reported case in the U.K. has ruled squarely on the question of the **12–49** applicability of a best endeavours provision as part of a trade mark licence. Nevertheless, it is possible to understand such a clause from the general principles that have been developed in respect of such a provision.

The meaning of 'best endeavours' under law in the United Kingdom was extensively considered in the case of *IBM United Kingdom Ltd v. Rockware Glass Ltd*.[80] The provision at issue was in connection with an agreement for the sale of land, and tied the obligation of the vendor to sell the property to the best endeavours of the purchaser to obtain planning permission.[81]

Planning permission was not obtained, and the parties disputed whether the best endeavours provision obliged the purchaser to appeal to the Secretary of State. The Court of Appeal held that the purchaser's failure to appeal to the Secretary of State was a breach of its obligations under the provision. There was a general agreement among the three judges in their understanding of the meaning of 'best endeavours'. Buckley J. was of the view that it meant that the purchaser:

> '... was bound to take all those steps in their power which are capable of producing the desired results, namely the obtaining of planning permission, being steps which a prudent, determined and reasonable owner, acting in his own interests and desiring to achieve the result, would take...'[82]

He was joined in this analysis by Goff J.[83] Lane J. expressed a similar view.[84] However, Lane J. admitted that the precedents available were of little use in assisting the court in determining the meaning of the provision with respect to the particular contract in issue.

---

[79] Shifley and Holbert, ' "Best Efforts" May Not Be the Best Advice,' *Les Nouvelles*, xxvii, 1, March 1992, p. 38.

[80] [1980] F.S.R. 335 (C.A. 1976). See also *Overseas v. Granadex*, 1980–2 Lloyd's Rep. 608.

[81] The provisions in question were as follows:
7.1 '... [T]his agreement is conditional upon the purchaser obtaining planning permission.'
7.2 '... [T]he purchaser will make an application for planning permission and use its best endeavours to obtain the same ...'
7.3 'In the event of planning permission not being obtained ... by November 1st 1975 the vendor shall be entitled to serve notice to rescind this agreement.'

[82] p. 343.

[83] p. 348.

[84] In Lane J.'s view, best endeavours obligated the purchaser 'to take all those reasonable steps which a prudent and determined man, acting in his own interests and anxious to obtain planning permission, would have taken' (p. 345).

It was left for Goff J. to contend with the argument, which he himself had suggested in an earlier judgment,[85] that a 'best endeavours' clause of the type in issue may be unenforceable. Goff J. explained his earlier words as follows:

'I was not in any way suggesting that an obligation to use best endeavours is uncertain and cannot be enforced. The difficulty over uncertainty in *Bower's* case was that the object which the best endeavours were to be used to promote was left wholly indefinite. It was an area unspecified as to type or size, and even that was only to be provided if practicable.'[86]

The result of this statement by Goff J. is that the subject matter of a best endeavours provision must be reasonably certain and defined, and it should relate to a specific aspect of the agreement. In addition, the provision should, if possible, indicate an objective measure of best endeavours. A general obligation to use one's best endeavours in the performance of the agreement may not be given effect because it is too vague to be enforceable.

Comparison with U.S. Formulations of Best Efforts

12–50 It is useful to compare various judicial formulations of the provision under U.S. law (where it is typically referred to as a 'best efforts' clause). Thus, it has been variously described as an obligation 'to act with good faith in light of one's own capability';[87] 'to make more than a good faith effort';[88] and to 'bring to, and devote to, the business the ability suggested by ... previous experience in ... the line of work'.[89]

Best Endeavours and Best Efforts in a Trade Mark Licence

12–51 The meaning and enforceability of a best endeavours provision in the context of a trade mark licence agreement have been the subject of a number of decisions in the U.S. These decisions point to the uncertainties that are connected with the enforcement of such a provision.

Objective versus Non-Objective Measure of Best Endeavours

12–52 It is commonly stated that a best endeavours provision should be tied to an objective measure of performance. The case of *Craig Food Industries v. Taco Time International, Inc.*,[90] suggests, however, that this is not a panacea for a licensor disenchanted with the performance of his licensee. In this case, the court declined to enforce several best endeavours obligations contained in the franchise agreement. It did so by adjusting the operative standard of the best endeavours in accordance with the subject matter of each obligation, and then ruling that in each case the licensee had satisfied the standard. For

---

[85] *Bower v. Bantam Investments Ltd* [1972] 1 W.L.R. 1120.
[86] *Supra*, n. 85, at 348.
[87] *Bloor v. Falstaff Brewing Co.*, 601 F.2d 609, 613 n. 7 (2nd Cir. 1979).
[88] *Grossman v. Melinda Lowell, Attorney at Law, P.A.*, 703 F. Supp. 282 (S.D.N.Y. 1989).
[89] *Walter v. Silvers*, 177 P.2d 40 (Cal. App. 1947).
[90] 469 F. Supp. 516 (N.D. Utah 1979).

example, one provision stated that the master franchisor for a given area:

> '... shall use its best efforts to collect royalties and shall advise [the franchisor] of all collection activities undertaken by [the franchisees].'[91]

The court held that there was no evidence that the master franchisor had not used its best efforts to collect royalties from the franchisees, despite the abundance of late payments. The objective failure of the franchisees to make timely payment was apparently insufficient to establish a lack of best endeavours on the part of the person collecting the royalties.[92] The court further held that despite late payments of royalties by many franchisees, the master franchisee was not in breach of its obligation regarding advising the franchisor of all collection activities undertaken. The court stated that the provision did not adequately specify the precise standard by which its best endeavours to advise the franchisor regarding collection procedures was to be measured.[93]

Lack of Certainty

A judgment reported from New Zealand, although not directly involving a **12–53** best endeavours clause, is also noteworthy.[94] In that case, the parties entered into a complex distribution and licensing agreement. The licensee/distributor undertook not to '... [u]se any of the trade marks or otherwise act in a manner detrimental to the interests of the [licensor] as registered proprietor of the trade marks or otherwise act in a manner detrimental to the interests of the [licensor].'

When the licensee began to sell and promote a competing brand, the licensor sought to terminate the agreement. The court refused to find that the provision supported the termination. It noted as follows:

> 'Nowhere in the contract is there any guide as to what was an acceptable minimum performance, what sales had to be achieved, what degree of promotion was required in respect of one product or against another.'[95]

It is suggested that a similar lack of certainty could be fatal to the enforcement of a best endeavours clause.

Best Endeavours and Non-Competition

A best endeavours clause is often viewed by the licensor as a substitute for a **12–54** non-competition undertaking by the licensee. The court may refuse to enforce the provision in the absence of a breach of a specific non-competition provision.

---

[91] 469 F. Supp. at 527.
[92] 469 F. Supp. at 528.
[93] Id.
[94] *Talleys-Fisheries Ltd v. Petersville Industries Ltd* (Nelson Registry, 5/8/88).
[95] *Talleys Fisheries Ltd, supra*, n. 94, transcript at p. 16.

Best Efforts Means Exclusive Efforts

12–55 In once case, *Joyce Beverages of N.Y. v. Royal Crown Cola,*[96] the court considered an obligation by the licensee-bottler to '... employ its best efforts to market the [licensor's trade-marked] products.' The question posed was whether the bottler's handling of a competing product breached this provision.

The court noted that it was not *per se* a breach of the best endeavours provision to handle a competing line. Here, however, the facts pointed to the fact that the licensee's activities in connection with the competing line 'diluted' its efforts in favour of the licensor's products.[97]

In effect, the licensee created a situation of dual loyalty. The court rejected the claim that 'best efforts' meant merely 'even-handed efforts' with respect to the competing products.[98] Under these circumstances, the court was prepared to hold that 'best efforts' meant nothing less than 'exclusive efforts.'

Best Efforts Not Enforced As Substitute for Non-Competition

12–56 On the other hand, in *Conan Properties Inc. v. Mattel Inc.,*[99] the court interpreted the 'reasonable efforts' provision contained in a copyright and trade mark licence agreement so as not to prevent the licensee from engaging in development of its own *He-Man* toy, despite its licence to market the licensor's *Conan* toy. The *Conan Properties* court pointed to express language in the licence agreement reserving certain rights to the licensee, and noted that the parties were aware of the licensee's development of the *He-Man* toy at the time that the licence agreement was entered into.[1]

Another court, in the case of *Merle Norman Cosmetics, Inc. v. Martin*, refused to impose a non-competition obligation when another clause already prohibited the licensee from carrying merchandise bearing a marking which was confusingly similar to the licensed trade mark.[2] There, the agreement contained a broad best endeavours undertaking to the effect that the licensee would 'use [its] best efforts to promote the sales of [the licensor's] products.' This was followed by a separate undertaking by the licensee not to carry any merchandise whose marking was likely to cause confusion under the U.S. trade mark laws.[3]

The *Merle Norman* court noted that the prohibition against carrying non-confusing merchandise was 'strange', in that it did not prohibit the carrying of competing products by the licensee *per se*. Nevertheless, given this provision, the court would not impose an additional obligation of non-competition on the basis of a best endeavours provision. It noted that the licensor had not otherwise made clear to the licensee where it had failed to use its best endeavours in the promotion of the licensor's products.[4]

In the *Craig Food Industries* case, the master franchisee had stated that it

---

[96] *Joyce Beverages of N.Y. Inc. v. Royal Crown Cola*, 355 F. Supp. 271 (S.D.N.Y. 1983).
[97] *Joyce Beverages*, supra, n. 96, at 276.
[98] *Joyce Beverages*, supra, n. 96, at 236, n. 1.
[99] 13 U.S.P.Q. 2d 1017, 1025 (S.D.N.Y. 1989).
[1] 13 U.S.P.Q. 2d *supra*, n. 99, at 1026.
[2] 18 U.S.P.Q. 2d 1848 (9th Cir. 1990).
[3] *supra*, n. 2, at 1850.
[4] *ibid.*

'... will use its best efforts to secure operators in this area.'[5] The master franchisee had met its contractual quota by opening a specified number of stores each year. However, the franchisor attempted to argue that the provision had been breached because the master franchisee had engaged in competing enterprises outside the contract territory. This claim was rejected by the court. The court pointed to the fact that the master franchisee had satisfied its objective obligations under the contract in connection with the opening of new stores. In the absence of an explicit non-competition provision, the court would not impose such a provision by virtue of the best endeavours provision.[6]

Best Endeavours and E.C. Competition Rules

'Best endeavours' has also been addressed by the European Commission.[7] **12–57** Most notably, the E.C. block exemption on franchising states that it is presumptively valid to include a provision in a franchise agreement that the franchisee '... shall use its best endeavours to sell the goods or provide the services that are the subject-matter of the franchise; to offer for sale a minimum range of goods, achieve a minimum turnover, plan its orders in advance, keep minimum stocks and provide customer and warranty services'.[8] A specific exemption for a non-competition clause is also included in the franchise block exemption.[9]

It remains uncertain to what extent the exemption for a best endeavours clause adds anything in substance to the other provisions exempted by Article 3(1)(c), all the more so since a non-competition clause is separately exempted in Article 3(1)(c). In contrast, the block exemption for a know-how licensing agreement explicitly bans a non-competition provision. The same article also exempts a best endeavours clause from the ambit of the prohibition, such a clause being 'without prejudice to an obligation on the licensee to use his best endeavours to exploit the technology...'[10]

In the European Commission decision regarding the validity of the licence for the *Moosehead* trade mark, it found that a provision in the licence obliging the licensee not to produce or promote any other beer identified as a Canadian beer was a form of non-competition which contravened Article 85(1). The Commission went on, however, to exempt the provision on the ground that it was pro-competitive in the circumstances.[11] It is questionable whether a general best endeavours provision would have been similarly treated, given that the Commission ruled that the licence agreement was not governed by any of the block exemptions.[12]

---

[5] *supra*, n. 90, at 539.
[6] *supra*, n. 90, at 540–541.
[7] See, *infra*, Chap. 13, for discussion generally on the principles guiding E.C. law in connection with trade mark licensing.
[8] Commission Regulation 4087/88, Art. 3(1)(e).
[9] Commission Regulation 4087/88, Art. 3(1)(c).
[10] Commission Regulation 556/89, Art. 3(9).
[11] [1990] O.J. L100/32, para. 7(5), 15, 16(2).
[12] [1990] O.J. L100/32, para. 16(1).

Should a Best Endeavours Provision be Included in a Trade Mark Licence?

12–58 The foregoing discussion raises the question of under what circumstances a best endeavours provision should be included in the trade mark licence agreement, the ultimate criterion being the enforceability of the obligation. The following observations may serve as guidelines:

(a) If the best endeavours provision refers to the performance of the trade mark licensee generally (*e.g.* 'the licensee will use its best endeavours in carrying out the provisions of this agreement'), the extent to which a court will be prepared to enforce the provision is uncertain.

(b) If the best endeavours provision can be reduced to an objective measure with respect to a defined performance, then the provision is probably unnecessary to secure the performance of this measure. For example, if the provision specifies a minimum number of sales of trade-marked goods by the licensee under the licence agreement, it is arguable whether an undertaking of best endeavours in this connection creates an additional enforceable obligation on the part of the licensee.

(c) In the absence of a defined measure of performance, the best endeavours provision may serve to oblige the licensee to take whole-hearted steps, perhaps greater than if it were acting in mere good faith, in carrying out the provision. For example, if the provision states that 'the licensee shall use its best endeavours to increase the number of retailers within the territory that shall market and sell the goods under this Agreement,' lackadaisical or sporadic approaches by the licensee to a small number of potential retailers could be in breach of the obligation.

(d) In the absence of an express undertaking of non-competition by the licensee, it is questionable whether a best endeavours provision would enable the licensor to prevent the licensee from engaging in activities that deleteriously compete with the interests of the licensor.

13. Trade Mark Licensing: The European Community Dimension

INTRODUCTION

The licensing of intellectual property rights has posed special problems under **13–01** the law of the European Community (or, as it is now formally called, the European Union). These problems arise from the interplay between two principles: the existence of intellectual property rights under the national laws of the various Member States, and the exercise of those national rights against the backdrop of the Treaty of Rome, both providing for the free movement of goods between the member states of the European Community and prohibiting anti-competitive and monopolistic behaviour.

National Protection of Intellectual Property Rights

On the one hand, the Treaty of Rome gives recognition to the national **13–02** character of intellectual property rights. Article 222 states that the Treaty of Rome 'shall in no way prejudice the rules of Member States governing the system of property ownership.' This is presumed to include the national protection of intellectual property rights, including trade marks.

Further, the protection of intellectual property rights may be invoked as an exception to the principle of the free movement of goods. Article 30 of the Treaty of Rome prohibits '[q]uantitative restrictions on imports and measures having equivalent effect', *i.e.* measures which prevent the free movement of goods. However, Article 36 provides that such restrictions on the free movement of goods between Member States may be justified for 'the protection of industrial and commercial property' (in this context, industrial property is another name for intellectual property. As now interpreted, the scope of Article 36 extends only to the safeguarding of the specific subject matter of the particular intellectual property right involved.[1]

These provisions, Articles 222 and 36, emphasise the national character of intellectual property rights. Even though intellectual property rights may be restrictive, or even to some extent monopolistic, this alone does not render them invalid under European Community law.

---

[1] *S.A. CNL-Sucal NV v. HAG GF AG* [1990] C.M.L.R. 59(4) at 580, Opinion of the Advocate General (hereinafter: *HAG II*). See also *Deutsche Renault v. Audi* [1993], European Court of Justice, stating in para. 31 that 'the detailed rules for protection of trade marks ... are a matter for national law.'

Limitations on the Exercise of Intellectual Property Rights

13–03 However, the provisions giving recognition to national intellectual property rights have been held to refer only to the actual existence of those rights.[2] Set against the existence of national intellectual property rights, the Treaty of Rome has recognised two principles which apply to the promotion of competition within the European Community generally. The effect of these principles is to limit the exercise of national intellectual property rights.

First, the Treaty of Rome prohibits certain kinds of anticompetitive or monopolistic conduct (much as the Sherman and Clayton Acts prohibit similar conduct under U.S. law). Thus, Article 85 prevents concerted anticompetitive conduct between undertakings, while Article 86 prohibits the abuse by an undertaking of a dominant market position. To the extent that the exercise of an intellectual property right has an anticompetitive or monopolistic effect, it is possible it may be held invalid.[3]

Secondly, as noted above, Articles 30–34 of the Treaty of Rome prohibit acts which may have the effect of inhibiting the free movement of goods between Member States. This includes, in principle, a prohibition against using the enforcement of national intellectual property rights to prevent the free movement of goods. Unless the exception set out in Article 36 is deemed applicable, the prohibition against actions that deter the free movement of goods may serve as a limitation on the exercise of national intellectual property rights.

Trade Mark Licensing Addresses Both Free Movement of Goods and Anti-Competitive Behaviour

13–04 The licensing of intellectual property rights, including trade marks, may touch on both the principle of the free movement of goods and the prohibition against anti-competitive behaviour.

The trade mark licensor, having permitted the licensed use of its trade mark in one Member State, may, by attempting to enforce its national trade mark rights, seek to prevent those licensed goods from being imported into other Member States. Such conduct by the licensor may be in conflict with the principle of the free movement of goods.[4] Secondly, the trade mark licence agreement may be deemed to contain with respect to the licensee certain restrictive provisions, that have an anti-competitive effect. Here, the trade mark licensor must walk a narrow line in imposing restrictions upon the licensee with respect tot he use of the mark. To be acceptable under the competition rules of the Treaty of Rome, the restrictions must either be in

---

[2] *HAG II, supra*, n. 1, at 580.
[3] Regarding competition law in the European Community generally, see Bellamy and Child, *Common Market Law of Competition* (3rd ed., 1987); Whish, *Competition Law* (3rd ed., 1993); Singleton, *Introduction to Competition Law* (1992).
[4] See, *infra*, paras. 13–05 to 13–11, for further discussion of this point.

direct furtherance of the protection of the trade mark right and/or promote economic efficiency in production or distribution.[5]

Thus, the validity of a trade mark licence under European Community law must navigate between what is permitted by virtue of the existence of the intellectual property right, and the limitations in the exercise of that right which derive from the trade and competition rules of the Treaty of Rome.[6]

RESTRICTIONS ON COMPETITION AND THE FREE MOVEMENT OF GOODS

The central question regarding the relationship between national trade mark   13–05
rights, on the one hand, and the competition rules and the free movement of goods, on the other, is this: Can a trade mark proprietor or licensee prevent the parallel importation of goods bearing the same trade mark?

If the answer is yes, the ability to move the licensed products freely from country to country within the European Community will be severely curtailed. If the answer is no, the exercise of national trade mark rights may serve as a restriction on the free movement of goods. The answer to this question lies at the heart of the concept of the European Community a transnational economic community.

Restrictions on Competition: The Consten and Grundig Decision

As early as 1966, the European Court of Justice set out the basic principles   13–06
concerning the right of a trade mark proprietor to enforce its trade mark rights in order to prevent parallel importation.[7] The German manufacturer Grundig appointed a sole distributor for its products in France, Saar and Corsica. Like all other distributors, the French distributor could not sell competing products, nor make deliveries of the product outside of France. The purpose of this arrangement was to grant to the French distributor (as well as the distributors in other Member States) absolute territorial protection.

In addition to the *Grundig* mark, which belonged to the German manufacturer, the company also made use of the mark *GINT*. To strengthen the French distributor's position, Grundig permitted the distributor to register

---

[5] See, *infra*, paras. 13–12 to 13–43, and 13–47 to 13–57, for further discussion on this point. Art. 85 may also be deemed not to apply to an agreement of minor importance, which is defined as an agreement between parties which do not have more than 5 per cent of the total market for the goods or services in the affected area of the Common Market, and whose aggregate annual turnover does not exceed 200 million ECU. Commission Notice of September 3, 1986.

[6] It should be noted that the distinction drawn between the existence and exercise of intellectual property rights has sometimes been criticised as conceptually flawed, if not unworkable and result-oriented. Korah, *An Introductory Guide to EEC Competition Law and Practice* (4th ed.) at 157 ('In legal theory, it is impossible to draw the line between existence and exercise, except at the extremes.') While these criticisms are not without merit, the distinction between 'existence' and 'exercise' is helpful in attempting to define the boundaries of these national rights against a broader regional framework.

[7] *Establishments Consten S.A.R.L. and Grundig-Verkaufs – Gm.B.H. v. Commission of the European Economic Community*, Nos. 56/64 and 58/64 [1966] E.C.R. 299; [1966] C.M.L.R. 418.

the *GINT* trade mark in France in its own name. The aim of this was to allow the distributor to sue any parallel importer for trade mark infringement, if the importer attempted to bring Grundig goods bearing the *GINT* trade mark into France. The goods that were the subject of the infringement action in France had been obtained for import into France from German distributors, despite the contractual prohibition imposed on them against export.

The Commission ruled that the arrangement by which the French distributor sought to prevent the parallel import of the products 'restrict[ed] and distort[ed] competition within the Common Market . . .'[8] The Court of Justice agreed. It held broadly that:

> '[T]he contract between Grundig and Consten, on the one hand by preventing undertakings other than Consten from importing Grundig products into France, and on the other hand by prohibiting Consten from re-exporting those products to other countries of the common product, indisputably affects trade between Member-States.'[9]

Thus, the territorial exercise of trade mark rights cannot be used in a way that restricts trade, such as partitioning the Common Market into a series of impregnable national markets.[10]

Competition Principle Extended to Assignments

13–07 This principle was extended by the Court of Justice in the *Sirena* decision. A U.S. company had assigned its trade mark rights in Italy in the 1940s. The Italian assignee subsequently sought to prevent the parallel importation of the product obtained from a licensee in Germany, where the mark had not been assigned but only licensed. The Court of Justice did not permit the Italian assignee to restrict importation of the trade marked product. Again, the assignment was viewed as an attempt to partition markets by preventing parallel imports in contravention of the competition principles of Article 85.[11]

Exhaustion of Rights

13–08 It should be carefully noted that the *Grundig* case was decided under the competition rules. Later decisions have emphasised the principle of the exhaustion of rights in the context of the free movement of goods under Article 30–36. This principle has been generally expressed by the Advocate General in the *HAG II* case as follows:

---

[8] Decision of the Commission No. IV-A/00004–03344, September 23, 1964 [1964] O.J. 2525.
[9] *Grundig*, above, n. 7, [1966] C.M.L.R. at 472.
[10] Under the reasoning of this case, the restraint on competition must result from concerted activity, and not simply from the fact that a national industrial property right is involved. *Parke, Davis & Co. v. Probel*, No. 24/67 [1968] E.C.R. 55; [1968] C.M.L.R. 47.
[11] *Sirena Srl. v. Eda Srl*, Case No. 40/70 [1971] E.C.R. 5. The *Sirena* decision is also notable for its characterisation of trade mark rights. In its view, trade marks are less worthy of protection than other forms of intellectual property. *Sirena*, at para. 7. this position has changed. In the *HAG II* case, it was noted by the Advocate General that '. . . at least in economic terms, and perhaps also 'from the human point of view', trade marks are no less deserving of protection, than any form of intellectual property.' [1990] 3 C.M.L.R. at 583.

'The exclusive right conferred on the owner of intellectual property is exhausted in relation to the products in question when he puts them into circulation anywhere within the Common Market. Spelt out more fully, the proprietor of an industrial or commercial property right protected by the legislation of a member-State may not rely on that legislation in order to oppose the importation of a product which has lawfully been marketed in another member state by, or with the consent of, the proprietor of the right himself or a person legally or economically dependent on him' (see, for example, Case 144/81 *Keurkoop v. Nancy Kean Gifts*, ... [,] confirming a principle first developed in the *Deutsche Grammophon* case).'[12]

Exhaustion and Trade Marks

The principle has been further explained by the Court of Justice with reference **13–09** to the specific subject-matter of trade marks.

'In relation to trade marks, the specific subject-matter of the industrial property is the guarantee that the owner of the trade mark has the exclusive right to use that trade mark, for the purpose of putting products protected by the trade mark into circulation for the first time, and is therefore intended to protect him against competitors wishing to take advantage of the status and reputation of the trade mark by selling products illegally bearing that trade mark.'[13]

The exhaustion principle applies only to goods bearing the trade mark which are put into commercial circulation in a Member State, either directly by the proprietor of the mark or with his consent. The situations in which consent is deemed to occur include products put into commerce by the same undertaking, by a licensee, a corporate parent, a subsidiary or an exclusive distributor.[13a] In all such cases, the proprietor cannot prevent the importation of the goods into other Member States, even if he also is the proprietor of the trade mark in those other Member States.

Exhaustion Principle Applies to Licensing

The exhaustion principle includes the authorised licensed manufacture and **13–10** sale of the goods. As well, it prevents the trade mark licensee in the importing country from preventing parallel importation from another Member State, if the goods were put into commerce by the proprietor or with his consent. The proprietor's consent is expressed through his ability to control the quality of the licensee's products, thereby ensuring that the mark continues to designate a single source.[13b] Thus, the exhaustion principle applies to the trade mark licensee both in the Member State of export and that of import.

---

[12] *HAG II*, *supra*, n. 1, Opinion of the Advocate General, at 580.
[13] *Centrafarm BV v. Winthrop BV*, no. 16/74 [1974] E.C.R. 1183 at 1194; [1976] 1 C.M.L.R. 1.
[13a] *IHT Internationale GmbH v. Ideal-Standard GmbH*, C-9/93 (ECJ, June 22, 1994), para. 34.
[13b] *IHT Internationale*, *supra*, n. 13a at para. 31.

Limitations on the Exhaustion Principle

13–11 The exhaustion principle does not apply to goods which originate from outside the Common Market.[14] Furthermore, and in a rare instance of reversal, the Court of Justice now holds that it does not apply where there has been a forcible split of ownership, and no common origin is deemed to exist.[15]

THE BLOCK EXEMPTIONS

Introduction

13–12 Equally important to trade mark licensing is whether the licence agreement is deemed to constitute a restraint on competition. The Commission of the European Community has, by issuing regulations (so-called 'block exemptions') sought to clarify that Article 85(1) does not apply to certain kinds of agreements, including various types of licensing agreements in the intellectual property area.[16] Block exemptions in this context have been issued for patents,[17] franchises,[18] and know-how.[19] In addition, block exemptions have been issued regarding exclusive distribution agreements[20] and exclusive purchasing agreements.[21]

The block exemptions typically provide a list of provisions which are exempted from the reach of Article 85(1) (the so-called 'white list'), those that are not exempted (the so-called 'black list'), and certain other specified provisions that are generally not restrictive of competition, depending upon the circumstances (the so-called 'grey list'). A block exemption, if applicable to a given type of transaction, may provide a greater degree of certainty when structuring the provisions of the licence.

Only One Block Exemption May Apply

13–13 Only one block exemption may apply to a given arrangement. For example, if a licence deals both with a patent and know-how, it will have to be decided which block exemption, patent or know-how, applies. The structure of a

---

[14] *E.M.I. Records Ltd v. CBS United Kingdom Ltd*, No. 51/75, June 15, 1976 [1976] E.C.R. 811; [1976] 2 C.M.L.R. 235.

[15] *HAG II*, *supra*, n. 1, has been extended to apply as well when the splitting of ownership of the trade mark on a territorial basis (*i.e.* country by country) is by way of a voluntary act rather than by sequestration (*IHT Internationale*, *supra*, n. 13a).

[16] The authority to issue these Regulations is based on Council Regulation No. 19/65. Regulations are binding on the Member States without any requirement that they be adopted by the national legislatures. *cf.* with Directives, *infra*, paras. 13–44 to 13–46, which require implementation by the Member States.

[17] Commission Regulation 2349/84 of July 22, 1984.

[18] Commission Regulation 4087/88 of November 30, 1988.

[19] Commission Regulation 556/89 of November 1988.

[20] Commission Regulation 1983/83 of June 22, 1983.

[21] Commission Regulation 1984/83 of June 22, 1983.

licence may thus be crafted to take into account the perceived advantages or disadvantages of the various block exemptions.[22]

Trade Mark Licence May be Ancillary

The trade mark licence may be subject to the provisions of a block exemption **13–14** if it is ancillary to a patent or know-how licence. In these cases, the applicable block exemption contains provisions that address aspects of trade mark licensing. The trade mark licence is not, however, the principal component of the arrangement.

Patent Licensing

A patent licence may include ancillary provisions regarding trade mark **13–15** licensing. In such a case, the following provisions will govern the treatment of the trade mark licence as part of the broader patent licensing arrangement.

Scope of Ancillary Trade Mark Licence

Recital 10 of the patent licensing block exemption describes the scope of **13–16** ancillary trade mark licensing as part of a patent licence.

> 'It is also appropriate to extend the scope of the Regulation to patent licensing agreements containing ancillary licensing provisions relating to trade marks, subject to ensuring that the trade-mark licence is not used to extend the effects of the patent license beyond the life of the patents. For this purpose it is necessary to allow the licensee to identify himself within the 'licensed territory,' *i.e.* the territory covering all or part of the common market where the licensor holds patents which the licensee is authorised to exploit, as the manufacturer of the 'licensed product', *i.e.* the product which is the subject matter of the licensed patent or which has been obtained directly from the process which is the subject matter of the licensed patent, to avoid his having to enter into a new trade-mark agreement with the licensor when the licensed patents expire in order not to lose the goodwill attaching to the licensed product.'

Perhaps the key point of Recital 10 is that the trade mark licence is intended to further rights in the trade mark, and not to extend the life of the patent licence beyond the term of the patent itself. In particular, the Recital points out that the patent licensee may continue to enjoy valuable rights in the

---

[22] For instance, the view is sometimes taken that the block exemption for know-how is more advantageous than the one relating to patents, with the result than when both a patent and know-how are involved in a particular license, is usually preferable to attempt to bring the arrangement under the know-how block exemption. Singleton, *supra*, n. 3, at 193. Note, however, that the separate block exemptions for patent and know-how, respectively, are scheduled to be replaced by a single Technology Transfer block exemption. Reference will be made to the text of the draft dated September 30, 1994.

goodwill earned in the trade mark after the expiry of the patent.[23] Articles 1(1)(7) and 2(1)(6) of the Regulation embody the principles expressed in Recital 10.

Use of the Licensor's Trade Mark or Get-Up

13–17 Article 1(1)(7) permits a provision that provides for 'an obligation on the licensee to use only the licensor's trade mark or the get-up determined by the licensor to distinguish the licensed product, provided that the licensee is not prevented from identifying himself as the manufacturer of the licensed product.' Note that the subject matter of this provision is not limited to a registered trade mark, and extends to get-up as well. A similar provision is contained in Article 2(12) of the draft of the Technology Transfer block exemption.

Identity of the Licensor

13–18 Article 2(1)(6) states that 'an obligation on the licensee to mark the licensed product with an indication of the patentee's name, the licensed patent or the patent licensing agreement' will not be deemed to be unduly restrictive.

Know-How Licensing

13–19 This block exemption applies to a know-how licence, or to a mixed know-how and patent licence which is not subject to the patent block exemption. Again, the block exemption addresses trade mark licensing that is ancillary to the know-how licence.

There is no recital in the know-how block exemption similar to Recital 10 of the patent block exemption. It has been suggested that Recital 10 may perhaps apply to those provisions in the know-block exemption which track its wording.[24] Further, Article 1(1) states that the know-how block exemption applies to agreements which also contain 'ancillary provisions relating to trademarks or intellectual property rights...'[25]

Use of the Licensor's Trade Mark or Get-Up

13–20 Article 1(1)(7) permits 'an obligation on the licensee to use only the licensor's trade mark or get-up determined by the licensor to distinguish the licensed product during the term of the agreement, provided that the licensee is not prevented from identifying himself as the manufacturer of the goods.' This

---

[23] Korah, *Patent Licensing and EEC Competition Rules*, Regulation 2349/84, at p. 53. For example, consider the continued use of the trade mark 'NutraSweet' after the expiry of the patent under which the artificial sweetener has been manufactured. Art. 1(1) of the draft of the Technology Transfer block exemption provides in a similar fashion that it shall not apply to 'ancillary provisions relating to [other] intellectual property rights.' See also, *infra*, para. 13–19.

[24] *Know-how Licensing Agreements and the EEC Competition Rules*, 556/89, p. 165.

[25] *cf.* with the Commission decision in the *Whitbread* case, *infra*, para. 13–25, where the trade mark was not considered ancillary to the know-how portions of the licence. Accordingly, the know-how block exemption was held not to apply.

provision is identical to Article 1(1)(7), with the addition of the reference to the term of the agreement. A quite similar provision is contained in Article 1(7) of the draft of the Technology Transfer block exemption.

Use of the Licensor's Name

Similar to Article 2(1)(6) of the Patent block exemption, Article 2(1)(11) **13–21** further permits 'an obligation on the licensee to mark the licensed product with the licensor's name.' The scope of this obligation is more limited than the corresponding provision in the patent licensing block exemption, reflecting perhaps the confidential nature of the know-how.

Quality Specifications

It has been observed that care should be taken to avoid the prohibition of **13–22** Article 3(3)(3) which blacklists unwarranted quality specifications or ancillary restrictions relating to goods or services.[26] The quality control provisions of a trade mark licence will typically include specifications, and may also require the purchase of ancillary products. The suggestion has been made that this prohibition may be overcome by including an express declaration regarding the appropriateness of the quality specifications for the licensing of the trade mark.[27]

Franchising

Trade Mark Licence May Be Central

Even in situations where, in contrast with a patent or know-how licence, the **13–23** use of a trade mark is more central, the trade mark licence may still be governed by a separate block exemption. This is the case when a trade mark licence is part of the business format franchise agreement that is deemed to be subject to the franchise block exemption.

In this context, it would be incorrect to say that the trade mark licence is ancillary to the other intellectual property rights which are part of the franchising block exemption. The trade mark licence is no less important than the know-how and commercial and technical assistance components of the franchise. Nevertheless, the franchise block exemption applies.[28]

The Block Exemption itself

The subject matter of the franchise block exemption is described in Recital 5 **13–24** as follows:

'This Regulation covers franchise agreements between two undertakings,

---

[26] Korah, *supra*, n. 24, pp. 124–125.
[27] Korah, *supra*, n. 24, p. 125. *cf.* with the *Moosehead/Whitbread* decision given by the European Commission, *infra*, paras. 13–52 to 13–56.
[28] Art. 5(4) of the draft of the Technology Transfer block exemption provides that the block exemption shall not apply to the licensing of other intellectual property rights, including trade marks. On the franchise block exemption, see generally Korah, 'Franchising and the EEC Competiton Rules Regulation' 4087/88 (1988).

the franchisor and the franchisee, for the retailing of goods or the provision of services to end users, or a combination of these activities, such as the processing or adaptation of goods to fit specific needs of their customers. It also covers cases where the relationship between franchisor and franchisee is made through a third undertaking, the master franchisee. It does not cover wholesale franchise agreements because of the lack of experience of the Commission in that field.'[29]

Trade Marks and Franchising: a Definition

13–25 The use of a trade mark by the franchisee is central to the retail sales or service franchise covered by the block exemption. This may be seen from the definition of franchise under Article 3(a) of the Regulation. This Article defines a franchise to mean 'a package of industrial or intellectual property rights relating to trade marks, trade names, shop signs, utility models, designs, copyrights, know-how or patents, to be exploited for the resale of goods or the provision of services to end users.'

It is clear that the provision of goods and services is often intertwined in such a franchise arrangement. This means that both trade marks and service marks may be involved.

The Franchisee's Minimum Obligations

13–26 Article 1(3)(b), in its definition of "francise agreement", sets out the franchisee's minimum obligations under the franchise arrangement:

(a) Use of a common name or sign;
(b) Uniform presentation of premises or means of transport;
(c) Disclosure by the franchisor to the franchisee of know-how;
(d) Continuing provision of commercial or technical assistance by the franchisor to the franchisee.

All of these obligations may be said to be embodied in the goodwill represented by the trade mark. However, while the franchisee's licensed use of the trade mark is an essential element of a franchise arrangement, it is not the sole factor which defines the franchise. The transfer of know-how and the provision of technical assistance are equally as important. Other intellectual property rights may also be licensed to the franchisee.

In summary, a franchise agreement, as defined, will include a trade mark licence as a component part, but not every trade mark licence amounts to a franchise agreement.

Franchise Block Exemption is Instructive Regarding Permitted Trade Mark Licensing

13–27 Despite the fact that not all trade mark licences form part of a franchise as defined by the block exemption, the centrality of the trade mark licence to a

---

[29] The block exemption does not apply to a manufacturing or production franchise, such as that in *Campari, infra*, paras. 13–48 to 13–51.

franchise makes this block exemption particularly instructive in understanding what is permitted and prohibited in the trade mark licensing context. The following key provisions are noted.[30]

Exempted or Permitted Provisions

Sole and Exclusive Franchise

The agreement may provide for the grant of an exclusive franchise. This **13–28** means that the franchisor will not itself exploit the franchise, supply the franchisor's goods to a third party, or grant a franchise to any third party.[31]

Quality Control and Procurement Requirements

The following obligations may be imposed on the franchisee, provided that **13–29** they are necessary to protect the franchisor's industrial and intellectual property rights, or to maintain the common identity and reputation of the franchised network.

(a) The franchisee may be obliged to sell, or use in the provision of services, only goods which match minimum objective quality specifications set down by the franchisor.[32]

(b) The franchisee may be obliged to sell, or use in the provision of services, goods manufactured by the franchisor or a designated third party, where it is impracticable, owing to the nature of the goods, to apply objective quality specifications.[33] This provision, which is a form of tie-in, comes into play only if the quality specifications themselves are necessary.[34]

There is no requirement to show that the following quality control provisions are necessary to protect the trade mark or other intellectual property rights of the franchisor.

(a) The franchisee may be obliged to comply with the franchisor's standards regarding equipment and mode of presentation of the premises.[35]

(b) The franchisor may be allowed to carry out inspections of the premises, in order to check on the goods sold, the services provided, and the franchisee's inventory and accounts.[36]

---

[30] Special attention should be paid to the treatment of services under a franchise, since the relatively recent adoption of service marks under the Trade Marks Act 1938 put a licence for service marks on the same footing as that of a trade mark licence. Under the Trade Marks Act 1994, licensing of both trade marks and service marks are recognised. See *supra*, Chap. 1, para. 1–27.

[31] Art. 2(a).

[32] Art. 3(1)(a).

[33] Art. 3(1)(b).

[34] *cf.* the quality specification under the quality control requirements of the registered user or registered licence provisions, *supra*, Chap. 6, para. 6–15.

[35] Art. 3(2)(g).

[36] Art. 3(2)(h). But see Art. 3(2)(h), which suggests that this obligation is conditional on the franchisor's inspection of the premises being in furtherance of the protection of its intellectual property rights.

    (c) The franchisee may be obliged to attend training courses arranged by the franchisor.[37]

    (d) The franchisee may be obliged to use the franchisor's commercial methods, and to use the franchisor's intellectual property rights.[38]

Non-Competition

13–30 The franchisee may be prohibited from handling goods which compete with the franchisor's goods,[39] from competing with the franchisor for up to a year after the termination of the franchise,[40] or from acquiring a financial stake in a competitor which would enable it to influence the conduct of the competitor.[41]

Active Sales

13–31 The franchisee may have to refrain from seeking customers outside the territory for the goods or services which are the subject matter of the franchise.[42]

Performance Requirements

13–32 The franchise may be bound to adhere to the following performance requirements:

    (a) To use its best endeavours to sell the goods or provide the services;

    (b) To offer for sale a minimum range of goods;

    (c) To achieve a minimum turnover;

    (d) To maintain minimum stocks;

    (e) To provide customer and warranty services.[43]

Advertising

13–33 The franchisee may also be obliged to carry out advertising, subject to the franchisor's approval.[44]

Third Party Infringement

13–34 The franchisee may have an obligation to inform the franchisor of infringement by a third-party of the franchisor's intellectual property rights, and either to take action or to assist the franchisor in so doing.[45]

---

[37] Art. 3(2)(e).

[38] Art. 3(2)(f).

[39] Art. 2(e).

[40] Art. 3(1)(c).

[41] Art. 3(1)(d). The restrictions contained in n. 40 and n. 41 are conditioned on their necessity to protect the franchisor's intellectual property interests.

[42] Art. 2(d).

[43] Art. 3(1)(g).

[44] Art. 3(1)(g). The restrictions contained in n. 43 and n. 44 are conditioned on their necessity to protect the franchisor's intellectual property interests.

[45] Art. 3(2)(c).

Know-How

(a) The franchisee may be obliged to keep the know-how of the franchisor 13–35 confidential, even after the termination of the franchise.[46]
(b) The franchisee may be prohibited from using and exploiting the know-how other than in connection with the franchise.[47]

Assignment

The franchisee may be required to obtain the franchisor's permission before 13–36 assigning its rights and obligations.[48]

Prohibited Provisions

The following provisions do not fall within the scope of the franchising block 13–37 exemption.

Resale Price Maintenance

The franchisor is not permitted to determine the sales prices for the goods or 13–38 services which that are the subject matter of the franchise. The franchisor is permitted, however, to recommend sales prices.[49]

Market Sharing

Franchise agreements entered into between competing manufacturers or sup- 13–39 pliers of services are not permitted.[50]

Foreclosing Suppliers

(a) Provisions which prevent the franchisee from obtaining supplies of 13–40 goods substantially equivalent to those offered by the franchisor are prohibited.[51]
(b) Provisions which obligate the franchisee to use or sell goods manufactured by the franchisor or a party designated by him, other than to protect the franchisor's intellectual property rights or its common identity and reputation, are prohibited.[52]

Post-Termination Use of the Know-How

The franchisee may not be prohibited from using the know-how after 13–41 termination, if the know-how has become publicly available.[53]

---

[46] Art. 3(2)(a).
[47] Art. 3(2)(d).
[48] Art. 3(2)(j).
[49] Art. 5(e).
[50] Art. 5(a).
[51] Art. 5(b).
[52] Art. 5(c), *cf.* Art 2(e).
[53] Art. 5(d).

No Challenge Clauses

13–42 The franchisor is not allowed to prevent the franchisee from challenging the validity of the industrial property rights. However, the franchisor may provide that in the event of such a challenge, the agreement may be terminated.[54]

Exclusive Distribution Agreements

13–43 Use of the trade mark by an exclusive distributor is addressed in several places in the block exemption for exclusive distribution agreements. It is assumed that such use by a distributor is not tantamount to licensed use of the mark.[55] Nevertheless, these provisions regarding trade mark use still merit brief attention.

Article 2(3)(b) permits an obligation on the exclusive distributor 'to sell the contract goods under trademarks, or packed and presented as specified by the other party.' Here, the obligation is intended to enable the manufacturer to enhance the goodwill in its mark through the distribution of the goods under the mark.

Article 2(3)(c) allows an obligation on the exclusive distributor 'to take measures for promotion of sales in particular: to advertise ...' Here as well, the required use of the mark is designed to promote the manufacturer's goodwill in it.

Similar provisions regarding trade mark use are contained in Articles 2(3)(c) and (d) of the block exemption for exclusive purchasing agreements.[56]

The Trade Mark Directive as a Source of Law

Introduction

13–44 An additional potential source of EC law regarding trade mark licensing is the Council Directive of December 21, 1988 to approximate the laws of the Member States relating to trade marks, the so-called Trade Mark Directive. The Trade Mark Directive is a form of secondary EC legislation.

As a Directive of the European Community, its terms must be implemented by each of the Member States. The purpose of a Directive is to bring about the harmonisation of national laws, in this case national trade mark laws, throughout the Community. Trade mark harmonisation was supposed to

---

[54] Art. 5(f); *cf.* the decision of the Commission of the European Community regarding *Moosehead/Whitbread, supra*, Chap. 9, paras. 9–47 to 9–50, where a no challenge clause was upheld in a pure trade mark licence.

[55] See, *supra*, Chap. 7, paras. 7–10 to 7–15, regarding trade mark use in distribution agreements.

[56] See above, n. 21.

have been achieved by December 31, 1992, but the Directive has not yet been implemented by all of the Member States.[57]

Licensing under the Trade Mark Directive

Licensing is expressly covered by the Trade Mark Directive. Article 8(1) **13–45** permits licensing:

(a) for some or all of the goods or services for which the mark is registered;
(b) for all or a part of a Member State;
(c) on either an exclusive or a non-exclusive basis.

Article 8(2) provides that a breach of the following provisions of the licence agreement will give rise to a claim of infringement:

(a) duration;
(b) the form in which the mark is permitted to be used;
(c) the scope of the goods or services;
(d) the territory;
(e) the quality control provisions.

This list is seen as potentially expanding the potential grounds on which a trade mark proprietor can invoke his trade mark rights against a breaching licensee.

---

[57] The time limit for implementation was extended by Council Directive 92/101 of December 19, 1991. The enactment of the Trade Marks Act 1994 constitutes implementation of the Directive by the U.K.

On December 23, 1993, the European Community promulgated Council Regulation (EC) No. 40/94 on the Community trade mark.

The effect of this Regulation is to create the framework for a Community-wide trade mark. Recital 5 of the Regulation states that the Community-wide trade mark will 'not replace the laws of the Member States on trade marks', and 'national trade marks continue to be necessary for those undertakings which do not want protection of their trade marks at the Community level.'

At least two Articles of the Regulation are directly relevant to the issue of licensing and use of the Community trade mark by a third party:

Licensing – Art. 2(1) and (2) provide for licensing of the Community trade mark in a manner similar to that provided by Art. 8(1) and (2) of the Trade Mark Directive. Further, Art. 22 contains three additional provisions regarding licensing:

  1. Art. 22(3) provides as follows:
     a. Subject to the provisions of the licensing agreement, the licensee may bring an action for infringement of the Community trade mark only with the consent of the proprietor of the mark.
     b. Notwithstanding, an exclusive licensee may bring a proceeding for infringement if the proprietor does not himself bring such proceedings within an appropriate period after receipt of formal notice.
  2. Art. 22(4) provides that a licensee is entitled to intervene in infringement proceedings brought by the proprietor of the mark for the purpose of obtaining compensation suffered by the licensee.
  3. Art. 22(5) provides that a licence, or the assignment thereof, may be registered on the register.

Exhaustion – Art. 13 provides for exhaustion of the rights conferred by a Community trade mark in a manner similar to the provisions for exhaustion under Art. 7 of the Trade Mark Directive. See *supra*, Chap. 7, paras. 7–28 to 7–29.

Is the Trade Mark Directive Compatible with Article 85?

13–46 It has been suggested that the Trade Mark Directive is presumed to be 'consistent with the practice of the Commission and the Court and is compatible with the EEC Treaty.'[58] If this is correct, a trade mark licence that contains any of the provisions specified in Article 8 is presumed not to fall foul of Article 85, and the breach of any of them is also an infringement of the licensor's trade mark rights. Whether this presumption of compatibility with Article 85 is correct remains open to question. For example, it is not clear what is meant by quality control under the Trade Mark Directive, and whether all acts allegedly relating to quality control are permitted by virtue of Article 8. It would appear that quality control provisions must still be determined by reference to the competition rules of the Treaty of Rome.[59]

LICENCE AGREEMENTS: THE CAMPARI AND MOOSEHEAD/WHITBREAD DECISIONS

General Competition Rules apply If No Block Exemption is relevant

13–47 In those situations where no block exemption applies, a trade mark licence will be evaluated under the general competition rules of the Treaty of Rome.[60] The Commission has on two occasions given decisions regarding a trade mark licence which offer some guidance in this resect.[61] Still, the absence of a block exemption for a trade mark licence *per se* makes it more difficult to set down definitive rules regarding what is permitted and prohibited in such an arrangement.[62]

The Campari Decision

Background

13–48 Campari-Milano established a network of licensees to manufacture and sell its aperitif products in various countries in the EC. It granted an exclusive right to use the trade mark, in conjunction with the use of its know-how, and it undertook not to manufacture the aperitif itself in those territories in which it had granted exclusivity.

---

[58] United States Trade Mark Association, Guidelines for Trade Mark Licensing in the European Community, August 1992 (USTA Guidelines), at n. 15.

[59] *cf.* also the treatment of an exclusive licence under the *Campari* and *Moosehead/Whitbread* decisions with the provisions of Art. 8(1)(iii).

[60] See, generally, Joliet (now Justice Joliet of the European Court of Justice), 'Trademark Licensing Agreements under the EEC Law of Competition,' *Northwestern Journal of International Law & Business*, 5:775 (1983), and 'Territorial and Exclusive Trademark Licensing under the EEC Law of Competition,' *IIC*, Vol. 15, no. 1/1984. See discussion, *supra*, paras. 13–05 to 13–11.

[61] These two decisions are the *Campari* decision of the Commission of December 23, 1977; [1977] O.J. L70/69, as reconfirmed in the Commission's 18th Report on Competition Policy, 1988, p. 71, and the *Moosehead/Whitbread* decision of the Commission, March 23, 1990; 1990 O.J. L100/32. See, *infra*, paras. 13–48 to 13–56, for discussion of these decisions.

[62] See generally, USTA Guidelines, *supra*, n. 58.

Each licensee operated within a single Member State. Certain other provisions regarding the relationship between the licensor and licensee were also contained in the licence agreement. The question was whether the trade mark licence was permitted under Article 85.[63]

Provisions held to be caught by Article 85(1)

The following provisions were found to restrict competition under Article **13–49** 85(1):

Exclusivity The exclusive nature of the licence, which had the effect of keeping out other available licensees, as well as precluding the licensor itself from acting in the territory.

Non-Competition This provision prohibited the licensee from manufacturing or selling competing products.

No Active Sales Policy Outside the Territory The licensee was prohibited from actively seeking customers outside the territory.

Provisions Found Acceptable Under Article 85(3)

The restrictive provisions listed above were, nevertheless, found to be accept- **13–50** able under Article 85(3), since they were deemed essential to induce the parties to enter into and to invest in the licence arrangement. Thus, the exclusivity provisions were held to improve production and distribution, and to induce the necessary investment and effort in the territory. The prohibition on carrying competing products was also found to enhance distribution, and ensured that the licensee would devote its reasonable efforts to the manufacture and sale of the product.

The non-competition clause was also found to contribute to a more rational distribution system. This type of provision in a trade mark licence was distinguished from a non-competition clause in the context of a patent licence. Similar reasoning was applied to the prohibition against maintaining an active sales policy outside the territory.

Provisions Not Covered by Article 85(1)

Other provisions in the *Campari* trade mark licence agreement were held not **13–51** to be caught by Article 85(1).

Export Ban Outside the European Community. This restriction was held not to amount to a material restriction on the licensees.

Quality Control and Know-How. The permitted provisions included the following:

---

[63] This decision was given in 1977, more than a decade before the know-how block exemption was issued, *supra*, n. 19.

(a) A restriction on plants which were permitted to manufacture the product.

(b) The obligation to follow the licensor's instructions regarding manufacture and to buy secret raw materials from the licensor.

(c) The licensees were prohibited from disclosing the manufacturing process to third parties.

(d) The licensee had a duty to maintain regular contact with customers, and to spend a fixed sum on advertising.

Limitation on Assignment

The licensor is allowed to choose its licensee. Therefore, free assignability by the licensee is properly prohibited.

The Moosehead/Whitbread Decision

Background

13–52 Over a decade later, the Commission had occasion to consider once again, this time in the *Moosehead/Whitbread* decision, a trade mark licence for the manufacture of the licensor's product under the trade mark. This case involved an agreement whereby Moosehead Breweries Ltd., a well-known Canadian beer manufacturer, granted to Whitbread and Company plc an exclusive license to brew and sell beer in the United Kingdom under Moosehead's trade marks.[64] The beer sold under the trade mark was deemed to have a taste distinctive of Canadian lagers.

The agreement between the parties consisted of three contracts: (a) A Marketing and Technical Agreement; (b) A Trade Mark User Agreement; (c) An Assignment. Taken together, these contracts contained certain provisions regarding the use and ownership of the licensed trade mark, and the reassignment of rights on termination. In addition, they set out various requirements concerning Whitbread's use of the technical and commercial knowhow.

Trade Mark is the Essential Element of the Licence

13–53 The first question was whether any block exemption, notably the know-how block exemption, applied to this arrangement. The Commission ruled that the agreement did not fall under the know-how block exemption. It reasoned that the exploitation of the trade mark was central to the agreement, rather than being ancillary to the know-how agreement. '[T]he Canadian origin of the mark is crucial to the success of the marketing campaign.'[65] Thus, despite the fact that the licensed know-how was made available to the licensee, the agreement was evaluated under the rules of competition of the Treaty of

---

[64] See generally, Subioto, 'Moosehead/Whitbread: Industrial Franchises and No-Challenge Clauses Relating to Licensed Trade Marks under EEC Competition Law,' [1990] 9 E.I.P.R., 334; Rothnie, 'EC Competition Policy, the Commission and Trade Marks,' *International Business Lawyer*, November 1991, p. 495.

[65] [1990] O.J. L100/36, at para. 16.

Rome, rather than under the know-how block exemption.[66]

Provisions Cleared by the Commission

The Commission cleared the following provisions of the agreement in the 13–54
Moosehead/Whitbread case.

Quality Control and Know How

Compliance with Directions The licensor would provide the licensee with the
relevant know-how to make the beer. In return, the licensee was obliged to
comply with the directions of the licensor regarding the know-how.

Purchase of Essential Supply The licensee had to purchase the yeast essential to
the making of the beer from the licensor or its designated supplier.

Duty of Confidentiality The licensee was permitted to use the know-how only
for the manufacture of the beer, and was obliged to maintain the confidentiality
of the know-how.

These provisions seem to be consistent with the ruling in the *Campari*
decision.

Non-Challenge Clause In perhaps the most significant part of the decision, the
no-challenge clause against the licensee was held not to restrict competition.
This applied to both the validity and the ownership of the mark.[67]

Provisions Held to be Restrictive of Competition

The Commission followed its lead in *Campari* in finding that the following 13–55
provisions were restrictive of competition under Article 85(1). An individual
exemption was therefore required for each provision.

Exclusivity and Prohibition against Active Sales outside the Territory

The Commission found that these two provisions, exclusivity and prohibition
against active sales outside the territory, were restrictive of competition under
Article 85(1), but were exempted under Article 85(3).[68]

---

[66] Query how the practitioner can in advance structure the agreement in such a way as to
increase the likelihood that the trade mark, or the know-how, is the principal element of the
agreement. One suggestion is to include in the agreement a specific recitation stating which
element is of primary importance. The efficacy of such a recitation is far from assured,
however; see Rothnie, *supra*, n. 64, at 497. It is probably more correct to say that classification
of such an arrangement lies at the mercy of the Commission.

[67] See, *supra*, Chap. 9, paras. 9–40 to 9–50, for further discussion of this provision.

[68] *cf.* the treatment of these two issues under the franchising block exemption, *supra*, paras. 13–
28, 13–31. *cf.* also the treatment of exclusive licences under Art. 7(1) of the Trade Mark
Directive and Art. 22(1) and (3) of the Trade Mark Regulation, *supra*, paras. 13–44 to 13–46,
and accompanying notes.

Non-Competition

Similarly, the non-competition clause was held to be restrictive of competition under Article 85(1).

Summary

13–56 In the main, therefore, this decision is consistent with the *Campari* decision. The novel points of interest are the decision's treatment of the no-challenge clause, and the finding that the know-how block exemption did not apply, thus necessitating an analysis under the competition principles of the Treaty of Rome.

The continuing treatment of the exclusivity provision, the ban against active sales outside the territory, and the non-competition obligation as being caught by Article 85(1) continues to introduce an element of uncertainty about the scope of permissible provisions in a trade mark licence.

Additional Permitted Provisions under E.C. Law

13–57 It has been suggested that at least two basic provisions in a trade mark licence agreement are permitted under E.C. law due to the very nature of trade mark rights and intellectual property licensing. These provisions are:

(a) The right of the licensor to impose restrictions on the use of the mark by the licensee;
(b) The right to collect royalty payments.[69]

These two provisions can be said to define the heart of the licensee's obligations under a trade mark licence, at least where the parties are unrelated, and a genuine arms length transaction is involved.

---

[69] USTA Guidelines, *supra*, n. 58, at 2.

14. Collateral Aspects of Trade Mark Licensing

This chapter will consider three important collateral aspects of trade mark **14–01** licensing – insolvency, product liability, and taxation.

INSOLVENCY AND TRADE MARK LICENSING

Introduction

The control of trade mark rights in the context of insolvency has taken on **14–02** increased importance in recent years. There are two interrelated reasons for this.

First, intellectual property rights, in general, and trade mark rights, in particular, have become a more significant portion of the assets of many companies. In some instances, as highlighted by the multi-billion dollar leveraged buy-out of the R.J. Reynolds company, trade mark rights constitute perhaps the most important asset in the transaction.[1] Secondly, the economic stagnation of the late 1980s and 1990s has placed the disposal of intellectual property assets at the centre stage of numerous company insolvencies. Just as the acquisition of trade mark rights had led to a reappraisal of what constitutes a company's value and worth, the disposal of those rights has led to a heightened interest in how the insolvency laws treat them.[2]

The Key Issue: Waiver or Rejection of the Licence During Insolvency Proceedings

Perhaps the most important question is the continuing validity of the trade **14–03**

---

[1] For a sweeping but critical account of this transaction, see Burrough and Helver, *Barbarians at the Gate: The Fall of RJR Nabisco* (1990).
[2] See, *e.g.* Hull, 'Is There Life for UK Trademarks after an Insolvency?' *Managing Intellectual Property*, No. 9, 1991, pp. 36–41.

mark licence once insolvency proceedings have commenced.[3] Under certain circumstances, it may be possible for the insolvent party in insolvency proceedings, typically the licensor, to disclaim (or in the language of U.S. law, to 'reject') the intellectual property licence, thereby depriving the licensee of the rights in which it may have invested extensive time and resources. Thus, the licensee could easily find itself deprived of the right to use the licensed rights in the trade mark.

The Lubrizol Problem

14–04 The possibility that a licensee can lose its rights to the use of the intellectual property was brought into prominence by a decision of the United States Fourth Circuit Court of Appeals in the *Lubrizol* case.[4] That decision held that by virtue of section 365 of the United States Bankruptcy Code, the licensor of certain know-how could reject a non-exclusive licence, thereby depriving the licensee of its use of the know-how.

Rejection of an Executory Contract

14–05 Section 365 provides that an 'executory contract' may be rejected by the debtor or trustee-in-bankruptcy. An executory contract has been defined as a contract under which both parties have material obligations of performance.[5] The effect of an executory contract is that no further performance is owning under the agreement, and the rejected party is left with an unsecured claim for damages.

The court in the *Lubrizol* case held that the licence agreement was an executory contract, with continuing obligations of performance on both sides.[6] Once an executory contract was established, the licensor satisfied the conditions for rejection of the licence, based on the exercise of its business

---

[3] The U.K. Insolvency Act 1986 provides for three basic types of procedural devices when a company becomes insolvent. These are a winding-up of the company, either voluntary or involuntary, with a view to its ultimate liquidation (s.73), putting an administrative receiver in charge, (s.42), or asking for a court-appointed administrator (s.8).

The trademark licence will not automatically terminate in the event of insolvency. See *Accurist Watches v. King* [1992] F.S.R. 80, where the contract manufacturer repossessed watches made to order under reservation of title clauses upon the insolvency of the party that had placed the order. See Nissen, 'The Effect of Insolvency on Trade Mark Licences,' paper presented at the 7th Annual Waidering Conference, Waidering, Austria, sponsored by McGeorge School of Law, 1993, pp. 14–15.

The main procedural vehicle in the U.S. is the Bankruptcy Code, 11 U.S.C. 101 *et seq.*, which provides for liquidation under chap. 7, and reorganisation under chap. 11.

[4] *Lubrizol Enterprises Inc. v. Richmond Metal Finishes, Inc.*, 756 F.2d 1043 (4th Cir. 1986).

[5] The leading definition of an 'executory contract' is as follows: '[A] contract under which the obligations of both the bankrupt and the other party to the contract are so far unperformed that the failure of either to complete performance would constitute a material breach excusing performance of the other.' Countryman, 'Executory Contracts in Bankruptcy,' 57 Minn. L.R. 439, 460.

[6] Note that the licensee's continuing performance was not merely the obligation to pay royalties, which might not be enough on its own to establish an executory contract, but also the licensee's duty to report use of the technology.

judgment that the rejection was advantageous to the estate.[7] The licensee was accordingly deprived of any further right to use the know-how.

Lubrizol *Reversed by Amendments to the Bankruptcy Code*

The result reached in the *Lubrizol* decision has largely measure been reversed   **14–06** by the enactment in 1988 of an amendment to the U.S. Bankruptcy Code, which significantly strengthens the ability of a licensee to exercise election and thereby to continue to enjoy the licenced rights even after rejection.[8] In particular, the licensee may elect to continue to pay royalties, in exchange for a continaton of the licence.[9]

Amendments Do Not Apply to a Trade Mark Licence

However, the 1988 amendment does not extend to a trade mark licence. The   **14–07** omission of trade marks was intentional, and reflects the special concern of quality control in trade mark licensing. The argument was successfully made that a licensor which was forced to monitor a trade mark licence that it either could not, or did not wish to, maintain, might show so little interest that abandonment of the trade mark might result, thereby leading to the loss of the very right on which the licence relied.[10]

This means that the *Lubrizol* principle is still relevant for determining the treatment of a trade mark licence under U.S. bankruptcy law. Two cases highlight the treatment of a trade mark licence in the context of bankruptcy.

Rejection of Trade Mark Licence Under the Bankruptcy Code

In the case of *Chipwich*,[11] the bankruptcy court, citing the *Lubrizol* decision,   **14–08** held that the two trade mark licences were executory contracts. The debtor-licensor was therefore entitled to reject the agreements in the exercise of its business judgment. More recently, in *Blackstone Potato Chip Co.*,[12] the court permitted the trade mark licensor to reject the licence, despite the fact that the licensor had misrepresented certain facts in connection with its obligations under the agreement. The fact that the licensor had not exercised quality control did not affect its right to reject the licence.

As a result of these cases, a trade mark licensee must be alert to the possibility that, under the principles of the *Lubrizol* case, the licence might be rejected by a licensor subject to bankruptcy proceedings.

---

[7] It was noted that the licensor would then be able to license the technology to other licensees on more favourable terms. The harm likely to be incurred by the licensee as a result of the rejection was not deemed to be relevant.

[8] See, *infra*, n. 10.

[9] Bankruptcy Act, s. 365(n).

[10] See generally, Wilkof, 'Bankruptcy and Creditor's Rights under U.S. Law: an IP Perspective', *Managing Intelletual Property*, No. 26, January–February 1993, p. 7.

[11] *Re Chipwich, Inc.*, 54 B.R. 427 (1985).

[12] *Re Blackstone Potato Chip Co.*, 109 B.R. 557 (1990).

Rejection of the Licence Might Be subject to Two Sets of Rules

14–09 Moreover, if the licence also involves the grant of other intellectual property rights, such as a patent, copyright or know-how, the rejection of the licence in bankruptcy might be subject to two sets of rules. The trade mark licence would continue to be governed by the right of rejection under *Lubrizol* and the decision which followed it, while the other intellectual property rights would be subject to the right of election in accordance with the amendment to the Bankruptcy Code under section 365(n).

Precautionary Measures by the Licence: Security Interest or Conditional Assignment

14–10 Thus, under U.S. law, a trade mark licensee might consider such precautionary measures as taking a security interest in the trade mark, or couching the arrangement as a conditional assignment rather than as a licence. These steps might prevent the disruption or rejection of the licensee's right to use the trade mark.[13]

Is There a Parallel to the Lubrizol Under Law in the United Kingdom

14–11 The possibility of a similar result under British law has been considered. In particular, it has been suggested that section 178 of the Insolvency Act 1986 may be relevant. This section empowers the liquidator to disclaim 'onerous property' of the insolvent estate, where onerous property includes 'any unprofitable contract'. Section 179 addresses disclaimers of property of 'a leasehold nature', which could be viewed perhaps as applying to a licence of intellectual property.

These provisions appear to establish a more demanding standard for disclaimer than under section 365 of the U.S. Bankruptcy Code, which merely calls for proof of an 'executory contract', together with the exercise of business judgment in rejecting the licence. The Insolvency Act 1986 is not meant to provide the liquidator with a broad statutory authority to deprive a licensee of its rights under a licence agreement.[14]

---

[13] The recordal of a security interest in a trade mark is governed by Art. 9 of the Uniform Commercial Code, which in similar form has been adopted in all states of the U.S., except Louisiana. Generally speaking, property rights in the U.S. are created under state, rather than federal law, and the registration of a security interest is recorded with the appropriate state authority.

There is some difference of opinion, however, over whether such a registration must also be made with the Patent and Trademark Office, as well as with the state registry, when a federally-registered trade mark under the Lanham Act is involved. The better view appears to be that no such additional registration is necessary, although caution might still dictate making the further registration. In *Re Peregrine Entertainment Ltd*, 16 U.S.P.Q2d 1017, 1023 (C.D. Cal. 1990.) See generally, Bramson, 'Intellectual Property as Collateral – Patents, Trade Secrets, Trademarks and Copyrights,' *The Business Lawyer*, Vol. 36, July 1981.

See also s.24(4) of the Trade Marks Act 1994, which provides that the assignment provisions with respect to a registered trade mark 'apply to assignment by way of security as in relation to any other assignment.'

[14] In the words of one commentator, s. 178 *et al.* are intended as a 'shield and not a sword.' Rome, 'The Lubrizol enterprises case – an English view,' *Computer Law & Practice*, September/October 1987, p. 9.

Might Quality Control Be Onerous?

As a result, it appears that the Insolvency Act 1986 does not usually allow **14–12** the disclaimer of an intellectual property licence in the manner recognised under the *Lubrizol* case. However, it may be possible to distinguish a trade mark licence form other types of intellectual property licensing on the basis that the licensor's obligation to maintain quality control is indeed 'onerous'.

Under this argument, an unwilling trade mark licensor might have to devote precious resources to maintaining quality control, when such resources could be more usefully allocated elsewhere. In addition, the failure to exercise quality control could lead to an abandonment of the mark, to the detriment of the estate. A similar suggestion has been made in connection with the right of a licensor of computer software to disclaim its duty to maintain the software.[15]

The argument that quality control is 'onerous' has been put forward in connection with the question of how a receiver may dispose of associated trade marks to different purchasers, when the law requires that the marks should not be separated. This may occur when a company with several divisions is being sold to different purchasers, and each division is identified by a similar mark. The Trade Marks Act 1938 did not permit these marks to be separated.[16]

One suggested solution is to assign all of the marks to one purchaser, who then licences the marks in the 'unsold' part of the business back to the receiver, who in turn assigns the licence to the purchaser of the other division of the company. One drawback of this arrangement is that it may burden the receiver with 'an onerous licence which imposes severe quality control provisions in respect of goods covered by the marks.'[17] In this situation, the undesired burden is on the licensee rather than the licensor. The important thing to remember, however, is that the quality control requirements in the context of an insolvency may impose unwanted responsibilities on both the licensor and licensee, depending upon the circumstances.

Mortgage of a Trade Mark as a Possible Solution

The possibility that a trade mark licence might be deemed 'onerous' under **14–13** certain circumstances raises the question of whether the licensee should consider taking precautions similar to those mentioned above in the context of U.S. practice, namely a mortgage over the trade mark.[18] The law and practice of security interests in trade marks was not well-settled under the Trade Marks Act 1938.

The Trade Marks Act 1938 did not explicitly provide for the creation or recordal of a security interest. Nevertheless, it may have been possible to

---

[15] Sandison, H., 'The Insolvency of a Software Licensor', 1991 (unreported).
[16] See, s. 23 of the Trade Marks Act 1938, for a discussion on associated marks. The Trade Marks Act 1994 does away with the provisions regarding associated trade marks.
[17] Hull, *supra*, n. 2, at p. 41.
[18] See, *supra*, para 14–10. It was argued that a mortgage rather than a charge is the appropriate arrangement for taking security in a trade mark under the Trade Marks Act 1938. Henry, 'Mortgages of Intellectual Property in the United Kingdom', [1992] 5 EIPR 158.

record a memorandum of the mortgage under section 34(1)(e) of the Trade Marks Act 1938. This section permitted the Registrar at his discretion to enter on the register a memorandum relating to a trade mark, provided that the memorandum does not extend the rights conferred by the registration. In this case, the memorandum would detail the mortgage as a restriction on the use of the trade mark. There was a requirement to advertise the memorandum in the Trade Marks Journal.[19]

The Trade Marks Act 1994 now makes it clear that a security interest over a registered trade mark is a 'registrable transaction'. Section 25(2) provides that a registered trade mark may be the subject of a security interest. Section 25(2) further provides that the particulars of 'any security interest (whether fixed or floating) over the registered trade mark or any right under it' may be registered upon application to the registrar.'[20] Registration of the security interest appears to constitute notice to third parties regarding the grant of the interest. Conversely, until the security interest is registered, the transaction is ineffective against an innocent third party that in the meantime acquires a conflicting interest.[21] Rules are to be promulgated relating to the amendment or removal from the register of particulars relating to the security interest. Such amendment or removal may be effected either by application or consent of the person who is entitled to the benefit of the security interest.[22]

Trade Mark Licensing and Product Liability

Introduction

14–14 A matter of increasing concern to the trade mark licensor is potential civil liability due to injury caused by defective products made and sold under the licensed mark. Such liability is popularly called 'product liability'.[23] A plaintiff in such circumstances may seek to expand the circle of actionable defendants, and thereby to improve his chances of recovery, by seeking to hold the licensor, as well as the licensee, liable for the injury. The key question is to what extent the licensor can be held responsible for the acts of the licensee.

Both tort and contract have been relied upon as bases for product liability. However, the application of these principles to the liability of a trade mark licensor is not settled. It is an accepted view that the licensor-licensee relationship is not that of partners, master and servant or principal and agent.[24] What then is the source of the licensor's liability for a defective product?

---

[19] Henry, *supra*, n. 18, at p. 160.
[20] Trade Marks Act 1994, ss.25(2).
[21] Trade Marks Act 1994, ss.25(3).
[22] Trade Marks Act 1994, ss.25(5), (6).
[23] In the U.S., the term is also referred to as 'products liability.'
[24] Adams, 'The Liability of a Trade Mark or Name for the Acts or Defaults of his Licensees,' [1981] 11 E.I.P.R. 314.

Liability Based on Control

One suggestion is that the licensor's liability rests on its control over the **14–15** manufacture of the licenced product. The issue raised here is the relationship if any, between quality control for the purposes of the trade mark laws, and control over the design and manufacture of the product for the purposes of product liability.

Quality control over the licensee's manufacture or selection of the licensed product is central to a trade mark licence.[25] Without at least some control, a trade mark licence may be found to be invalid. The argument is made, therefore, that the licensor's quality control over the licensee is a sufficient basis to impose liability on the licensor for injury caused by defective goods. Thus, in one frequently cited review of the case law on such liability under U.S. law, it was concluded: 'Liability under a strict products liability theory seems impossible to avoid ... [and] turn[s] on factors inherent in the franchise or trademark license relationship,' namely the benefit of royalties and the need for supervision.[26] Under this view, quality control is integrally related to product liability.

Does Quality Control Give Rise to Liability?

However, this conclusion can be questioned. Quality control serves to identify **14–16** the source of the goods by indicating a certain level of quality that is associated with the trade mark. Quality control does not necessarily serve as a warranty that the goods are free from defects.[27] Moreover, the extent to which actual quality control is practised will differ from situation to situation.[28]

It appears facile, therefore, to conclude that the mere fact of quality control in the trade mark sense implies the kind of control that gives rise to tortious liability. The amount of actual control must be taken into account.

Test for Control

One way to view the quantum of control required to establish the necessary **14–17** link between the licensor and licensee for the purposes of tortious liability is to consider the overall licence arrangement. The following factors have been deemed to support a finding of actual control: (a) regulating the licensee's hours of operations; (b) going beyond the specification of standards by laying down methods for preparing or providing the goods or services; (c) detailing methods of operation; (d) designating the stock to be carried; (e) specifying the suppliers.[29]

Factors that argue against a finding of control have been identified as

---

[25] See generally, *supra*, Chap. 6, for discussion on quality control.
[26] Borchard and Ehrlich, 'Franchisor Tort Liability: Minimizing the Potential Liability of a Franchisor for a Franchisee's Torts,' 69 *The Trademark Reporter* 127.
[27] See, however, Goldstein, 'Products Liability and the Trademark Owner: When a Trademark is a Warranty,' 67 *The Trademark Reporter* 587, for the opposing view that a trade mark serves a warranty function which is compatible with the notion of civil liability.
[28] See *supra*, Chap. 6, paras. 6–34 to 6–41.
[29] Adams, *supra*, n. 24, p. 315; see also Borchard and Ehrlich, *supra*, n. 36.

follows: (a) the absence of any salary or commission received by the licensee from the licensor; (b) the operation by the licensee of his business independently of the licensor, including hiring and firing of staff, and retaining profits; (c) the lack of any reporting system between the licensee and the licensor.[30]

Two words of caution must be mentioned in connection with these lists. First, they tend to be applicable more to a fully-fledged franchise arrangement than to a trade mark licence agreement. Secondly, the lists are based primarily on the results of U.S. judgments. The number of English cases on this subject appears to be negligible.[31]

To What Extent is the Licensor Connected with the Manufacture?

14–18 Another way to view the control test is to examine the extent to which the licensor can be deemed to be connected to the manufacture of the product. This approach can be seen by comparing the results reached in two U.S. decisions; liability was found in one case, but was rejected in the other.

Torres: The Parent Exercises Overall Control

14–19 The first case is *Torres v. Goodyear Tire & Rubber Co.*[32] The court found that under the common law of the State of Arizona as well as under that state's product liability statute, the Goodyear Tire & Rubber Co. was liable for the injury caused by a tread separation in a tyre bearing its trade mark.

The defendant attempted to argue that since the research, design, manufacture, distribution and sale of the product were all carried out through its wholly-owned subsidiaries, it itself could not be held liable, despite the fact that it was the proprietor of the trade mark which appeared on the product. The defendant claimed that no there is no hard-and-fast rule that a trade mark licensor should be held strictly liable. Rather, the test was the extent to which the licensor had been involved in overall production and manufacture.[33]

The court did not make an express finding on the extent to which an inquiry into control is appropriate, but it disagreed with the defendant on the application of this test to the facts. In graphic language, the court found the defendant liable as follows: 'Certainly the brain that so competently and thoroughly directs the entire enterprise must be liable for the acts of its appendages.'[34]

The Burkert Case: The Manufacturer is Too Far Removed from the Defective Product

14–20 The *Torres* decision was subsequently distinguished by the Supreme Court for the State of Connecticut.[35] This case involved the manufacture by third

---

[30] Adams, *supra*, n. 24, p. 315.
[31] *ibid.*
[32] 14 U.S.P.Q. 1522 (9th Cir. 1990).
[33] *Torres, supra*, n. 32, at 1526.
[34] *Torres, supra*, n. 32.
[35] *Burkert v. Petrol Plus of Naugatuck, Inc.*, 40 PCTJ 327 (1990).

parties of automatic transmission fluid under the licensed trade mark Dexron II, which was owned by General Motors Corporation('GM').

GM put the licensed fluid through 20 performance tests carried out by a GM-approved laboratory. Once it had passed these tests, however, GM exercised no material control over the makeup, production or distribution of the product, nor did it issue any warning to purchasers concerning potential problems. GM earned no royalties from the licensed manufacture and sale of the product. One of the licensees substituted a lesser quality lubricant for Dexron II. The question was whether the distributor could seek an indemnification from GM as well as from the offending licensee.

The plaintiff argued that, by virtue of its quality control obligations, the licensor had a duty to police misleading uses of its mark, including tortious acts by the licensee. The court rejected this claim. The penalty for inadequate quality control by a licensor is the abandonment of its exclusive rights in the trade mark, not tortious liability for a defective product. A claim for breach of warranty was also rejected. The defendant had not been adequately involved in the manufacturing chain in respect of the licensed product to give rise to such liability.

Liability Based on Holding Out

It has also been argued that circumstances may occur when it can fairly be **14–21** stated that a third party 'has no reason to suppose the name and mark associated with the licensor are being used other than by the licensor itself.'[36] A version of this rationale can also be found in the notion of vicarious liability, where one party is held liable for something done by another.

The *Burkert* case concluded that GM could not be found to have 'held out' the defective fluid to the public, since it was in no way involved in the sale, lease, gift or loan of the defective fluid.[37] Another example can be found in a Canadian case, *Fraser v. U-Need-A-Cab*.[38] The licensor operated a cab service. It would receive an order for a cab , and then either summon one of its own cabs, or despatch an independently owned cab which used the trademark and the insignia of the licensor. The plaintiff was injured as a result of a defective door of a cab that had been ordered through the cab service.

The court found the licensor liable on the ground that there was an implied warranty that the cab carrying the plaintiff was safe. The court reasoned that a customer could not distinguish between a cab owned by the licensor and one that was licensed to use its mark and insignia. In both situations, the licensor held itself out to be, and was perceived by the consuming public to be, the source of the cabs identified by its mark.

---

[36] Adams, *supra*, n. 24, p. 316.
[37] *supra*, n. 35.
[38] Reported in *Blakes Report*, January/February 1990, Vol. 5, No. 1.

Holding Out: the Relationship with Quality Control

14–22 The licensor's liability under this rationale is concerned more with the manner in which the licensor portrays itself as being responsible for the goods bearing its trade mark. A licensor concerned about liability on the ground of holding out could consider dividing up its business among several entities, with one company holding the trade mark, another exercising quality control on behalf of the proprietor, and another being licensed to use the mark. However, the risk here is that if too many entities are involved, the arrangement could conceivably weaken a licensor's claim that it was exercising overall quality control.[39]

Consumer Protection Act 1987

14–23 Under the Consumer Protection Act 1987, enacted in the light of the EC directive to harmonise national laws in this area, English law has established civil liability without the need to meet the traditional negligence standard of tortious liability for defective products.[40]

No Proof of Negligence Required

14–24 Under section 1 of the Consumer Protection Act, a 'producer' will be held liable for damage caused by a defect in his product. A product is defective if 'it does not provide the safety which a person is entitled to expect.'[41] Neither a contractual relationship, nor an obligation to establish fault, is necessary to hold a producer liable. The producer cannot exclude liability by a contract term, notice or similar device.[42] All that the plaintiff needs to show is damage, a defect, and the causal link between them. No proof of negligence, the traditional test to establish tortious liability, is required.[43]

Liability for a Party Which Holds Itself Out as the 'Producer'

14–25 The idea of a producer is not limited to the person who is actually responsible for manufacturing the goods. Section 2 of the Consumer Protection Act treats several other categories of persons as liable for damage caused by defects as if they were the actual producers of the goods. Section 2(2)(b) is particularly relevant. It imposes liability on '(b) any person who, by putting his name on the product, or using a trade mark or other distinguishing mark in relation to the product, has held himself out to be the producer of the product.'

---

[39] Adams, *supra*, n. 24, p. 317.
[40] Directive of July 25, 1985 (85/374/EEC) on the approximation of the laws, regulations and administrative provisions of the Member States concerning liability for defective products. See generally, Wright, *Product Liability*, 1989. Any general statement about the status of strict liability under U.S. law is impossible. There is no federal law of product liability, with the result that products liability in the U.S. is a patchwork of case law and statute, as it has developed in each of the 50 states. See, generally, Phillips, *Products Liability* (3rd ed.), 1988.
[41] s. 3.
[42] s. 7.
[43] Wright, *supra*, n. 40, p. 36.

The reference to 'holding out' as a producer would appear to distinguish between a situation in which the product bears only the name of the trade mark proprietor, and where the goods specify or suggest that another party is the actual manufacturer. It may not be enough that the actual manufacturer is capable of being identified, if the goods or packaging do not provide any indication of this fact. The test is the perception of the reasonable consumer regarding the identity of the manufacturer of the goods.

Holding Out and Labelling

The following three examples of package labels have been suggested. Only in **14–26** the first example is the identity of the producer (XYZ Ltd), being a person other than the trade mark proprietor (ABC Ltd), clearly identified.

Example 1 – 'Made for ABC Ltd. by XYZ Ltd.'

Example 2 – 'Specially made for ABC Ltd.'

Example 3 – 'ABC Ltd. – genuinely approved parts.'[44]

Is a Licensor Liable under the Act?

There is nothing in the language of the provision that would appear necessarily **14–27** to exclude a trade mark licensor from the ambit of this provision, since his trade mark will obviously appear on the goods. The question is under what conditions the licensor can be deemed to have held himself out as the manufacturer of the goods. This potential liability also extends to the licensor of other intellectual property rights whose mark or name appears.[45]

Liability under E.C. Directives

The Consumer Protection Act was implemented in response to the Product **14–28** Liability Directive issued in 1985.[46] The sections of the Consumer Protection Act discussed above are similar to the relevant provisions in the Directive.[47] Two additional pieces of secondary legislation or proposed legislation of the European Community are worthy of mention.

Directive on General Product Safety

The Directive on General Product Safety is intended to standardise safety **14–29** requirements for products by imposing a general duty on producers and others.[48] This Directive was formally adopted in 1992, and provides for a

---

[44] Wright, *supra*, n. 40, p. 42.
[45] See generally, Good and Easter, 'Product Liability and Product Safety: The Implications for Licensing' [1993] E.I.P.R. 10.
[46] 85/374/EEC (1985) O.J. L210.
[47] It is noted that the Directive has not been implemented in all Member States, and even in those Member States in which implementation has taken place, such as the U.K., challenges have been made as to the adequacy of the implementation. See *Francovich & others v. Italian Republic* C-6/90 and 9/90, as reported in Good and Easter, *supra*, n. 45, at p. 11, n. 4.
[48] See Good and Easter, *supra*, n. 45, p. 11.

two-year period for implementation by the Member States.

It contains a definition of 'producer' which is similar to that contained in the Directive on Product Liability. Thus, a producer includes 'any person presenting himself as the manufacturer by affixing his name, trade mark or other distinctive mark on the product.'[49] The use of the word 'affixing' raises the question of whether actual affixation must take place, or whether the mere authority to do so is sufficient. A similar question was once asked regarding the definition of a trade mark, and it is now accepted that actual affixation is not required in that context. It is unlikely that a different answer will apply here.[50]

A further question is whether the 'affixation' requirement, together with the phrase 'presenting himself', denotes a narrower definition for 'producer' than the parallel provision in the Consumer Protection Act.

Liability of Suppliers of Services

14–30 The draft Directive on Liability of Suppliers of Services is intended to hold suppliers liable for direct damage caused in connection with the provision of their services.[51] Unlike the Product Liability Directive, this Directive does not impose strict liability.

Article 3(2) defines a supplier as '[a]ny person who provides a service by using the services of a representative or other legally independent intermediary.' Particularly noteworthy in this context is Article 8, which extends liability to a franchisor, master franchisor and franchisee under specified circumstances. There is some doubt, however, whether this Directive will be adopted in its current form.[52]

Measures to Protect the Licensor against Liability

14–31 It is widely accepted that whatever basis is relied upon, there is no foolproof way by which a licensor can prevent liability for injury caused by the defective products of its licensee.[53] A number of measures have been employed by licensors to mitigate the risk. These measures depend upon the jurisdiction involved, the nature of the product or service, and the custom in the particular industry. Nevertheless, they can be viewed as useful guidelines to assist the concerned licensor.

(a) Insurance: It is frequently recommended that a licensor should seek insurance as protection against liability, particularly if the goods are such that bodily injury may result from a defect. In some circumstances, the licensor may prefer to self-insure the risk, although this form of insurance might serve as a disincentive to a potential licensee or distributor.

(b) Indemnification: the licensor might seek an indemnity from the licensee.

---

[49] Art. 2(d).
[50] Good and Easter, *supra*, n. 45, p. 11.
[51] COM (90)482 final, O.J. C12/8.
[52] Good and Easter, above, *supra*, n. 45, p. 13.
[53] Borchard and Ehrlich, *supra*, n. 26, p. 127.

As an additional form of protection, it could also ask for additional security from the licensee, such as a letter of credit or a pledge of assets.

(c) Liability and warranty disclaimer: The licensor might consider inserting in the licence agreement a disclaimer against liability and from all possible express and implied warranties. While it is doubtful whether such disclaimers will be effective against third parties, they might prove useful if the licensee itself seeks to bring a counterclaim or a similar action against the licensor.

(d) Warnings: The licensor should insist that appropriate warnings appear on the product.

(e) Compliance with Regulations and Standards: The licensor should require the licensee's compliance with the appropriate standards and regulations.

(f) Termination clause: the licensor might include a provision in the licence which authorises him to terminate the agreement if the licensee does not comply with the appropriate standards. It is doubtful however, whether the exercise of such a provision would help the licensor in a claim for injury resulting from a failure to comply.[54]

Measures to Protect the Licensee against Liability

The above provisions have been looked at from the viewpoint of the licensor, **14–32** but it may be the licensee itself which seeks to assert liability against the licensor. A licensee which finds itself named as a sole defendant may seek to bring a separate action against the licensor or to join the licensor into the action as a co-defendant. This will be particularly so if the licensee can show that the alleged defect arose from standards, designs, or other measures imposed upon it by the licensor under the terms of the licence.

A concerned licensee in such circumstances might consider relying on one or more of the measures suggested above to protect its own interest. In particular, provisions regarding insurance, indemnity and disclaimers may be relevant. Much will depend, however, on the relative bargaining power of the licensee and the licensor.

Tax Aspects of a Trade Mark Licence

Introduction

Trade marks and service marks may be very valuable items of property in a **14–33** commercial sense, but there is practically no mention of them as such in the United Kingdom Taxes Acts. There are therefore no provisions as there are

---

[54] See generally, Schwartz, 'Product Liability, Indemnities and Insurance,' Paper Delivered at the USTA 113th Annual Meeting, 1991; 'Licensing and Products Liability,' *Les Nouvelles*, March 1985, p. 41; Good and Easter, *supra*, n. 45, p. 14.

with patents and know-how, taxing capital receipts as income.[55] Conversely, there is no mechanism for spreading receipts from the exploitation of trade marks over a period, as there is with copyright,[56] public lending rights,[57] designs[58] or artists' receipts.[59] There are no provisions treating royalties received on licensing trade marks as annual payments, as there is for a patent royalty[60] nor any withholding requirement where the owner of the trade mark is resident outside the United Kingdom as there is with copyright.[61] Because trade marks and service marks have an indefinite life, licensing, often as part of a franchise arrangement, can be very advantageous commercially.

Licensing Income

14–34 Although it is conceivable that income from licensing trade marks or service marks could be investment income, assessable under Schedule D, Case III under T.A. 1988, s.18(3), it is much more likely that it will constitute trading receipts under Schedule D, Case I, also under T.A. 1988, s.18(3). The income would normally be paid as a licence fee, computed by reference to the time during which the trade mark was used by the licensee or by reference to the products or services supplied by the licensee in the period. Where the amounts received are anything other than insignificant, the Revenue will expect them to be brought into account on an accruals basis by reference to the period during which they were earned, and not by reference to the period in which the royalty is actually received.

However, in complex cases of international licensing, particularly where sub-licensing is concerned, it may not be practical to include royalties receivable in the theoretically correct accounting period because the recipient does not normally know the amount of the licence fee that is due to be received until the licensee reports on his production figures, which will normally be subject to some form of auditing by the licensor. In such cases, it is normal practice to include in the accounting year royalties received during the year and royalties relating to the year reported within a reasonable period after the year end, which would be known to the licensor by the time its accounts are drawn up for the accounting period. If royalties are received in advance, any element relating to a period beyond the accounting date would be carried forward as a receipt in advance and related to the period to which the advance related.

Annual Payments

14–35 Although a trade or service mark royalty is not by definition an annual payment, it could be an annual payment under general principles if it were

---

[55] T.A. 1988, ss.524, 525, 531.
[56] T.A. 1988, ss.534, 535.
[57] T.A. 1988, s.537.
[58] T.A. 1988, s.537A.
[59] T.A. 1988, s.538.
[60] T.A. 1988, s.349(1)(b).
[61] T.A. 1988, s.536.

pure income profits of the licensor. The definition of pure income profit in the hands of the recipient has been considered in cases such as *I.R.C. v. National Book League*,[62] *Earl Howe v. I.R.C.*[63] and *Campbell v. I.R.C.*[64] In this last case, Lord Donovan stated at page 446:

'the test must be applicable to all annual payments and the problem must continue to be resolved, in my opinion, on the lines laid down by Scrutton L J in Earl Howe's case. One must determine in the light of all the relevant facts whether the payment is a taxable receipt in the hands of the recipient without any deduction for expenses or the like, whether it is in other words pure income or pure profit income in his hands as those expressions had been used in the decided cases. If so, it will be an annual payment under Case III. If on the other hand it is simply gross revenue in the recipient's hands out of which a taxable income will emerge only after his outgoings have been deducted, then the payment is not such an annual payment. This, of course, has been said often enough before, but the judgement under review makes it necessary I think to say it again. The test makes it necessary to decide each case on its own facts'.

Advertising and Promoting

In the case of a trade mark or service mark, the licensor is normally providing **14–36** substantial services in the form of advertising and promoting the goods or services protected by the mark, and the royalties received from the licensee would have the character of trading receipts, not pure income profit.

Secret Processes

There is no jurisprudence on the point, but it has been held in *Delage v.* **14–37** *Nugget Polish Co Ltd*[65] that royalties paid for the use of secret processes were annual payments taxable on the recipient under Schedule D, Case III. It is arguable that this case was in any event wrongly decided, as attributing the royalties to a source in the United Kingdom as Schedule D, Case III would have no application if the source were outside the United Kingdom.

Deduction of Tax by Licensee

If the royalties were annual payments, then the licensee would deduct tax at **14–38** source from the payment under T.A. 1988, s.348(1) or 349(1)(a).

T.A. 1988, s.348 applies where the payment is by an individual or partnership and income tax at the basic rate is deducted by the payer. If, therefore, the royalty was £1,000, the payer would withhold an amount equivalent to the basic rate of 25 per cent *i.e.* £250 and pay over £750 to the licensor. The licensor would treat the amount received of £750 as an amount from which tax at the basic rate had been deducted; that is, a receipt of £1,000, in respect

---

[62] (1957) 37 T.C. 455.
[63] (1919) 7 T.C. 289.
[64] (1968) 45 T.C. 427.
[65] (1905) 21 T.L.R. 454.

of which he was entitled to a tax credit of £250. The licensee would give to the licensor a certificate of deduction of tax on form R185AP in accordance with T.A. 1988, s.352. Tax deducted in excess of the taxable income of the licensor could be recovered. The licensee would claim a deduction for the royalty paid only for the excess of higher rates of tax over the basic rate and would not claim relief for tax at the basic rate, the relief having been given by reducing the amount payable to the licensor. The tax so held in charge is effectively accounted for to the Revenue, by the licensee not claiming a basic rate deduction and therefore paying more tax on his profit.

Tax Paid Over to Revenue

14–39 Clearly, this system breaks down if the licensee's tax liability is less than the amount of tax withheld, or if the licensee is a corporation not subject to income tax. In both cases the tax withheld from the payment to the licensor, and not accounted for to the Revenue by being held in charge to tax, has to be paid over to the Revenue under T.A. 1988, s.349 and s.350. In the case of a company, the mechanics of paying over the tax are set out in T.A. 1988, s. 349(4) and Schedule 16, which requires the company to make quarterly returns on form CT61 for each period of three months ending with March 31, June 30, September 30 or December 31 within its accounting period. If its accounting period does not end on one of those dates, a further return is required made up from the latest quarterly date to the accounting date and there are therefore five return periods in each 12 month accounting period for such companies.

In accounting to the Revenue for tax deducted from annual payments on a CT61, it may take credit for tax deducted from annual payments received in the return period. Any excess of tax deducted from receipts over tax deducted from payments will be treated as a payment on account of corporation tax for the period in which the royalty is received under T.A. 1988, s. 7(2).

Charges on Income

14–40 If the royalty is an annual payment, the licensee will not be able to claim a deduction as a trading expense in view of T.A. 1988, s. 74(m) which prevents a deduction for an annuity or other annual payment, but will be able to claim relief as a deduction from total income under T.A. 1988, s. 338(3)(a). This in turn involves a complication in that if the royalties paid exceed the total income of the company, there would be an excess charge rather than a trading loss. An excess charge can be treated as if it were a loss for tax purposes under T.A. 1988, s. 393(1). It is, however, only available to carry forward against future profits under T.A. 1988, s. 393(9) and cannot unlike trading losses be carried back against earlier years' profits under T.A. 1988, s. 393A. In the case of unincorporated businesses, excess charges may be carried forward as trading losses against future profits under T.A. 1988, s. 387.

Deduction Errors

If the licensee should have deducted tax from the royalty as an annual **14–41** payment, but failed to do so, the Revenue can nonetheless still assess the licensor.[66] However, the licensee is not entitled to deduct tax from future royalty payments if his failure to do so was a mistake of law.[67] A mistake of law would be where, for example, the licensee did not appreciate that tax should have been deducted from the royalty payment.[68] If tax had not been deducted from the royalty due to a mistake of fact, for example on the assumption that it was a franchise fee rather than a royalty, the tax which the licensee failed to deduct could be deducted from future payments.[69]

The rate of tax which the licensee should use when deducting tax from an annual payment is that applicable to the fiscal year in which the royalty becomes due for payment if the tax is held in charge by a sole trader or partnership.[70] If, on the other hand, the tax is withheld and accounted for to the Revenue under T.A. 1988 s.349 and s.350, the rate of tax to be deducted is that for the fiscal year in which the royalty is actually paid, irrespective of when it was due.[71]

Non-Resident Licensor

It will be appreciated that the tax treatment of a trade mark or service mark **14–42** royalty becomes of major importance where the recipient is outside the United Kingdom. In such a case, if the royalty were payable as a United Kingdom annual payment because the licence agreement was in the United Kingdom, the royalty would have to be paid under deduction of tax which would equate with a 25 per cent withholding tax as far as the licensor was concerned, unless this could be reduced under the royalty article in an appropriate double tax treaty. The Financial Intermediaries and Claims Office, International Division can authorise the licensee to deduct tax from an annual payment to a licensor resident in a treaty country at a reduced rate under the double Taxation Relief (Taxes on Income) General Regulations 2(2).[72]

Fortunately, the considerable complexities of dealing with trade mark royalties as annual payments is not normally necessary as the services provided by the licensor to ensure they are not pure income profit. If they are not annual payments, there is no withholding tax on payment to an overseas licensor even if resident in a tax haven, provided that the licensee and the licensor are unconnected and therefore outside the transfer pricing provisions of T.A. 1988 ss. 770, 772 and 773, and are incurred wholly and exclusively

---

[66] *Glamorgan County Quarter Sessions v. Wilson* (1910) 5 T.C. 537; *Grosvenor Place Estates Ltd v. Roberts* (1960) 39 T.C. 433.
[67] *Shrewsbury v. Shrewsbury* (1907) 23 T.L.R. 224.
[68] *Barclays Bank Ltd v. W.J. Simms* [1980] Q.B. 677.
[69] *Re Musgrave Machell v. Parry* (1916) 2 C.H. 417; *Turvey v. Dentons (1923) Ltd* (1952) 31 A.T.C. 470.
[70] T.A. 1988, s. 4(2)(a).
[71] T.A. 1988, s. 4(2)(b); *Re Sebright Public Trustee v. Sebright* (1944) 23 T.C. 190; *Regal (Hastings) Ltd v. Gulliver* (1944) 44 A.T.C. 297.
[72] (S.I. 1970 No. 488).

for the purpose of the licensee's trade and therefore allowable under T.A. 1988 s. 74.

Lump Sum Receipts

14–43 It is by no means uncommon, particularly in franchise agreements, for the licensee to pay a lump sum under the franchise agreement for the right to use the franchised name and logo which is obviously subject to trade mark protection. It then becomes necessary to consider the precise nature of the payment and the allocation where there is a composite sum.[73]

Capital Receipts

14–44 If the licensor is effectively disposing of the trade mark, either wholly or in part, it is likely to be a capital receipt. There are no cases in relation to trade marks, but this would seem to follow from the position with regard to designs[74] and the know-how cases.[75] Further support comes from patent cases such as *I.R.C. v. British Salmson Aero Engines Ltd*,[76] *Desoutter Brothers Ltd v. J.R. Hanger & C. Ltd*.[77]

A lump sum payable by instalments can still be a capital payment.[78] If the lump sum is related to a keep out covenant under which the trade mark owner agrees not to compete with the licensee in a particular area, it is again likely that the payment would be regarded as capital.[79] With copyright, an absolute assignment was treated as a capital receipt in *Beare v. Carter*[80] and *Nethersole v. Withers*.[81]

Trading Receipts

14–45 If, however, the lump sum is merely for the right to use the trade mark in a particular area, as would be normal under a franchise arrangement, it is probable that the lump sum would be treated as a trading receipt. Again, there is no jurisprudence in relation to trade marks, but by analogy with patent cases, such as *Constantinsco v. R*,[82] *Mills v. Jones*,[83] *I.R.C. v. Rustproof Metal Window Co Ltd*,[84] *Harry Ferguson Motors Ltd v. I.R.C.*,[85], *Reece Roturbo Development Syndicate v. Ducker*,[86] *Wild v. Ionides* [87] and *Brandwood*

---

[73] *Paterson Engineering Co. Ltd v. Duff* (1943) 25 T.C. 43.
[74] *Handley Page v. Butterworth* (1935) 19 T.C. 328.
[75] *Evans Medical Supplies Ltd v. Moriarty* (1957) 37 T.C. 540 and *Wolf Electric Tools Ltd v. Wilson* (1968) 45 T.C. 326.
[76] (1938) 22 T.C. 29.
[77] (1936) 15 A.T.C. 49.
[78] *William John Jones v. I.R.C.* (1919) 7 T.C. 310.
[79] *Murray v. Imperial Chemical Industries Ltd* (1967) 44 T.C. 175; *Kirby v. Thorn E.M.I. plc* (1987) S.T.C. 621; *Margerison v. Tyresoles Ltd* (1942) 25 T.C. 59.
[80] (1940) 23 T.C. 353.
[81] (1948) 28 T.C. 501.
[82] (1927) 11 T.C. 730.
[83] (1929) 14 T.C. 769.
[84] (1947) 29 T.C. 243.
[85] (1951) 33 T.C. 15.
[86] (1928) 13 T.C. 366.
[87] (1925) 9 T.C. 32.

v. Banker[88] supports this treatment. A similar stream of copyright cases included lump sums, in particular for the sale of film rights, as receipts of the author's profession in *Billam v. Griffiths,*[89] *Glasson v. Rougier,*[90] *Mackenzie v. Arnold,*[91] *Household v. Grimshaw*[92] and *Howson v. Monsell.*[93] In the case of disposals, know-how lump sums have been treated as trading receipts where there is no absolute disposal to the exclusion of the transferor, in *Jeffrey v. Rolls-Royce Ltd,*[94] *Musker v. English Electric Co Ltd,*[95] *Coalite & Chemical Products Ltd v. Treeby,*[96] *Thomsons (Carron) v I.R.C.,*[97] *John E Sturge Ltd v. Hessel*[98] and *British Dyestuffs Corporation (Blackley) Ltd v. I.R.C..*[99] This last case again confirmed that the method of payment, *i.e.* as a single payment or by instalments does not determine whether the receipt is capital or income.

In most cases, it can be assumed that if the trade mark or service mark is sold outright and assigned to the purchaser, the receipt will be capital and if the trade mark is licensed so that the licensee has use of the trade mark for a restricted area or period of time with the licensor retaining ultimate ownership of the trade mark, the disposal will give rise to a trading receipt.

Expenses

The only section of the Taxes Acts which specifically refers to trade marks is 14–46 T.A. 1988, s. 83 which provides that fees or expenses incurred in the registration of a design or trade mark, including a service mark, or a renewal of the registration of a trade mark may be treated as a trading expense. This provision is necessary where the trade mark would be held as a capital asset, as expenditure which gives rise to a capital asset would otherwise be disallowed under T.A. 1988, s. 74(f).

Dealing in Trade Marks

Because of the nature of trade marks and the old prohibition against 14–47 trafficking, it is extremely unlikely that trade marks would be acquired and sold in the course of a trade of dealing in trade marks.

Relief to Purchaser

Where a trade mark is acquired on assignment, it is necessary to consider 14–48 what relief, if any, is due to the purchaser. In many cases, the acquisition will be a straightforward purchase of a capital asset and there is no provision in

---

[88] (1928) 14 T.C. 44.
[89] (1941) 23 T.C. 757.
[90] (1944) 26 T.C. 86.
[91] (1952) 33 T.C. 363.
[92] (1953) 34 T.C. 366.
[93] (1950) 31 T.C. 529.
[94] (1962) 40 T.C. 443.
[95] (1964) 41 T.C. 556.
[96] (1971) 48 T.C. 171.
[97] [1976] S.T.C. 317.
[98] [1975] S.T.C. 573.
[99] (1924) 12 T.C. 586.

the Taxes Acts giving any capital allowances or the equivalent on such a purchase, as there is in the case of patents under T.A. 1988, ss. 520 to 523, or know-how as in T.A. 1988, s. 530. The only relief in such circumstances is therefore as a deduction from the sale proceeds in the chargeable gains computation on disposal of the trade mark acquired. The normal computational rules, including indexation, would apply in the same way as for any other capital asset not eligible for capital allowances.

Deferred Revenue Expenditure

14-49 It may be possible however, to argue that the acquisition of the trade mark or service mark is expenditure which should be written off over a limited period as deferred revenue expenditure. This will depend on the ongoing life of the trade mark and whether an asset or advantage has been brought into existence for the enduring benefit of the trade, which would result in the disallowance of the expenditure as capital, following *Atherton v. British Insulated & Helsby Cables Ltd*[1] and *R T Z Oil & Gas Ltd v. Ellis*.[2]

In this latter case, Vinelott J stated at page 541: 'It is elementary that although it may be necessary in order to give a true and fair view of the profits earned by a trade in a given year to make an allowance for the depreciation of a wasting asset on which capital has been expended, no such allowance can be made in ascertaining the taxable profit for that year. The disallowance has always been found in cases within Case I of Schedule D, in that part of Rule 3 of the rules applicable to that case', which is now reproduced (though modified so far as concerns the deduction of interest on capital) in T.A. 1988, s. 74(f).[3] On page 546 he continued: 'The legislature has not left the allowance of depreciation to be determined in accordance with accountancy principles and practice. Instead, it has imposed a general prohibition and has, since 1886, dealt with the question whether a depreciation allowance should be made in a particular case by a separate, detailed and frequently amended code. The question whether that code should not be further amended to permit the deduction claimed in the instant case is one which must be determined by the legislature and not by the Court'. This does not seem very helpful, but the treatment of such expenditure is not entirely without precedent.

Film Production and Computer Software

14-50 The Inland Revenue statement of Practice No 9 of 1979 stated 'in the accounts of film production companies, the cost of making films is normally treated as deferred revenue expenditure, *i.e.* it is not written off immediately but spread over a period of years starting with the release of the film, on the principle of matching expenditure with receipts to produce a true view of the profit or loss arising from the production of the film. The writing off of the expenditure in the accounts has normally been followed for tax purposes'. Such treatment

---

[1] (1925) 10 T.C. 155.
[2] [1987] S.T.C. 512.
[3] See, in particular, *Alianza Co. Ltd v. Bell* (1906) 5 T.C. 172.

was subsequently enacted in what is now C.A.A. 1990, s. 68. Similarly, with computer software the Revenue was asked on October 1, 1980 to confirm: 'having regard to the Statement of Practice (SP 9/79) dated August 10, 1979, it would seem that the cost of software in connection with installing a computer system should be regarded as plant for capital allowance purposes, such software having a life of not less than two years. The software comprises the cost of engaging an organisation to devise and rewrite programmes. There is also the cost of systems analysis'.

The reply dated November 18, 1980 was as follows: 'If software is purchased at the same time as the hardware, then we would normally treat the whole of the expenditure as capital expenditure on the provision of plant on which capital allowances are due. Where software is purchased independently we would normally treat the cost as a revenue expense either in the year of purchase or if the purchaser so chooses by amortisation of the expenditure over a period relating to its expected life. As an alternative to writing off the expenditure to revenue if the user opted to capitalise it to claim capital allowances, we would not normally object provided the life of the software was expected to exceed two years'. Again, the treatment of computer software has now been legislated for under C.A.A. 1990, s. 67A, but the principle that deferred revenue expenditure is acceptable treatment for tax purposes seems firmly entrenched.

Written Off or Amortised Expenditure

The question therefore comes back to whether the expenditure on the 14–51 acquisition of the trade mark is of value for a relatively limited period, in which case it should be written off as deferred revenue expenditure over this period, both in the accounts and for tax purposes, or whether it gives rise to a capital asset which would be amortised over its commercial life with no allowance for tax purposes. If the decision is taken to amortise the cost of the trade mark in the purchaser's accounts, it does not necessarily mean that the cost would be reduced for chargeable gains purposes as a wasting asset under T.C.G.A. 1992, s. 44.

A trade mark is not obviously within the definition of an asset with a predictable life not exceeding 50 years because it lasts indefinitely and its life is difficult, if not impossible, to predict. If the commercial view is that it has a short life, then the argument for treatment as deferred revenue expenditure is thereby increased. If the decision is taken to amortise it over, say, 25 years as a matter of conservative accounting, it does not follow that it has a predictable life of less than 50 years and as a consequence its base value for chargeable gains purposes should be depreciated as a wasting asset. It would be perfectly compatible for the chargeable gains base value to increase by indexation at the same time as the commercial value was decreased by amortisation. The same, of course, applies for goodwill written off in a company's accounts.

Location

14–52 As a capital asset, a trade mark or service mark is situated where it is registered and the rights or licences to use a trade mark or service mark are situated in the United Kingdom if they, or any right derived from them, are exercisable in the United Kingdom under T.C.G.A. 1992, s. 275(h).

Chargeable Gains

14–53 Consideration for the disposal of a trade mark or service mark which is taxed as income is excluded from any chargeable gains charge by T.C.G.A. 1992, s. 37. If it is within the chargeable gains provisions, capital expenditure not allowed as a revenue expense in acquiring or disposing of the trade mark would be deductible under T.C.G.A. 1992, s. 38.

Inheritance Tax

14–54 On February 25, 1983, the Financial Secretary to the Treasury confirmed that *'the value of copyright for capital transfer tax (inheritance tax) is the price a property might reasonably be expected to fetch if sold in the open market at the time of the transfer'.*[4] There is no reason to believe that a trade mark or service mark is any less an asset for inheritance tax purposes than is copyright. A trade mark owned by a business would normally be valued as part of the business and qualify for business property relief under I.H.T.A. 1984, ss. 103 to 114.

Valuation

14–55 If it does become necessary to value a trade mark or service mark for capital gains tax purposes, T.C.G.A. 1992, s. 272(1) provides that the value means the price which it might reasonably be expected to fetch on a sale in the open market. For inheritance tax purposes a similar valuation is given under I.H.T.A. 1984, s. 160.

Trade marks as assets would fall within the normal capital gains tax and inheritance tax rules, and consideration would therefore have to be given to such matters as retirement relief under T.C.G.A. 1992, ss. 163, 164 and Schedule 6, roll-over relief on reinvestment under T.C.G.A. 1992, s. 164A to N, and roll-over relief on transfer of a business under T.C.G.A. 1992, s. 162, but it should be noted that a trade mark is not within the relevant class of asset for roll-over relief for business assets under T.C.G.A. 1992, s. 155. Similarly, for inheritance tax purposes, matters such as related property under I.H.T.A. 1984, s. 161 have to be considered.

Trade marks owned by a company would naturally be included in the valuation of the company's shares and not treated as a separate asset of the shareholder. The mechanics of valuing a trade mark for tax purposes will be the same as for any other form of intellectual property, that is the present value of the income stream that could be generated from the asset in question.

---

[4] *Hansard*, H.C. Vol. 37, col. 562.

In the case of a trade mark, it might be difficult to isolate the income stream derived from the trade mark itself, compared with the income arising from the general goodwill of the business and the know-how and reputation of the business in the market. The fact that it is difficult to value does not mean that it is not valuable; for some businesses the trade marks are easily the most valuable assets.

Stamp Duty

An exclusive non-revocable licence or assignment of a trade mark would be **14–56** subject to ad valorem duty as a conveyance on sale under Stamp Act 1891 ss. 59 and 62, but a revocable assignment or non-exclusive licence is not subject to duty. If an assignment is subject to duty, this would be calculated on any lump sum, together with the amount of the future royalties, if ascertainable, payable within 20 years of the assignment or licence under SA 1891, s. 56.[5] Duty is charged at 1 per cent where the consideration is in excess of £30,000. Where only the minimum payment is shown on the document, that is the amount subject to duty. If a basic consideration is obtainable from the document that amount is subject to duty.[6] Where the quantum of royalties is wholly unascertainable, it is arguable that no Stamp Duty is payable as there is no consideration which can be ascertained from the document.

Value Added Tax

Under the Value Added Tax (Place of Supply of Services) Order 1992[7] services **14–57** supplied where received, including transfers and assignments of trade marks and similar rights under V.A.T.A., 1994, Sched. 5, para. 1, are treated from January, 1993 as made where the recipient of the services belongs; that is, where the licensee belongs,[8] provided that the licensee belongs in a Member State of the European Union carrying on a business there with a VAT registration number and is not within the United Kingdom reverse charge provisions under V.A.T.A. 1994, s. 8. Similar provisions apply where the licensee belongs in a country other than the Isle of Man outside the European Union.

Rates

The effect of these rules is that the place of supply will be in the United **14–58** Kingdom in the unlikely event of the licensee belonging in another Member State of the European Union but not VAT registerable, or if he belongs in the United Kingdom. In such cases VAT at the standard rate of 17.5 per cent would be charged on licence royalties.

Where no VAT is charged in respect of a trade mark licence to a registered

---

[5] *Underground Electric Railways Co of London Ltd v. I.R.C.* [1906] A.C. 21; *Glyn Mills Currie & Co v. I.R.C.* [1916] 1 K.B. 306.
[6] *I.T.A. v. I.R.C.* [1961] A.C. 427.
[7] S.I. 1992 No. 3121.
[8] *ibid.*, reg. 16.

business in another Member State of the European Union, such a supply would be outside the scope of the United Kingdom VAT but input tax credit would still be available under V.A.T.A. 1994, s. 25(2)(b). Where the licensee belongs outside the European Union, the supply would also be outside the scope of U.K. VAT and the above provisions would apply.

Transfer of Business as a Going Concern

14–59 If the assignment of a trade mark takes place in conjunction with the sale of the business or part of the business as a going concern, the transfer is primarily a supply made in the course of furtherance of the business under V.A.T.A. 1994, s. 94(6). However, V.A.T.A. 1994, s. 49(2) provides for regulations in connection with transfers of going concerns. The transferee can take over the transferor's registration number under the Value Added Tax (General) Regulations 1985, regs. 4(4) to (8).[9] It is, however, unusual for the transferee to take over the transferor's registration, as he would also take over any outstanding VAT liabilities and he would therefore normally register independently. In such cases, the transfer of the business as a going concern, including the trade marks, would be outside the scope of VAT under the Value Added Tax (Special Provisions) Order 1992.[10] This means that VAT would not be charged by the transferor, nor recoverable by the transferee.

International Tax Planning

14–60 Because trade marks have no limited life and there is normally no requirement to deduct tax on paying a royalty for the use of a trade mark to an overseas company, they are particularly useful in the field of international tax planning within a group of companies. Provided that the royalty is commercial for the use of a valuable trade mark or service mark, the paying company should be entitled to a deduction as a trading expense of the royalty payable even where the recipient is a connected party and resident in a tax haven. Clearly, if the royalty is excessive for the value of the trade mark, the deduction would be challenged under the transfer pricing provisions of T.A. 1988, s. 770. The trade mark royalty, however, does avoid the necessity of relying on a double tax treaty to eliminate or reduce withholding taxes which would be necessary in the case of patents and most forms of copyright.

It is often helpful for the trade marks and service marks in the group to be held through a company in, for example, the Netherlands Antilles, which would be responsible for the international promotion of the goods covered by the trade mark in question. This in turn would be licensed either directly where trade mark royalties can be paid without any withholding tax as in the United Kingdom, or through a sub-licensing company in, say, the Netherlands, Denmark or Austria, which in turn would licence the trade mark where the licensee would be required to deduct withholding tax.

Trade mark royalties are within the definition of royalties covered by

---

[9] S.I. 1985 No. 886.
[10] S.I. 1992 No. 3129.

almost all double taxation treaties and careful routing of trade mark royalties should therefore ensure a deduction in the paying company and a tax-free, or nearly tax-free receipt in the recipient company. Ultimately, the controlled foreign company legislation or its equivalent might require the payment back to the ultimate holding company of a dividend from the tax haven trade mark holding company, but the process should generate at the very least a worthwhile deferral of tax.

Tax Aspects of Trademarks in USA

In many respects the tax treatment of trademarks in the USA is the same as **14-61** that for intangible assets generally. A notable difference, however, is that trademark expenditure cannot be depreciated because of the absence of a predictable life for such expenditure. By contrast, patents and copyrights, which do have a clearly defined life, may be depreciated.

Trademark Expenditure

Expenditure directly connected with the acquisition, protection, expansion **14-62** registration or defence of a trademark is regarded as capital expenditure. Prior to October 2, 1989, such expenditure was specifically non-depreciable for tax purposes. The prohibition was repealed but it appears that the IRS view is that this expenditure remains non-depreciable despite the absence of a specific prohibition.

Trademark Royalties

Royalties received from trademark licences are taxable as income. The basis **14-63** of taxation depends on whether the taxpayer is a cash or accruals basis taxpayer. As a general rule individuals may opt for taxation on either basis. Whichever basis is chosen applies to all income and should be consistently applied. It is possible to change from the cash to the accruals basis and vice versa with IRS permission. Companies (apart from 'S' corporations) must normally use the accruals basis.

Following on from this, the position relating to payments of trademark royalties is a mirror image in that they will be deductible on a cash or accruals basis, according to the basis adopted generally by the taxpayer.

Non-Residents

Trademark royalties paid to a non-resident constitute fixed or determinable **14-64** annual or periodical income of the non-resident and as such are subject to deduction of tax at source at a rate of 30 per cent. This may be reduced by the provisions of a double taxation agreement. For instance, under the United Kingdom/USA double taxation agreement the withholding tax is reduced to nil where the beneficial owner of the royalty is a resident of the United Kingdom.

The same applies under the Netherlands/USA double taxation agreement, although in this case there are extensive anti-treaty shopping provisions designed to ensure, broadly, that treaty benefits are only enjoyed by individual Dutch residents, companies controlled by them or Dutch quoted companies. Because of the complexity of these provisions they should be consulted in every case to ascertain whether relief is available.

Under the Malta/USA agreement the rate of withholding tax on trademark royalties is reduced to $12\frac{1}{2}$ per cent. The reduction does not apply where the recipient is a Maltese company and 25 per cent or more of its capital is owned directly or indirectly by individuals who are not-resident in Malta; by reason of special measures the royalties are subject to tax which is substantially less than the tax generally imposed in Malta on company business profits. As Malta applies an imputation system to non resident shareholders it may be possible to recover tax paid by the company in the hands of the shareholder and limit the effective tax to the $12\frac{1}{2}$ per cent withholding tax.

Transfer

14-65 The disposal of trademarks gives rise to a capital gain unless the transferor retains any significant power, right or continuing interest with respect to the subject matter of the trademark, in which case the receipt is taxed as income. A significant power, right or continuing interest includes, but is not limited to, the following rights with respect to the interest transferred:

(a) a right to disapprove of any assignment of such interest, or part thereof;
(b) a right to terminate at will;
(c) a right to prescribe the standards of quality of products used or sold;
(d) a right to require the transferee only to sell or advertise products or services of the transferor;
(e) a right to require the transferee to purchase substantially all of his supplies and equipment from the transferor;
(f) a right to payments contingent on the productivity, use, or disposition of the subject matter of the interest transferred, if such payments constitute a substantial element under the transfer agreement.

When trademark royalties are paid to a non-resident and the payer and recipient are owned or controlled directly or indirectly by the same interests, the transfer pricing provisions of Section 482 IRC will apply. As a general rule, the regulations issued under this section apply normal arm's length principles to transactions, including transactions involving intangibles. In cases, however, where intangibles are transferred by a US taxpayer, these principles are modified. In cases where an intangible is transferred under an arrangement that covers more than one year, the consideration may be adjusted to ensure that it is commensurate with the income attributable to the intangible. Different adjustments can be made under this criterion in different years. No adjustment may be made where the taxpayer has entered into a comparable uncontrolled transaction, as defined.

15. Annotated Sample Trade Mark Licence Agreement

This chapter sets out a sample trade mark licence agreement with annotations and cross references. It is not intended to represent the only possible form of trade mark licence. There will obviously be many different versions, given the diversity of circumstances in which trade mark licensing takes place. The sample agreement is intended to highlight the main aspects which may need to be included in a trade mark licence.

> **THIS AGREEMENT** is made on the [   ] day of [   ], 19[ ]
>
> **by and between**
>
> **ABC Ltd.**, a company incorporated in [   ], whose registered office is located at 123 Feather Lane,
> Anywhere (hereinafter: 'ABC' or 'the Licensor'), of the first part,
>
>   **and**
>
> **XYZ Ltd.**, a company incorporated in [   ], whose registered office is located at 100 Drury Street,
> Somewhere (hereinafter: 'XYZ' or 'the Licensee'), of the other part.

Comments

1. The parties should be accurately described and identified. When a large corporation with numerous subsidiaries is involved, particular care should be taken to ensure that the corporate entity which is the proprietor or licensee of the mark is correctly identified. The parties need not be corporate entities; any person with legal capacity can be a party to the agreement. An unincorporated division selling its products under a particular trade mark will usually not have legal capacity.

2. Care should be taken that the addresses of the respective parties are correctly stated. This will enable written notice to be provided in a timely manner under the terms of the agreement, and preclude any potential dispute on this point.

3. There are advantages and disadvantages to identifying the parties by

their respective names, rather than simply referring to them as 'Licensor' and 'Licensee'.

(i) On the one hand, the use of the names of the parties obviates the risk that the terms 'Licensor' and 'Licensee' will be inadvertently confused in the Agreement.

(ii) On the other hand, the terms 'Licensor' and 'Licensee' may facilitate understanding of the respective rights and obligations of the parties, particularly when the identity of one or both parties is likely to change during the term of the Agreement.

Sometimes, a combination of the two methods is adopted. For example, the Licensor maybe referred to by its name ('ABC'), while the other party may simply be referred to as 'the Licensee'.

PREAMBLE

WHEREAS, ABC is the proprietor of the Trade Marks (as set out in Schedule A) registered in the Territory (as hereinafter defined) in respect of certain Goods and Services (as set out in Schedule B); and

WHEREAS, the Licensee wishes to use the Trade Marks in the Territory in relation to the Goods and Services; and

WHEREAS, ABC is willing to grant to the Licensee a licence to use the Trade Marks on an exclusive basis throughout the Territory, in accordance with the terms and conditions of this Agreement, as hereinafter set forth.

NOW THEREFORE, IN CONSIDERATION FOR THE MUTUAL COVENANTS AND PROMISES HEREINAFTER SET FORTH, THE PARTIES AGREE AS FOLLOWS:

Comments

1. These provisions constitute the basic recitals of a trade mark licence agreement. Additional recitals may be included, if the parties so desire. It is arguable, however, whether there is any point in reciting additional matters which are covered elsewhere in the Agreement.

2. If the parties intend the licence to be recorded under the registered user, or similar provision, the second recital might also include the following:

'... the Licensee is desirous of being registered as a licensee or a registered user of the Trade Marks under the provisions of the applicable provisions of trade mark law.'

3. If the licence is based on an application under a statutory provision such as section 29(1)(b) of the Trade Marks Act 1938, the first recital will be modified to reflect the fact the Licensor is an applicant for registration, rather than the proprietor of a registered trade mark.

4. If the licence is non-exclusive rather than exclusive, the recital should be changed accordingly.

5. If a licensing agent is used, the licensor should make certain that it, and not the licensing agent, is the party that enters into the licence agreement. The licensor should make clear contractually with the licensing agent that any understanding reached by the licensing agent with a prospective licensee is subject to the licensor's approval. See Daniel, 'Dealing with Canadian Licensing Agent,' *Blake's Report: Intellectual Property*, January/February 1994.

Cross References

1. Principles of a trade mark, Chap. 1, paras. 1–10 and 1–11.
2. Registered user provisions, Chap. 3, paras. 3–01 to 3–13.
3. Practice under section 29 of the Trade Marks Act 1938, Chap. 3, paras. 3–20 to 3–24.
4. Nature of the trade mark licence, Chap. 10, paras. 10–01 to 10–06.

1. DEFINITIONS AND INTERPRETATION

1.1 In this Agreement, the following expressions shall have the respective meanings assigned to them:

Trade Marks: The registered trade marks and service marks, as set out in Schedule A to this Agreement, as may be changed from time to time in writing.

Goods and Services: The goods and services described in Schedule B to this Agreement and to which the Trade Marks are applied or otherwise used under the provisions of this Agreement.

Territory: The territory of [   ].

Confidential Information: All information, advice, knowledge, trade secrets and know-how which is disclosed by ABC to the Licensee, and without derogating from the generality of the foregoing, methods, processes, designs and improvements in connection with the manufacture of the Goods or furnishing of the Services, whether tangible or intangible.

Net Sales: The sum total of all amounts invoiced by the Licensee for sales of the Goods and Services, less freight charges and excise taxes, and less all usual discounts, allowances and refunds.

1.2 The Recitals contained in the Preamble shall be taken into account in the interpretation and construction of this Agreement.

1.3 The headings in this Agreement are for ease of reference only and shall not affect its construction.

1.4 In this Agreement, if the context so requires, references to the singular shall include the plural and vice versa.

Comments

1. There are three approaches to the handling of definitions in the agreement.

(i) Provide a comprehensive set of definitions at the outset of the agreement.

(ii) Provide definitions of the most important terms, and leave other terms to be defined as required in the context of specific provisions.

(iii) Do not include a definitions section, and define all terms as they are needed in the context of specific provisions.

The sample agreement has adopted the second approach.

2. The definition of Trade Marks refers to registered marks only. It is possible that unregistered marks may also be covered by the Agreement. In the event that unregistered marks are covered, the definition may include additional wording such as the following:

> 'Trade Marks shall also mean all other trade marks, service marks, trade names, styles, logos and other trade symbols which are under the control or proprietorship of the Licensor, and which are to be used in connection with the Goods and Services under this Agreement.'

The rights of the parties with respect to these unlicensed marks will differ from country to country.

3. However the trade marks are defined, the definition should be carefully worded, so that the parties are clear about which marks are subject to the licence, and in what form.

4. If the agreement is intended to cover only a single country, it is better to specify the territory in the definition. If, however, the agreement covers more than one country, it may be preferable to describe the territories separately in a Schedule. The defined territory may be narrower than the entire territory of the jurisdiction in which the marks are registered. When the legal status of a territory is disputed or is in doubt, the licensee should verify that the registered trade marks are in fact duly recorded in that territory.

5. The definition of 'confidential information' is particularly important when the licensor is furnishing know-how, whether as part of the exercise of quality control or otherwise. The licensee may also own significant confidential information in connection with the manufacture of the goods or the provision of the services, and it will want to limit the disclosure of such confidential information to the licensor. The licensee should make certain that the licensor is the proprietor of all of the 'confidential information'. If not, the licensee will have to procure an additional licence with respect to the confidential information that is not directly owned by the licensor.

6. The definition of 'net sales' is fundamental to the calculation of royalties. The precise definition will depend upon the nature of the goods or services which are subject to the licence. For example, it is possible to define net sales in terms of units sold, less returns, rather than on the basis of the aggregate amount invoiced.

7. The parties should make it clear whether they want the recitals to form an operative as part of the agreement.

8. Schedules are often used to indicate the trade marks that are included in the arrangement and, if more than one country is involved, the territories that are covered. These schedules are too often left uncompleted during drafting, and are either finished in haste immediately prior to the execution of the agreement, or are even left to be completed at some later time. Both circumstances are undesirable. It is advisable to treat the schedules with the same attention as the rest of the agreement.

Cross References

1. Licensing of unregistered trade marks, Chap. 3, paras. 3–11 to 3–19.
2. Know-how licensing, Chap. 1, paras. 1–16 to 1–20; Chap. 13, paras. 13–19 to 13–22.
3. Principles of a trade mark, Chap. 1, paras. 1–27 to 1–29.

2.0 THE GRANT

2.1 The Licensor hereby grants to the Licensee, and the Licensee hereby accepts, an exclusive licence to use the Trade Marks for the manufacture, promotion, sale and distribution of the Goods and Services within the Territory during the term of this Agreement.
2.2 As long as this Agreement is in effect, or unless otherwise provided, the Licensor shall not use, or authorise any person or entity to use, the Trade Marks within the Territory on or in connection with the Goods or Services.

Comments

1. This provision should state whether the grant is exclusive, sole or non-exclusive. The sample clause has provided for an exclusive grant, whereby the licensor is also prohibited from using the licensed trade mark during the term of the agreement. By contrast, a sole licence prohibits the licensor from granting additional licences, but it still allows the licensor itself to use the licensed trade mark in the territory.

2. It is possible for the same agreement to provide both for exclusive and non-exclusive use by the licensee, depending upon the particular goods or services involved. For example, the licensee could be granted an exclusive licence to use the trade mark for women's casual wear, and a non-exclusive licence to use the trade mark for bathing suits.

3. If the licence grant is for export as well, it should be so indicated. The territories into which the export is authorised should be carefully set out in the definition of 'Territory'.

Cross References

1. Conceptual foundations of a trade mark licence regarding the basic elements of the grant, Chap. 10, paras. 10–04 to 10–06.
2. Trade mark licensing distinguished from other forms of intellectual property licensing, Chap. 1, paras. 1–05 to 1–24.
3. Exclusive and non-exclusive licensees, Chap. 4, paras. 4–07 to 4–11, and Chap. 10, paras. 10–20 to 10–22.

3. TERM OF THE AGREEMENT

3.1 Subject to the provisions for earlier termination set out hereunder, this Agreement shall be in effect for an initial period commencing on the execution date and expiring on December 31, 199[ ].
3.2 Subject to the provisions for earlier termination set out hereunder, this Agreement shall automatically be extended for additional periods of five years each, provided that neither the Licensor nor the Licensee furnishes the other party with written notice of termination not less than six months prior to the expiry of the initial period referred to in paragraph 3.1, or the expiry of any subsequent renewal period under this paragraph.

Comments

1. The parties may wish to define further the term 'execution date' if there is any likelihood of uncertainty, as there may be if, for example, the parties are located in different countries, and they sign the agreement at different times.
2. The parties may provide for an initial term based on a fixed period of time, such as five years, rather than a beginning and end date.
3. There are a number of ways of providing for renewal of the agreement. Some of them are as follows:

(i) No provision for renewal is included and the agreement is in effect for a single fixed term. At the expiry of the fixed term, the parties will have to take steps either to execute a new agreement or to provide for the renewal or extension of the old agreement.
(ii) The renewal of the agreement is tied to the licensee's satisfactory performance of certain obligations, typically the attainment of a certain level of sales, or the payment of minimum royalties. If these criteria are met, the licence is renewed, unless the licensee otherwise elects not to continue. It is possible that the number of renewals may be limited.
(iii) The licence remains in effect without limitation, subject only to the continuing validity of the underlying trade mark rights.

4. Grounds for premature termination will be contained in the termination clause or other similar provisions of the agreement. See, *infra*, clauses 19 and 20 of the sample Agreement.

Cross References

1. Renewal and termination of licence, Chap. 12, paras. 12–13 to 12–19.

4. ROYALTIES AND PAYMENT

4.1 In consideration for the grant of the licence in clause 2, the Licensee undertakes to pay the Licensor an amount equal to the Royalty Percentage.

4.2 If the Licensor determines that the Royalty Percentage should be adjusted, it shall notify the Licensee of the adjustment no later than [　] months prior to the expiry of the current term of the Agreement. If neither party terminates this Agreement in accordance with clause 3, the revised Royalty Percentage shall be in effect for an additional [　] period.

4.3 The payment of royalties in accordance with paragraph 4.1 above shall be made on a [　] basis, commencing on [　] [　] 199[　], and at the end of each [　] period thereafter. Payment shall be made by the Licensee in [　] [designate the currency] no later than [　] days after the end of each such period to such place as shall be designated by the Licensor in writing.

4.4 Payment shall be net of withholding or any other tax as required by the applicable law of the Territory. If required by the Licensor, the Licensee shall furnish the Licensor with a suitable tax invoice.

Comments

    1. In the sample provision, it is presumed that the agreement defines the term Royalty Percentage, based on whatever form of royalty rate is adopted.
    2. The Royalty Percentage can be fixed in various ways. The sample clause has set out the basic royalty provisions, but each agreement will tailor this paragraph to its particular needs.
    3. Some of the most popular royalty arrangements are as follows:

(i) Initial lump-sum payment (which may be deemed an advance) plus continuing royalties.
(ii) Fixed percentage irrespective of the number of units sold.
(iii) Increasing percentage as higher sales levels are reached.
(iv) Decreasing percentage as higher sales levels are reached.
(v) Minimum royalties.
(vi) Maximum royalties.

    4. Royalties can be calculated on the basis of units sold, or on the basis of some sales price.
    5. The royalty rate and the provisions for payment have been dealt with in a single paragraph. However, if the provisions are more complicated it may be preferable to set out each of them in a separate paragraph.
    6. If currency restrictions are an issue in the Licensee's jurisdiction, the

agreement may provide either that the licensee is permitted to pay in an alternative currency, subject to the licensor's approval, or that the licensee can pay the royalties into a designated bank account in the name of the licensor.

7. The agreement may provide for a minimum sales target for the licensed products. Failure to reach these targets may provide a ground for termination by the licensor. The licensor may soften this provision by permitting the licensee to pay the minimum royalty as if it had attained the minimum sales target, thereby keeping the licence agreement in force.

8. If a licensing agent is used, the licensor will typically wish to provide that payments be made directly to the licensor, who then pays the licensing agent his fee or commission. In this way, the licensor protects himself from bankruptcy or insolvency of the licensing agent. However, considerations of convenience of the licensees may dictate in certain circumstances that payment be made directly to the licensing agent. See Daniel, *supra*, Clause 1, Comment 5.

Cross References

1. Taxation of licensed income, Chap. 14, paras. 14–33 to 14–65.
2. Conceptual foundations of a trade mark licence, the contractual and proprietary nature of royalties, Chap. 10, paras. 10–24 and 10–25.
3. Termination of a licence, Chap. 12, paras. 12–24 and 12–25.
4. Bankruptcy and insolvency, Chap. 14, paras. 14–02 to 14–13.

5. RECORDS AND ACCOUNTS

5.1 The Licensee shall maintain accurate and complete records regarding the manufacture, import, sale and distribution of the Goods and Services in accordance with this Agreement, including such information as is necessary for the calculation and payment of royalties.

5.2 The Licensor, or his agent or representative, shall have the right to inspect the relevant records and accounts of the Licensee during regular business hours throughout the term of this Agreement, and to make copies of any books of account, or other materials, relating to the sale of the Goods and Services. The right of inspection shall remain in effect under the same conditions for a period of one year after termination of this Agreement.

5.3 In the event that the Licensor causes an audit to be performed, and the audit discloses that the Net Sales as reported to the Licensor are understated, the Licensee shall immediately pay the Licensor the additional royalty payment owed, plus interest thereon. If the Net Sales are understated by [ ] or more, the Licensee shall also pay for the cost of the audit. If at any time it becomes known that the Licensee has knowingly withheld or understated Net Sales, the Licensor shall be entitled to terminate this Agreement immediately.

5.4 In addition to any other report required to be submitted by the Licensee under this Agreement, the Licensee shall deliver to the Licensor, no later than 90 days after the end of each calendar year, an audited statement of the Net Sales for the just-concluded calendar year.

Comments

1. The mechanics of recording and verifying the amount of royalty payments owing to the licensor should be carefully specified to avoid disputes.

2. The penalties to be imposed for errors in the calculation of the royalties owing to the licensor can be adapted to suit the particular circumstances.

3. It has been argued that the audited statement provided for in paragraph 5.4 may be an unnecessary expense. One way to address this concern is to provide for the parties to share the cost of the audit.

4. Interest may be specified on the basis of a recognized rate, such as LIBOR, subject to any maximum interest that may be imposed by the law of the territory.

Cross Reference

1. Termination based on failure to satisfy reporting requirements, Chap. 12, paras. 12–25.

6. QUALITY CONTROL

6.1 The Licensor shall advise the Licensee of the standards and specifications for the Goods and Services subject to this agreement. Subject to clause [   ] below [Confidential Information] and the rights of any third party to intellectual property of whatever kind relating to the Goods and Services, the Licensor shall make available to the Licensee all necessary information, and supply all necessary materials, to enable the Licensee to meet these standards and specifications. If the Licensor changes or modifies any such standard or specification, he shall give the Licensee reasonable notice, who shall thereafter act in conformity therewith.

6.2 To the extent permitted by the law of the Territory, the Licensor shall take steps to ensure that the Goods and Services as manufactured or provided are in conformity with the Licensor's standards and specifications as aforesaid.

6.3 Without derogating from the generality of paragraph 6.2, the Licensee, upon request, shall at its own expense furnish the Licensor with randomly selected samples and packaging of the Goods and Services. The Licensor, at its sole expense, shall also have access to the Licensee's premises during reasonable hours in order to inspect samples, and the methods of manufacture, storage and distribution, and to remove a reasonable number of samples at no charge for further examination.

6.4 The Licensor may reject any such samples by furnishing the Licensee with written notice of rejection no later than 30 days after removal of the samples. If such written notice of rejection is furnished, the Licensee may not distribute the Goods and Services until the Licensee takes such steps as are necessary to meet the Licensor's objections, and the Licensor furnishes the Licensee with written authorisation. In the absence of the Licensor furnishing written notice of rejection within 30 days as aforesaid, the samples shall be deemed to be approved by the Licensor.

6.5 The obligations of the Licensee hereunder shall apply mutatis mutandis to any contract manufacturer.

6.6 The Licensor's failure to reject a sample shall not be construed to mean that the Licensor has determined that the sample conforms to applicable local laws, rules and regulations.

Comments

1. Quality control is the central component of a trade mark licence. The forms of quality control are as diverse as the types of goods and services that may be licensed under a trade mark or service mark.

2. The sample provisions address the typical elements of a quality control programme. This does not mean that even these provisions are in any way standard. For example, the licensee may be reluctant to allow the inspection of its premises by the licensor. The licensor, for its part, may be wary of disclosing confidential information to the licensee, unless it receives appropriate assurances.

3. The licensor may take wish to have a more active involvement in the manufacture of the goods than merely exercising a right of inspection of the licensee's premises. If the parties agree, a provision such as the following could be included:

> 'The Licensor shall have the right to send up to [ ] employees to supervise the initial manufacture of the Goods and related operations by the Licensee. Thereafter, it shall be entitled to send up to [ ] employees for a period of not more than [ ] days each year to review the manufacturing, marketing and other practices of the Licensee. All expenses in connection with such supervision shall be borne solely by the Licensor.
>
> In addition, the Licensee may at all reasonable times request the Licensor to provide one or more persons, depending upon need and availability, to assist the Licensee in carrying out its obligations under this Agreement. Such persons shall be paid by the Licensee at the rate of [   ]% of their regular salary, from the time that the person leaves his regular position and until his return, plus all reasonable expenses and travel costs.'

4. The obligations to furnish samples and allow for inspection may also

apply to a contract manufacturer. Some form of control may also be present in a certification mark relationship.

5. Although this paragraph is entitled 'quality control', other provisions in the agreement will also be relevant to the issue of quality control.

6. The extent to which explicit contractual provisions for maintaining quality control between a parent and subsidiary are necessary will depend upon the particular jurisdiction involved. Prudence dictates that some form of written licence agreement, with suitable provisions for quality control, is almost always advisable, even when the principal basis for control is financial rather than contractual.

7. Should the licensee be the assignor of trade mark rights by virtue of an assignment and licence back arrangement, effective control may be exercised by the licensee.

Cross References

1. Quality control generally, Chap. 6, paras. 6–01 to 6–47.
2. Quality control in the context of the registered user provisions, Chap. 3, paras. 3–01 to 3–34.
3. Quality control of related companies under U.S. law, Chap. 5.
4. Trademark use by distributors, Chap. 7.
5. Assignment and licence back, Chap. 6, paras. 6–48 to 6–63.
6. Contract manufacturer and quality control, Chap. 8, paras. 8–01 to 8–16, and control and certification marks, Chap. 8, paras. 8–17 to 8–30.
7. Quality control provisions in the context of the European Commission, Chap. 13, paras. 13–23 to 13.57.
8. Quality control and product liability, Chap. 14, paras. 14–14 to 14–32.
9. Quality control in written form, Chap. 10, paras. 10–04 to 10–06, 10–23.
10. Quality control and unwritten licence, Chap. 11, paras. 11–01 to 11–26.
11. Quality control as basis for trade mark licensing, Chap. 2, paras. 2–01 to 2–26.

7. ADVERTISING AND PROMOTION

7.1 The Licensee may use the Trade Marks in the promotion and sale of the Goods and Services. All advertising and promotional materials containing the Trade Marks shall be furnished to the Licensor for inspection and approval. If the Licensor disapproves of any of these materials, it shall notify the Licensee in writing no later than 15 days after receipt. The Licensee shall not use any materials in the promotion and advertising of the Goods and Services which have not been approved by the Licensor.

7.2 The Licensor shall not unreasonably withhold approval of the materials. It shall not be unreasonable for the Licensor to withhold approval if the Licensor believes in good faith that the materials would adversely affect the reputation and image of the Licensor or of the Trade Marks. Failure by the

Licensor to notify the Licensee within the said period of time shall be deemed to constitute acceptance of the materials.

7.3 Acceptance by the Licensor under this paragraph shall not be construed to mean that the Licensor has determined that the materials conform to applicable local law, rules and regulations.

Comments

1. The extent to which the licensor may in practice monitor advertising and promotional materials will depend upon the circumstances of the licence agreement. The advertising function of trade marks cannot be overlooked, however, and the licensor should be careful to control these uses of the trade mark.

2. The licensor may wish to obtain a warranty from the licensee regarding the ownership of any copyrighted material contained in the promotional materials submitted to the licensor.

3. A franchise arrangement often provides for a central advertising fund to which all franchisees contribute. The franchisor then operates this fund generally for the benefit of all the licensees in connection with the advertising and promotion of the trade marks. An advertising fund may also be created and maintained by a licensor which has granted a number of non-exclusive licences within the territory. An example of such an advertising provision is as follows:

> 'The Licensee shall contribute to the advertising and promotion of the Trade Marks an amount equal to [ ]% of Net Sales. This fund shall be maintained at the sole discretion of the Licensor. This payment shall be made at the same times and under the same terms and conditions as the payment of royalties under clause 4.'

If such a fund is established, attention should be paid to whether a franchise arrangement is created, particularly under U.S. law.

4. The licensor may also include one or more clauses which provide for a degree of control over the manner in which the licensee markets the licensed products. If such a provision is included, care should be taken that the licensor does not seek to control the price of the licensed products.

Cross References

1. Advertising function of trade marks, Chap. 2, paras. 2–27 to 2–30.
2. Quality control, see Cross References in connection with Clause 6.
3. The licensing of copyright, Chap. 1, paras. 1–21 to 1–24.
4. EC block exemptions for exclusive distribution, exclusive purchase, and franchise agreements, Chap. 13, paras. 13–23 to 13.57.

8. TRADE MARK RIGHTS

8.1 The Licensor warrants and represents that it is the proprietor of the Trade Marks. The Licensor at its sole discretion may, upon written notice to the Licensee, add or remove any trade marks or service marks to or from Schedule A.

8.2 The Licensor will take all steps required to maintain existing registrations of the Trade Marks and to prosecute to completion any pending applications. The Licensee will provide all necessary assistance to the Licensor in maintaining and obtaining such registrations, provided that all reasonable expenses incurred by the Licensee shall be borne by the Licensor.

8.3 Nothing herein confers, or shall confer upon the Licensee, any right, title or interest in any of the Trade Marks during the term of this Agreement or any time thereafter. All use of the Trade Marks by the Licensee shall be in strict accordance with the provisions of this Agreement.

8.4 All use of the Trade Marks by the Licensee under this Agreement shall insure solely to the benefit of the Licensor. The Licensee will take all steps required to avoid abandonment of the Trade Marks for any reason including, but not limited to, non-use.

8.5 The Licensee acknowledges that the Trade Marks are the exclusive property of the Licensor, and that it will not assert any claim of ownership to the Trade Marks, or to the goodwill or reputation thereof, by virtue of the Licensee's use of the Trade Marks, or otherwise.

8.6 The Licensee will not do any act, or permit any act or thing to be done or carried out in derogation of any of the rights of the Licensor in the Trade Marks, either during the term of this Agreement or thereafter.

8.7 The Licensee shall not dispute or challenge the validity of the Trade Marks, or any of the rights of the Licensor thereto, during the term of this Agreement or thereafter.

Comments

1. These provisions attempt to make it clear that the licensee obtains no rights in the trade marks, other than the right to use them in accordance with the licence agreement.

2. The extent to which the agreement can prevent a licensee from challenging either the validity or proprietorship of the trade marks is not fully settled.

3. See Comment 8 to Clause 1 regarding the importance of completing promptly and completely the schedule of trade marks.

Cross References

1. Nature of the licensee's right in the trade mark, Chap. 10.
2. Right of the distributor in the trade mark, Chap. 7.
3. No challenge clauses and licensee estoppel, Chap. 9, paras. 9–40 to 9–59.
4. Trade mark rights of contract manufacturer and certification mark, Chap. 8.

9. USE OF THE TRADE MARK BY THE LICENSEE

9.1 All Goods and Services made and sold by the Licensee under this Agreement must bear the appropriate Trade Mark. The Licensee shall apply such Trade Mark to the Goods and Services only in the form and manner specified by the Licensor.

9.2 The Licensee shall indicate that the Trade Marks are the property of the Licensor by the use of the ® symbol, if permitted by the law in the Territory, or the words 'Registered Trade Mark of [the Licensor], or similar indication permitted by law.'

9.3 No other marks, symbols or other wording shall appear on the Goods or in relation to the Services, without the prior written approval of the Licensor.

9.4 Notwithstanding the foregoing, the Licensee is permitted to use its trade name or service mark [specify name or mark] on packaging materials, and in advertising on promotional materials.

9.5 The Licensee shall as far as is reasonably practicable use the Trade Marks on labelling and packaging in accordance with the provisions of this paragraph. The Licensee shall comply fully with any additional requirements under the applicable local law with respect to the labelling and packaging of the goods.

9.6 The Licensee shall not use the Trade Marks, in whole or in part, in its company, corporate or trade name.

Comments

1. The licensor may wish to impose a more extensive legend in order to clarify that the mark is being used under licence. An example is as follows:

'Made in [identify the place] by the [Licensee] under Licence from [the Licensor]', together with the ® symbol, if appropriate, or the legend 'Registered Trade Mark of [the Licensor].'

2. If the goods are intended for export, the countries of destination may have additional requirements in connection with the marking of the goods.
3. There may be additional requirements under local law with respect to

the labelling and packaging of the goods. The parties should make clear how compliance with these requirements will be ensured.

4. The licensor should not allow a licensee to include the trade mark as part of the licensee's company name. The risk is that the terminated licensee will claim a continuing right in the name after its commercial relationship with the licensor has come to an end. The same holds true for a terminated distributor. The one possible exception to this rule of practice is where the licensee is the wholly-owned subsidiary of the licensor. Here, as well, there is a risk that the subsidiary may later be separated from the parent, and together with it the rights in the trade mark.

Cross References

1. Joint marking of goods by the licensor and the licensee, Chap. 7, paras. 7–20 to 7–25.
2. Distributor's rights in a trade mark, Chap. 7, paras. 7–40 to 7–64.
3. Nature of the rights of the licensor and the licensee, Chap. 10, paras. 10–07 to 10–35.
4. Split of proprietorship of trade mark under E.C. law, Chap. 13, paras. 13–05 to 13–11.

10. THIRD-PARTY INFRINGEMENT

10.1 If the Licensee becomes aware of any infringement, actual or suspected, or any other unauthorised use of the Trade Marks by another person within the Territory (hereinafter 'the Unauthorised Use'), the Licensee shall promptly give notice to the Licensor in writing specifying the particulars of the Unauthorised Use.

10.2 The Licensor, at its sole discretion, shall take whatever action it deems advisable in connection with the Unauthorised Use, and it shall notify the Licensee of its decision within [   ] days of being informed by the Licensee of the Unauthorised Use in accordance with paragraph 10.1 above.

10.3 If the Licensor decides to take action of any kind against the Unauthorised Use, the Licensor shall have sole control of the conduct of any such action. The Licensor shall bear the entire cost and expense associated with the conduct of any such action, and any recovery or compensation that may be awarded as a result of such action, including but not limited to any settlement that may be reached, shall belong to the Licensor.

10.4 The Licensee, if called upon in writing by the Licensor, shall cooperate fully with the Licensor, at the Licensor's sole expense, in the conduct of any such action. Such cooperation shall not entitle the Licensee to any claim for recovery or compensation in respect thereof, and all such recovery or compensation shall belong solely to the Licensor.

10.5 If the Licensor notifies the Licensee, in accordance with paragraph 10.2 above, that it has elected not to take action against the Unauthorised Use, or if the Licensor fails to notify the Licensee within [   ] days as provided in paragraph 10.2 above, the Licensee may, at its sole discretion, take action against the Unauthorised Use.

10.6 If the Licensee elects to take action of any kind against the Unauthorised Use, it shall promptly notify the Licensor and the provisions of paragraphs 10.3 and 10.4 above shall apply to the Licensee as if it were the Licensor. Action taken by the Licensee under this paragraph shall be in the name of the Licensee and, if required by the law of the Territory, on behalf of the Licensor. The Licensor shall also be joined as a party to any suit initiated by the Licensee, if required by the law of the Territory.

Comments

1. The Trade Marks Act 1994 has swept away the framework of section 28 of the Trade Marks Act 1938 in connection with the licensee's right to bring an action for infringement under the trade mark licence. Subject to any agreement to the contrary between the licensor and the licensee, these sections of the Trade Marks Act 1994 will apply. Under the Trade Marks Act 1994, the parties enjoy a broad right to override by agreement the statutory provisions regarding right to bring suit. The model provision should be carefully compared with the statutory provisions of the Trade Marks Act 1994, or the relevant act of the jurisdiction involved.

2. The licensor may also seek to oblige the licensee actively to investigate acts of infringement. Such a provision may provide as follows:

> 'The Licensee shall take reasonable measure to identify any infringement, actual or suspected, or any other unauthorised use of the Trade Marks by another person within the Territory.'

3. Two questions are raised by such a provision:

(i) Why is the provision necessary? Under this view, clause 10.1 should be primarily concerned with setting out the manner in which notification of the infringement is to be given. It is assumed that by virtue of the nature of the licence relationship, it is in the mutual interests of the parties to monitor suspected infringement activity.

(ii) Even if the provision is deemed desirable, is it too vague to be enforceable? If so, it may be difficult to express the obligation with any greater certainty in order to enhance its enforceability.

4. The licensee may not wish to broaden the scope of its obligations beyond acts of infringement to include other unlawful acts in connection with the trade mark, such as dilution under U.S. law or passing-off.

5. If the parties wish to share in the expenses and, as a consequence, in any recovery resulting from a successful action, such a provision should be expressly included. The provision should specify exactly how the expenses and recovery are to be shared. In the absence of a provision limiting the

recovery, under U.K. law, the provisions of the Trade Marks Act 1994 will apply.

6. It is worth checking whether the law in the Territory allows the licensee to take immediate action contrary to the statutory timetable, such as injunctive relief, in the event that the licensor does not take action, and there is a real risk of irreparable damage to the trade marks. For instance, the 1994 Trade Marks Act permits an exclusive licensee to apply alone for interlocutory relief.

7. If a licensee decides to take action in accordance with the law of the territory, should he undertake to indemnify the licensor? In addition, should the licensor undertake to assist and cooperate with the licensee in the maintenance of any action?

8. An additional question is whether a licensee, if it maintains an action alone and at its sole expense, is still obliged to pay the licensor an amount equal to the royalties to which the licensor would have been entitled had the infringer paid such royalties? The Trade Marks Act 1994 permits the court to apportion recovery on account of infringement, subject to an agreement between the licensor and licensee.

9. The licensor may not wish to provide the licensee with any right of action. However, when the law of the Territory contains a provision similar to section 28(3) of the Trade Marks Act 1938, which granted the registered user a statutory right of action under specified conditions, the licensor must explicitly provide that the licensee shall have no right of action other than its statutory right of action.

Cross References

1. Registered licensee and right of action generally, Chap. 4, paras. 4–07 to 4–31.
2. The proprietary and contractual aspects of infringement generally, Chap. 10, paras. 10–07 to 10–34.
3. Allocation of proceeds from settlement or recovery, Chap. 4, paras. 4–14 to 4–18 and Chap. 10, paras. 10–27 to 10–30.

11. INFRINGEMENT ACTION AGAINST THE LICENSEE

11.1 If legal action is commenced or threatened against the Licensee as a result of its authorised use of the Trade Marks or the Confidential Information, the Licensee shall promptly notify the Licensor in writing.

11.2 Upon receipt of written notice as a foresaid, the Licensor, at its sole expense, shall have the obligation to take whatever steps are necessary to protect and defend the Licensee against such claim, suit or demand. If called upon by the Licensor, the Licensee shall furnish all reasonable assistance at the Licensor's expense.

11.3 The Licensor shall indemnify the Licensee against any loss, cost or expense incurred by the Licensee as a result of such action. The Licensee shall have no authority to settle or compromise any such claim, and the Licensor shall enjoy any recovery or settlement awarded or otherwise received in respect of such action.

Comments

1. It is possible to provide that the licensor may, but is not obliged to, defend any such action. In such a situation, the agreement may provide as follows:

> 'If the Licensor elects not to defend such action, the Licensee shall bear all the costs of defence, and shall be responsible for any award against it, provided that the Licensor shall provide the Licensee with all reasonable assistance at the Licensee's expense. Any recovery or award paid to the Licensee shall belong solely to the Licensee.'

2. A successful action brought by a third party may amount to a breach of the licensor's warranty of good title, or some similar warranty, and may even be a ground for termination if the licensee is no longer permitted to use the licensed mark.

3. The licensor's obligations apply only if the licensee uses the trade marks in an authorised manner under the licence agreement. Should the licensee use the licensed trade marks in an unauthorised manner, the licensee may be liable both for infringement of the trade marks rights of a third party, and breach of the licence agreement.

Cross References

1. The proprietary and contractual rights of the licensor and licensee under a licence agreement, Chap. 10, paras. 10–15 to 10–23.
2. Termination, Chap. 12, paras. 12–01 to 12–12.

12. SUBLICENCES

12.1 The rights granted under this Agreement may be sublicensed by the Licensor to one or more persons as proposed by the Licensee. The appointment of any such sublicensee shall be subject to the sole discretion of the Licensor.

12.2 The Licensee shall determine that a prospective sublicensee has the financial resources, and the requisite experience, skills and qualifications, to carry out the use of the Trade Marks in an appropriate manner.

12.3 The Licensee shall furnish to the Licensor for its approval the proposed form of sublicence agreement. The sublicence agreement shall be in accordance with all of the provisions of this Agreement. Without derogating from the generality of the foregoing, the sublicence agreement shall provide for termination simultaneously with the termination of this Agreement.

12.4 The Licensor hereby appoints the Licensee as its representative to ensure that the sublicensee satisfies all of the quality control requirements set out in this Agreement.

Comments

1. The right of the licensee to grant a sublicence was uncertain under the Trade Marks Act 1938, and it was clearly not recognised under the registered user provisions. The Trade Marks Act 1994 explicitly provides that a sub-licence may be granted.

2. In those jurisdictions where the right of sublicence has not been fully resolved, a three-way arrangement is possible, where the grant of the right to use the trade mark runs directly from the licensor to the sublicensee, while the actual control over the sublicensee is exercised by the licensee/sublicensor, as the representative of the licensor. The licensor should also reserve the right to exercise quality control on its own behalf.

3. There has been a suggestion under U.S. law that the licensor is a third party beneficiary of the sublicence. This relationship is sometimes expressly provided for in the main licence agreement itself.

4. Royalties may be collected by the licensee, so that the licensee retains any royalty income received from the sublicensee the amount owing to the licensor in respect of the sale of the licensed products. Alternatively, it may be possible for payment to be made directly by the sublicensee to the licensor, with a set-off against amounts owing to the licensor by the licensee.

5. The right of sublicence agreement should mirror as far as possible the provisions of the licence agreement.

Cross References

1. Conceptual foundations of a trade mark licence, Chap. 10, paras. 10–07 to 10–25.
2. Quality control, see Cross References in connection with Clause 6.
3. Origins of licensing under the registered user provisions, Chap. 2, paras. 2–18 to 2–26.
4. Sublicensing under the Trade Marks Act 1994, Chap. 4, para. 4–50.

13. CONTRACT MANUFACTURE

13.1 If the Licensee wishes to enter into a sub-contract with a manufacturer within the Territory to manufacture the goods and to apply the Trade Marks to them, the Licensee shall enter into a written agreement with the manufacturer subject to the prior approval of the Licensor.

13.2 Such agreement shall contain provisions addressing the following subjects:

(i) **The mode of application of the Trade Marks on the Goods.**
(ii) **Quality control in the manufacture of the Goods.**

(iii) **Disclosure of Confidential Information.**

Comments

1. An agreement between the Licensee and the contract manufacturer will probably include certain provisions which have reference to the trade mark licence. These include at a minimum the issues addressed in paragraph 13.2 of the Sample Agreement.

Cross References

1. Contract manufacture, Chap. 8, paras. 8–01 to 8–16.
2. Licensing of trade secrets and know-how, Chap. 1, paras. 1–16 to 1–20.
3. Know-how licensing in the European Community, Chap. 13, paras. 13–15 to 13–22.

14. ASSIGNMENT

14.1 The Licensor may assign any of its rights or delegate any of its duties under this Agreement.

14.2 The Licensee may not assign any of its rights or delegate any of its duties under this Agreement without the prior written consent of the Licensor, and provided that such assignment is not otherwise contrary to law.

Comments

1. A licensee is generally selected because he is perceived by the licensor to have particular qualities. For this reason, the licensee will not usually be granted an unrestricted right of assignment.
2. In addition, the assignment of rights by the licensee may otherwise be prohibited by law, such as under the Trade Marks Act 1938, which prohibited an assignment by a registered user. No such restriction appears to apply to the assignment by a registered licensee under the Trade Marks Act 1994.
3. The licensor may wish to include a provision under which he is appointed to carry out all necessary acts to effect the assignment. Alternatively, the parties may execute assignment documents at the same time as they enter into the agreement. Such assignment documents would then be held by a fiduciary under appropriate instructions.

Cross Reference

1. Assignment by a registered licensee, Chap. 4, para. 4–50.
2. Assignment distinguished from a licence, Chap. 1, para. 1–37.
3. Assignment distinguished from a consent, Chap. 9, para. 9–02.

15. CONFIDENTIAL INFORMATION

15.1 Confidential Information, as defined in paragraph 1 of this Agreement, shall be disclosed to the Licensee only for such purposes as shall be set out in this Agreement, and such Confidential Information may only be disclosed by the Licensee to those persons for whom such disclosure is necessary in the carrying out of their duties.

15.2 The restrictions on disclosure under this paragraph shall not apply to any Confidential Information that is in the public domain, which the Licensee has otherwise received lawfully from a third party, or was in the possession of the Licensee prior to the disclosure, or which has been disclosed other than due to the fault of the Licensee.

Comments

1. The agreement assumes that there is disclosure of confidential information from the licensor to the licensee. If there is to be mutual disclosure, the paragraph should be modified as appropriate.
2. A licensor may wish to include a provision whereby it disclaims any warranty regarding the efficacy of the confidential information, particularly in connection with anticipated business success. An example of such a provision would be as follows:

'The Licensor makes no warranty regarding the completeness or accuracy of the Confidential Information in connection with the subject matter of this Agreement.'

3. See Comment 5 to Paragraph 1 in relation to the definition of Confidential Information.

Cross References

1. Introduction, know-how licensing, Chap. 1, paras. 1–16 to 1–20.
2. Know-how licensing in the European Community, Chap. 13, paras. 13–15 to 13–22.
3. Quality control, see Cross References in connection with Clause 6.

16. NO AGENCY CREATED

16.1 Nothing in this Agreement shall make one party the agent of the other, and neither party has power or authority to bind the other in respect of any of the rights or duties hereunder.

Comments

1. The argument has occasionally been made that a licence creates an agency relationship between the licensor and the licensee. See *Re Silenus*

Wines, Inc., 194 U.S.P.Q. 261, 263, n. 2 (C.C.P.A. 1977) ('Whether the "related company" doctrine preempts general agency law concerning when the acts of a party are legally the acts of another, and whether such use by a mere agent can create registration rights, are questions we do not reach.')

2. This paragraph makes it clear that the parties to the licence arrangement do not intend to create an agency relationship between the licensor and licensee.

Cross References

1. Rights in a trade mark licence other than contractual or proprietary rights, Chap. 10, paras. 10–26 to 10–30.
2. 'Related company' doctrine under U.S. law, Chap. 1, para. 1–36.

17. INSURANCE AND INDEMNIFICATION

17.1 The Licensee shall, at its own expense, carry comprehensive general liability insurance and product liability insurance covering the Goods made and the Services rendered in connection with the Trade marks under this Agreement, in the amount of $/£[ ], with a deductible of no more than $/£[ ]. The insurance policy shall include insurance coverage for the Licensee's obligation to indemnify the Licensor in accordance with paragraph 17.5 below.

17.2 The insurance policy shall be for the benefit of the Licensee and shall name the Licensor as co-insured. The insurance policy shall remain in effect for as long as any of the Trade Marks are used in accordance with this Agreement, and for a period of [ ] months/years thereafter.

17.3 The insurance policy shall provide that [ ] days' written notice be furnished to the Licensor prior to cancellation, or prior to any material modification or change.

17.4 Upon the execution of this Agreement, the Licensee shall promptly furnish the Licensor with a certificate evidencing that insurance has been effected in accordance with the provisions of this paragraph.

17.5 Subject to the provisions of clause 11, the Licensee agrees to defend, indemnify, and hold harmless the Licensor, including all subsidiaries, affiliates and assignees of the Licensor, against all claims, judgments, actions, debts or rights of action, of whatever kind, and all costs, including reasonable legal fees, arising out of the manufacture, promotion, marketing, distribution or sale of the Goods or Services by the Licensee under this Agreement.

Comments

1. The insurance and indemnification provisions may be set out in separate paragraphs.

2. The scope of the indemnity of the licensor and the licensee, respectively, should be carefully drafted. Compare the licensor's indemnity in clause 11.3 and its disclaimer in clause 18.1 with the licensee's indemnity in clause 17.5 and its warranty in clause 18.2.

3. The insurance clause should be carefully tailored to the particular requirements of the insurance laws in the Territory. Bear in mind, however, that in the U.S. insurance is currently regulated primarily by state rather than federal law.

Cross Reference

1. Product liability, Chap. 14, paras. 14–14 to 14–32.
2. See indemnification, Chap. 4, para. 4–25.

18. DISCLAIMERS AND WARRANTIES

18.1 The Licensor makes no representation or warranty with respect to any Goods sold or Services rendered under this Agreement, and disclaims all liability arising out of or in connection with such Goods and Services.

18.2 The Licensee warrants that it will use the Trade marks only as authorised under this Agreement, and that it will comply with and follow all appropriate laws, regulations, guidelines and rules, and the standards of any appropriate professional association in the Territory in respect of the Goods and Services.

Comments

1. These provisions are intended primarily to limit the licensor's exposure to a product liability claim.

2. The provisions of this paragraph are not the only measures that the licensor may take to limit its exposure to a product liability claim. See the additional measures discussed in Chap. 14, paras. 14–31 and 14–32.

Cross References

1. Product liability, Chap. 14, paras. 14–14 to 14–32.

19. TERMINATION

19.1 Notwithstanding the provisions of clause 3 of this Agreement, or except as otherwise provided, either party may terminate this Agreement:

(i) **In the event that the other party is in breach of any provision of this**

Agreement, and the breaching party fails to cure such breach within 30 days after receipt of written notice from the non-breaching party regarding such breach;

(ii) The other party is unable to pay its debts as they fall due, suspends or threatens to suspend the making of payments, takes steps to cease or ceases to carry out its business as a going concern, enters into winding-up, liquidation, or bankruptcy proceedings, either voluntary or involuntary, or enters into an arrangement for the benefit of creditors;

(iii) A receiver or administrator is appointed over all or part of the assets of the other party.

19.2 Without derogating from the provisions of paragraph 19.1, this Agreement may be terminated by the Licensor in the event that:

(i) The Licensee is in default of its obligation to pay royalties or to satisfy any other monetary obligation under this Agreement, and it fails to cure such default within 48 hours of written notice from the Licensor;

(ii) There is a change in the control of the Licensee which, in the sole opinion of the Licensor, has materially affected the ability of the Licensee to carry out its obligations under this Agreement in a manner satisfactory to the Licensor;

(iii) The Licensee has willingly understated or withheld the reporting of Net Sales.

19.3 Without derogating from the provisions of paragraph 19.1, this Agreement may be terminated if it fails in its essential purpose, including, but not limited to, circumstances involving a breach by the Licensor of paragraph 8.1.

19.4 The exercise of the right of termination by either party shall be without prejudice to the right to collect all sums due and owing to it, to seek monetary relief for the breach of any of the provisions of this Agreement, or to enforce any other right which arose prior to termination.

Comments

1. The grounds for termination will depend upon the details of the licence agreement. The sample clause has included those provisions which frequently appear.

2. Another provision which often triggers termination is the failure of the licensee to meet minimum sales or royalty payments. Such a provision may permit the licensee to avoid termination by paying the minimum royalty as if he had attained the minimum sales target. See also Comment No. 7 to clause 4 above.

3. The right of a party to terminate the licence due to bankruptcy proceedings may be restricted under the relevant bankruptcy or insolvency laws.

Cross References

1. Termination, Chap. 12.
2. Bankruptcy and the disclaimer or rejection of a trade mark licence, Chap. 14, paras. 14–02 to 14–13.
3. Proprietary versus contractual rights in a licence in the event of termination, Chap. 10, paras. 10–07 to 10–31.

20. RIGHTS AND OBLIGATIONS UPON EXPIRY OR TERMINATION

20.1 Upon the expiry or termination of this Agreement, for whatever reason, the Licensee shall immediately cease its use of the Trade Marks, and shall have no further right to use the Trade Marks, except as otherwise specified under this paragraph. The Licensee shall dispose of all promotional and other materials bearing or relating to the Trade Marks in accordance with the Licensor's instructions.

20.2 The Licensee shall return to the Licensor all Confidential Information, in whatever form, and all copies thereof, and make no further use thereof.

20.3 The Licensee shall execute all documents necessary for cancellation of the Licensee as a registered user or registered licensee, and shall refrain from engaging in any act which would lead a person to think that the Licensee is still associated or connected with the Licensor.

20.4 If this Agreement expires at the end of the term in accordance with clause 3, the Licensee shall be permitted for a period of [   ] months thereafter to take and fulfill orders for inventory existing as of the date of expiry, provided that the pre-termination manufacture of this inventory does not exceed reasonable quantities.

20.5 The Licensee shall be liable to the Licensor for the payment of royalties and all other payments in accordance with clause 4 for all inventory sold during this post-termination period referred to in clause 4.

Comments

1. The termination of the Agreement may not necessarily result in the immediate cessation of all use of the licensed trade marks by the licensee. Rather, as shown in the sample provision, there will be a transition period during which the licensee may be permitted to sell its remaining inventory, without prejudicing the licensor's proprietorship in the licensed trade marks.

2. In this situation, the parties must clarify what, if any, post-termination activity by the licensee is permitted. This is particularly important for the licensee, since any post-termination use outside the provisions of this clause put him at risk of infringement.

3. It is advisable to have the documents cancelling the registered user registration prepared and signed at the time that the agreement is executed. These documents can then be held by a fiduciary, who will submit them to the Registry when instructed that the agreement has expired or been terminated. This practice is advisable as well for the registration of a licensee under the Trade marks Act 1994.

4. The return of the Confidential Information assumes that the disclosure was made by the licensor to the licensee. If mutual disclosure has taken place, the clause should be modified as appropriate.

Cross References

1. Termination, Chap. 12.
2. Disposal of inventory by a contract manufacturer, Chap. 8, paras. 8–12 to 8–16.
3. See Comments to clause 15 regarding Confidential Information.
4. Registration of registered user and registered licensee, Chap. 4, paras. 4–19 to 4–20, 4–32 to 4–39, 4–48 to 4–51.
5. Rights of licensor and licensee upon breach, Chap. 10, paras. 10–07 to 10–31.

21. GOVERNING LAW AND JURISDICTION

21.1 This Agreement shall be governed by and construed under the laws of [ ].

21.2 The courts of [ ] shall have exclusive jurisdiction over any dispute between the parties arising out of or under this Agreement.

Comments

1. It should be kept in mind that the governing law question is separate and distinct from the issue of jurisdiction. In the absence of a provision specifying the governing law of the agreement, the choice of law rules will determine the issue.

2. The provision of a governing law of the agreement is also distinct from the issue of the governing law in respect of the determination of the validity or infringement of the trade mark.

3. When the licensor and the licensee are from two different countries, the issues of governing law and agreed place of jurisdiction can be thorny. One solution is to provide for arbitration. It is now recognised that trade mark issues can be resolved by arbitration.

4. There are numerous arrangements for arbitration. Among the principal points to be considered in drafting the arbitration clause are the following:

(i) Applicable arbitration rules.
(ii) Place of arbitration.

(iii) Subject matter to be adjudicated by arbitration.
(iv) Exclusivity of arbitration.
(v) Finality of the arbitral award.
(vi) Number and selection of the arbitrators.
(vii) Language of the arbitration.

5. Attention should be paid to the recent opening of the WIPO (World Intellectual Property Organization) Arbitration Centre in Geneva. The center offers services for the resolution of intellectual property disputes between private parties.

Cross Reference

1. See *Apple T.M.* case, Chap. 9, para. 9–26.

22. NOTICE

22.1 All notices required or permitted under this Agreement shall be made in writing, and shall be deemed to have been given and delivered in accordance with the following:

(i) By registered mail, [   ] days after despatch.
(ii) By commercial courier, [   ] days after despatch.
(iii) By facsimile transmission, the next business day following that on which the transmission was sent.
(iv) By personal delivery, immediately thereupon.

22.2 The addresses and numbers for telecopier transmission for the purposes of notice are as follows:

22.3 Either of the parties may change the address or telephone number for telecopier transmission for notice provided in paragraph 22.2 by furnishing the other party with written notice of such change.

Comments

1. The importance of notices in the licence agreement requires that the parties be clear as to how notice is to be given, and to what address the notice is to be sent.
2. As an alternative formulation for provision of notice by telecopier transmission, the agreement may state that 'a confirmation copy of the telecopier transmission is immediately thereupon sent by a commercial courier service.'

Cross Reference

1. Notice of renewal and termination, Chap. 12, paras. 12–13 to 12–19.

23. MISCELLANEOUS

23.1 The Licensee's obligations shall be excused to the extent that its performance is prevented by war, fire, strike, flood or other natural disaster, or other similar event beyond the control of the Licensee. In such an event, the obligations of the Licensee shall be suspended for such time as the performance thereof is thereby prevented.

23.2 This Agreement, and the schedules hereto, constitute the entire agreement between the parties with respect to the subject matters contained herein.

23.3 No modification or other amendment to this Agreement shall be valid unless reduced to writing and signed by both parties.

23.4 No waiver by either party of any breach or default by the other party shall constitute a waiver of the provisions of this Agreement with respect to any subsequent breach thereof.

23.5 To the extent permitted by law, all provisions of this Agreement shall be severable and no provision shall be affected by the invalidity of any other provision.

23.6 This agreement may be executed in counterparts, each of which shall be deemed an original.

IN WITNESS WHEREOF, the parties hereto have executed this Agreement as of the date first written above.

Licensor   Licensee

By: By:

Comments

1. These various provisions are often referred to as 'boilerplate' clauses. Despite this characterisation, these provisions are important and the parties should ensure that due thought is given to which such boilerplate provisions should be included.

2. In the event that the licensor and the licensee are located in different countries, and the agreement has been translated into a foreign language for the convenience of one of the parties, it may be advisable to make clear which language version of the agreement is binding.

SCHEDULE A
The Trade Marks

Mark   Registration no./   Country   Class[catagory of goods/services
        Application no./   to which the mark applies]

SCHEDULE B
The Goods and Services

[include a brief description of the goods and services]

Appendix:
Sample Consent Agreement

Introduction

Set forth below is a sample consent agreement. This agreement should be read in conjunction with Chapter 9, 'Consent and Delimitation Agreements. Licensee Estoppel and No Challenge Clauses.'

Particular attention should be paid to the symmetry between the undertakings of the two parties to the agreement. As described in para. 9–31 there are various other ways for the two parties to delimit the scope of the use of their respective trade marks, depending upon the circumstances.

CONSENT AGREEMENT

This Agreement is made this [   ] day of [   ], 19[   ]

by and between

ABC Ltd: a company incorporated in [   ], whose registered office is located at 123 Feather Lane, Anywhere (hereinafter referred to separately and jointly with its subsidiaries, affiliates, successors and assigns: 'ABC'), of the first part,

and

XYZ Ltd: a company incorporated in [   ], whose registered office is located at 100 Drury Street, Somewhere (hereinafter referred to separately and jointly with its subsidiaries, affiliates, successors and assigns: 'XYZ'), of the other part.

WHEREAS, ABC has adopted the trade mark MOOSE for use in connection with [describe goods] (hereinafter: ABC's Goods), and such trade mark is the subject of various registrations and applications in the name of ABC in the United Kingdom and elsewhere, as set forth in Exhibit A to this Agreement; and

WHEREAS, XYZ has adopted the trade mark MOOSE for use in connection with [describe goods] (hereinafter: XYZ's Goods), and such trade mark is the subject of various registrations and applications in the name of XYZ in the United Kingdom and elsewhere, as set out in Exhibit to this Agreement; and

WHEREAS, the parties wish to define and delimit the scope of the use of their respective trade marks in order to eliminate any reasonable likelihood of confusion, and to amicably resolve any controversy between them in connection with their respective trade marks.

NOW THEREFORE. THE PARTIES HEREBY AGREE AS FOLLOWS:

1. XYZ recognises, acknowledges and consents to the right of ABC to use the trade mark MOOSE, or any trade mark that incorporates the word MOOSE, on or in connection with ABC's Goods throughout the world.

2. XYZ agrees not to contest or challenge the use of the MOOSE trade mark by ABC on ABC's Goods.

3. ABC recognises, acknowledges and consents to the right of XYZ to use the trade mark MOOSE, or any trade mark that incorporates the word MOOSE, on or in connection with XYZ's Goods throughout the world.

4. ABC agrees not to contest or challenge the use of the MOOSE trade mark by XYZ on XYZ's Goods.

5. ABC warrants and declares that Exhibit A is a complete and accurate list of all registrations or applications on its behalf for the MOOSE trade mark, or that incorporates the word MOOSE, in respect of ABC's Goods. XYZ warrants and declares that Exhibit B is a complete and accurate list of all registrations or applications on its behalf for the MOOSE trade mark, or that incorporates the word MOOSE, in respect of XYZ's Goods.

6. The parties agree that each of them will cooperate fully with the other, including the provision of a Letter of Consent or any similar document as may be reasonably required, in order to enable each of them to register and maintain its respective trade mark in such jurisdictions as it may choose. In the event that, for whatever reason, only one of the parties is permitted by the competent administrative jurisdiction to register its trade mark, the party whose trade mark is so registered shall take no steps to impede or hinder the use by the other party of the other party's trade mark in that jurisdiction.

7. Each of the parties agrees to withdraw all oppositions or other actions that it has brought in any jurisdiction in connection with the registrability, validity or enforceability of the trade mark of the other party in accordance with this Agreement. A complete and accurate list of all such oppositions and other actions is attached hereto as Exhibit C.

8. The parties acknowledge that the scope of the use of their respective trade marks, as set forth in this Agreement, does not constitute a present likelihood of confusion. As well, it is believed that any future expansion by one party with respect to its activities under the MOOSE trade mark shall not constitute

a likelihood of confusion. Notwithstanding this, the parties agree to take all reasonable steps, including consultation, to ensure that any such future expansion of the use of the trade mark does not create a likelihood of confusion.

9. This Agreement shall extend to and be effective throughout the world.

10. This Agreement shall be subject to the laws of England, and any dispute concerning its construction, performance or validity shall be adjudicated in the courts of England.

11. If any part, term or provision of this Agreement shall be held to be illegal, unenforceable or in conflict with the law of any relevant jurisdiction, the validity or enforceability of the remainder of this Agreement shall not be affected thereby.

12. This Agreement is binding upon the parties, their respective subsidiaries and affiliates, on their respective successors and assigns. Any of the rights or duties under this Agreement may be assigned, provided that the assignee undertakes in writing to be bound by the terms and conditions of this Agreement in respect of the assignment.

13. The preamble to this Agreement is an integral part thereof.

[   ]
ABC Ltd.
By:

[   ]
XYZ Ltd.
By:

Index

Note. References are to paragraph numbers, except for those within chapter 15, the sample licence agreement, which are to chapters and clause numbers and denoted by the suffix "cl." The suffix "n" denotes a reference to a footnote.

Holding companies. *See* Associated companies
House marks, 2–21

Identification of ownership, 2–04—2–05
Implied licences,
  employees, 11–20—11–22
  infringement defence, 11–15—11–19
  oral licences contrasted, 11–26
  post-termination, 11–23
  pre-formal agreement, 11–21—11–22
  proprietorship claims, 11–25
  quality control, 11–24, 11–26
  See also Constructive licences
Implied terms,
  exclusivity, 10–22
  post-termination use, 12–10—12–11, 12–19,
    12–28—12–30
  termination, 12–14—12–17
Implied trusts, 11–33
Importers. *See* Distributors
Imports. *See* Parallel imports
Income tax,
  amortised expenditure, 14–51
  annual payments, 14–35—14–42
  basis of assessment, 14–34
  capital allowances, 14–48
  chargeable gains, 14–53
  deduction at source, 14–38—14–42
  deductions, 14–40, 14–46
  deferred revenue expenditure, 14–49—
    14–50
  franchise agreements, 14–43—14–46
  location, 14–52
  lump sum receipts, 14–43—14–47
  non-resident licensors, 14–42
  planning, 14–60
  U.S., 14–61—14–64
  written off expenditure, 14–51
Indemnities, 15–17cl
  infringement proceedings, 4–25
  product liability, 14–31, 14–32
India,
  registered users, 4–51n
Individual licensors, 5–40—5–42
Infringement, 15–10—15–11cl
  advertising, 7–14, 7–20
  assignment and licence back, 6–63
  consent agreements, 9–27, 9–30—9–31
  contract manufacturers, 8–12—8–17
  defences, 4–10
  distributors, 7–12—7–19
    U.S., 4–28, 4–30
  franchising, 13–34
  implied licences, 11–17—11–19
  labelling, 7–15n
  meaning, 10–02—10–03
  notification, 4–23, 13–34
  packaging, 7–15n
  post-termination use, 10–24—10–25,
    12–02—12–08
  quality control, 4–38n
  registered licensees' rights, 4–06—4–12,
    4–20—4–25
  registered users' rights, 4–19, 4–32n

Infringement—*cont.*
  sub-licensees, 4–50
  Trade Marks Directive, 13–45
  unregistered trade marks, 3–14, 4–29
  U.S., 4–26—4–31
  See also Breach of contract; Infringement
    proceedings
Infringement proceedings,
  account of profits, 4–14—4–18
  costs, 4–10, 4–25
  damages, 4–11—4–17
  eligibility, 4–03
  exclusive licensees, 4–07—4–12, 4–32n
  indemnities, 4–25
  interlocutory relief, 4–08, 4–10, 4–11
  joinder of proprietors, 4–10—4–12
    U.S., 5–43
  notification, 4–23
  sub-licensees, 4–50
  See also Breach of contract
Ingredient control, 5–05, 6–14
  See also Foreclosure of suppliers
Inheritance tax, 14–54—14–55
Injunctions, 4–08, 4–10, 4–11
Insolvency,
  disclaimer of licences, 14–11—14–13
  effects on licences, 14–03
  rejection of licences, 14–04—14–10
  trade mark disposal, 14–12
Inspection, 6–10, 6–14
Insurance, 14–31, 14–32, 15–17cl
Intellectual property licences, 1–08—1–11
Intent-to-use applications, 1–35, 5–30
Interlocutory relief, 4–08, 4–10, 4–11
International tax planning, 14–60
Israel,
  registered users, 3–01

Joinder of parties, 4–10—4–12, 5–43
  product liability, 14–32

Know-how, 1–16, 1–17, 1–19
  franchising, 13–35
  See also Know-how licences
Know-how licences, 1–19—1–20
  block exemption, 12–57, 13–19—13–22
  relation with trade mark licences, 1–07,
    1–18
  trade mark use, 13–20

Labelling, 7–15n, 7–21—7–25
  See also Marking
Licences. *See* Trade mark licences
Licences in gross, 5–12
Licensee estoppel, 9–51—9–54, 11–12—11–13
  certification marks, 8–21
  U.S., 9–55—9–59
  See also No challenge clauses
Licensees,
  contractual rights, 10–15—10–23, 10–26—
    10–29, 10–35
  See also Registered licensees; Registered
    users